DEVELOPING READING VERSATILITY

FIFTH EDITION

W. Royce Adams

Santa Barbara City College

HOLT, RINEHART AND WINSTON, INC.

New York   Chicago   San Francisco   Philadelphia
Montreal   Toronto   London   Sydney   Tokyo

Publisher, Humanities: Charlyce Jones Owen
Senior Project Editor: Lester A. Sheinis
Senior Production Manager: Nancy Myers
Design Supervisor: Gloria Gentile
Text Designer: Barbara Bert
Cover Painting: Robert Andrew Parker

Library of Congress Cataloging-in-Publication Data

Adams, W. Royce.
    Developing reading versatility/W. Royce Adams.—5th ed.
        p.   cm.
    Includes bibliographical references.
    1. Reading (Higher education)   2. Reading comprehension.
    I. Title.
    LB2395.3.A33   1989
    428.4'07'11—dc19   88–20999
                                                        CIP

ISBN 0-03-023739-4

Printed in the United States of America

9 0 1 2   084   9 8 7 6 5 4 3 2 1

Holt, Rinehart and Winston, Inc.
The Dryden Press
Saunders College Publishing

Preface

Since the first appearance of *Developing Reading Versatility* back in 1973, as well as all later editions, the intent has been to teach students to read better inductively by "doing" rather than by reading "how to." That emphasis still remains in this fifth edition, but more skills explanations, made as inductive as possible, appear in this edition. Introductions to various drills at the literal, critical, and affective levels of comprehension have been expanded and, in most cases, require student responses followed by explanations in order to assure clarity. Thus, the basic philosophy behind this edition remains the same.

We have tried to respond to the many suggestions of users and reviewers of *Developing Reading Versatility*. Where possible, all reading selection favorites have been retained, although their position and use may be changed, and those lacking favor have been dropped. All Inventory and Progress checks have been changed, as well as all key drills that might be used for grading purposes. More work has been added in the areas of vocabulary development, main ideas, mapping, and test-taking strategies. The unit on critical reading has been tightened, with an entire chapter on inference and drawing conclusions. Drills on figurative language now appear in Unit II as well as Unit III. This edition contains ten chapters rather than eleven. Nearly three fourths of the readings or drill sources are new and range in variety from textbook passages to poetry.

As before, there is more material here than can be covered in a reading course, allowing for selectivity. Not all students will need to do all the drills provided. Proper diagnosis will place students in their areas of need. It is hoped that in using this book students will develop the awareness that nobody has a single fixed reading rate, that reading is complex, that purposes and motivation determine comprehension, that there are no true or false answers to some questions, and that it is not too late to learn to read better.

Reviewers are split on whether or not answers to the drills should be supplied to students. For those who prefer students to have an answer key, answer keys will be made available to the department. For more information, write to the English Editor, Holt, Rinehart and Winston, 111 Fifth Avenue, New York, N.Y. 10002, or contact your sales representative.

It is, of course, quite gratifying that *Developing Reading Versatility* has been well received over the past sixteen years. I would like to express my appreciation to my students and my colleagues for their help with this edition. The following reviewers are to be thanked: Linda Briggs, Sacramento City College; Nancy Kolk, Clinton Community College; Evelyn Dandy, Armstrong State College; Minna Lee, Brookdale Community College; Marilyn Lyons, Clinton Community College; and David Sellars, Nashville State Technical Institute. At Holt, I wish to thank Charlyce Jones Owen, Lester A. Sheinis, Tod Gross, Nancy Myers, and Gloria Gentile.

WRA

Your "No Money-Back Guarantee"

"We guarantee your money will be refunded in full if you fail to double your reading rate with no loss in comprehension in just one lesson!"

Ever hear or read an ad like that? You probably have. They seem to appear everywhere. Maybe you've even signed up for a course that made such claims. But if you did, it obviously didn't work or you wouldn't be reading this book. Every year, thousands of dollars—most of them wasted—are spent on books, courses, and gadgets that claim to double or triple reading powers. Some readers do increase their reading ability during these courses, but the majority of them drop right back to their original reading habits when the course is over or the gadget wears out.

This book offers you no money-back guarantee if you fail to read any better after completing it than you do now. It is quite possible that you could do well on every exercise in this book and still continue to read the way you do now. Why? Because you might fail to *use* the information gained from this book when you read material outside the book. In other words, unless you practice in *all* your reading what you do and learn in this book, there will be no transfer of skills. You will just be kidding yourself that you are reading better. Thus, while we can guarantee that the book may be helpful, we can't be sure of *you*. So, no money-back guarantee.

However, to get the most for your money, here are some points and suggestions for you to consider.

1. Turn to the Contents. Notice that this book is divided into three units. Each unit provides you with a variety of exercises in one level of comprehension. Together, these three different levels of understanding will bring you closer to a total comprehension of what you read. Actually, no Great Reading God in the Sky said, "Let there be three levels of comprehension. Zap!" These divisions are made only to help you see the many facets of comprehension.
2. Don't feel obligated to do every exercise in each unit. The preunit inventories are guides to how well you function at these different levels. How much practice you need depends on how much

more competent you want to be in each area.

3. Some of the early drills in Unit I deal more with the development of visual perception than with comprehension. If you are a very slow reader—averaging, say, 150 words per minute—you will find these drills very beneficial. It is suggested that you don't try doing them all as a group. Use them as warm-up exercises before reading. You will find that they help you break your slow reading rate habit.
4. Some of the drills in this book are timed for speed. The pressure of speed is used to prod you from your normal reading habits. But don't make speed your goal. Your speed will automatically increase as a by-product of the good reading habits you will learn here. Reading speeds vary depending on purpose, material, and vocabulary levels.
5. Don't expect overnight miracles. Lifetime results can be obtained from the drills you do here if you learn from your mistakes as well as your successes. It takes time, effort, and patience to change reading habits you have developed over many years.
6. Some of the drill questions can't be answered in a key, and in these cases the class should discuss them. Discussion is necessary for developing comprehension skills. Engage in class discussion; don't just sit back and listen to others, especially when you are working in Unit III.
7. Three record charts are provided so that you can keep a record of your various drill work. Don't be worried about ups and downs in rate and comprehension scores. It's normal to fluctuate. Also, don't be fooled into thinking that because your scores go up on the chart that you are reading better in materials outside the text. Only you can actually determine how much success you are feeling.

With these things said, you are ready to get down to work. Just remember, the responsibility for learning and transfer of learning is yours. Are you willing to place a money-back guarantee on yourself?

Contents

Chapter 4 Developing Skimming and Scanning Skills 172

Chapter 5 Developing Speed of Comprehension 216

UNIT II
CRITICAL COMPREHENSION 261

Chapter 6 Distinguishing Fact from Opinion 270

Chapter 7 Recognizing Intent, Attitude, and Tone 304

Chapter 8 Recognizing Inferences and Drawing Conclusions 339

UNIT III
AFFECTIVE COMPREHENSION 393

Chapter 9 Developing Affective Awareness 402

Chapter **10**   **Reading Affectively Effectively**   433

APPENDIX   491

UNIT I

LITERAL COMPREHENSION

LITERAL COMPREHENSION INVENTORY

Before you begin work in this unit, use the following reading selection to take inventory of your reading ability at the literal comprehension level. The selection is from a typical college textbook. Read it the way you normally read, since the object is to see what skills you have and which ones you need to develop as you work through this text. Here is what the inventory measures:

1. *Reading speed.* You will want to time yourself or have someone time you as you read to get some idea of your reading rate for material of this type.
2. *Literal comprehension ability.* After you time your reading, answer the questions based on the material without looking back. This will let you know how well you understand what you read at that rate of speed.
3. *Vocabulary level.* After the comprehension check you will answer some questions about words from the reading selection.
4. *Skimming/scanning ability.* You will be asked to skim and scan to answer some questions based on the reading selection in order to see how fast and how accurate your skills in this area are.
5. *Personal evaluation.* When you are finished, you will be asked to write down what problems you had while doing this inventory and what you feel you need to learn in this unit.

This is not a test, so don't be intimidated by this inventory. The information gathered here will be helpful to both you and your instructor. Upon completion of this unit, you will be given a progress check similar to this one so that you can see your growth in these areas. Relax now, and read in your normal fashion.

When you are ready, write your starting time in the blank below. Try to begin exactly on the minute.

Begin timing. Starting time: _____

GROUPS: THE SOCIOLOGICAL SUBJECT

Rodney Stark

1   A **group** consists of two or more persons who maintain a stable pattern of relations over a significant period of time. Some groups, such as a married couple, are tiny. Other groups, such as the workers in a factory, are large. However, not just any gathering of people qualifies as a group in the sociological sense.

2   In everyday speech we often refer to ten people standing on the corner waiting for the walk light as a "group." But sociologists would call them an **aggregate** of individuals. They have come together only briefly and accidentally. They are not acquainted with one another, and they may not even notice one another. For sociologists, people constitute a group only when they are *united by social relations*. If the ten people waiting for the walk light were all members of the same family or baseball team, then they would be a group in the sociological sense of the term.

DYADS AND TRIADS

3   The smallest sociological group is the **dyad:** a pair of individuals who engage in social relations. As we shall see in Chapter 3, an analysis of the basic properties of two-person relationships gives sociology the tools for building a theory of human interaction— for explaining how we influence one another and thereby construct and enforce rules governing social life. Much of our behavior is governed by our need to exchange with others, whether we exchange apples or affection. Such exchanges are possible only if we can anticipate how the other person will respond and vice versa.

4   However, if the dyad is the fundamental building block of sociology, it is not its primary object of interest. Human social relations do not consist mainly of isolated pairs, but of multiple relations involving every individual with a number of others. And, as soon as we shift our focus from dyads to social relations involving three or more individuals, some very interesting and complex patterns emerge. As a preview, let's consider **triads:** social relations among three persons.

5   Let's imagine a triad of three women: Ann, Betty, and Cindy. This triad, like all others, includes not one, but three relationships. In other words, relationships exist between Ann and Betty, between Betty and Cindy, and between Ann and Cindy. Sociologists have discovered many rules about the behavior of triads. Let's consider two of them.

6   *Transitivity*   Triads demonstrate the **transitivity** rule governing human relations. . . . The rule is simple: Relations among members of a group will tend to be balanced or consistent. This idea is captured by everyday sayings such as "Any friend of yours is a friend of mine," "My enemy's friends are my enemies," "Your enemies are my enemies," and "If you like her, you're no friend of mine." It follows then, . . . that if Ann likes Betty and Betty hates Cindy, Ann will also be apt to hate Cindy. Or, if Ann likes Betty and Betty likes Cindy, chances are that Ann will like Cindy too. Also, if Ann hates Betty and Betty likes Cindy, Ann probably will also hate Cindy. Such patterns of relationships in a triad are said to be transitive, because there are no strains on relations between any pair caused by contrary relations with the third person (Heider, 1946; Newcomb, 1953; Davis and Leinhardt, 1972).

7   Now suppose a triad of three close friends: Andy, Bubba, and Cal. One day Andy and Bubba get raging mad at each other and never speak again. But both are still buddies of Cal. This is an *intransitive* triad. Now whenever Andy goes bowling with Cal, Bubba is resentful—"How come my buddy bowls with my worst enemy?" Or, whenever Bubba and Cal go fishing, Andy grumbles about friends who let you down.

8   Intransitive triads are unstable and usually break up. Sooner or later Cal is going to have to stop seeing either Andy or Bubba, or both. Trying to be friends with two people who hate each other causes too much tension.

9   *Coalition formation*   Suppose Cal decides to go along with one of his buddies and gang up on the other. Maybe he joins Andy as an enemy of Bubba. Now we can say that Andy and Bubba have formed a **coalition.** They have combined to oppose someone else.

10   Now let's introduce *power* into this triadic relationship. Sociologists define power as the ability to get one's way over the opposition of others (see Chapter 9). Many things can cause some people to be more powerful than others, but for now let's limit our attention to physical strength. If all three guys are of equal physical strength, we cannot predict whether Cal will

From Rodney Stark, *Sociology*, 2nd ed., Wadsworth Publishing Co., 1987, pp. 8–12.

choose to line up with Andy or Bubba if there is going to be a fight. Either choice is equally likely.

11   Suppose, however, that Bubba is huge and could easily beat up either Andy or Cal, while Andy and Cal are equally matched. Suppose too that Bubba couldn't beat up both Andy and Cal at the same time. Now we can predict that Andy and Cal will gang up on Bubba—that they will form a coalition (Caplow, 1968). Why? Because if Cal chose to join Bubba he would still be at Bubba's mercy after Andy was beaten. The same goes if Andy joins Bubba against Cal. But if Andy and Cal gang up on Bubba they are safe—safe from Bubba and safe from one another, because they are too evenly matched to want to risk a showdown.

12   Transitivity and coalition formation are but two of a multitude of principles governing social relations in small groups. I have discussed them here to offer a sample of what micro sociologists study. However, principles such as these are not limited to the behavior of triads. The intimate connections between micro and macro sociology can be seen if we realize that rules such as those above apply equally well to large groups. To illustrate, let's see how intransitivity and coalition formation shape the internal structure of larger groups.

NETWORKS

13   All groups consist of social relations among members, whether the group contains three or three thousand members. The patterns of relations among members of a group are often called **social networks.** Ideally, even a large group is transitive, with all members liking one another. However, the ideal is rarely realized. Some members do not like others, and thus relations inside a group can become intransitive. And just as intransitivity can lead either to the breakup of a triad or to coalition formation, so can it cause people in large groups to readjust their relations. Intransitivity leads to the formation of internal clusters within the network of the group—clusters composed of persons who like one another and have few friends outside their own cluster. These clusters are often called internal factions or **cliques.** When a pattern of cliques has developed, transitivity is restored: People no longer attempt to remain friends with people who are also friendly with their enemies.

14   To study the structure of group networks, sociologists often use **sociograms** to chart relationships within a group. For example, a sociologist may ask members of a fourth-grade class, a sorority, or a business office to list the individuals whom they like or admire most in the group (or whom they dislike most). The lines of friendship can then be drawn on a chart. Usually several individuals stand out as "sociometric stars" because they are often chosen as the most liked. If these stars also like one another, then an integrated network exists. People who admire one star will also tend to like another star as well as group members who like other stars.

15   For example, suppose George and Mary are the two most popular kids in the fourth grade and also like each other. Then those who like George will also tend to like Mary and the other kids who regard Mary as the star. Many bonds of friendship exist between members, and no clear lines of separation exist within the group.

16   Intransitivity arises, however, when two stars become enemies—when, in our example, Mary and George suddenly decide they can't stand each other. For then they impose strains between their respective followers just like the strains created in the triad when Andy and Bubba got mad at each other. And, just as the intransitive triad led to a coalition, so does intransitivity in larger networks produce a choosing up of sides. Such networks display clearly separated patterns of social relations—distinct cliques or factions. When more than two such internal factions exist, coalition formation is likely: Several factions will cooperate against other factions. Here, too, the coalition rule outlined above applies. But, whether or not coalitions form, internal factions always threaten to produce internal conflict, and in some cases they can cause the group to break up.

PRIMARY AND SECONDARY GROUPS

17   Not all groups are of equal importance to their members. For example, we will more willingly withdraw from a group made up of persons working in our office than from one made up of family or intimate friends. This distinction is captured by the notions of primary and secondary groups.

18   **Primary groups** are characterized by great intimacy among the members. People in these groups do not merely know one another and interact frequently, but they know one another well and have strong emotional ties. As a result, people gain much of their self-esteem and sense of identity from primary groups—as we shall consider in depth in Chapter 3. For example, when retired athletes report how much they miss belonging to a team, they are telling of the pains of leaving a primary group.

19   The family is the most common primary group, but many other groups can also become so. Indeed, Charles H. Cooley, who coined the term *primary group,* said a group is primary if its members refer to themselves as "we." Primary groups involve "the sort of sympathy and mutual identification for which 'we' is the natural expression" (Cooley, 1909).

20   **Secondary groups** consist of less intimate social networks within which people pursue various collective goals but without a powerful sense of belonging. Business organizations, political parties, even model

railroad clubs are typically secondary groups. People find it relatively easy to switch from one secondary group to another and refer to themselves and group members as "we" only in a mild sense of the term. However, as we shall see in Chapter 19, primary groups often form *within* secondary groups—a process that can produce internal strains. For example, a group of close friends within a business may promote one another to the disadvantage of other employees and perhaps cause the company to operate less efficiently.

21   Groups, then, are the primary subject matter of sociology. The aim of sociologists is to construct a science of groups, of human social relations. However, not everyone believes that it is possible to achieve a science of social relations.

Finishing time: _____

Starting time: _____

Reading time: _____ (Subtract starting time from finishing time.) Check page 499 for your reading rate, or words per minute.

WPM: _____

Now answer the questions that follow without looking back at the reading material.

LITERAL COMPREHENSION INVENTORY

Part A

Directions: In the space provided, write a summary of the reading selection you just read.

Part B

Directions: Answer the following questions without looking back at the reading selection.

1. State in your own words what you think is the main idea of the reading

    selection. _____

    _____

    _____

2. What is the sociological definition of a group? _____

_____

_____

3. Define a dyad. _____

_____

4. Define a triad. _____

_____

5. Explain the transitivity rule governing human relations. _____

_____

_____

6. Are intransitive triads stable or unstable? _____

Explain. _____

_____

7. When two or more people combine forces to oppose someone else, what is

that called? _____

8. Explain what is meant by a social network. _____

_____

_____

9. What group is the most common "primary group"? _____

_____

10. What is the aim of sociologists? _____

_____

_____

VOCABULARY INVENTORY

Part A

Directions: Define the following underlined words as they are used in context.

1. maintain a <u>stable</u> pattern of relationships

   _____

2. their annoying <u>vociferous</u> chatter

   _____

3. a <u>lethal</u> weapon

   _____

4. speaking <u>candidly</u> about it

   _____

5. in an <u>articulate</u> manner

   _____

6. <u>frugal</u> with his money

   _____

7. makes <u>astute</u> observations

   _____

8. hordes of <u>indigent</u> people

   _____

9. a <u>morose</u> story

   _____

10. acted with startling <u>impudence</u>

    _____

Part B

Directions: Define the following word parts.

1. bio _____

2. in _____

3. un _____

4. anthrop _____

5. ist _____

6. trans _____

    7. pre _____

    8. vis _____

    9. logy _____

  10. psych _____

SKIMMING/SCANNING INVENTORY

Directions: Take no more than two minutes to scan the reading selection that you read earlier on page 4 for the answers to the following questions. You may want to have someone time you.

    1. What are the titles of the two subheadings under the major heading "Dyads

    and Triads"? _____

    and _____

    2. According to paragraph 8, why are intransitive triads unstable?

    _____

    3. How do sociologists define power according to paragraph 10?

    _____

    4. What two types of groups are discussed in this selection?

    _____ and _____

    5. Why is Charles Cooley mentioned in paragraph 19?

    _____

    Once this inventory has been scored, enter the results on the Inventory Progress Chart on page 493. When you have finished working in this unit, you will take a progress check so that you can compare your pre- and postunit scores.

PERSONAL EVALUATION OF SCORES

Directions: In the space provided, write down your evaluation of the inventory results, what difficulties you may have had, what strengths you have, or anything that might help your instructor provide you with the type of practice you need.

INTRODUCTION TO LITERAL COMPREHENSION

Comprehension is the act of understanding or the capacity to understand. But as you know, the act of understanding is not always simple. In order to help you develop your ability to comprehend better, this book is divided into three levels of comprehension: literal, critical, and affective. None of these levels is actually a separate entity. All three depend on the other. Think of total comprehension as a diamond. If we want to look more closely at that diamond, we can look separately at each of its facets or polished sides. The more facets, the more glimmer to the diamond.

You are going to be working separately with three facets of comprehension. Each of the three facets will be further broken down so that you can "polish" the skills necessary to get maximum comprehension of what you read. If you look at the diagram that follows, you will notice that each leg of the triangle represents one level of comprehension. Literal comprehension is at the bottom of the triangle; it's the most basic, the foundation for understanding. Making up literal comprehension skills are such things as vocabulary knowledge, visual perception, understanding main ideas and supporting details, skimming and scanning skills, and study skills. All of these will be taught in Unit I.

The second leg of the triangle is critical comprehension, which requires separating fact from opinion; recognizing an author's intent, attitude, tone, and bias; being able to draw inferences; and drawing conclusions. All of these skills are presented for your practice in Unit II, as well as continued practice in the skills from Unit I.

The third part of the triangle represents affective comprehension, which requires an understanding of figurative language, use of the im-

agination and feelings, and an awareness of the aesthetics of imaginative and expository writings. Unit III deals with these skills. By the time you have finished with the last unit, you will have had continual practice using all three levels of comprehension. It is important as you work through this book to keep in mind that each skill eventually builds upon the other.

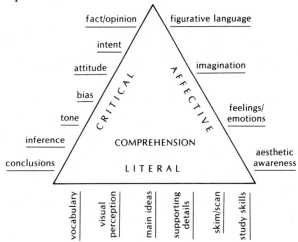

WHAT IS LITERAL COMPREHENSION?

This first unit deals with just one of three complex levels of total comprehension, the literal level. Literal comprehension is that basic level of understanding that entails the ability to recognize words accurately, to identify main ideas and supporting details, to understand sequence of events, to recognize cause-and-effect relationships, to interpret directions, and to understand organizational

11

patterns used in various types of reading matter. It is the level of comprehension you use when you follow a cooking recipe or the directions for putting a swing set together. It is also the level of comprehension necessary for understanding the main ideas in a news story, a magazine article, or a chapter from a textbook. More simply put, it is the most basic level of understanding, providing the foundation for the development of the two higher levels, namely, critical and affective comprehension.

Of the three levels of comprehension, literal comprehension is probably the most used. That is because everyday reading skills, such as skimming and scanning telephone directories, catalogues, movie and television listings, and even reading the newspaper or a favorite magazine, seldom require anything but literal comprehension. In addition, most training in reading courses from the early grades through college classes places a larger emphasis on literal recall than on critical or affective comprehension. This is not to say that there is no training in these areas, but an examination of materials and tests used in reading courses, as well as in other subjects, reveals a strong reliance on literal comprehension with more stress on recall than on forming judgments, evaluations, or personal reactions at the critical and affective levels. But in spite of daily use, most people do not read as well as they could at the literal level.

Reading is much more than recognizing words on a page. Knowing the meaning and function of words you are reading is naturally basic, but you must also understand those words in their context. Then it becomes important to understand the author's main points, the details and how they are being used, and the organization of the material. When these basics are mastered, speed of comprehension is increased and the basis is laid for developing your critical and affective levels of awareness.

WHAT DOES THIS UNIT COVER?

In this unit the exercises deal with the development of all facets of literal comprehension. Drill goals are as basic as improving eye movement and as complex as learning to separate main ideas from supporting details and recognizing writing patterns. An attempt has been made to provide a variety of reading experiences.

There are five chapters in this unit. Chapter 1 offers methods for vocabulary development, an important area for the improvement of reading at any level. Chapter 2 deals with the development of literal recall, stressing reading for main ideas and supporting details, understanding paragraph patterns writers use, and recognizing an author's thesis. Chapter 3 offers you practice in developing study-reading skills, including the famous SQ3R method, reading-notetaking methods such as marking, underlining, and mapping techniques, and test-taking skills. Chapter 4 offers skimming and scanning practices, using textbook and reference materials. Chapter 5 is concerned with developing speed of comprehension by helping you to overcome any barriers to your speed of comprehension. All chapters contain reading practices of various styles and subject matter with comprehension and vocabulary practice.

There are two points about these drills that can't be overstated. One is that you should not worry about mistakes you make. Turn your mistakes into "learning experiences." When you miss a question, learn from it. Try to understand what caused you to make an error. If you can't figure it out on your own, get help from your instructor. The second point is to take what you learn here and apply it to your reading outside this text. Whether or not this text helps you to read any better is really up to you. While many students do well as they proceed through the work required of them in this book, they fail to apply the techniques to other required or pleasure readings. This book is designed to develop an awareness of what is required of an intelligent person when reading certain types of materials. Apply this awareness to all of your readings.

WHAT SHOULD YOU KNOW AFTER COMPLETING THIS UNIT?

Even though it may take quite a while to complete the exercises that will be assigned to you, in this unit you should have some goals and objectives in mind that you want to achieve before going on to the next unit. Here are some objectives to consider. You may want to add some of your own. When you have finished this unit, you should be able to:

1. Write a thorough definition of literal comprehension.
2. Select a method that aids you in the continuing development of your vocabulary and use it regularly.
3. Perceive words and phrases more accurately and rapidly than you do now.
4. Define the difference between skimming and scanning as well as know when and how to do both properly.
5. Identify the following writing patterns as an aid in comprehension: definition, illustration/example, cause/effect, comparison/contrast, description, and sequence of events.
6. Read expository reading matter at least 100 words per minute faster with no loss in literal comprehension.

These are not unrealistic objectives to keep in mind as you work through this unit. With proper practice, you will achieve them all. If you have any objectives of your own, write them down below and share them with your instructor.

Personal reading objectives for Unit I:

_____

_____

_____

CHAPTER 1

Developing Vocabulary Skills

One of the first places to begin developing reading versatility is with vocabulary development. Obviously, without a good vocabulary, reading comprehension is poor and slow. In order to understand what you read, you need to recognize not only the definitions of the words being read, but more importantly, the way words are used in context. As a first step in developing reading versatility, this chapter will provide you with some methods and drills in the areas of sight recognition of words, understanding words in context, learning word parts and roots, and dictionary usage.

Vocabulary development means more than just adding new words to those you already know. It also means learning how to change words to different parts of speech, how to add or delete prefixes and suffixes, how to recognize the root elements of a word and its relationship to other words with that root, how synonyms and antonyms form families of words, as well as how to use words correctly in your own speech and writing.

While this book is not a vocabulary textbook, a strong emphasis is placed on vocabulary building because no real reading improvement can take place without it. Several approaches for building your vocabulary are presented. Some may seem more helpful to you than others, but give them all a try. Many words will be presented not only in this chapter but throughout the book as part of the reading comprehension and vocabulary drills. Be selective and learn words that you feel you need to learn. You might want to start with those words you "sort of" know but can't really use. Devote some part of your day to working on your vocabulary. There is no getting around the work part. Building up your vocabulary is like staying in shape. It requires concentrated effort and regular workouts. No one can do it for you.

The first part of this chapter presents three methods for learning words you really want to make your own. Try all three methods before deciding which one you will use during this course.

The second part deals with words in context. For instance, the word *run* can have many different meanings, depending on how it is used in context. Notice these examples:

There was a run on the bank.
She had a run in her stocking.
Run to the store for me.

In each case, and there are many others with the word *run*, the meaning is different, depending on the contextual use of the word. Learning to use contextual clues can also save you many trips to the dictionary.

The third section of this chapter deals with word structure, that is, prefixes, roots, and suffixes. Learning how words are structured and what certain commonly used prefixes, roots, and suffixes mean can help you unlock the meanings of many unfamiliar words. Useful Greek and Latin word roots are presented in drills to help you develop this aspect of vocabulary building.

The fourth section of this chapter develops your dictionary skills. Exercises are presented that will help you interpret the symbols and abbreviations in the dictionary.

Vocabulary development is a lifelong process. This chapter is meant only to get you started, not to be a complete course. It will be up to you to continue to use the information provided in this chapter. As you begin work, keep in mind Objective 2 listed in the introduction of this unit: "Review or discover methods for vocabulary development."

A. Learning New Words: 3 Methods

METHOD 1: A VOCABULARY NOTEBOOK

One way to develop your vocabulary is to keep a notebook of the words you want to learn. An 8½ × 11 spiral notebook is best. In it you can write the words you want to learn, their definitions, and sentence examples using the words. For instance, a typical entry might look like this:

> *perspicacious* = having keen insight, judgment, or understanding; shrewd
>
> If he had been more perspicacious, he might not have lost so much money on the stock market.

Of course, what type entries are made is up to you. Some students prefer to include the sentence where the word is first encountered and then write an example sentence of their own. In addition, some students also write in the phonetic spelling of the word, especially if it is one that has never been heard before.

The advantages to this method are that it is a convenient way to keep all new words together and a good source for constant review of older entries as new ones are made. The disadvantage is that the notebook can, if you let it, become nothing more than a list of words unless you take the effort to review your words constantly.

METHOD 2: THE COLUMN FOLDS

With this method you take a regular piece of notebook paper and fold it into three or four columns, three if you do not need to learn the phonetic spelling of the word you want to learn. In the first column you write the words you wish to learn. In the second column you write the phonetic spelling. In the third column you write the definition of the word, and in the fourth column, an example sentence using the word, but instead of writing in the word you place a blank. You can usually get about ten or twelve words on one sheet of paper.

You can then practice learning the words in several ways. One way is to fold the paper so only the words show. You then see if you can remember the definitions; if not, you unfold the paper and check the answer. Another way is to fold the paper so only the definitions show and see if you can identify the word that belongs to that definition. Still another way is to fold the paper so only the sentences show and try to remember the word that goes in the blank. And still another way is to fold the paper so that the phonetic spelling shows and try to pronounce the word and give its definition.

The advantage to this method is that it provides you with a means of studying with immediate feedback to the answers. The disadvantage is that the paper can become rather tattered after a while if you require much time to learn the words.

METHOD 3: VOCABULARY CARDS

You have probably seen boxed sets of vocabulary cards for foreign languages as well as for English. In such sets, each card has a word on one side and its definition on the other. These ready-made cards can be helpful, but chances are you will already know many of the words on the cards.

You can easily personalize the vocabulary card method by making up your own 3 × 5 index file cards. Here's all you need to do:

1. On the front of a card, print the word you want to learn. Use ink so that after much use it will still be legible. Underneath the word print the phonetic spelling unless you already know how to pronounce the word.
2. On the back of the card put as much information as needed to help you learn the word. It is recommended that besides the definition you include a synonym (a word that has a similar meaning) and an antonym (a word that has the opposite meaning) if possible. A sentence using the word is also advised, either the sentence in which you found the word or an example of your own.

> *mnemonic*
>
> *(nē mon´ ik)*

Front of Card

> *aiding or designed to aid the memory: a device to help remember*
>
> *Vocabulary cards are mnemonic devices used to remember newly learned words.*

Back of Card

3. Be selective and make vocabulary cards only for the words you want to overlearn. It is important to overlearn new words, not just memorize them, because you will gradually forget their meanings if you do not use them. All the words you presently know you have already overlearned and use without thinking. The only way to have a truly larger vocabulary is to overlearn new words the way you have with the ones you now use regularly.
4. Try to learn at least five new words a week, more if you can. Practice daily by quickly flashing only the front of the vocabulary card and pronouncing the word to yourself and the word's meaning. Try not to refer to the back of the card unless you can't recall the definition.
5. Carry a small stack of cards around in your purse or pocket so you can refer to them often. At odd times during the day—between classes, while waiting for a friend, on a bus, during a boring class lecture—practice flashing your cards. If

you have a friend who is also using this method, practice flashing each other's cards. The more you practice, the sooner you will begin to overlearn the words and recognize them by sight.

6. As the weeks go by and you accumulate fifty to a hundred or so cards, put aside the cards for words you feel you know very well and probably will never forget. At a later date, review the cards you put aside and see if you still remember them. If there are some you don't remember, put them back in your active stack of cards.

The advantage to this method is that it is a convenient way to learn words. If you have your cards with you, practice can take place anywhere, anytime. Rather than learning words from a list where association with other words on the list takes place, flash cards can be shuffled and mixed up. Once you have all the information you need on a card, you never have to look up the word again. The disadvantage is that making up cards does take time, but the advantages far outweigh this one.

All this may seem like too much work. Perhaps it's not the method for you, but it has worked very well for many students. Of the three methods mentioned, the personalized vocabulary card method is the one most recommended.

CHECK TEST

Directions: Answer the following questions in the blanks provided.

1. What is meant by vocabulary development? _____

_____

2. What are the three methods just discussed for developing vocabulary? ___

_____

3. Explain Method 1. _____

_____

_____

4. Explain Method 2. _____

_____

_____

5. Explain Method 3. _____

_____

_____

6. Which method is most recommended? _____

_____

7. Why is this method recommended over the others? _____

_____

_____

8. What is meant by overlearning new words? _____

_____

_____

9. Why is developing your vocabulary vital to developing reading versatility?

_____

_____

10. Which method do you think you will use once you have tried all three?

_____ Why? _____

_____

_____

NAME _____ SECTION _____ DATE _____

VOCABULARY CARD RECORD SHEET

Directions: You or your instructor may wish to check your personalized vocabulary cards on a regular basis. Use the following form to keep track of your progress.

Check #1

Date _____

Number of cards _____

Number correct _____

Checked by _____

Check #2

Date _____

Number of cards _____

Number correct _____

Checked by _____

Check #3

Date _____

Number of cards _____

Number correct _____

Checked by _____

Check #4

Date _____

Number of cards _____

Number correct _____

Checked by _____

Check #5

Date _____

Number of cards _____

Number correct _____

Checked by _____

Check #6

Date _____

Number of cards _____

Number correct _____

Checked by _____

Check #7

Date _____

Number of cards _____

Number correct _____

Checked by _____

Check #8

Date _____

Number of cards _____

Number correct _____

Checked by _____

Check #9

Date _____

Number of cards _____

Number correct _____

Checked by _____

Check #10

Date _____

Number of cards _____

Number correct _____

Checked by _____

Check #11

Date _____

Number of cards _____

Number correct _____

Checked by _____

Check #12

Date _____

Number of cards _____

Number correct _____

Checked by _____

Check #13

Date _____

Number of cards _____

Number correct _____

Checked by _____

Check #14

Date _____

Number of cards _____

Number correct _____

Checked by _____

Check #15

Date _____

Number of cards _____

Number correct _____

Checked by _____

Check #16

Date _____

Number of cards _____

Number correct _____

Checked by _____

Check #17

Date _____

Number of cards _____

Number correct _____

Checked by _____

Check #18

Date _____

Number of cards _____

Number correct _____

Checked by _____

B. Learning Words in Context

This section provides practice in figuring out a word's meaning by its use in context. A close look at the context in which a word is used can often, though not always, eliminate the need to use a dictionary.

CONTEXTUAL HINTS

There are several different types of context clues which will be covered in this section, but let's look at one: *contextual hints*. For instance, in the following sentence notice how the meaning of the word "lucid" is hinted at:

His lucid lectures, along with his clearly presented explanations, made it easy to take notes.

The phrases "clearly presented explanations," and "easy to take notes" give clues to the meaning of the word "lucid"—easy to understand, clear. Thus, it's generally a good idea not to stop on words you don't know, but rather to read on a bit and see if hints or other clues to the word's meaning might be given.

Here's another sentence written with a contextual hint to a key word's meaning:

It was imprudent for Lisa to skate on the ice without checking to see how thick it was.

Since we know that skating on ice without making sure it is thick enough is dangerous, we can guess that Lisa was not very wise, perhaps foolish for doing so. Therefore, "imprudent" must mean unwise, rash, or foolish.

Drill B-1: CONTEXTUAL HINTS

Directions: See if you can define the italicized words in the following sentences and explain the contextual hints.

1. Their *vociferous* chatter made me wish I had earplugs.

   a. *vociferous* means _____

   b. The clue is _____
2. He was so *impudent* to his mother that I would have spanked him if he talked to me that way.

   a. *impudent* means _____

   b. The clue is _____
3. When asked if she liked her aunt's new hat, she *candidly* replied, "No, it's awful."

   a. *candidly* means _____

   b. The clue is _____

4. That toy is a *lethal* weapon; the kid almost killed me with it!

    a. *lethal* means _____

    b. The clue is _____

5. My dad is so *punctilious* that he always corrects my sloppy speech or points out my incorrect use of certain words.

    a. *punctilious* means _____

    b. The clue is _____

6. They think of themselves as the *elite* group on campus, looking down their noses at others.

    a. *elite* means _____

    b. The clue is _____

Make vocabulary cards for any words that gave you trouble, or use whatever method you have decided to use to develop your word power.

SIGNAL WORDS

Sometimes there are contextual *signal words* in a sentence that indirectly help define an unknown word. Signal words are just that: words that signal to you that a change is about to occur. Just as stoplights and road signs signal that you should slow down, look for curves, and watch out for cross streets while you're driving, signal words are used by writers to help you follow their thoughts. For instance, consider the following sentence:

While his subjects were grieving over their dead, the king was filled with exultation over his military victory.

Notice how the signal word "while" contrasts the way the subjects feel with the way the king feels. The subjects are grieving (sad) while the king is exulting (happy). So if we didn't know what exultation meant, the signal word "while" alerts us that it means the opposite of grieving.

Here's another example:

Despite his fear of the snake, Paul managed to subdue his true feelings as it coiled around his arm.

The signal word here is "despite," meaning in spite of, or even though. Here we have someone who has a fear of snakes, but despite that fear he subdues or, as we can guess from the context, manages to control his true feelings.

Here are some signal words that you probably already know but may never have thought about using in this way. In the future, let them help you unlock the meanings to words you may not know.

Signal Words

but	despite	yet	although
however	even though	in contrast	instead
nevertheless	in spite of		
while	rather		

Drill   B-2: SIGNAL WORDS

Directions: Using the signal words, see if you can figure out the meaning of the italicized words in the following sentences.

   1.   Although the patient is usually *morose*, she seems happy today.

     a.   *morose* means _____

     b.   signal word _____

   2.   He is usually *loquacious*, but tonight he's rather silent.

     a.   *loquacious* means _____

     b.   signal word _____

   3.   The boxer *feigned* a punch with his left rather than actually jabbing.

     a.   *feigned* means _____

     b.   signal word _____

   4.   Even though our camp spot was rather *remote*, I was afraid other people might discover it.

     a.   *remote* means _____

     b.   signal word _____

   5.   She usually is a *laggard*; however, today she was energetic and did her share.

     a.   *laggard* means _____

     b.   signal word _____

   6.   Although his parents were *indigent*, they somehow managed to provide Tommy with proper food and clothing.

     a.   *indigent* means _____

     b.   signal word _____

Make vocabulary cards or use some other method to learn any words that gave you trouble.

CONTEXTUAL EXAMPLES

Another way you can frequently determine an unknown word's meaning is through *contextual examples*. Writers often provide examples of things or ideas that help define a word. For instance, look at this sentence:

Luis must be very affluent. He wears expensive clothes and jewelry, drives a Rolls-Royce convertible, and owns a $1,750,000 house in Beverly Hills.

Notice all the examples that help define the word "affluent": expensive clothes, jewelry, car, house in Beverly Hills. All of these are items that require money or wealth. So it doesn't take much to figure out that affluent means wealthy or well-to-do.

Let's look at another example of the use of contextual examples:

The navy recruiting officer offered him several inducements to join up, such as the promise of a college education, the opportunity to fly jets, and the chance to be stationed in Hawaii.

If the word "inducements" is unclear to begin with, a look at the examples of what the recruitment officer promised gives us a hint that the word must mean reasons or motives to join the navy.

Now try using this technique on the following sentences.

Drill B-3: CONTEXTUAL EXAMPLES

Directions: Define the italicized words in the following sentences and give the example clues.

1. In order to show *clemency*, the judge reduced the fine to one dollar and merely gave the man a warning.

   a.   *clemency* means _____

   b.   example clues _____

2. Burning the village to the ground, shooting all the villagers, and plundering the area for valuables, the rebels committed one of the most *heinous* acts of the war.

   a.   *heinous* means _____

   b.   example clues _____

3. Sara is very *astute*; she borrowed money at a very low interest rate and built it into a small fortune through wise investments.

   a.   *astute* means _____

   b.   example clues _____

4. Jerry is so *indolent*! He sleeps late, never does chores unless yelled at, and would rather lounge around the house than look for a job.

   a.   *indolent* means _____

   b.   example clues _____

5. Carnegie was very *frugal*. Even though he earned little, he saved most of his money and lived on very little until he saved $10,000 for the investment that was to make him rich.

   a.   *frugal* means _____

   b.   example clues _____

6. They *enhanced* the property by pulling weeds, mowing the lawn, and planting trees around the house.

    a. *enhanced* means _____

    b. example clues _____

Make vocabulary cards or use some other method to learn the words that gave you trouble.

DEFINITION CLUES

The easiest of context clues to recognize is the *definition clue*. Often overlooked by readers, some sentences actually define the unknown word right in the sentence itself. Notice how that is done in the following example:

Sue, serving as the chairperson, presided at the meeting.

The phrase "serving as chairperson" actually defines the word "preside," which means to hold the position of authority, to be in charge.

Here's another example of a definition clue in a sentence:

Luke's pretentious manner, standing up and shouting at Sue that he should be running the meeting just to give her a bad time, didn't win him any friends.

Based on Luke's bad manners, we can guess that pretentious has something to do with claiming or demanding something when it's unjustified.

While context clues are not always there to help you with unfamiliar words, they do appear with frequency. Take the time in your future readings to look for the various types of clues covered in this section.

Drill B-4: DEFINITION CLUES

Directions: Define the italicized words in the following sentences.

1. I *presumed* or guessed that something was wrong when I smelled the smoke.

    presumed means _____
2. I always felt the *rapport* between us was good, based on a relationship of trust.

    rapport means _____
3. The most *salient* feature on his face is his chin; it's quite prominent.

    salient means _____
4. Sherry's anger, or more accurately, *malevolence* toward her brother became obvious when she tried to push him down the stairs.

    malevolence means _____
5. Bret's *jocose* manner soon had all of us laughing and joking.

    jocose means _____

6. Hans Zinsser said, "The rat, like men, has become practically *omnivorous*—it eats anything that lets it."

omnivorous means _____

Make vocabulary cards or use some other method to learn the words that gave you trouble.

Drill   B-5: CONTEXTUAL CLUES IN PARAGRAPHS

Directions: Read the following paragraphs. Then choose the correct definitions for each of the underlined words as they are used in context.

Paragraph 1

I became increasingly frustrated at not being able to express what I wanted to *convey* in letters that I wrote. . . . In the street, I had been the most *articulate* hustler out there—I had *commanded* attention when I said something. But now, trying to write simple English, I not only wasn't articulate, I wasn't even *functional*. How would I sound writing slang the way I would say it, something such as, "Look, daddy, let me pull your coat about a cat." (From Malcolm X with Alex Haley, *Autobiography of Malcolm X.*)

Circle the correct response.

1. convey	**2.** articulate	**3.** commanded	**4.** functional
a. transport	**a.** funny	**a.** ordered	**a.** workable
b. communicate	**b.** mean, tough	**b.** overlooked	**b.** not usable
c. believe	**c.** clear	**c.** exercised authority	**c.** worthy

Paragraph 2

This anti-literature attitude includes the idea that reading of literature is impractical, unproductive and perhaps slightly *immoral* or at least *effeminate*, because it is basically a pleasure-centered, leisure-time activity. Many people think that literary interests are undemocratic, *pseudo-aristocratic* and *pretentious* because of "upper-class" and "*elite*" connotations, and because some people have attempted to use "culture" and literary knowledge in a snobbish way for social-climbing and as a status symbol. (From Hugo Hortig, "Why Do They Hate Literature?" *Reading Improvement,* Vol. 2, No. 2, Winter 1965, p. 39.)

Circle the correct response.

1. immoral
  a. sexually attractive
  b. long-lasting
  c. wicked

2. effeminate
  a. tiresome
  b. womanly
  c. sinful

3. pseudo-aristocratic
  a. falsely proud or pretending "upper-classness"
  b. not genuine
  c. abnormal, according to accepted standards

4. pretentious
  a. false
  b. showy
  c. taken for granted

5. elite
  a. a type size
  b. choicest part
  c. enlightened

Paragraph 3

The "RED DEATH" had long devastated the country. No *pestilence* had ever been so fatal, or so hideous. Blood was its Avatar and its seal—the redness and horror of blood. There were sharp pains, and sudden dizziness, and then *profuse* bleeding at the pores, with *dissolution*. The scarlet stains upon the body, and especially upon the face of the victim, were the pest *ban* which shut him out from the aid and from the sympathy of his fellowmen. And the whole seizure, progress and *termination* of the disease, were the incidents of half an hour. (From Edgar Allan Poe "The Masque of the Red Death.")

Define the following words as they are used in context in the passage:

1. pestilence _____

2. profuse _____

3. dissolution _____

4. ban _____

5. termination _____

Paragraph 4

. . . Your brain has the capacity to hold billions of items of information, and research has shown that the millions of facts *acquired* from infancy and then apparently forgotten are actually *indelibly imprinted* on the mind. Any problems which occur when you try to *recall* something you have just seen or heard arise not from an inability to *retain* information, but from difficulties of *retrieval*. (From D. Lewis and J. Green, *Thinking Better,* Rawson, Wade Publishers, 1982.)

Substitute the following words from the passage with one-word synonyms:

1. acquired _____

2. indelibly _____

3. imprinted _____

4. recall _____

5. retain _____

6. retrieval _____

Paragraph 5

. . . Language is our unique gift from nature, and we use it for exploring. More than this, we have spontaneously arranged ourselves in *dense* clusters, cities, for all the world like *ganglia*, all over the surface of the earth. We are becoming a live network of thought, a meshwork of messages, measuring things, turning things over, talking forever to each other, *gabbling* sometimes, but thinking all the way. Maybe, with luck and long enough survival, we could turn out to be a kind of consciousness for the whole System. Maybe everything you say, perhaps even everything you think, is zipping around out there in the network, making up parts of the thought and memory of the whole creature. Maybe that is how we survive, in real life. I view this as a practical, down-to-earth, nonmystical notion. Nature is *profligate* in many ways, with seeds for instance, but *parsimonious* with mechanisms that require a great deal of energy. I cannot imagine anything more specialized and harder to make than a thought. (From Lewis Thomas, "The Strangeness of Nature," *The New England Journal of Medicine*, Vol. 298, No. 26, June 29, 1978.)

Define the following words from the paragraph:

1. dense _____

2. ganglia _____

3. gabbling _____

4. profligate _____

5. parsimonious _____

Paragraph 6

In the *melting-pot* America legend, plunging straight into the English language in school was a matter of pride and *sheer* survival. The pain of learning, and of leaving one's immigrant parents behind, was justified as necessary for progress and *assimilation*. But by the 1970s, *prevailing* notions about education and *ethnicity* had changed. It was believed that the cultural heritage of each student should be preserved. Accordingly, new *waves* of immigrant children, the majority of them Hispanics, were provided with bilingual education as the Federal Government *prodded* schools to give them instruction primarily in their own language until they acquired English skills. But many students stayed in such classes for years. (From "Taking Bilingualism to Task," *Time*, April 19, 1982.)

Define the following words as they are used in the paragraph:

1. melting-pot _____

2. sheer _____

3. assimilation _____

4. prevailing _____

5. ethnicity _____

6. waves _____

7. prodded _____

After your answers have been checked, make vocabulary cards or use some other method to learn the words that gave you trouble.

Drill B-6: QUICK QUIZ

Directions: The following words are from the drills you've been doing on context clues. Define each word and then write a sentence using it correctly in context.

1. articulate

   a. definition _____

   b. sentence _____

   _____

2. pretentious

   a. definition _____

   b. sentence _____

   _____

3. jocose

   a. definition _____

   b. sentence _____

   _____

4. rapport

   a. definition _____

   b. sentence _____

   _____

5. indolent

   a. definition _____

   b. sentence _____

   _____

6. astute

   a. definition _____

   b. sentence _____

   _____

7. frugal

   a. definition _____

   b. sentence _____

   _____

8. loquacious

   a. definition _____

   b. sentence _____

   _____

9. laggard

   a. definition _____

   b. sentence _____

   _____

10. vociferous

   a. definition _____

   b. sentence _____

   _____

Turn the quiz in to your instructor.

C. Learning Word Parts and Structure

Another good way to develop your vocabulary is to learn some of the basic word parts that make up the English language. Many of our words are derived from other languages, and many prefixes, suffixes, and root word parts come from Latin and Greek. You probably already know many of them but have never taken the time to see how frequently they appear in our language or why certain words mean what they do. In this section you will review and learn some of the commonly used word parts in English.

No doubt you know the word "phonograph." This common word in English is actually made up of two Greek word roots—*phon*, meaning sound, and *graph*, meaning write or record. Technically, the grooves in a recording are a record of sound, or, if you will, sound written on a record. The advantage of knowing the meaning to word parts is that you can often figure out what an unknown word means by looking at its parts. Look at some of the words that contain the word part *phon:*

> phone = informal verb meaning to telephone someone as well as the informal word for telephone
> phonate = to utter speech sounds
> phoneme = one of the set of the smallest units of speech that distinguishes one utterance or word from another; the *b* in bat and the *m* in mat are phonemes.
> phonemics = the study of phonemes
> phonetic = representing the sounds of speech with distinct symbols
> phonetician = an expert in phonetics
> phonic = having sound
> phonics = the study or science of sound
> phonogram = a character or symbol representing a word or phoneme
> phonology = the science of speech sounds
> phonotype = text printed in phonetic symbols
> symphony = a long sonata for orchestra (*sym* means together or in harmony)
> euphony = good, pleasant sounds (*eu* means good)
> cacophony = harsh, unpleasant sound (*caco* means bad)

Even though some of these words are speciality words, you are one step ahead when you know that all the words have something to do with sound.

Many words in English are made up of *prefixes* (small but meaningful letter groups added before a base word or root that change the root's meaning) and *suffixes* (letter groups that are added to the end of a base word or root). Learning the meaning of these word parts, together with the meaning of common base words and Greek and Latin roots, will give you the key for unlocking the meanings of hundreds of words.

Following are several drills dealing with word parts and structure. Some you will know, some will be new to you. It is suggested that you make vocabulary cards for those you want to overlearn, or use whatever method you have decided upon for enlarging your vocabulary.

Drill C-1: PREFIXES THAT EXPRESS NEGATIVITY AND REVERSAL

Directions: There are several prefixes (letter groups added before a root word that change the root's meaning) that have to do with negation or reversal. For instance, placing the prefix *dis* in front of the root word *approve* creates the word *disapprove*, changing the word to a negative one. Placing the prefix *dis* on the root word *arm* creates the word *disarm*, reversing the root's meaning.

Below there are three columns. Column 1 contains some prefixes that express negative or reverse meanings. Column 2 contains words you should know. In column 3 you should write in the words from column 2, adding to each what you think is the correct prefix from column 1 to the root word's meaning. The first one has been done for you. Clues for using *il, im,* and *ir* are

use *il* with words beginning with *l*
use *im* with words beginning with *b, m,* and *p*
use *ir* with words beginning with *r*

Column 1	Column 2	Column 3
a	active	1. _____ *inactive* _____
counter	comfortable	2. _____
de	expensive	3. _____
dis	logical	4. _____
non	violent	5. _____
il	fair	6. _____
im	regulate	7. _____
in	typical	8. _____
ir	pleasant	9. _____
un	settle	10. _____
	proper	11. _____
	legal	12. _____
	regular	13. _____
	polite	14. _____
	desicive	15. _____
	easy	16. _____
	movable	17. _____
	possible	18. _____

rational   **19.** _____

legitimate   **20.** _____

Drill C-2: PREFIXES THAT EXPRESS TIME AND PLACE

Directions: Below are some commonly used prefixes that express time and place. Study them carefully. Then fill in the blanks in the numbered exercises. The first one has been done for you.

Prefix	Meaning
intro, intra	inside, within
inter	between, among
pre	before
de	away, undo
ex	out, not any longer
post	after
re	back, again
super	above
trans	across
sub	under
retro	back, backward
circum	around

1. What is the opposite of *inflate* (to fill)? _____ *deflate* _____

2. If a patriot is a loyal countryman, what is an *expatriate?* _____

3. What is the opposite of *activate?* _____

4. If import means to bring in, *export* means _____

5. If urban refers to the city, what is an *intraurban* truck line? _____

6. Is *postgraduate* work done before or after you graduate from college? ____

_____

7. A *prefix* is called what it is because it is fixed _____ the root word.

8. If the root word *vive* refers to life, what does *revive* mean? _____

_____

9. A *transatlantic* voyage would take you _____

10. If you *intercede* during an argument, what are you doing? _____

_____

_____

11. *Intercollegiate* sports are activities that take place _____
different colleges.

12. *Intracollegiate* sports are activities that take place _____ .

_____

13. Is the *pre-Victorian* period before or after the Victorian period? _____

14. *Mortem* refers to death; what is a *postmortem?* _____

_____

15. Who is higher in rank, a *subprincipal* or a principal? _____

16. What is meant by a *superhuman* effort? _____

_____

17. What would it mean if your boss said you had some *retroactive* pay coming to

you? _____

_____

18. What's the difference between *circumference* and *diagonal* measurements?

_____

_____

19. Why are *subways* called what they are? _____

_____

20. What is the difference between *interisland* ships and those that *circumnavi-*

gate? _____

Drill   C-3: MISCELLANEOUS PREFIXES

Directions: Study the following miscellaneous prefixes and their meanings.
Then answer the questions that follow. The first one has been done for you.

Prefix	**Meaning**
anti	against
auto	self
bene	good, well
bi	two
eu	good, nice
hetero	different
mis, miso	wrong; hatred
mal	bad, wrong
poly	many

1. If a newspaper is printed *bimonthly,* it is printed *twice a month.*

2. If *phon* means sound, what does *euphonious* mean? _____

_____

3. If *toxin* means poison, what does *antitoxin* mean? _____

_____

4. If *gen* refers to types or kinds, what does *heterogeneous* mean? _____

_____

5. If *homogeneous* is the opposite of *heterogeneous*, what does it mean? _____

_____

6. If *sect* means to cut or divide, what does *bisect* mean? _____

_____

7. If *caco* means bad, or unpleasant, how would you form a word that means the

opposite of *euphony?* _____

8. Since *gam* refers to marriage, *misogamy* means _____

_____

9. Since *gyn* refers to women, a *misogynist* is _____

_____

10. What is a *polygamist?* _____

_____

11. Why is an *automatic* transmission called what it is? _____

_____

12. Which is better, a tumor that is *malignant* or *benign?* _____

_____

13. What is *malpractice?* _____

_____

14. Why are fund-raisers often called *benefits?* _____

_____

15. Why is someone who donates money called a *benefactor?* _____

_____

Drill C-4: QUICK QUIZ

Directions: Define the following prefixes and write a word that contains each prefix.

Prefix	Definition	Word Using Prefix
1. auto		
2. il		
3. intra		
4. in		
5. un		
6. ir		
7. anti		
8. a/an		
9. bi		
10. de		
11. dis		
12. hetero		
13. bene		
14. eu		
15. sub		
16. im		
17. mis		
18. post		
19. trans		
20. re		

Turn in the quiz to your instructor.

NAME _____ SECTION _____ DATE _____

Drill C-5: NOUN SUFFIXES

Directions: A noun, as you may remember, is frequently defined as a person, place, or thing: woman, John, city, farm, hammer, car—all are nouns. There are some suffixes (letters at the end of a word) that change root words into nouns. For instance, *er* on the end of the word *teach* (a verb) forms the word *teacher,* a noun. The suffix *dom* on the end of *free* creates the noun *freedom.*

Study the following list of suffixes. They all mean "a person who is or does something." Then answer the questions that follow. The first one has been done for you.

ent	ess
er	ist
or	ee
ant	ard
ar	

1. Someone who acts is an _____ *actor, actress* _____.

2. A person who is paid to serve in a household is a _____.

3. Someone who gets drunk much of the time is a _____.

4. A person who practices science is _____.

5. A woman who waits on tables in a restaurant is a _____.

6. One who begs is a _____.

7. A person who resides in an apartment is called a _____.

8. One who is elected to preside over an organization is called the _____

    _____.

9. A payer _____ while a payee _____.

10. Someone who commits anarchy is an _____.

11. A friend who keeps your confidence is called a _____.

12. One who sails is a _____.

13. Someone who practices biology is a _____.

14. A person who narrates is a _____.

15. One who studies is a _____.

Drill C-6: MORE NOUN SUFFIXES

Directions: Column 1 contains a list of suffixes that mean a state or quality of being. For instance, *violence* is the state of being *violent; loyalty* is the state of being *loyal.* Column 2 contains some words that can be changed to nouns by adding the suffixes from column 1. Using the suffixes in column 1, write in the correct noun form in column 3. The first one has been done for you.

Column 1	Column 2	Column 3
ance	fail	1. _____ *failure* _____
ation	hero	2. _____
dom	amuse	3. _____
hood	friend	4. _____
ion	free	5. _____
ism	tense	6. _____
ity	necessary	7. _____
ment	repent	8. _____
ness	starve	9. _____
ty	royal	10. _____
ship	happy	11. _____
ure	seize	12. _____
	lively	13. _____
	content	14. _____
	moderate	15. _____

Drill C-7: MISCELLANEOUS SUFFIXES

Directions: Study the following list of suffixes and their definitions. Then, using the list, add suffixes to the words that follow. Some words may take more than one suffix. The first one has been done for you.

Suffix	Definition	Suffix	Definition
able, ible	able to	less	without
cy	state or condition	ize	to make
ful, ous	full of	ly	a characteristic or in
ic, al	related to		a certain manner
ish, ive	inclined to; similar		

1. care   *careful, careless, carefully, carelessly*

2. depend   _____

3. instruct _____

4. infant _____

5. vocal _____

6. expend _____

7. form _____

8. permanent _____

9. care _____

10. tropic _____

11. active _____

12. popular _____

13. combat _____

14. compete _____

15. caution _____

16. word _____

17. history _____

18. wonder _____

19. nature _____

20. defense _____

Drill C-8: ROOTS

Directions: Using the list below of word roots and their definitions, answer the questions that follow.

Root	Definition	Root	Definition
aud	hear	graph	write, record
chron	time	man, manu	hand
cred	belief	mort	death
dent	tooth	phil	love
dict	tell, say	phon	sound

1. If *meter* means measure, a chronometer _____

_____.

2. If something is audible, you can _____ it.

3. *Incredulous* means _____

_____.

4. The suffix *ist* refers to a person; that's why someone who works on your teeth

is called a _____.

5. If *contra* means against or opposite; *contradict* means _____

_____.

6. A chronograph is _____

_____.

7. The opposite of *automatic* is _____

_____.

8. Does a postmortem occur before or after death? _____.

9. If *anthrop* refers to man or mankind, what is a philanthropist? _____

_____.

10. What is a dictaphone? _____

_____.

Drill   C-9: MORE ROOTS

Directions: Define the following words. Don't look back at any previous exercises. You should be able to define all of these words if you learned from the
previous drills.

Root	Definition	Root	Definition
biblio	book	phobia	fear
bio	life	poly	many
gam	marriage	port	carry
gen	kinds, types	tele	far, distance
log(y)	study of	theo	god
mono	one	vis	see

1. bibliography   _____

2. biology   _____

3. biography   _____

4. monogamy   _____

5. polyphonous _____

6. heterogeneous _____

7. bibliophobia _____

8. portable _____

9. televise _____

10. theology _____

Drill C-10: QUICK QUIZ

Directions: Define the following words. Don't look back at any previous exercises. You should be able to define all of these words if you learned from the previous drills.

1. illogical _____

2. irrational _____

3. atypical _____

4. bimotored _____

5. euphonious _____

6. antitheological _____

7. heterogeneous _____

8. deflate _____

9. intraoffice _____

10. misanthropist _____

11. autograph _____

12. monogamy _____

13. submariner _____

14. audiometer _____

15. incredulous _____

16. bibliophile _____

17. philanthropist _____

18. bibliography _____

19. credible _____

20. dictation _____

Turn in the quiz to your instructor. Make vocabulary cards for any words you missed or need to learn better.

D. Learning Dictionary Skills

There comes a time when context clues and knowledge of word parts is not enough to help you understand an unknown word's meaning. That usually means a trip to the dictionary. The dictionary is more than a recorder of a word's meaning. It gives information on the word's origin, its various meanings, pronunciation, parts of speech, spellings, synonyms and antonyms, and its formal and informal usage. If you don't have a good, up-to-date dictionary, you should get one. (In a later drill you will read an essay entitled "What You Should Look for in a Dictionary" by Robert M. Pierson that will help you select one appropriate for you.)

Here is a typical dictionary word entry:

> **ap·peal** (ə-pēl′) *n.* **1.** An earnest request. **2.** An application to a higher authority, as for a decision. **3.** The power of arousing interest. **4.** *Law.* **a.** Transfer of a case from a lower to a higher court for a new hearing. **b.** A request for a new hearing. —*v.* **1.** To make an earnest request, as for help. **2.** To be attractive. **3.** To transfer or apply to transfer (a case) to a higher court for rehearing. [< Lat. *appellare,* to entreat.] —**ap·peal′a·ble** *adj.* —**ap·peal′er** *n.* —**ap·peal′ing·ly** *adv.*

Copyright © 1983 by Houghton Mifflin Company. Reprinted by permission from *The American Heritage Dictionary,* paperback edition.

In almost all dictionaries, the main word appears in bold type and is divided into syllables by dots. Following in parentheses are the pronunciation symbols. If you are unfamiliar with the symbols and their sounds, a pronunciation key appears either at the bottom of the page and/or near the front of the dictionary. It usually looks like this:

ă pat   ā pay   â care   ä father   ĕ pet   ē be   ĭ pit   ī tie   î pier   ŏ pot   ō toe   ô paw, for   oi noise   ŏŏ took
ōō boot   ou out   th thin   *th* this   ŭ cut   û urge   yōō abuse   zh vision   ə about, item, edible, gallop, circus

---

Copyright © 1983 by Houghton Mifflin Company. Reprinted by permission from *The American Heritage Dictionary,* paperback edition.

Notice that very basic words are used in order to make certain you can easily figure out how to pronounce an unknown word.

Next, abbreviated, is the word's part of speech. The *n.* means noun, but if you look more closely after definition 4b, a -*v.* appears. That's because the word can also be used as a verb. It's important to understand what part of speech a word is so that you can use it correctly.

Notice that there are four definitions given for *appeal* as a noun. The fourth definition is actually divided in two, showing how it is used in law terminology. Then three definitions are given for the word's use as a verb.

The bracketed section that appears after the definition provides the word's etymology or its historical origin. In this case, the word originally came from the Latin *appellare,* meaning to entreat.

Finally, in bold print, the spellings of the word being used as other parts of speech are given.

Unfortunately, the definitions given for words in some dictionaries are not always easy to understand. Frequently, a word that is being used in a definition must also be looked up in the dictionary! All dictionaries are not the same, so be selective in your choice.

The following drills should help you become more familiar with how to get the most from whatever dictionary you buy.

Drill   D-1: PRONUNCIATION KEYS

Directions: Using the pronunciation key on the opposite page, answer the following questions. Answers with explanations follow each question.

1. The first *o* in the word *loquacious* (lō-kwā´-shəs) is pronounced like the *o* in the key words

   _____ and _____.
   The key words used are *toe* and *horse*. Since the first *o* in loquacious is marked ō, it is necessary to scan the dictionary symbol column and find an ō listed. Such a symbol appears in the second column. This sound is called the long *o* sound. The symbols appearing over the vowel letters are called diacritical marks.

2. The *a* in the word *loquacious* is pronounced

   like the *a* in the key word _____.
   The key word is pay. The answer is found in the first column, second listing. This sound is called the long *a* sound.

3. The ə symbol used in the pronunciation clues (lō-kwā´-shəs) symbolizes the sound of the let-

   ter _____ as in the word *circus*.
   The symbol ə represents several sounds depending on what letter of the alphabet it represents. In this case it represents the *u* sound as in the word circus.

4. The symbol ə is called a _____.
   You may have known the answer to this without finding it in the chart. However, the schwa is defined in the explanatory notes under the chart.

5. The *a* in the word *chartreuse* (shär-tro͞oz´) is

   pronounced like the *a* in the word _____.
   The two small dots give the *a* a completely different sound which is sometimes called the short vowel sound. The word *father* is the answer indicated in the first column.

6. The o͞o sound in *chartreuse* is pronounced

   like the double *o* in the word _____.
   The word *boot* contains the o͞o sound. See the middle column.

7. The first *e* in the word *incertitude* (insûr´-tə-to͞od) is pronounced like the *e* in the word

   _____.
   The *cer* portion of the word *incertitude* is pronounced *sûr.* The *û* sound, as the column shows, is pronounced like the *e* in *term. Term* is the correct answer.

8. The second *i* in the word *incertitude* is pro-

   nounced like the *i* in the word _____.
   Here you need to refer back to *incertitude* in parentheses in question 7 above; then scan the chart for the sound of the schwa ə as used to replace the letter *i. Edible* is the answer.

9. The *dg* in a word such as *judge* is replaced by

   the symbol _____ as a pronunciation clue.
   Unless you already knew the answer, you needed to scan the key word column for a quick answer to this question and look for the word *judge.* Fifth from the bottom of the first key word column is the word *judge.* To the right is the symbol *j,* meaning *dg* is sounded as a *j* sounds.

10. Does the (´) mark mean the accent should be placed on the syllable before or after the mark

    appears? _____
    The mark means the accent should be on the syllable before the mark.

PRONUNCIATION KEY

A shorter form of this key appears across the bottom of each lefthand page. The symbols marked with an asterisk are discussed in the explanatory notes following the pronunciation key.

spellings	symbols	spellings	symbols
pat	ă	noise	oi
pay	ā	took	o͝o
care	*âr	boot	o͞o
father	ä	out	ou
bib	b	pop	p
church	ch	roar	*r
deed, milled	d	sauce	s
pet	ĕ	ship, dish	sh
bee	ē	tight, stopped	t
fife, phase, rough	f	thin	th
gag	g	this	*th*
hat	h	cut	ŭ
which	hw	urge, term, firm,	*ûr
pit	*ĭ	word, heard	
pie, by	ī	valve	v
pier	*îr	with	w
judge	j	yes	y
kick, cat, pique	k	abuse, use	yo͞o
lid, needle	*l (nēd′l)	zebra, xylem	z
mum	m	vision, pleasure,	zh
no, sudden	*n (sŭd′n)	garage	
thing	ng	about, item, edible,	*ə
pot, *horrid	ŏ	gallop, circus	
toe, *hoarse	ō	butter	*ər
caught, paw, *for	ô		

STRESS

Primary stress ′   **bi·ol′o·gy** (bī-ŏl′ə-jē)
Secondary stress ′   **bi′o·log′i·cal** (bī′ə-lŏj′ĭ-kəl)

EXPLANATORY NOTES

ə: This nonalphabetical symbol is called a *schwa*. The symbol is used in the Dictionary to represent only a reduced vowel, i.e., a vowel that receives the weakest level of stress (which can be thought of as no stress) within a word and therefore nearly always exhibits a change in quality from the quality it would have if it were stressed, as in *telegraph* (tĕl′ĭ-grăf′) and *telegraphy* (tə-lĕg′rə-fē). Vowels are never reduced to a single exact vowel; the schwa sound will vary according to its phonetic environment.

ĭ: This symbol is used to represent the second vowel in **artist** (är′tĭst), a vowel that has been only partially reduced and therefore cannot be represented by the schwa. The choice between schwa (ə) and "breve i" (ĭ) to represent reduced vowels is arrived at through a complex set of considerations. In nearly every case in which (ĭ) appears, there is also a variant pronunciation closer to (ə). As long as reduced vowels receive no stress, the surrounding sounds will lead the reader to produce either (ə) or (ĭ), according to his regional speech pattern.

âr   These symbols represent vowels that have been altered by a following *r*.
îr   This situation is traditionally exemplified by the words *Mary, merry*, and
ôr   *marry*. In some regional varieties all three are pronounced alike: (mĕr′ē).
ōr   However, in a broad range of individual American speech patterns cutting
ûr   across regional boundaries the three words are distinguished. It is this pattern that the Dictionary represents, thus: *Mary* (mâr′ē), *merry* (mĕr′ē), *marry* (măr′ē). Some words, however, are heard in all three pronunciations, indistinctly grading one into another. For these words the Dictionary represents only (âr), for example, *care* (kâr), *dairy* (dâr′ē).

Abbreviations and Symbols

abbr.	abbreviation	freq.	frequentative
adj.	adjective	comp.	comparative
adv.	adverb	dial.	dialectal
cent.	century	dim.	diminutive
fem.	feminine	ety.	etymology
fut.	future	pl.	plural
gerund.	gerundive	poss.	possibly
imit.	imitative	pr.	present
imper.	imperative	pr.p.	present participle
M	Middle	prob.	probably
masc.	masculine	redup.	reduplication
Med.	Medieval	sing.	singular
Mod.	Modern	St.	Saint
n.	noun	superl.	superlative
naut.	nautical	transl.	translation
O	Old	ult.	ultimately
obs.	obsolete	v.	verb
orig.	origin, originally	var.	variant
p.	past		
p.p.	past participle		
p.t.	past tense	<	derived from
perh.	perhaps	+	combined with

Abbreviations of Languages

Afr.	Afrikaans	Louisiana Fr.	Louisiana French
Am. E.	American English	LG	Low German
Am. Sp.	American Spanish	MDu.	Middle Dutch
AN	Anglo-Norman	ME	Middle English
Ar.	Arabic	Med. Lat.	Medieval Latin
Aram.	Aramaic	Mex. Sp.	Mexican Spanish
Balt.	Baltic	MHG	Middle High German
Brit.	British	MLG	Middle Low German
Can. Fr.	Canadian French	NLat.	New Latin
Cant.	Cantonese	Norman Fr.	Norman French
Celt.	Celtic	Norw.	Norwegian
Chin.	Chinese	ODan	Old Danish
Dan.	Danish	OE	Old English
Du.	Dutch	OFr.	Old French
Egypt.	Egyptian	OHG	Old High German
E.	English	OIr.	Old Irish
Finn.	Finnish	OItal.	Old Italian
Flem.	Flemish	ON	Old Norse
Fr.	French	ONFr.	Old North French
G.	German	OProv.	Old Provençal
Gael.	Gaelic	OSp.	Old Spanish
Gk.	Greek	Pers.	Persian
Gmc.	Germanic	Pidgin E.	Pidgin English
Goth.	Gothic	Pol.	Polish
Heb.	Hebrew	Port.	Portuguese
HG	High German	Prov.	Provençal
Hung.	Hungarian	R.	Russian
Icel.	Icelandic	Rum.	Rumanian
Ir.	Irish	Sc.	Scottish
Iran.	Iranian	Scand.	Scandinavian
Ir. Gael.	Irish Gaelic	Sc. Gael.	Scottish Gaelic
Ital.	Italian	Skt.	Sanskrit
J.	Japanese	Slav.	Slavic
Lat.	Latin	Sp.	Spanish
LGk.	Late Greek	Swed.	Swedish
Lith.	Lithuanian	Turk.	Turkish

xiii

Drill D-2: ABBREVIATIONS

Directions: Dictionaries must use many abbreviations because of space and
size limitations. Using the chart on the opposite page, find what the following
abbreviations mean. Write your answers in the blanks.

1. ME _____

2. pl. _____

3. obs. _____

4. Heb. _____

5. G. _____

6. Brit. _____

7. OFr. _____

8. Sp. _____

9. v. _____

10. ety. _____

11. naut. _____

12. adv. _____

13. p. _____

14. Gk. _____

15. transl. _____

16. adj. _____

17. Sc. _____

18. cent. _____

19. + _____

20. dial _____

21. Lat. _____

22. orig. _____

23. E. _____

24. n. _____

25. fem. _____

26. < _____

27. var. _____

28. obs. _____

29. pr. _____

30. masc. _____

Drill D-3: WORD ENTRY KNOWLEDGE

Directions: Using the following dictionary word entry, answer the questions
that follow.

out·side (out-sīd′, out′sīd′) *n.* **1.** An outer surface or side; exterior. **2.** The space beyond a boundary or limit. **3.** The utmost limit; maximum: *We'll be leaving in ten days at the outside.* —*adj.* **1.** Acting, occurring, originating, or existing at a place beyond certain limits; outer; foreign: *outside assistance.* **2.** Of, restricted to, or situated on the outside of an enclosure or boundary; external: *an outside door lock.* **3.** Extreme; uttermost: *The cost exceeded even my outside estimate.* **4.** Slight; remote: *an outside chance.* —*adv.* On or into the outside; outdoors: *Let's go outside.* —*prep.* **1.** On or to the outer side of: *outside the playing field.* **2.** Beyond the limits of: *outside the rules.* **3.** With the exception of; except: *no information outside the figures given.*

Copyright © 1983 by Houghton Mifflin Company. Reprinted by permission from *The American Heritage Dictionary,* paperback edition.

1. In total, how many definitions are given for the word *outside?* _____

2. For how many parts of speech can *outside* be used? _____

3. Two ways to pronounce *outside* are given. What is the difference between the

    two? _____

    _____

4. What does it mean to say there is an outside chance you might win? _____

    _____

5. A sentence using *outside* in context is provided after the third definition of the

    word as a noun. Explain in your own words what the sentence means. ____

    _____

    _____

6. What is the etymology of the word *outside?* _____

    _____

7. Use *outside* in four different sentences, each one as a different part of speech:

    a. as a n. _____

        _____

    b. as an adj. _____

        _____

    c. as an adv. _____

        _____

    d. as a prep. _____

        _____

Drill   D-4: FINDING INFORMATION

Directions: Using the dictionary excerpt on the opposite page, look for the
answers to the following questions. Write your answers in the blanks.

1. What is the difference between *Babel* (capital *B*) and *babel?*

    _____

    _____

2. What is the origin of the word *baby?* (You may need to use the abbreviation

    chart on page 46.) _____

Bb

b or **B** (bē) *n., pl.* **b's** or **B's.** **1.** The 2nd letter of the English alphabet. **2.** The 2nd in a series. **3.** The 2nd-highest grade in quality.
B The symbol for the element boron.
Ba The symbol for the element barium.
baa (bă, bä) *n.* The bleat of a sheep. —**baa** *v.*
Ba·al (bā′əl) *n., pl.* **-al·im** (-ə-lĭm). **1.** Any of various fertility and nature gods of the ancient Semitic peoples. **2.** A false god or idol.
Bab·bitt (băb′ĭt) *n.* A smug, provincial member of the American middle class. [< the main character in *Babbitt* by Sinclair Lewis (1885–1951).]
bab·ble (băb′əl) *v.* **-bled, -bling.** **1.** To utter indistinct, meaningless sounds. **2.** To talk foolishly; chatter. **3.** To make a continuous low, murmuring sound. [ME *babelen.*] —**bab′ble** *n.* —**bab′bler** *n.*
babe (bāb) *n.* **1.** A baby. **2.** An innocent or naive person. [ME.]
Ba·bel (bā′bəl, băb′əl) *n.* **1.** In the Old Testament, the site of a tower where construction was interrupted by God who caused a confusion of tongues. **2. babel.** A confusion of sounds, voices, or languages.
ba·boon (bă-boon′) *n.* A large African monkey with an elongated, doglike muzzle. [< OFr. *babuin.*]
ba·bush·ka (bə-boosh′kə) *n.* A head scarf, folded triangularly and tied under the chin. [R., grandmother.]
ba·by (bā′bē) *n., pl.* **-bies.** **1.** A very young child; infant. **2.** The youngest member of a family or group. **3.** One who acts like a baby. **4.** *Slang.* A young girl or woman. **5.** *Slang.* An object of personal concern: *The project was his baby.* —*v.* **-bied, -by·ing.** To treat oversolicitously. [ME *babie.*] —**ba′by·hood′** *n.* —**ba′by·ish** *adj.* —**ba′by·ish·ly** *adv.* —**ba′by·ish·ness** *n.*
Syns: *baby, coddle, indulge, mollycoddle, pamper, spoil* **v.**
Bab·y·lo·ni·an (băb′ə-lō′nē-ən) *n.* **1.** A native or inhabitant of Babylonia. **2.** The Semitic language of the Babylonians, a form of Akkadian. —**Bab′y·lo′ni·an** *adj.*
ba·by's-breath (bā′bĕz-brĕth′) *n.* Also **babies'-breath.** A plant with numerous small white flowers.
ba·by-sit (bā′bē-sĭt′) *v.* To care for children when the parents are not at home. —**baby sitter** *n.*
bac·ca·lau·re·ate (băk′ə-lôr′ē-ĭt) *n.* **1.** The degree of bachelor conferred upon graduates of colleges and universities. **2.** An address delivered to a graduating class at commencement. [Med. Lat. *baccalaureatus.*]
bac·ca·rat (bä′kə-rä′, băk′ə-) *n.* A gambling game played with cards. [Fr. *baccara.*]
bac·cha·nal (băk′ə-năl′, bä′kə-näl′, băk′ə-nəl) *n.* **1.** A drunken or riotous celebration, orig. in honor of Bacchus. **2.** A participant in such a celebration. **3.** A reveler. —**bac′cha·na′lian** (-năl′yən, -nā′lē-ən) *adj.*
Bac·chus (băk′əs) *n. Rom. Myth.* The god of wine. —**Bac′chic** *adj.*
bach·e·lor (băch′ə-lər, băch′lər) *n.* **1.** An unmarried man. **2. a.** A college or university degree signifying completion of the undergraduate curriculum. **b.** A person with this degree. [< Med. Lat. *baccalarius.*] —**bach′e·lor·hood′** *n.*
bach·e·lor's-but·ton (băch′ə-lərz-bŭt′n, băch′-lərz-) *n.* The cornflower.

3. Who is Bacchus? _____

4. What is a *bacchanal?* _____

5. From where does the definition of Babbitt come? _____

_____

6. How is *baby* defined in this example: "The project was his baby"? _____

_____

7. According to the dictionary, is it acceptable English to use the word *baby* to

refer to a girl or a woman? _____

8. Is *Babylonian* a person or a language? _____

   9. What is the origin of *babushka?* _____

   _____

   10. What suffixes are used to change *baby* to different parts of speech? _____

   _____

Drill   D-5: QUICK QUIZ

Directions: On the opposite page there is an excerpt from a dictionary with some items marked for your identification. Look at the circled material and fill in the blanks with the letter of the items listed below that best describes it. The first one has been done for you. When finished, turn the exercise in to your instructor.

   a. pictures or illustrations
   b. definitions based on parts of speech
   c. parts of speech
   d. contextual examples of word usage
   e. etymology or word history
   f. formal and informal usage of a word
   g. the preferred pronunciation of the word
   h. slang definitions
   i. word meaning in its original language

person. [< OE *swēte.*] —**sweet·ly** *adv.*
—**sweet′ness** *n.*

sweet·bread (swĕt′brĕd′) *n.* The thymus or pancreas of an animal, used for food.

sweet·bri·er (swĕt′brī′ər) *n.* Also **sweet·bri·ar.** A rose with prickly stems, fragrant leaves, and pink flowers.

sweet corn *n.* The common edible variety of corn, with kernels that are sweet when young.

sweet·en (swĕt′n) *v.* **1.** To make sweet or sweeter. **2.** To make more valuable or attractive. —**sweet′en·er** *n.*

sweet·en·ing (swĕt′n-ĭng) *n.* **1.** The act or process of making sweet. **2.** Something used to sweeten.

sweet·heart (swĕt′härt′) *n.* **1.** One who is loved by another. **2.** A lovable person.

sweet·meat (swĕt′mēt′) *n.* **1.** Candy. **2.** Crystallized fruit.

sweet pea *n.* A climbing plant cultivated for its variously colored, fragrant flowers.

sweet pea   sweet William

sweet potato *n.* **1.** A tropical American vine cultivated for its thick, orange-colored, edible root. **2.** The root of this plant, eaten cooked as a vegetable.

sweet-talk (swĕt′tôk′) *v.* To coax or cajole with flattery. —**sweet talk** *n.*

sweet tooth *n.* *Informal.* A fondness or craving for sweets.

sweet Wil·liam (wĭl′yəm) *n.* A widely cultivated plant with flat, dense clusters of varicolored flowers.

swell (swĕl) *v.* **swelled, swelled** or **swol·len** (swō′lən), **swell·ing.** **1.** To increase in size or volume. **2.** To increase in force, number, or intensity. **3.** To bulge out; protrude. **4.** To fill or become filled with an emotion: *swelled with pride.* —*n.* **1.** A swollen part. **2.** A long wave that moves continuously without breaking. **3.** *Informal.* **a.** A fashionably dressed person. **b.** A person prominent in fashionable society. —*adj.* **-er, -est.** **1.** *Informal.* Fashionably elegant; smart; stylish. **2.** *Slang.* Fine; excellent. [< OE *swellan.*]

swell·ing (swĕl′ĭng) *n.* **1.** The act of expanding. **2.** Something that is swollen.

swel·ter (swĕl′tər) *v.* To suffer oppressively from heat. [< OE *sweltan,* to die.]

swept (swĕpt) *v.* *p.t. & p.p.* of **sweep.**

swerve (swûrv) *v.* **swerved, swerv·ing.** To turn aside from a straight course; veer. [< OE *sweorfan,* to rub.] —**swerve** *n.*

swift (swĭft) *adj.* **-er, -est.** **1.** Moving or able to move with great speed. **2.** Occurring or accomplished quickly. —*n.* Any of various dark-colored birds with long, narrow wings and a relatively short tail. [< OE.] —**swift′ly** *adv.* —**swift′ness** *n.*

1. _____ *g* _____

2. _____

3. _____

4. _____

5. _____

6. _____

7. _____

8. _____

9. _____

NAME _____ SECTION _____ DATE _____

E. Reading Practices

Below are two reading selections. Both are followed by comprehension and vocabulary checks. Always make certain that you understand why you may have missed any questions. Your scores at this point are less important than understanding why you may have missed a question. Learn from your mistakes.

Drill   E-1

Directions: The following selection is from *The Autobiography of Malcolm X,* written with the assistance of Alex Haley, who later wrote *Roots*. Malcolm X was a controversial Black Muslim leader who, raised in a world of crime, drugs, and prison, became one of the most powerful and articulate blacks in the 1960s until he was shot to death while giving a speech in Harlem. This portion tells of an important turning point in his life.

HOW I DISCOVERED WORDS: A HOMEMADE EDUCATION

Malcolm X

1   It was because of my letters that I happened to stumble upon starting to acquire some kind of a homemade education.

2   I became increasingly frustrated at not being able to express what I wanted to convey in letters that I wrote, especially those to Mr. Elijah Muhammad. In the street, I had been the most articulate hustler out there—I had commanded attention when I said something. But now, trying to write simple English, I not only wasn't articulate, I wasn't even functional. How would I sound writing in slang, the way I would *say* it, something such as, "Look, daddy, let me pull your coat about a cat. Elijah Muhammad—"

3   Many who today hear me somewhere in person, or on television, or those who read something I've said, will think I went to school far beyond the eighth grade. This impression is due entirely to my prison studies.

4   It had really begun in the Charlestown Prison, when Bimbi first made me feel envy of his stock of knowledge. Bimbi had always taken charge of any conversation he was in, and I had tried to emulate him. But every book I picked up had few sentences which didn't contain anywhere from one to nearly all of the words that might as well have been in Chinese. When I just skipped those words, of course, I really ended up with little idea of what the book said. So I had come to the Norfolk Prison Colony still going through only book-reading motions. Pretty soon, I would have quit even these motions, unless I had received the motivation that I did.

5   I saw that the best thing I could do was get hold of a dictionary—to study, to learn some words. I was lucky enough to reason also that I should try to improve my penmanship. It was sad. I couldn't even write in a straight line. It was both ideas

together that moved me to request a dictionary along with some tablets and pencils from the Norfolk Prison Colony school.

6   I spent two days just riffling uncertainly through the dictionary's pages. I'd never realized so many words existed! I didn't know *which* words I needed to learn. Finally, just to start some kind of action, I began copying.

7   In my slow, painstaking, ragged handwriting, I copied into my tablet everything printed on that first page, down to the punctuation marks.

8   I believe it took me a day. Then, aloud, I read back, to myself, everything I'd written on the tablet. Over and over, aloud, to myself, I read my own handwriting.

9   I woke up the next morning, thinking about those words—immensely proud to realize that not only had I written so much at one time, but I'd written words that I never knew were in the world. Moreover, with a little effort, I also could remember what many of these words meant. I reviewed the words whose meanings I didn't remember. Funny thing, from the dictionary first page right now, that "aardvark" springs to my mind. The dictionary had a picture of it, a long-tailed, long-eared, burrowing African mammal, which lives off termites caught by sticking out its tongue as an anteater does for ants.

10   I was so fascinated that I went on—I copied the dictionary's next page. And the same experience came when I studied that. With every succeeding page, I also learned of people and places and events from history. Actually the dictionary is like a miniature encyclopedia. Finally the dictionary's A section had filled a whole tablet—and I went on into the B's. That was the way I started copying what eventually became the entire dictionary. It went a lot faster after so much practice helped me to pick up handwriting speed. Between what I wrote in my tablet, and writing letters, during the rest of my time in prison I would guess I wrote a million words.

11   I suppose it was inevitable that as my word-base broadened, I could for the first time pick up a book and read and now begin to understand what the book was saying. Anyone who has read a great deal can imagine the new world that opened. Let me tell you something: from then until I left that prison, in every free moment I had, if I was not reading in the library, I was reading on my bunk. You couldn't have gotten me out of books with a wedge. Between Mr. Muhammad's teachings, my correspondence, my visitors—usually Ella and Reginald—and my reading of books, months passed without my even thinking about being imprisoned. In fact, up to then, I never had been so truly free in my life.

COMPREHENSION CHECK

Directions: Answer the following questions about the selection you just read.

1. Where was Malcolm X during the time he discusses in the essay?

_____

2. How many years of formal education did Malcolm X receive?

_____

3. How did Malcolm X begin his "homemade education"?

_____

4. How much of the dictionary did Malcolm X eventually copy?

_____

5. Why did copying the dictionary change Malcolm X's life?

_____

6. We are not told in this portion of the autobiography who Bimbi is, but we can infer or guess. Who is Bimbi?

   _____

7. What person is mentioned who had a strong influence on Malcolm X? ____

   _____

8. Besides learning to read better, what other skills did Malcolm X develop as he copied the dictionary?

   _____

9. In how many prisons do we know from this account did Malcolm X serve

   time? _____

10. Explain what you think is meant by the last sentence.

   _____

   _____

VOCABULARY CHECK

Directions: Define the following underlined words as they are used in the excerpt.

1. I wanted to <u>convey</u> in letters

   _____

2. I . . . wasn't <u>articulate</u>

   _____

3. his <u>stock</u> of knowledge

   _____

4. tried to <u>emulate</u> him.

   _____

5. going through <u>book-reading motions</u>

   _____

6. just <u>riffling</u> uncertainly through

   _____

7. that "<u>aardvark</u>" springs to mind

   _____

8. every <u>succeeding</u> page

   _____

9. it was <u>inevitable</u>

   _____

10. the most articulate <u>hustler</u>

   _____

Record the results of these checks on the Student Record Sheet on page 495. For any questions that you may have missed, make certain that you understand why before going on. Remember to make vocabulary cards for any words you need to overlearn, or use whatever method you are using to add new words to your word repertoire.

Drill E-2

Directions: Read the following selection and answer the questions that follow.

WHAT YOU SHOULD LOOK FOR IN A DICTIONARY

Robert M. Pierson

1   First, does it describe or prescribe? Does it tell you how words *are* used or does it tell you how its compiler thinks words *should* be used? Most modern dictionaries do the former—most of the time. They are—or strive to be—objective reports of the state of the language. (The big exceptions are usage manuals and stylebooks—on which more below.) Editors of today's dictionaries may privately shudder at *presently* for *now,* at *hose* for *stockings,* at *cremains* for *ashes of people who have been cremated,* at *home* for *house.* But if Americans choose to use words so, editors are honor-bound to record that fact. The day is therefore past when you can defend the artistic effect of your use of a word by saying, "But I found it in the dictionary."

2   It was not always so. In centuries past, dictionaries existed primarily to establish and maintain good French—or whatever. Sometimes the motive was to replace Latin (a nearly frozen language) with something just as stable and "classic"; sometimes, to make one dialect (that of the capital?) supreme; sometimes, to encourage the use of a national language (as opposed to that of a foreign oppressor). Times have indeed changed.

3   Not that today's dictionaries are completely value-free. They identify some uses as slang, some as obsolete, some as dialectal, some as illiterate—and some words as taboo, even offensive. But even here they strive to explain how society in general views words, not how *the dictionaries* view them. They are not saying that it is "bad" to use *smashed* for *drunk*—only that most people will regard *smashed* as an informal way of putting it. Only you and your editor can decide whether, in a particular situation, you should write *smashed* or *drunk*—or *blotto* or *feeling no pain* or *intoxicated* or *inebriated* or *under the influence* (without, perhaps, saying of what!).

4   Some other points to note in dictionaries:
        1.   Their scope. Are they *general* or are they in some way *specialized?* Do they cover the language as a whole or are they in some way limited? Do they, for example, cover new words only? or slang only? or only the special vocabulary of science—or of one particular science? As a writer, you will surely want a general dictionary—plus one or more specialized ones, depending on your interests.
        2.   Their scale (a result of their *degree of selectivity*). Are they more or less complete—*unabridged*—or are they selective—*abridged?* If the latter, is abridgement

Excerpted from "A Writer's Guide to Dictionaries" by Robert M. Pierson. Originally published in *Writer's Digest,* November 1983, pp. 34–38, 49.

a matter of less information about the same number of words or a matter of the same amount of information about fewer words—or, as is usually the case, mostly the latter but with some of the former? As a writer you may, deep in your heart, want an unabridged dictionary, plus a revolving stand to mount it on. But you will probably find that an abridged dictionary designated, in its title, as "college" or "collegiate" will meet your needs well enough—and with less pain to your wallet and your arm muscles. If you can afford to do so, get two such dictionaries and, when a problem arises, compare what they have to say.

 3. Their intended readership. Are they for children or for adults? If for adults, for adults of what level of sophistication? Again, the "collegiate" dictionaries will probably best suit you as a writer: they will give you not only *the* meaning of each word they list but also other meanings, with labels to alert you to how words are likely to be received. They will also tell you a little about the origins and histories of the words they list.

 4. Their overall arrangement. Basically, are they in one alphabetical sequence or in several? Opinions differ as to which way is best. Should place-names be in a separate list? What about personal names? foreign words widely used in English? abbreviations? How about new words and new uses of old words? Some dictionaries merge all categories into (as information scientists say) one file. Others lift out one or more categories and file them separately. The best solution, so far as users of dictionaries are concerned, is to look, first of all, at each dictionary's table of contents. And once you are within an alphabetical sequence, remember what I said before about word-by-word, letter-by-letter, and keyword-by-keyword alphabetizing. Remember, too, that *Mc* and *Mac* names may be filed as spelled, filed separately, or all filed as if spelled *Mac* (which is how most library catalogs do it, by the way). Again don't struggle to remember which system is used: just be ready to shift gears.

 5. The order in which they list multiple definitions. Here are two main sequences: "historical" sequence, with oldest extant uses defined first, newest last; and "frequence" sequence, with most common first, least common last. Historical sequence tends to be featured in Merriam-Webster titles; frequency, in most others. As a writer, you must be aware of all the ways in which the words you use *may* be understood, so always read the whole entry. Just bear in mind that the first meaning listed may or may not be the one most likely to come to mind.

 6. The readability of their definitions. One of the attractive features of the *American Heritage* titles is their sheer readability. Occasionally, if the editors of dictionaries are not watchful, circular definitions, which leave you where you were, creep in—e.g., calling a *prosthesis* a *prosthetic appliance*. Sometimes definitions will seem duskier than the words they are said to illumine. On the other hand, dictionaries tend to be brief—and who said brevity always leads to clarity? If dictionary editors spun out their definitions to make them more readable, their products would weigh and cost much more. Still and all, try looking up some words in fields you know a *little* about and see how they read: if you look up words you already know a lot about, you may "read in" meaning not provided by their definitions; and if you look up totally unfamiliar words, you will be in no position to judge. Either way, try not to mistake over-simplification for genuine clarity: sure, it's "readable" to call an apricot "a delicious fruit of a pale creamy pinky yellow," but would not that definition apply equally well to nectarines and some grapefruits?

 7. Their labeling of meanings and uses. As suggested earlier, it is helpful to know that *braces* in the sense of *suspenders* is British, as is *suspender* in the sense of *garter*—that in botanical usage, the Irish potato is a *stem*, a strawberry not essentially a *fruit*, and a tomato only a *berry*! The constant reminder as to what is *standard* (unlabeled) and what is not really keeps us on our toes—as writers. Not that labeling is always perfect: one dictionary I reviewed several years ago carefully labeled racial and religious slurs as offensive, e.g., *nigger* and *kike*, but did not so label *broad* ("woman") and *queer* ("homosexual")—surely just as offensive to those to whom the words are applied—though just possibly, I grant, those particular words are not always *intended* to be offensive. But surely that is just the point. As writers, we need to express ourselves, yes, choosing the words that most exactly say—to us—what we mean; but if we are to communicate successfully, we must also think of how our words are likely to be received, regardless of our intentions. Hence the usefulness of labels. By the way, the *American Heritage* titles are particularly strong in respect to usage, with more concerning the "social status" of words than you find in other general dictionaries.

8. What they may tell words besides their meanings. Pronunciation, syllabification, grammatical inflections (plurals, past tense forms, etc.), origins and histories—and, of course, spelling!: all these are likely to be indicated in "collegiate" dictionaries. Often the presentation of this material is extremely condensed and literally hard to read: I know one dictionary whose print is so small and so dull that it is hard to tell whether the little marks between syllables are only raised periods (meaning, in that dictionary, syllabic division) or actual hyphens (meaning to spell with hyphens). In an age when we are encouraged to read faster and faster, you may need to slow down, as if reading the thorniest Rossetti or Hopkins sonnet! And be sure to study the system of symbols used—e.g., > for "derived from" and the "schwa" (ə) or the "uh" sound—and abbreviations too, like *O.F.* for "Old French." There may well be a key at the bottom of the page. Just don't assume that every new dictionary—or dictionary new to you—is, in this respect, like one you are used to.

9. Their references to related words. Often defining a word precisely is very difficult. One solution to that problem is to refer to words of more or less similar meaning (from *awkward* to *clumsy*, from *rude* to *boorish*, from *immaculate* to *clean*) or to words of opposite meaning (from *calm* to *agitated*, from *mellifluous* to *harsh*). The more a dictionary does this—and the more it explains subtle differences—the better for you as a writer. Sensitivity to such matters will give your writing precision.

10. Their use of examples—including quotations—to clairfy meaning. These may be "made-up" illustrations of usage or they may be quotations from published material. If the latter, observe their age. As a reader of old and new material, you may be helped by a quotation from the Bible or from Shakespeare. As a writer, you may be more helped by a quotation from *Time* or *Natural History* or *Organic Gardening*. In any case, quotations—giving words in context—may hint at shades of meaning exceedingly difficult to convey otherwise.

11. Their use of graphics, especially line drawings. Again, the more the better—to label the parts of a Greek column, for instance, or the components of a threshing machine. I do not share the view that a picture is always worth a thousand words; but sometimes a picture can do what dozens of words fail to do—at least as you and I use them.

12. The presence of encyclopedia information. In theory, a dictionary is a word book; an encyclopedia, a subject-matter book. When you define *grizzly bear* so as to make it clear how grizzlies differ, basically, from American black bears, you are doing only what dictionaries traditionally do; when you tell what they feed on (cow parsnips, I am told) and how many are left—and go on to mention a good book on the subject—you are doing, in addition, what encyclopedias do. Some dictionaries go very far along this line, even to the point of giving lists of chemical elements, evolutionary trees for animals and plants and languages, maps of continents, rules of grammar and punctuation, even the text of the Constitution—you name it; some dictionary—some "word book"—will provide it. And when you get into specialized subject dictionaries, the tendency is even more marked—with *dictionary* used to designate just about any book featuring alphabetical sequence. When it comes to selecting a general English-language dictionary of "desk size," my advice is this: don't buy a book on the basis of bonus features unless you really need the bonus features. How much space do you have for other books? Do you already own an encyclopedia? How far do you live from the public library?

5   My advice, then, is this: Get to know your dictionaries. Look at *all* their parts—

including those little appendices and supplements at the back. Imagine how you might use what you find. Keep your dictionaries at hand, and form the habit of consulting them often. And read them for pleasure. Though not set up for consecutive reading, as are novels and treatises, they can be read in much the same way. Read in them again and again—and note your findings, whether in your "writer's journal," on note cards for orderly filing, or in that secret file at the back of your mind. Save all these bits and pieces. You never know when they will rise to the surface for you to hook them. They will be there "for you," like old friends, to enrich your creative output; to help you say what you mean, not just something close; to help you convey a sense of truth-telling, not of weary echoing of the thoughts and feelings of others; to help give your writing the sheen, the glow, the magic that we all of us strive for but so seldom achieve, let alone sustain.

COMPREHENSION CHECK

Directions:　In the spaces provided, answer the following questions about the article you just read.

1.　Are dictionaries supposed to tell how words are used or tell how they are

supposed to be used? _____

Explain. _____

_____

The following are some of the points the author says to note when looking for a good dictionary. Explain briefly what he means by each:

2.　scope _____

_____

3.　scale _____

_____

4.　intended readership _____

_____

5.　overall arrangement _____

_____

6.　What are the ways some dictionaries list multiple definitions? _____

_____

_____

7.　Explain what the author means by circular definitions. _____

_____

_____

8. What dictionary does the author recommend for strength in respect to readability? _____

_____

9. What does the author say is the difference between an encyclopedia and a dictionary? _____

_____

10. T/F   The author believes you should read a dictionary for pleasure. _____

Go on to the Vocabulary Check.

VOCABULARY CHECK

Directions: Define the following underlined words from the article.

1. does it describe or <u>prescribe</u>

_____

2. develop a <u>repertoire</u> of possibilities

_____

3. <u>inebriated</u> or under the influence

_____

4. an <u>unabridged</u> dictionary

_____

5. with oldest <u>extant</u> uses defined first

_____

6. as if reading the <u>thorniest</u> Rossetti sonnet

_____

7. the trouble with <u>conventional</u> dictionaries

_____

8. they may <u>lament</u> the growing use of

_____

9. <u>abide</u> by the manual

_____

10. those little <u>appendices</u>

_____

After the results of the Comprehension Check and Vocabulary Check have been scored, record them on the Student Record Chart on page 495. Each answer for both checks is worth 10 percent for a total of 100 percent possible for comprehension and 100 percent for vocabulary.

Remember to make vocabulary cards for any words that gave you trouble.

CHAPTER 2

DEVELOPING LITERAL RECALL

A. Separating the Main Ideas from Details

One of the keys to good comprehension is the ability to separate main ideas from details. Sometimes the main idea in a passage is easy to identify, sometimes not. Usually, though not always, the best place to look for the main idea is the first sentence in a paragraph, but it can come in the middle, at the end, or not at all. Such sentences are called *topic sentences*. However, some main ideas are implied, not stated directly in any sentence. Your comprehension can be enhanced if you understand how writers form paragraphs, so let's look at some examples of writers at work.

Read the following paragraph:

Some words are loaded with pleasant associations. Such words as *home, happiness, tenderness, contentment, baby,* and *mother* usually bring out favorable feelings or connotations. The word *mother,* for instance, makes most people think of home, safety, love, care, food, security, and the like.

What would you say the paragraph is about? _____

_____

What evidence is supplied to support the main idea? _____

_____

_____

The paragraph's main idea is located in the first sentence: some words express pleasant associations. The rest of the paragraph provides support with examples of words that bring out favorable associations. An outline of the paragraph would look something like this:

Main idea: Some words are loaded with pleasant associations.
Supporting details:
    1.   Examples: home, happiness, tenderness, contentment, baby, mother
    2.   Specific example: mother, creating thoughts of home, safety, love, etc.

Notice that the topic sentence, or sentence with the main idea in it, is more general. The other sentences are more specific and provide us with supporting details.

Here's another paragraph example. See if you can find the main idea, or topic sentence.

A major part of our self-image is shaped by the work we do. Consider how we describe ourselves: "I'm just a janitor." "I'm only a housewife." "I'm senior vice president of the company." "I'm out of work right now." "I'm the boss here." Even our friends and fellow workers refer to us by our status (teacher, student, lawyer, doctor, pilot) and by what we do.

What is the main idea of this paragraph? _____

_____

What evidence does the author provide to support this idea? _____

_____

_____

An outline of the preceding paragraph looks like this:

Main idea: The work we do shapes a major part of our self-image.
Supporting details:
1. consider our self-description
    a. just a janitor
    b. only a housewife
    c. senior vice president
    d. out of work
    e. boss
2. friends and fellow workers refer to us by our status/job
    a. teacher
    b. student
    c. lawyer
    d. doctor
    e. pilot

Again, the main idea is more general, with specific details supporting the topic idea.
Find the main idea in this paragraph:

A young college student is constantly discouraged, irritable, and unable to sleep. Frequent crying spells have ended, but she's still very unhappy. A middle-aged man has become increasingly indecisive in business affairs. He has strong feelings of worthlessness and guilt, and has lost interest in sex. An elderly woman complains of fatigue and lack of appetite. Her weight has been dropping steadily. Three different problems? Not really. These people—and millions like them—suffer from the most common mental ailment in the book: depression. (From Maxine Abram, "Rx for Depression," *TWA Ambassador* magazine, January 1987.)

Main idea or topic: _____

Supporting details: _____

_____

The main idea in this paragraph comes in the last sentence. Everything up to it is an example that supports the main point. Here's a brief outline of the paragraph:

Main idea: millions of people suffer from depression, a common ailment
Supporting details:
1. young college student's problems
2. middle-aged man's problems
3. elderly woman's problems

Of course, you could list the specific ailments of each of the three people if you wanted a more complete outline. What's important here is to realize that each of the three people and the problems mentioned are supporting details for the main idea—that depression is common. Notice, too, that the author used a young person, a middle-aged person, and an elderly person to show the wide range of depression.

See what you think is the main idea of this paragraph:

> This is the story of a sturdy American symbol which has now spread throughout most of the world. The symbol is not the dollar. It is not even Coca-Cola. It is a simple pair of pants called blue jeans.... Blue jeans are favored equally by bureaucrats and cowboys; bankers and deadbeats; fashion designers and beer drinkers. They draw no distinctions and recognize no classes; they are merely American. Yet they are sought after almost everywhere in the world—including Russia, where authorities recently broke up a teenaged gang that was selling them on the black market for two hundred dollars a pair. They have been around for a long time, and it seems likely that they will outlive even the necktie. (From Carin Quinn, "The Jeaning of America—and the World," *American Heritage*, April 1978.)

What is this paragraph about? _____

What are some of the author's supporting points? _____

_____

_____

_____

While the opening sentence in the paragraph states that "this is the story of a sturdy American symbol," it isn't until the fourth sentence that we are told the symbol is a pair of blue jeans. So no one sentence is the topic sentence here. In effect, the paragraph is about the popularity of blue jeans around the world. The author provides us with examples of their popularity with various classes of people around the world, including Russia, to support her main idea.

Here's one last paragraph example, taken from a history textbook. Don't try to remember all the facts and figures for this reading; just look for the main idea in it:

> In 1840, only one-twelfth of the American population lived in cities of 8,000 or more. By 1860, the proportion of city-dwellers had grown to one-sixth, and by 1900 to one-third of the population. In 1900, more than 25 million Americans were living in cities, most of them in the metropolises that had grown so lustily in the preceding 50 years. In 1850, New York City and independent Brooklyn together had a population of 1,200,000. By 1900 (after official consolidation in 1898), their population had soared to over 3 million. In the same period, Philadelphia rose from 560,000 to 1,300,000. Most spectacular of all was Chicago. Starting out in 1831 as a muddy trading post on the prairie with 12 families and a meager garrison as its only inhabitants, Chicago had grown to 30,000 by 1850; 500,000 by 1880. In the next 20 years, its population soared to 1,700,000, a figure that placed it far ahead of Philadelphia and second only to New York in size. (From Hofstader, Miller and Aaron, *The United States: The History of a Republic*, Prentice-Hall, 1987, p. 510.)

What is the main idea of this paragraph? _____

Instead of the authors placing their main idea at the beginning, middle, or end of the paragraph, they simply left it out. Their main idea is *implied: In the last half of the nineteenth century, America became urbanized at a startling rate.* By providing us with dates and statistics, we are able to infer the main idea. Notice that all of the dates provided are between 1850 and 1900, the late or latter part of the nineteenth century. All of the cities (New York, Brooklyn, Philadelphia, Chicago) are examples of fast population growth during these dates. Because of these details, we see for ourselves, without the authors telling us, that America urbanized very rapidly during the last half of the nineteenth century.

As you can see, sometimes it is easy to figure out an author's main idea and separate it from details, but sometimes we have to be more alert to what is being said. As you work through the following drills, become more conscious of how writers express their main points and provide details to support them.

Drill A-1: RECOGNIZING MAIN IDEAS AND SUPPORTING DETAILS

Directions: Read the following paragraphs and in the appropriate blanks write the main idea and list the supporting details. The first one has been done for you.

Paragraph 1

Many of us impose unnecessary limitations on ourselves. We say, or think, we can't do something without checking. We hold ourselves back when we could move ahead. We assume that certain good occupations are closed to us, when they're really not closed at all. We think we're not as good as the next person when we really are.

Main idea: *Many of us limit our potential unnecessarily.*

Supporting details: *1. We say we can't without really knowing.*

2. We hold back.

3. We think we're not good enough for certain jobs.

4. We think we're not as good as others.

Paragraph 2

Nature has provided natural means to soothe the mind and body. Herbal remedies for sleeplessness have been used successfully for centuries. Valerian root, for example, lessens irritability and excitement in the nervous system by rebuilding frayed nerve endings. Scullcap produces a peacefully drowsy feeling and restful sleep. A cup of chamomile tea is also a sleep producer and is a delicious break from stimulating hot caffeine drinks at night. Other valuable herbs for relaxing include hops, yellow jasmine, and lady slipper. Herbs also offer the advantage of containing important vitamins and minerals, which further increases their benefit to your general mental and physical health. (From Josie Knowles, "The Big Business of Falling Asleep," *Soma,* September/October 1980.)

Main idea: _____

Supporting details: _____

_____

_____

_____

Paragraph 3

Sometimes we bury or hide our undesirable emotions. We do this because we have been programmed to do this. By the time we are five years old, our parents have influenced us to be affectionate, tender, angry, or hateful. We moralize our emotions. We tell ourselves it is good to feel grateful, but bad to feel angry or jealous. So we repress emotions we should release. We get into "value conflicts." Boys and men are not supposed to cry or show fear. So some men attempt to bury their true feelings and create a false self-image.

Main idea: _____

Supporting details: _____

_____

_____

_____

Paragraph 4

Cocaine has a long history of use and misuse in the United States. At the turn of the century, dozens of nonprescription potions and cure-alls containing cocaine were sold. It was during this time that Coca-Cola was indeed the "real thing." From 1886, when it was first concocted, until 1906 when the Pure Food and Drug Act was passed, Coca-Cola contained cocaine (which has since been replaced with caffeine). In the 1930s, the popularity of cocaine declined when the cheaper synthetic amphetamines became available. This trend was reversed in the 1960s when a federal crackdown on amphetamine sales made this drug less available and more expensive. Today, cocaine is becoming one of the most widely abused illegal drugs.

Main idea: _____

Supporting details: _____

_____

_____

_____

Paragraph 5

It is now believed that the earth's outer layer of rock, called the lithosphere, is divided into large, rigid plates that fit together like pieces of a huge jigsaw puzzle. There are twelve major plates (and numerous subplates), each about sixty miles thick and some almost as wide as the Pacific Ocean. They float on a layer of dense, viscous rock called the asthenosphere, which, in turn, surrounds the earth's hot core.

Main idea: _____

Supporting details: _____

_____

_____

_____

_____

Paragraph 6

Caffeine has various effects on the body. It speeds up the heart, promotes the release of stomach acid, and increases urine production; also, it dilates some blood vessels while narrowing others. In large amounts, caffeine may cause convulsions, but this is highly unlikely. It takes about 10 grams of caffeine, the equivalent of 100 cups of coffee, to run a serious risk of death. Psychologically, caffeine suppresses fatigue or drowsiness and increases feelings of alertness.

Main idea: _____

Supporting details: _____

_____

_____

_____

_____

Paragraph 7

In other words, "intelligence" is something we acquire from experience rather than an inborn ability. This does not mean that inheritance has no role to play in establishing levels of intellectual ability. Few would argue against the fact that the upper limits of human intellectual capacity are to a great extent determined by the physical structure of the brain and this, like every other structure in the body, develops directly from "blue prints" contained in the genes. It is also fair to assume that these upper limits will vary from one individual to the next, depending on the instructions contained in those blue prints.... Our contention is, however, that these genetically determined upper limits are of no practical significance to the person seeking to increase mental ability substantially. There are many reasons to believe that we never come anywhere near these limits and that man's ability to reason, to remember, and to learn expands as the need arises. (From D. Lewis and J. Green, *Thinking Better,* Rawson, Wade Publishers, 1982, pp. 6–7.)

Main idea: _____

Supporting details: _____

_____

_____

_____

Paragraph 8

You could not live without stress. Stress, like pain, begins at birth and remains common to the human condition throughout your life and that of every other human being who ever lived. It is not merely universal; it is endemic and omnipresent. In the functioning of our biological systems, normal stress is necessary and vital. Through variations on the themes of fight or flight, stress reactions mobilize us to adapt to changing stimuli. (From Richard A. Stein, *Personal Strategies for Living with Less Stress,* John Gallagher Comm., Ltd., 1983.)

Main idea: _____

Supporting details: _____

_____

_____

_____

Paragraph 9

Despite the central role breathing plays in our lives as organisms, few of us have been taught how to breathe. Most of us are unaware of the fact that we use probably only a third of our lung capacity. Our breathing is shallow and occurs about fifteen to seventeen times a minute, taking in about a pint of air each time. Yet your lungs can hold eight times as much air. Therefore, shallow breathing provides only a limited amount of fresh oxygen and doesn't fully expel all the burnt gases, such as carbon dioxide. (Stein, *op. cit.,* p. 1.)

Main idea: _____

Supporting details: _____

_____

_____

_____

_____

Paragraph 10

The proliferation of computers in recent years has been truly phenomenal. In 1978, there were about 5,000 desk-top computers in the United States. In 1982, there were 5 million. In 1980, there were 350,000 computer terminals communicating with a large machine elsewhere; by 1982, there were 3 million such terminals. By 1990, it is estimated there will be 80 million desk-top computers in the United States. By then, if you count microprocessors in weapon systems and home appliances, there will be a *billion* computers throughout the world. (From Michael Crichton, *Electronic Life: How to Think About Computers*, Knopf, 1983, p. 3.)

Main idea: _____

Supporting details: _____

_____

_____

_____

_____

Drill   A-2: SEPARATING MAIN IDEAS FROM SUPPORTING DETAILS

Directions: For each of the paragraphs that follow, underline the topic or main idea sentence. Then in the space provided write in your own words what you think the main idea is.

1.   Maybe the tequila boom is somehow related to the enthusiasm among college-age youths for Carlos Castenada's books about Aztec [*sic*] sorcery and spiritualism. More likely, in the opinion of most bartenders, the new generation has simply taken a deep fancy to the old Mexican taste mix of salt, tequila and lemon. (From Joe McCarthy, "Tequila," *Travel and Leisure*, November 1974.)

Main idea: _____

_____

2.   The computer differs from other machines in only one significant respect: its output is not a direct function of its input, but of a set of arbitrary instructions (called programs) previously input or built into the machine's structure. The computer is, therefore, able to transform information (data) from one representation to another by means of rules unrelated to the information to be processed. (From Monte Crowl, "Computers: What Are They?" *Now*, Spring 1975.)

Main idea: _____

_____

3.   Basically, there are two types of true protection from burns and other sun-penetrated damage. One is a sun-block—a substance that is completely opaque, totally blocking light rays. This is the sort of screen you see on lifeguards' noses; it's unsightly, but as the lifeguards know, it's thoroughly

dependable. . . . The second type, a chemical sunscreen, works by filtering out certain of the sun's rays. . . . (From Dodi Schultz, "Dangers of the Midday Sun," *Travel and Leisure,* July 1984.)

Main idea: _____

4.   *How to Make Love to a Single Girl* contains over 160 photos—each one just as clear and exciting as the photograph above. These photographs are large, beautiful, and incredibly frank. They show you—step by exciting step—exactly how to turn on a woman. And today that's more important than ever before. . . . (From an advertisement for *How to Make Love to a Single Girl.*)

Main idea: _____

5.   . . . There is no one of us who is always a teacher or always a learner. In fact, the children often teach us to look at something differently—a story or picture, which they see more clearly than we do. The other day I came upon Tonia and a six-year-old friend sitting in her bedroom reading a simple comic book. He was teaching her what he learned in school—pointing out words, reading sentences, explaining the story. He remembered what he picked up in school and being just a first-grader saw nothing wrong with sharing that knowledge. (From Herbert Kohl, *Reading, How To.*)

Main idea: _____

6.   In Chicago, a correspondence school took in more than $3 million a year from students enrolled in its law course, but not one graduate was able to qualify for the bar exam. A New York City nurses' training school collected $500 tuition fees for a course in nurse's aid, but not one graduate of the course could obtain a job in any New York hospital. A St. Louis school advertised an aircraft mechanics course that promised high pay and jobs at a time when the airlines were laying off mechanics. These are only a few of the many examples of the widespread cheating of students that the Federal Trade Commission has discovered.

Main idea: _____

7.   Problem readers may need a year just to learn the names and sounds of the letters of the alphabet and to learn to read a dozen words. They may need four or five more years to learn the basic vocabulary that allows them to read as well as the average second grader. During junior and senior high school, they may need instruction in the fundamental skill of reading the telephone directory, instruction manuals, catalogs, and newspapers. As adults, they will be able to read when they must, but problem readers are not likely to read material of any kind when they can avoid doing so. (From Joyce Hood, "Poor Readers II," *Today's Education,* September/October 1974.)

Main idea: _____

8.   Simply put, comprehension is the act of understanding or the capacity to understand. It can be divided into three levels: literal, critical, and affective. Literal comprehension is the basic level of understanding that entails the ability to identify main ideas and supporting details, to follow the sequence of events, to recognize cause-effect relationships, to interpret directions, and to perceive organizational patterns in various types of reading matter. Critical comprehension requires distinguishing opinion from fact, recognizing an author's intent, attitude, and bias, and making critical judgments. Affective comprehension is your intellectual and emotional response to what you read.

Main idea: _____

_____

9.   In other words, I think kids in the 1920s were very much like kids are in the 1980s—they were getting drunk, and they were flappers, or whatever. They drove fast cars. Many were concerned with death and suicide, just as they are now. The hippies in the '60s were just another variation. Today, MTV gives you a way to see what the kids are thinking and feeling, and I see a certain continuity and sameness. (From Joshua Hoffs, "Getting the Message Across," *Los Angeles Times Calendar,* July 8, 1984.)

Main idea: _____

_____

10.   The conditions of American pioneer life had fostered equality of the sexes, even to the franchise in New Jersey and Virginia. After the Revolution, however, the dependent and protected status of women was emphasized. In a legal sense a woman was a perpetual minor, with her property and wages at the absolute disposal of her husband. Also, he had the right of chastisement: halfway through the century he had the legal right to beat his wife with a reasonable instrument, which in one case was adjudged to be a stick no thicker than a man's thumb. Widows and unmarried women had more extensive rights over their own property and their own actions, but courts were not inclined to favor them. (From Leland D. Baldwin, *The Stream of American History,* vol. 1, American Book Co., p. 618.)

Main idea: _____

_____

Drill A-3: MORE ON MAIN IDEAS

Directions: Read the following article. At the end of each paragraph write a one-sentence statement in the blank, stating what you think is the main idea of the paragraph.

INTERVIEWING FOR A JOB

1.   One of the most important components of successful job hunting is the job interview. There are thousands of people entering new careers and searching for job placement. In order to give yourself an edge over others

applying for the job you want, it is important to create a solid impression during the job interview.

Main idea: _____

_____

_____

2.   Because what you say during an interview is so important, there are two rules to remember. One is to present yourself in a favorable way and stress your areas of competence. However, don't exaggerate; tell the truth. Second, listen carefully and get involved in what the interviewer is saying. Notice the interviewer's interests and relate your comments to them.

Main idea: _____

_____

_____

3.   The job interview is the time to "sell" yourself by giving examples of experiences you've had related to the job and by revealing your good points. It's a good idea to have handy your job résumé or a list of school courses that prepared you for the job. Don't exaggerate the truth. Be honest, but show confidence in yourself and your ability to do the job.

Main idea: _____

_____

_____

4.   If you are not certain what the job will require of you, ask questions to see whether you do feel qualified. Do more listening than talking. Don't be afraid to ask for a second interview if you need time to gather information that will be more useful in the second interview. Most interviewers will appreciate your questions and your ability to listen and respond.

Main idea: _____

_____

5.   Some people talk themselves out of a job by saying too much or by digressing from the point. Although it's important to talk about your successful experiences, don't come on too strong and sound like a braggart.

Main idea: _____

_____

_____

6.   Each of us has sensitive areas, and you might anticipate your responses in the event that you are asked about your own. Such questions could refer to your lack of an academic degree, a long period of unemployment, or lack of work experience if you are entering a new field. Answer sensitive questions briefly and positively, because even one negative example can create doubt in the interviewer's mind. If you believe that this area presents a real obstacle to a job offer, you could be communicating this doubt to the interviewer. Many times, however, an interviewer will override these sensitive areas if you have a confident, positive attitude.

Main idea: _____

_____

_____

7.   Making a favorable impression is especially important in light of recent estimates, which show that most hiring is done on an emotional rather than a factual basis. An interviewer who accepts you as a person and is emotionally on your side may consider you favorably for the job—even if you don't fit the pre-established qualifications.

Main idea: _____

_____

_____

_____

8.   The job interview is an important part of the job search because the attitude and impression you project can make the interviewer feel "with you" or "against you." Remember that you have the power to create a favorable impression. Interviewers have the intelligence to recognize genuine enthusiasm and interest.

Main idea: _____

_____

_____

_____

B. Reading for Main Ideas: Paragraph Patterns

Another way to distinguish between an author's main ideas and supporting points is to pay attention to the writing patterns used frequently by authors. Authors use a variety of writing patterns to develop their ideas: illustration or example, definition of terms, comparison or contrast, sequence of events, cause and effect, description, or a combination of these. These patterns are called rhetorical modes. They are useful not only in better understanding paragraphs, but entire reading passages. If you have taken an English composition course, you may already know the terms. They are frequently used to teach students how to write better. As a reader, your awareness of these patterns can help you more readily identify an author's main idea and supporting details. Let's examine each pattern.

ILLUSTRATION/EXAMPLE

One of the most widely used writing patterns is *illustration/example*. In this pattern, the author uses exmples to illustrate or support the main idea. Notice in the following example how the topic sentence, the first one, is made clearer and supported by examples:

It would seem **the lesson to be gained from famous love stories is that passionate love and marriage do not mix. For instance,** witness the ending to the stories of Antony and Cleopatra, Tristan and Isolde, Lancelot and Guinevere, Dante and Beatrice, and poor Cyrano and Roxanne. Even Romeo and Juliet ran into problems.

All of the names listed in the paragraph are given as examples to illustrate and support the main idea: marriage and passionate love don't seem to go together. Even if you don't know who all the characters listed are, you can infer that they were all passionate lovers who never got married, or if they did, presumably the marriages didn't last. Otherwise, the author wouldn't use them as examples to support the main idea.

A clue to the illustration/example pattern is usually given through what are called *signal words*. Signal words or phrases such as *for instance, for example, to illustrate, such as, much like,* and *similar to* all signal or alert you that examples are about to be given. If what follows is an example, then it can't be the main idea. Instead, it supports a main idea that you need to recognize.

DEFINITION

Another frequently used writing pattern is *definition,* or an attempt to explain what is being discussed through elaborate defining of terms. Here is an example:

A word generally has two meanings: a denotative meaning and a connotative meaning. The denotative meaning of a word is its most direct or literal meaning as found in the dictionary. What the word suggests or implies beyond its literal definition is its connotative meaning.

The author's main point here is to define the terms denotative and connotative.

Frequently, when authors define a word or term they also use examples. Notice in the following example how a definition of inference is provided, then an example of how we make inferences is given:

> An inference is a statement about the unknown made on the basis of the known. In other words, an inference is an educated guess. If a woman smiles when we see a man whisper something in her ear, we can infer or assume that she is pleased or amused. Because smiles generally mean pleasure and frowns generally mean displeasure, we can infer that she is pleased.

In this example the definition of inference is given, then an example of how we make inferences is given, thus combining both the definition and illustration/example patterns.

COMPARISON/CONTRAST

The comparison/contrast writing pattern is also used with some frequency. With this pattern authors attempt to develop the main point by either comparing or contrasting one thing or idea with another, or by using both. Here's an example of the use of comparison/contrast:

> Crime as presented on television is different from what it is in reality. On television, murder, assault, and armed robbery are the most common crimes. However, in reality, quiet burglaries, clever larcenies, unspectacular auto thefts, and drunkenness are the most common. Video detectives solve 90 percent of their cases. But in reality, the figure is much lower. On TV only 7 percent of violence occurs between relatives. In reality, this accounts for 25–30 percent of interpersonal violence.

Notice that what is being contrasted is crime as portrayed on TV and what it is like in reality. The author's main idea is that television does not portray crime realistically. To prove this, the author contrasts three points: the most common crimes as portrayed on TV with real crime, the difference in the number of cases detectives solve on TV and in reality, and the percentage of interpersonal violence on TV and in reality.

There are some signal words that alert you to the use of comparison/contrast. Notice in the example paragraph the use of such words as *different from, however,* and *but.* These signal a change or contrast will be made. Other signal words you may see that contrast are *more than, yet, opposite, though, less, more, in contrast, even though, on the other hand,* and *on the contrary.*

Words that signal comparison or more of the same are *and, too, also, same, like, similar, in comparison,* and *analogous to.* When you see such words being used you know that you are being provided with supporting details or information, not the main idea. The main idea will be whatever the comparison or contrast details are supporting.

SEQUENCE OF EVENTS

A fourth writing pattern is sequence of events. This is a pattern used when directions are given, when there is a certain order to events, or when chronology is important. Sometimes certain key words, such as *first, second, third,* or the numbers themselves ar used. Words such as *then, later, finally,* and *thus* also serve as guides to a sequence of events. Notice the sequence of events in the following example:

> Scientists now believe that there are four major stages of sleep. The first stage is light sleep. During this period a person can be awakened easily. But within fifteen or thirty minutes after the first stage, he falls quickly into stages two and three known as intermediate periods. These stages are short. Then he falls into the fourth stage, deep sleep. This final stage may last an hour or more and research shows this is a difficult period from which to awaken a person. (From "What Scientists Really Know About Sleep," *Good Housekeeping,* February 1986.)

The author has related the various sequences of stages involved in falling asleep. Numbers and words such as *then* and *final* aid the reader. An awareness of these things provides a pattern for understanding and helps you recall the information later.

CAUSE AND EFFECT

Still another writing pattern is the use of *cause and effect*. With this pattern the author attempts to show how one action or a series of actions causes something to happen. For instance, tapping a raw egg on a skillet causes it to crack. In a cause/effect paragraph, the author links what causes an event with the effects it brings. Here is an example of cause/effect relationship in a paragraph:

> The permissive nature of society in the United States is notorious. With Dr. Benjamin Spock's books on child raising, the Bible of the last generation of parents, family life has become very democratic. In recent decades, many school teachers have urged children to express themselves, to give their opinions rather than to regurgitate the rote recitations that used to characterize—and still characterize elsewhere—much of what we call education. The point is not that there is no discipline or authoritarianism in the family or school, but that there is considerably less than in the American past or in the present of most other nations. (From John Gillingham, "Then and Now," *Radical Reader.*)

Notice that the point of the paragraph is that permissiveness in the United States is greater than ever (effect). The use of Dr. Spock's books in rearing children (cause), and the urging of children by teachers to give their opinions rather than to learn by rote (cause), explain why discipline in the family and school is less than in the past. Thus, the author of the preceding paragraph sees the effect of two causes.

DESCRIPTION

The last writing pattern to be discussed here is the use of *description*. Usually the author is attempting to give you a visual picture or a feeling for something. Generally, but not always, there is no topic sentence. Notice this example:

> When I last checked into the Mandarin hotel, I found a boy on duty 24 hours a day to merely open my door and ring for the elevator. My laundry seemed to be done as it came off my back. Anything in need of repair was mended to perfection overnight. Room service turned out to be a ritual of

elegance involving a platoon of boys who appeared to be passing dishes along a human chain from the kitchen. (From "Hong Kong," *Clipper*, August–September 1980.)

As you can see, there is no topic sentence. The whole paragraph is a description of the excellent service the author got at the hotel where he stayed.

Your ability to understand what you read can be enhanced by an awareness of these writing patterns. The patterns themselves are not important, but an awareness of how an author presents information can aid comprehension. To help you develop this ability, the next drills provide practice in identifying writing patterns.

As you work through this section, keep in mind the last two objectives listed in the introduction to this unit. You should be able to identify the following writing patterns: illustration/example, definition, cause and effect, comparison/contrast, description, and sequence of events.

Drill   B-1: FINDING MAIN IDEAS THROUGH PARAGRAPH PATTERNS

Directions: For each of the following paragraphs, identify which of the organizational patterns listed best describes the paragraph. Then, in the spaces provided, write what you think is the main idea and key supporting points.

a.	illustration/example	**e.**	cause/effect
b.	definition	**f.**	description
c.	comparison/contrast	**g.**	combination (include the
d.	sequence of events		letters of the patterns)

Write the letter of the correct pattern in the blank before the paragraph.

1. _____   College athletes ought to be paid a salary on top of any scholarships and allowances they receive. Major college athletics is a form of entertainment. As with other entertainments, talented people perform for audiences who pay to watch. What universities are doing is using performance for publicity purposes. College athletes should be paid for their part in this. Other people in the collegiate-sport industry—coaches, athletic directors, trainers—are making a good living. Why not the athletes, the actual producers of the event?

Main idea: _____

_____

Supporting details: _____

_____

_____

_____

2. _____   College athletes should not be paid a salary on top of any scholarships and allowances they receive. A student athlete is a part of a university family, along with other students, the faculty, and so on. Only a handful of students—a maximum of 110 in men's football and basketball—play sports that generate revenue. A school's resources, regardless of how they are generated, should be used to benefit the entire college. To pay athletes in football and basketball—most of whom already receive full tuition and room and board—the institution would have to cut some nonrevenue sports or reassign resources from some other academic area. How about other athletes, like wrestlers, swimmers, softball players? They must train as rigorously and may receive only a partial grant or none at all.

Main idea: _____

_____

Supporting details: _____

_____

_____

_____

3. _____ Here is a four-step method to prevent your mind from wandering while reading. First, before you attempt to read anything, look over the length of the material to see whether you have time to read it all; if not, mark a spot where you intend to stop. Second, read the title and the first paragraph, looking for the main idea of the article. Next, read the boldface headings, if there are any, and the first sentence of each paragraph. Finally, read the last paragraph, which probably contains a summary of the material. These steps condition your mind to accept the material you want to read and keep it from wandering.

Main idea: _____

_____

Supporting details: _____

_____

_____

_____

4. _____ Irony may be defined as a contrast, a disparity between what actually is and what ought to be; it is one form of contrast and can be found in all aspects of modern fiction. You will find it in conflict; if, for example, you tell the story of a man who spends his life in the pursuit of money only to discover that the goal was not worth the struggle, this would be ironical.... (From Richard Altick, *Preface to Critical Reading*, 2nd ed., Holt, Rinehart and Winston, 1984.)

Main idea: _____

_____

Supporting details: _____

_____

_____

_____

5. _____   In the U.S., the age-old problem of excessive drinking is taking a disturbing new turn and affecting new kinds of victims. On a New York subway train, a school-bound 15-year-old holds his books in one hand, a brown paper bag containing a beer bottle in the other. He takes a swig, then passes the bottle to a classmate. In a San Francisco suburb, several high school freshmen show up for class drunk every morning, while others sneak off for a nip or two of whiskey during the lunch recess. On the campuses, the beer bash is fashionable once again, and lowered drinking ages have made liquor the high without the hassle.

Main idea: _____

_____

Supporting details: _____

_____

_____

_____

6. _____   But Walnut Canyon offered the Sinagua more than cozy home-sites. A dependable supply of water flowed along the streambed on the floor of the canyon. Fertile volcanic-cinder soil lay within about two miles of the canyon rim. A great variety of trees, for fuel and implements, grew within the canyon and on the mesa. Other wild plants, a source of food and medicines, lined the banks of the stream and blanketed the slope. Game, furred and feathered, abounded in the canyon and on the mesa top. (From *Walnut Canyon*, Superintendent of Documents, U.S. Government Printing Office, 1968.)

Main idea: _____

_____

Supporting details: _____

_____

_____

_____

7. _____   The patients wandered aimlessly about, mumbling incoherently. Violent ones were wrapped in wet sheets with their arms

pinned, or they wore straitjackets. Attendants, in danger of assault, peered at their charges through screens. The floor lay bare, because rugs would have quickly been soiled with excrement. The large mental institution of 30 years ago was a madhouse.

Main idea: _____

_____

Supporting details: _____

_____

_____

_____

8. _____   Because of the way prime-time television portrays them, America's elderly have a distorted image. Only 1 out of every 50 fictional television characters is over 65; in real life 1 out of every 10 persons has passed that age. Studies show that in 1365 nighttime programs, older people are portrayed as stubborn, eccentric, ineffectual, sexually unattractive, and sometimes silly. Older women appear on television shows seldom and in roles with few romantic possibilities. Old men are shown as having evil powers. Because the largest group of people watching television is over 55, television could end up alienating its most faithful viewers.

Main idea: _____

_____

Supporting details: _____

_____

_____

_____

9. _____   There are basically two different types of purchasers who respond to advertising. One type rushes out to buy 50 percent of all the products they see advertised. Such buyers help make advertising a highly successful, multibillion-dollar-a-year industry. People of the second type think they are immune to ads; they think most ads are silly, stupid, and "beneath their dignity." This type of purchaser believes ads are aimed at the "suckers" of the first type. Yet 90 percent of the nation's adults who believe themselves immune are responsible for about 90 percent of all purchases of advertised products.

Main idea: _____

_____

Supporting details: _____

_____

_____

_____

10. _____   Television is addictive. For example, when a set breaks, most families rush to have it repaired, often renting one if the repair process takes longer than a day or two. When "nothing's on TV," people experience boredom with their lives, not knowing what to do with themselves. Perhaps the best example of television addiction was an experiment in Germany where 184 volunteers were paid to go without television for a year. At first, most volunteers did well, reporting that they were spending more time with their children, reading, and visiting friends. Then, within a month, tension, restlessness, and quarreling increased. Not one volunteer lasted more than five months without a television set. Once the sets were on again, people lost their anxieties and returned to normal.

Main idea: _____

_____

Supporting details: _____

_____

_____

_____

Drill B-2: MAIN IDEAS IN LONGER PASSAGES

Directions: The following reading passages are longer than the ones in the previous drills. Read them and answer the questions that follow. Use what you have learned about main ideas, supporting details, and paragraph patterns.

Passage A:

The two most popular aerobic exercises are jogging and swimming. The latter is more enthusiastically recommended because it avoids the trauma to the legs and spine of jogging and utilizes the arms and chest muscles as well as the legs. It is done with the help, or buoyancy, of water. The gravitational force on your joints is not nearly so great as when standing out of water. Your weight in the water (with only your head and neck exposed) is only one-tenth what it is out of water.

Since the water, and not your body, bears much of your weight, swimming is an excellent exercise for those suffering with arthritis. At the same time the buoyancy also spares your knees, ankles, and lower back from the constant pounding associated with jogging. In fact swimming is often prescribed for those people who have suffered joint injuries from other sports or exercise activities. It strengthens the muscles of your abdomen and has been prescribed as the one exercise program for those with chronic back problems. (From Richard Stein, "What Is the Best Form of Exercise?" John Gallagher Communications.)

1. Which statement best describes the main idea of the passage?
   a. The two most popular aerobic exercises are jogging and swimming.
   b. Jogging is better than swimming.
   c. Swimming is more popular than jogging.
   d. Swimming is recommended over jogging.
2. The writing pattern most used in this passage is
   a. definition
   b. comparison/contrast
   c. cause/effect
   d. both b and c
3. In the space provided, list some of the details given to support your answer to

   question 1. _____

   _____

   _____

   _____

   _____

Passage B:

One of the important mechanisms by which the individual takes on the values of others is *identification.* The term is loosely used to sum up a number of different ways in which one person puts himself in the place of another. People are said to identify with others when they are able to feel sympathy for another's plight, to understand and perhaps even experience the emotions someone else is experiencing, and to treat others as they themselves would like to be treated.

The normal tendency of the child to take the same attitudes toward himself that others take toward him is also a form of identification. If the average child does not steal, it is not because he has reached the rational conclusion that it is unwise or inexpedient to do so. Rather he takes the same morally disapproving attitude toward such behavior that others take toward it. He identifies with the adult point of view, and the thought of stealing prompts feelings of guilt.

It is also normal for the child to take the same attitudes toward his environment that his "significant others" take toward him. The little girl who is spanked by her mother may in turn spank her dolls, acting toward her dolls as her mother acts toward her. She identifies with her mother according to her limited experience of what a mother does and feels. (From Leonard Broom and Philip Selznick, *Sociology,* 5th ed., Harper & Row, 1982, p. 103.)

1. Which is the basic pattern used in the above passage?
   a. illustration/example   c. cause/effect
   b. definition   d. comparison/contrast

2. Explain why you selected the writing pattern you circled.

_____

_____

_____

3. While the basic pattern is one of the choices in question 1, what other method is also used to a lesser degree?
   a. illustration/example   **c.** cause/effect
   b. definition   **d.** comparison/contrast
4. Explain your answer to question 3.

_____

_____

_____

5. What is the main idea of this passage?

_____

_____

_____

Passage C:

Modern unionism also concentrates power and control in industry and government. A union will attempt to establish uniform wage rates in all plants in which the majority of workers are members of that union. In competition with other unions for members and power, it cannot accept lower rates of pay than those secured by other unions, even in different industries. Union competition of this kind tends to equalize wage rates for comparable work throughout a given industry and ultimately narrows the spread between wages paid for similar skills in different industries. But it is the bigger and longer established companies which are in the best position to absorb added wage costs to production. A particular handicap is presented new companies, with limited capital, once they are caught in such a competitive wage spiral. The established corporation, with a quasi-controlled market, can invariably pass on added labor costs either to distributors or to consumers, which a new company is unable to do. The charge has been made that some big corporations welcome "another round" of wage increases that will eliminate newer companies from "free competition." (From Arnold Green, _Sociology: An Analysis of Life in Modern Society,_ McGraw-Hill, p. 265.)

1. What writing pattern is used in this passage?
   a. definition   **c.** comparison/contrast
   b. sequence of events   **d.** cause/effect
2. There are two results that occur when a union attempts to establish uniform wage rates in all plants in which the majority of workers are union members.

Name them.

_____

_____

3. State in your own words what you think the main idea of this passage is.

_____

_____

_____

Passage D:

The mass man has been described by David Riesman as "other-directed" in contrast to the "inner-directed" man of an earlier period. The behavior of the inner-directed man was governed by internal norms or values. His course through life was directed by the values—largely imposed by parents and Church—that had come to form the content of his conscience. These values, interiorized in the process of growing up, functioned in a manner analogous to the gyroscope, giving his behavior a self-contained equilibrium and direction.

The other-directed man, by contrast, has no fixed or definite standards of taste or judgment. He wants above all to belong, to be liked, not to stand out from the crowd. He seeks to conform his behavior to the constantly changing expectations of others, rather than to any internalized standards of right and wrong. The analogy here is not the gyroscope, but radar. In search of cues from the groups to which he belongs, he sends out signals and guides his behavior by what he interprets to be the expectations of his fellows. Professor Ray Ginger makes the same point in his study of Chicago when its leading public figures were such controversial men as the radical Governor Peter Altgeld and Clarence Darrow. However unlovely in certain respects these men's personalities may have been, the question they put to themselves was, "Am I right?" This is to be contrasted with the question that appears to dominate the lives of current residents of suburbia, "Am I covered?" (From Leonard Broom and Philip Selznick, _Sociology_, 5th ed., Harper & Row, p. 65).

1. In the space provided, list the differences and similarities under the headings below:

inner-directed man   _other-directed man_

_____

_____

_____

_____

_____

2. In the middle of the second paragraph, the authors say, "The analogy here is not the gyroscope, but radar." Explain what is meant.

_____

_____

_____

3. Which question is appropriate for the inner-directed man?
   a. "Am I right?"
   b. "Am I covered?"
4. What is the main point of this passage?

_____

_____

_____

Passage E:

1.   The need for effective public speaking will almost certainly touch you sometime in your life. When it does, you want to be ready. But even if you never give another speech in your life, you still have much to gain from studying public speaking. Your speech class will give you training in researching topics, organizing your ideas, and presenting yourself skillfully. This training is invaluable for every type of communication.

2.   There are many similarities between public speaking and daily conversation. The three major goals of public speaking—to inform, to persuade, to entertain—are also the three major goals of everyday conversation. In conversation, almost without thinking about it, you employ a wide range of skills. You organize your ideas logically. You tailor your message to your audience. You tell a story for maximum impact. You adapt to feedback from your listener. These are among the most important skills you will need for public speaking.

3.   Of course, public speaking is also different from conversation. First, public speaking is more highly structured than conversation. It usually imposes strict time limitations on the speaker, and it requires more detailed preparation than does ordinary conversation. Second, speechmaking requires more formal language. Listeners react negatively to speeches loaded with slang, jargon, and bad grammar. Third, public speaking demands a different method of delivery. Effective speakers adjust their voices to the larger audience and work at avoiding distracting physical mannerisms and verbal habits.

4.   One of the major concerns of students in any speech class is stage fright. Actually, most successful speakers are nervous before making a speech. Your speech class will give you an opportunity to gain confidence and make your nervousness work for you rather than against you. You will take a big step toward overcoming stage fright if you think positively, choose speech topics you really care about, prepare thoroughly, and concentrate on communicating with your audience. Like many students over the years, you too can develop confidence in your speechmaking abilities.

5.   The speech communication process as a whole includes seven elements—speaker, message, channel, listener, feedback, interference, and situation. The speaker is the person who initiates a speech transaction. Whatever the speaker communicates is the message, which is sent by means of a particular channel. The listener receives the communicated message and may provide feedback to the speaker. Interference is anything that impedes the communication of a message; and the situation is the time and place in which speech communication occurs. The interaction of these seven elements is what determines the outcome in any instance of speech communication.

6. Because speechmaking is a form of power, it carries with it heavy ethical responsibilities. Ethical speakers use sound means to achieve sound goals. They do this by being well informed about their subjects, by being honest in what they say, by using sound evidence, and by employing valid reasoning. (From *The Art of Public Speaking* by Stephen E. Lucas. Copyright © 1983 by Random House, Inc. Reprinted by permission of Random House, Inc.)

1. What is being compared in paragraph 2?

   _____

2. What is being contrasted in paragraph 3?

   _____

3. What is the cause and what is the effect being discussed in paragraph 4?

   _____

   _____

4. What is the basic writing pattern being used in paragraph 5?
    a. definition   **c.** description
    b. sequence of events   **d.** illustration/example

5. The topic of this passage is public speaking. What is the main point being made by the author about public speaking?

   _____

   _____

   _____

   _____

C. Finding an Author's Thesis

Every well-written essay or article contains a *thesis* or a main idea about the subject that the author wants the reader to accept or think about. A thesis is not the same as the subject. The *subject* of an essay is what the author is writing about, such as computers, good manners, horse racing, war, a country, and the like. Subjects for essays are limitless. A thesis is what the author wants to say about the subject, or the author's feelings about the subject.

Let's say you are reading an essay about grades and their value. That would be the subject of the essay. But you need to understand the main point the author is making about grades. Is the author in favor of grades or against them? Is the author presenting a new concept about grading that she or he wants the reader to accept? A thesis, then, is what the author wants to say about that particular subject. Recognizing an author's thesis is basic to developing good literal comprehension.

The next few drills provide practice in recognizing an author's thesis.

Drill C-1

Directions: As you read the following essay, look for the subject of the essay, the author's thesis, and the major details used to develop the thesis. Then answer the questions that follow.

STRIKE OUT LITTLE LEAGUE

Robin Roberts

1   In 1939, Little League baseball was organized by Bert and George Bebble and Carl Stotz of Williamsport, Pa. What they had in mind in organizing this kids' baseball program, I'll never know. But I'm sure they never visualized the monster it would grow into.

2   At least 25,000 teams, in about 5,000 leagues, compete for a chance to go to the Little League World Series in Williamsport each summer. These leagues are in more than fifteen countries, although recently the Little League organization has voted to restrict the competition to teams in the United States. If you judge the success of a program by the number of participants, it would appear that Little League has been a tremendous success. More than 600,000 boys from 8 to 12 are involved. But I say Little League is wrong—and I'll try to explain why.

3   If I told you and your family that I want you to help me with a project from the middle of May until the end of July, one that would totally disrupt your dinner schedule and pay nothing, you would probably tell me to get lost. That's what Little League does. Mothers and fathers or both spend four or five nights a week taking children to Little League, watching the game, coming home around 8 or 8:30 and sitting down to a late dinner.

4   These games are played at this hour because the adults are running the programs and this is the only time they have available. These same adults are in most cases

unqualified as instructors and do not have the emotional stability to work with children of this age. The dedication and sincerity of these instructors cannot be questioned, but the purpose of this dedication should be. Youngsters eligible for Little League are of the age when their concentration lasts, at most, for five seconds—and without sustained concentration organized athletic programs are a farce.

5   Most instructors will never understand this. As a result there is a lot of pressure on these young people to do something that is unnatural for their age—so there will always be hollering and tremendous disappointment for most of these players. For acting their age, they are made to feel incompetent. This is a basic fault of Little League.

6   If you watch a Little League game, in most cases the pitchers are the most mature. They throw harder, and if they throw strikes very few batters can hit the ball. Consequently, it makes good baseball sense for most hitters to take the pitch. Don't swing. Hope for a walk. That could be a player's instruction for four years. The fun is in hitting the ball; the coach says don't swing. That may be sound baseball, but it does nothing to help a young player develop his hitting. What would seem like a basic training ground for baseball often turns out to be a program of negative thoughts that only retards a young player.

7   I believe more good young athletes are turned off by the pressure of organized Little League than are helped. Little Leagues have no value as a training ground for baseball fundamentals. The instruction at that age, under the pressure of an organized league program, creates more doubt and eliminates the naturalness that is most important.

8   If I'm going to criticize such a popular program as Little League, I'd better have some thoughts on what changes I would like to see.

9   First of all, I wouldn't start any programs until the school year is over. Any young student has enough of a schedule during the school year to keep busy.

10   These programs should be played in the afternoon—with a softball. Kids have a natural fear of a baseball; it hurts when it hits you. A softball is bigger, easier to see and easier to hit. You get to run the bases more and there isn't as much danger of injury if one gets hit with the ball. Boys and girls could play together. Different teams would be chosen every day. The instructors would be young adults home from college, or high-school graduates. The instructor could be the pitcher and the umpire at the same time. These programs could be run on public playgrounds or in schoolyards.

11   I guarantee that their dinner would be at the same time every night. The fathers could come home after work and relax; most of all, the kids would have a good time playing ball in a program in which hitting the ball and running the bases are the big things.

12   When you start talking about young people playing baseball at 13 to 15, you may have something. Organize them a little, but be careful; they are still young. But from 16 and on, work them really hard. Discipline them, organize the leagues, strive to win championships, travel all over. Give this age all the time and attention you can.

13   I believe Little League has done just the opposite. We've worked hard with the 8- to 12-year-olds. We overorganize them, put them under pressure they can't handle and make playing baseball seem important. When our young people reach 16 they would appreciate the attention and help from the parents, and that's when our present programs almost stop.

14   The whole idea of Little League baseball is wrong. There are alternatives available for more sensible programs. With the same dedication that has made the Little League such a major part of many of our lives, I'm sure we'll find the answer.

15   I still don't know what these three gentlemen in Williamsport had in mind when they organized Little League baseball. I'm sure they didn't want parents arguing with their children about kids' games. I'm sure they didn't want to have family meals disrupted for three months every year. I'm sure they didn't want young athletes hurting their arms pitching under pressure at such a young age. I'm sure they didn't want young boys who don't have much athletic ability made to feel that something is wrong with

them because they can't play baseball. I'm sure they didn't want a group of coaches drafting the players each year for different teams. I'm sure they didn't want unqualified men working with the young players. I'm sure they didn't realize how normal it is for an 8-year-old boy to be scared of a thrown or batted baseball.

16   For the life of me, I can't figure out what they had in mind.

Now answer the following questions. Answers to some questions will require you to reread portions of the article.

1. The author's thesis or main idea is that
    a. Little League baseball was started by three men in Williamsburg, Pa.
    b. Little League baseball should be abolished.
    c. Little League has become a training ground for future proball players.
    d. Little League, as it is, is all wrong and should be changed.

2. Paragraph 2 contains many details. For what purpose does the author use

    them? _____

    _____

    _____

3. What is the main idea of paragraph 4? _____

    _____

    _____

4. According to the author, many good young athletes are turned off by the
    a. instructions they receive.
    b. pressure of organized ball playing.
    c. disruption of meals because of training schedules.
    d. lack of dedication of instructors.

5. List the changes the author would make in Little League. _____

    _____

    _____

    _____

    _____

    _____

    _____

6. What is the main idea of paragraph 15? _____

    _____

    _____

Let's look at the questions and your answers to make certain you have put to use what you have learned in previous drills. Finding the thesis in a reading selection, such as the one you just read, is similar to finding the main idea in paragraphs. The difference is that in a longer selection paragraphs are used to support the thesis, just as sentences are used in paragraphs to support the topic sentence.

The best answer for the first question is d. Paragraphs 2, 8, and 15, plus the clues in the title, support this answer. If you missed this question, look at those portions of the essay again.

To answer the second question, you should have said something to this effect: The details are used to show how popular and successful Little League is, which also lets us know the author is aware that his opinion is contrary to many others; yet despite its popularity, he is against Little League as it is now run.

In answering question 3, you need to say something such as: The dedication and sincerity of Little League instructors can't be questioned, but their purpose and qualifications as instructors should be. If this question gave you trouble, reread paragraph 4 again and notice the key words.

The best answer to question 4 is b; pressure is mentioned in paragraphs 7 and 13. The other options are mentioned but not in reference to what turns off young athletes.

The answer to question 5 begins with paragraph 9. You should have listed most of these:

    a.   games should be played in the afternoons

    b.   a softball should be used

    c.   boys and girls should play together

    d.   instructors should be young college students

    e.   use of public playgrounds or schoolyards

    f.   dinner would be at the same time every night

    g.   start training later, from ages 13–15

    h.   after age 16, work the kids hard, not before

The answer to question 6 is that it summarizes all the things the author finds wrong with Little League as it now is run. All the items he mentions are negative and help support his thesis.

Before going on to the next drill, make certain that you understand any mistakes or misinterpretations you may have made in answering the above questions.

Drill C-2

Directions: Follow the same directions as for the last drill; read carefully, looking for the subject, the thesis, and the supporting details in the essay. If you had any problems with the last two drills, make certain you understand your mistakes before going on.

WEEP NOT FOR THE WIZENED

James Dale Davidson

1   Have you ever wondered why the wealthiest man in the United States is entitled to ride for half-fare on any bus? Answer: He's over 65. He's also entitled to Social Security benefits (read windfalls) and taxpayer-subsidized medical treatment (Medi-

care), and he can see *Jaws 3-D* on a special senior discount at any American Multi-Cinema.

2   I don't begrudge anyone *Jaws 3-D*. Nor billions. Indeed, I wish everyone good health and a long life. What I don't understand is why I should be obliged to subsidize people who have a thousand times more assets than I—merely because they are old.

3   Being old is nothing to gripe about. It's far more appealing than the alternative: being dead. Lots of people do die before they reach old age. *They're* the ones I feel sorry for—those who are crippled or hurt or who lose their lives altogether in youth or middle age. Someone who is now elderly has already lived a long life. If it was not a full life, that's his fault. I see no good reason that the elderly should become our prime national charity—especially when many are not even poor.

4   Look at the figures, and you find that the oldest portion of the population is the richest. The richest. They own more of the nation's real estate, stocks, and businesses than people in any other age bracket. Most of the elderly actually own their homes. Because of the mess they left the country in, many young people never will own their homes.

5   Not all the old are wealthy, of course. But even those without wealth and with below-average income can realize a higher standard of living than most of the rest of the population. Much of the income of the elderly, in the form of Social Security benefits, is tax-free. And their other income is taxed at lower rates, because they have twice the number of exemptions as persons under 65.

6   Furthermore, the elderly have lower expenses than persons in other age brackets. Most don't work regularly and thus save thousands required for commuting, dressing for work, and having meals outside the home. Because they typically own their homes outright, having bought years ago at low interest rates, their housing costs, as a group, are lower.

7   In short, Grandpa and Grandma may deserve our love, and maybe even our pity if their health has started to fail. But not just because they are old. Not because they have lived a long life. There's nothing pitiful about that.

8   And if we really get down to cases, the elderly have as much to apologize for as to crow about. They're the ones who voted for the politicians who left the country in the shabby shape it's in today. In fairness, they should pay part of the cost rather than using the system to plunder those who were unlucky enough to come along later. They voted in the Social Security system but didn't put it on a sound footing—or pay taxes themselves that were in any way commensurate with the benefits they are now drawing. A man who turned 65 in 1982 and retired in that year with a nonworking spouse would have collected every penny he ever paid into Social Security by the end of March 1983. He and then his widow, when he dies, will continue to collect benefits until after the turn of the century.

9   Politicians are bidding against one another to make these windfalls even greater. The hoppers in Congress are filled with bills to give elderly persons up to $10,000 in income-tax exclusions, an exclusive right to deduct real-estate taxes paid on rented apartments, exemption from penalties for underpayment of estimated tax, special home health-care subsidies, subsidized home repairs, "grandparents rights," and more.

10   At the same time the politicians proclaim that the oldsters are so pitiful as to deserve all this bounty, they prohibit any presumption that the elderly are incompetent. Age can now be used as a basis for refusing employment only with the greatest difficulty. One might be obliged to hire an elderly accountant at the same time the politicians tell us that he, but not his young client, may be excused for not paying his estimated taxes. Figure that one out.

11   Politicians pander to the old because they tend not to work and therefore have a discoverable interest as recipients of benefits from the government. There are tens of thousands of occupations in America. Those of working age who fill those jobs tend to vote in ways that narrowly promote the interest of the groups to which they belong.

Farmers vote for price supports, auto workers for import quotas, doctors for restraint of trade in the medical industry, and so on. But retired farmers, auto workers, and doctors all want more benefits for retired people. In old age, they are united in greed, as they were once divided by it. The politicians sense this, which is why the oldest segment in our population will continue to exploit the rest of us; why we see the absurd spectacle of government investing more in the old than in the young.

12   While those who are not retired on Social Security will collect large multiples of the amount they paid into the system, those now working will be lucky to receive a large fraction of their contributions. The system is unfair and wrong. The next time someone proposes changing the national anthem, which happens every few years, I have a suggestion: that classic sung by the Ponytails in 1958, "Born Too Late."

Now answer the following questions. You may need to reread portions of the essay, especially when certain paragraphs are referred to.

1.   What is the thesis of the essay? _____

_____

_____

2.   In what paragraph is the thesis best stated? _____

3.   What is the main idea and supporting detail of each of the following paragraphs?

a.   *Paragraph 4*

Main idea: _____

Supporting details: _____

_____

_____

b.   *Paragraph 5*

Main idea: _____

Supporting details: _____

_____

_____

c.   *Paragraph 6*

Main idea: _____

Supporting details: _____

_____

4.   What reasons are given for politicians "pandering" to the old? _____

_____

_____

5. In paragraph 12, the author claims that the Social Security system is unfair

and wrong. What is it that he feels is specifically unfair and wrong? _____

_____

_____

6. What is your reaction to the essay?

_____

_____

D. Summarizing As a Way to Test Your Understanding

Frequently, instructors in your college classes will ask you to write summaries of reading assignments. In addition, many essay exams you will be required to take are really nothing more than a test of your ability to write summaries in answer to questions based on sections from your textbooks. What, then, *is* a summary and how do you write one?

A summary is a brief statement in your own words of the main ideas and support used in a reading selection. Writing summaries requires that you include only the most vital information presented in a piece of writing. The drills you have been doing that require you to separate the main ideas from details provide the basis for writing summaries.

There are three basic things to keep in mind when you write a summary: be brief, be complete, and be objective. This can sound easier than it is. If you are too brief, you may not be complete; if you try to be too complete, you may write too much; if you're not careful, you may slip into subjectivity, allowing your own feelings and opinions to creep in. A summary has no place for your views. As a guideline, a good rule of thumb in writing summaries is to make them no longer than one quarter of the length of the passage you are summarizing. But this may vary depending on the instructor's summary assignment.

Let's say you are asked to summarize the essay you read in Drill C-1, "Strike Out Little League," on page 86. The best way to get started is to begin with the author's thesis, which is reflected in his title. Roberts believes that the whole idea of Little League baseball is wrong. Why? What does he want to do about Little League?

As we look over the essay paragraph by paragraph, we see that the first paragraph begins with a brief history and his comment that it has grown into a "monster." The second paragraph provides information on what Little League has grown into, ending with the comment that it is "wrong." His position on Little League is clear after the first two paragraphs. Now we want to know why.

In paragraph 3 he begins to tell us. The schedule involved disrupts family life, keeping everyone out four or five nights a week. There's one reason.

In paragraph 4, more reasons are provided: most adults running the program are unqualified; adult supervisors are only available at night; and children eligible for Little League don't have the necessary concentration at that age.

Paragraph 5 gives more reasons: pressure is brought on the kids because most adult leaders don't understand that age level; kids are made to feel inferior or incompetent when they act their age.

Paragraph 6 gives still more: the fun of baseball is hitting the ball, but in Little League, most of the pitchers are older and throw too hard for the younger ones; the training doesn't help a player develop his hitting.

Paragraph 7 is a type of summary in which Roberts states the pressure, the lack of value as a training ground, and his belief that an organized league for young kids creates doubt and eliminates naturalness. With these three points, Roberts then prepares us for paragraph 8, which serves as a transition to the things he would like to see done instead. As we move through the paragraphs, we can list what he would change:

1. games would be played in the afternoon
2. a softball would be used
3. co-ed playing would be allowed
4. college students should be the instructors

5. public playgrounds or schoolyards would be used
6. training would start later, from ages 13–15
7. kids wouldn't be worked hard until they reach 16

His last two paragraphs summarize some of his reasons around his thesis.

Now, if we put all this together, we might have a summary that says something like this:

> In his essay "Strike Out Little League," Robin Roberts believes that Little League baseball, as presently organized, is wrong and should be changed. What's wrong is that present schedules keep the family out four or five nights a week, disrupting dinnertime. He also feels most adults running the programs are not qualified to work with the Little League age bracket. In addition, most children don't have the concentration necessary for rigid training, training which often takes the fun out of playing baseball. The pressure of the training to win also makes the unsuccessful children feel inferior or inept. To counter this, Roberts would change the playing schedule to afternoons, use college students as coaches, switch to the use of a softball, use public playgrounds or schoolyards, not start training until ages 13–15, and not work kids hard until they are at least 16 years old.

Obviously things have to be left out of a summary, but this example is brief, complete in presenting the thesis and support used by Roberts, and objective.

In order to write this summary, it was necessary for the author to go over the Roberts' essay very carefully. It required using the skills necessary for separating main ideas from details and identifying the author's thesis, both skills that were taught in this unit. The practice of writing summaries of what you read can be of great benefit to your literal comprehension development.

Drill D-1: PRACTICE IN SUMMARIZING

Directions: In the space provided, write a summary of passage B on page 81 which you have already read. You may want to use the answers to your questions as a guide.

Drill D-2: MORE SUMMARIZING

Directions: In the space below, write a summary of passage E on page 84 which you have already read. You may want to use your answers as a guide.

Drill D-3: AND STILL MORE ON SUMMARIZING

Directions: On another sheet of paper, write a summary of the essay on page 89, "Weep Not for the Wizened," and turn it in to your instructor.

E. Reading Practices

The next two drills give you the opportunity to use what you have learned about reading to find an author's thesis and use of main ideas and supporting details. Before you begin, it is recommended that you refer to the Student Record Chart on page 495 and review your scores for the reading selections in Chapter 1. Note your comprehension and vocabulary scores. Try either to match your scores or to do better this time. As you progress through this book, use these scores as a motivation and challenge to do better each time. Your only competition is yourself.

Drill E-1

Directions: As you read the following essay, distinguish between the subject and the thesis and note what main ideas and supporting details are used to back up the author's thesis.

THINKING: A NEGLECTED ART

Carolyn Kane

1   It is generally agreed that the American educational system is in deep trouble. Everyone is aware of the horrible facts: school systems are running out of money, teachers can't spell.

2   Most of us know, or think we know, who is to blame: liberal courts, spineless school boards, government regulations. It is easy to select a villain.

3   But possibly the problem lies not so much in our institutions as in our attitudes. It is sad that although most of us profess to believe in education, we place no value on intellectual activity.

4   We Americans are a charitable and humane people: we have institutions devoted to every good cause from rescuing homeless cats to preventing World War III. But what have we done to promote the art of thinking? Certainly we make no room for thought in our daily lives. Suppose a man were to say to his friends, "I'm not going to PTA tonight (or choir practice or the baseball game) because I need some time to myself, some time to think"? Such a man would be shunned by his neighbors; his family would be ashamed of him. What if a teen-ager were to say, "I'm not going to the dance tonight because I need some time to think"? His parents would immediately start looking in the Yellow Pages for a psychiatrist. We are all too much like Julius Caesar: we fear and distrust people who think too much. We believe that almost anything is more important than thinking.

5   **Guilty:** Several years ago a college administrator told me that if he wanted to do any serious thinking, he had to get up at 5:30 in the morning—I suppose because that was the only time when no one would interrupt him. More recently I heard a professor remark that when his friends catch him in the act of reading a book, they say, "My, it must be nice to have so much free time." And even though I am an English teacher—a person who should know better—I find myself feeling vaguely guilty whenever I sneak off to the library to read. It is a common belief that if a man is thinking or reading, he is

doing nothing. Through our words and our actions, we express this attitude every day of our lives. Then we wonder why our children refuse to take their studies seriously and why they say to their teachers, "This stuff won't do me any good because I'll never need to use it."

6   It is easy to understand the causes of this prejudice against thinking. One problem is that to most of us, thinking looks suspiciously like loafing. Homo sapiens in deep thought is an uninspiring sight. He leans back in his chair, props up his feet, puffs on his pipe and stares into space. He gives every appearance of wasting time; he reminds us more of Dagwood and Beetle Bailey than of Shakespeare and Einstein. We wish he would get up and *do* something; mow the lawn, maybe, or wash the car. Our resentment is natural.

7   But thinking is far different from laziness. Thinking is one of the most productive activities a human being can undertake. Every beautiful and useful thing we have created—including democratic government and freedom of religion—exists because somebody took the time and effort to think of it.

8   And thinking does require time and effort. It is a common misconception that if a person is "gifted" or "bright" or "talented," wonderful ideas will flash spontaneously into his mind. Unfortunately, the intellect does not work in this way. Even Einstein had to study and think for months before he could formulate his theory of relativity. Those of us who are less intelligent find it a struggle to conceive even a moderately good idea, let alone a brilliant one.

9   **Seclusion:** Another reason why we distrust thinking is that it seems unnatural. Human beings are a social species, but thinking is an activity that requires solitude. Consequently, we worry about people who like to think. It disturbs us to meet a person who deliberately chooses to sit alone and think instead of going to a party or a rodeo or a soccer match. We suspect that such a person needs counseling.

10   Our concern is misplaced. Intelligence is just as much a part of human nature as sociability. It would certainly be unnatural for a person to retreat into total seclusion. It would be equally unnatural for a person to allow his mind to die of neglect.

11   If Americans ever became convinced of the importance of thought, we would probably find ways to solve the problems of our schools, problems that now seem insurmountable. But how can we revive interest in the art of thinking? The best place to start would be in the homes and churches of our land. Ministers should admonish their congregations to do some purposeful procrastination every day, to put off one chore in order to have a few minutes to think. Family members should practice saying such things as, "I'll wash the dishes tonight because I know you want to catch up on your thinking."

12   This may sound un-American, possibly sacrilegious. But if we are to survive as a free people, we will have to take some such course of action as soon as possible, because regardless of what some advertisers have led us to believe, this country does not run on oil. It runs on ideas.

COMPREHENSION CHECK

Directions: Answer the following questions without looking back.

   1.   What is the *subject* of the essay you just read?

   _____

   2.   What is the *thesis* of this essay?   _____

   _____

3. According to the author, if someone is thinking or reading, that person is frequently thought of as
    a. weird   **c.** studying
    b. doing nothing   **d.** not using his or her time wisely

4. State two reasons the author gives for prejudice against thinking: _____

    _____

5. According to the author, thinking requires
    a. time   **c.** solitude
    b. effort   **d.** all four

6. The author uses Einstein as an example to support one of her main ideas.

    What point is she making? _____

    _____

    _____

7. If a person chooses to sit alone and think instead of going to a party or sports event, we tend to suspect that person
    a. is a nerd   **c.** needs counseling
    b. is another Einstein   **d.** none of these

8. How, according to the author, can we revive interest in the art of thinking?

    _____

    _____

9. T/F   The author claims that while we profess to believe in education, we place no value on intellectual activity.

10. The author concludes that this country runs on _____.

VOCABULARY CHECK

Directions: Define the following underlined words used in the essay.

1. <u>spineless</u> school boards

    _____

2. will flash <u>spontaneously</u> into his mind

    _____

3. he could <u>formulate</u> his theory

    _____

4. problems that now seem <u>insurmountable</u>

    _____

5. should <u>admonish</u> their congregations

    _____

6. some purposeful <u>procrastination</u>

    _____

7. may sound positively <u>sacrilegious</u>

_____

8. <u>shunned</u> by his neighbors

_____

9. Look again at all the underlined words above and write in all the prefixes and suffixes that appear.

_____

10. What is the root of the underlined word in item 4?

_____

Record the results of the comprehension and vocabulary checks on the Student Record Chart on page 495. Make certain you understand any mistakes you may have made before going on. Use whatever method you are using to learn any words you missed.

Drill   E-2

Directions: Read the following essay, noting the author's subject, thesis, main ideas, and details used to support the thesis.

PUTTING READING IN ITS PROPER PLACE

Dominic F. Martia

1   As more and more Americans depend exclusively on television for information and ideas, the nation's reading proficiency suffers—and so does society.

2   It isn't hard to see why TV is so appealing. It offers the immediacy of real life. Yet, TV doesn't merely give us real life. Events in real life occur without commentary. In contrast, televised events are often delivered from prefabricated perspectives. In real life, we are forced to make up our own minds as to the meaning of events. When we see televised news events, the meaning often is supplied through selection, angle, emphasis and accompanying narrative.

3   But the point isn't that TV may be biased. So may books, magazines or newspapers. The point is that television's seductive and misleading immediacy lulls our critical judgment. Watching TV requires much less effort than reading does. Our preference for TV as a source of information and ideas is a measure of intellectual laziness.

4   TV long ago won the battle for our attention. But the real loser has been our ability to read, which, like other learned abilities, needs regular practice to maintain its strength.

5   As we seek a better balance between our dependence on TV and our use of the

From *U.S. News & World Report*, Feb. 9, 1987, p. 6. Reprinted with permission of Dominic F. Martia.

print media, we will increase the time we spend reading. This will be a good start. If overreliance on TV has atrophied our reading skill, then reading more should help restore it. But besides reading more, we need to become more-selective and more-critical readers. Much of what we might read isn't worth reading. It panders to the same laziness that induces us to turn on the TV rather than open a book.

6   In a nation our size, it would be surprising if there weren't a persistent market for serious and high-quality publications. But the demise of many newspapers, the shaky economics of journals of opinion and the unprofitability of serious books indicate that the general level of reading taste has declined sharply since the '50s.

7   Our concern for providing basic literacy to adults seems to recognize the importance of reading. But let's also encourage people who are already literate to aspire to a higher level of reading skill and taste. It will take some thought, study and debate before we can decide exactly what should be done to achieve this goal. Schools, libraries and publishers would be the logical ones to begin the process, the guiding assumption of which is that reading is essential to education and to effective citizenship.

8   The issue is not a simple one of whether one source of information and ideas is better than another. We need them all. But intelligent use of our media requires the critical judgment that is best developed through reading. So let's put reading where it belongs—in first place.

COMPREHENSION CHECK

Directions: Answer the following questions without looking back.

1.   What is the *subject* of the essay you just read?

_____

2.   What is the *thesis* of this essay? _____

_____

3.   According to the author, TV, as opposed to reading, is appealing because
    a.   it forces us to make up our own minds
    b.   the meaning to events is supplied
    c.   we are intellectually lazy
    d.   all of the above

4.   T/F   The author believes TV is biased whereas reading books or newspapers or magazines is not.

5.   Because TV has won the battle for our attention, the author believes that the real loser is
    a.   our ability to read
    b.   our desire to read
    c.   our need to read
    d.   our children

6.   In order to maintain a proper balance between our dependence on TV and

our use of the print media, we need to increase the time we spend _____

_____

7.   According to the author, our reading skills require regular _____

_____.

8. Besides reading more, we need to become
    a. more selective in our reading
    b. more critical readers
    c. both a and b
    d. none of the above
9. What support does the author provide for his statement that the general level

    of reading taste has declined since the 1950s? _____

    _____

    _____

10. The author believes that reading
    a. is essential to education
    b. is essential to effective citizenship
    c. is essential to developing critical judgments
    d. all of the above

VOCABULARY CHECK

Directions: Define the following underlined words from the essay.

1. the nation's reading <u>proficiency</u> suffers

    _____

2. often delivered from <u>prefabricated</u> perspectives

    _____

3. it <u>lulls</u> our critical judgment

    _____

4. TV has <u>atrophied</u> our reading skill

    _____

5. it <u>panders</u> to the same laziness

    _____

6. the same laziness that <u>induces</u> us to turn on TV

    _____

7. the <u>demise</u> of many newspapers and high-quality publications

    _____

8. to <u>aspire</u> to a higher level of reading

    _____

9. the guiding <u>assumption</u>

    _____

10. intelligent use of our <u>media</u>

    _____

Record the results of the comprehension and vocabulary checks on the Student Record Chart on page 495.

Before you go on to the next chapter, make certain you understand any mistakes or problems you may have encountered in this one. It is important that you learn from mistakes, so don't despair when you make them. Accept mistakes as normal. It is often the best way to discover what you do and don't know.

CHAPTER 3

Developing Study-Reading Skills

In addition to being able to understand word meanings, recall main ideas and supporting details, and recognize the difference between a subject and a thesis (the content of Chapters 1 and 2), you need to develop a study-reading strategy. A study-reading strategy is a method or approach to studying that will offer you the best results for the time and effort you put into studying.

Textbooks and teachers are not all alike, as you well know. Therefore, you usually have to adapt or modify your study-reading approaches for different classes. Obviously, one of the best places to start is to familiarize yourself with each of the textbooks required for the classes you are taking. Most textbooks contain aids for students, but are often overlooked, ignored, or considered unimportant. The best thing you can do is to take the time to look over your textbooks to see what kinds of aids and information will be helpful when you study-read.

Almost all textbooks contain a table of contents, glossary, index, pictures, charts, and graphic aids. Often these items are designed as aids in studying, but not always. To find out how helpful such aids are, you should spend a few minutes looking over your books for such things as the

1. *title page;* it will give you the full title of the book, the edition, the authors and their school affiliation, and the publishing company. The complete title often helps you understand what the book will cover in regard to the subject. For instance, an introductory textbook is going to be more general than one that specifies a particular area. A history text that states "Volume 2" on the title page indicates an entire volume of history should have been studied before that one.
2. *copyright page;* this tells you when the book was published and the date of any previous editions, so you will have some idea how dated the information in the book is.
3. *preface;* this explains the author's purpose for writing the book, for what readers the book is intended, and usually includes an acknowledgment of those people who helped with the book.
4. *table of contents;* this shows how the book is organized, an outline of sorts. Some tables of contents are very comprehensive, some not; but at least they show you if the book is divided into units, chapters, sections, whether or not there is a glossary, index, appendix, and so on.
5. *index;* this is an alphabetical listing of the various topics covered in the book. Names, places, events, definitions of terms, and the like are usually listed. Looking over an index can give you an idea of the book's subject matter, plus call to mind anything you may already have studied in the past in another course.
6. *glossary;* the glossary is a small dictionary of sorts that usually defines the specialized terms covered in the book. It can save you from using the dictionary, but better yet, it defines the words and terms as they are used in the context of the book.
7. *appendixes;* textbooks frequently contain an appendix (sometimes more than one) that provides supplemental information related to the topic of the book. It is provided for the reader's use, but often overlooked.

How helpful these components of a textbook are varies from book to book. More often than not, they are not examined very thoroughly by students. This is unfortunate because as you progress through a particular course, these aids can sometimes be very beneficial. It is doubtful you would buy a car without driving it, looking it over carefully to see what features it has, and even comparing it with other cars. But when it comes to textbooks, most students buy them because they are required and never bother to get to know what they offer. More will be said about these aids in Chapter 4.

Another mistake some students make is to begin reading a textbook assignment without preparing to read it. They simply turn to the assigned pages and start reading. Soon they discover their minds have wandered and don't even remember what they have read up to that point. One of the most important parts of a good study strategy is to prepare to read an assignment. Just as you need to look over your textbooks to get to know their content, so should you look over any assignment before reading it to see how long it will take, what subject will be covered, and what aids are provided in the chapter to help you comprehend better.

This chapter is divided into five sections. Part A will offer you practice in preparing to read an assignment as well as providing you with a tried-and-true study strategy. Part B gives practice in marking and underlining textbooks for better comprehension. Part C provides practice in taking notes while reading, in case you are using a book you shouldn't or don't want to underline. Part D deals with clues for taking both objective and subjective tests. All of the reading selections in the drills from the first three sections are taken from actual college textbooks in various content areas. Part E, as in the first two chapters, provides reading practices containing both comprehension and vocabulary checks.

A. Study-Reading Strategies

Research has shown that the typical reader remembers only about half of what he or she reads when given a test right after reading an assignment. There are several factors that contribute to this, but one of the major ones is lack of preparation before beginning to study-read. In order to get the maximum efficiency from a study-reading session, it has been found that "looking before you leap," that is, surveying or looking over what has been assigned before trying to read it, is best.

To survey an assignment means that you should

1. *check the length of the assignment* by flipping through the assigned pages. Can you read it in one sitting or should you divide it up and cover a certain number of pages at a time? Don't try to take in too much at once, especially if it is a subject you don't know well or are having trouble understanding.

2. *read the title of the chapter and the subheadings carefully.* These serve as clues to what the assignment will cover. If you know anything about the subject, your memory will be triggered by the title and headings. If you know nothing about the contents of the assignment, carefully noting the chapter title and headings will help you focus on the subject of the chapter so that your mind will not wander. If something in the title or headings is unclear, make up a question about it that you can use as a guide when you are ready to read. In fact, the more questions you have about what you are going to study-read the better, since reading for the answers will keep your mind from wandering.

3. *look for any study aids the chapter may have.* See if there are any questions at the beginning or end of the chapter. Look them over before reading closely. Reading for answers will focus your attention on the subject matter. If there is a summary, read it to see what will be covered. Look for pictures and other visual aids. Read the captions under them. These types of aids help prepare you for better reading comprehension.

The next drill provides you with some practice in surveying a chapter from a textbook.

Drill   A-1: LOOK BEFORE YOU LEAP

Directions: The following reading selection is part of a chapter from a textbook entitled *Effective Study* by Francis Robinson. Professor Robinson devised a study strategy known as the SQ3R method. Since then many others have adapted his technique, but basically they all borrowed from him. In this drill, do not try to read the selection. You'll get to do that in the next drill. For now, just survey it: (a) check the length to judge how long it will take you to read; (b) read the title and subheadings carefully to see what you will be reading about in detail; (c) look for any study aids the chapter may provide. Remember, don't read the chapter selection, just survey it. Normally, a survey of material this length should take about two minutes or less and is well worth it in the long run. But for now, don't worry about how much time it takes. Just apply the survey steps correctly so that you will see their benefits.

C. Development of SQ3R Method

Many books have been written on special skills useful in reading books. Some have emphasized increased speed of reading; others, techniques for getting the most stimulation from an author's ideas. Students, however, want a skill that will be particularly effective when reading school textbooks.

A new technique must be devised, since the methods of good students are too often inefficient and no one of the experiments previously discussed has found the perfect method. The findings of these experiments, however, did contribute a scientific foundation from which a higher-level study skill could be devised. They showed that a quick survey of headings and summaries before starting to read gave an orientation that speeded up reading and aided retention. They showed that asking a question before starting each section also helped reading. They showed that the very rapid forgetting that is so typical after reading can be markedly slowed by the simple expedient of forcing oneself to recite from memory after reading. Other experiments showed when the best timing of this self-recitation would be during the study period. Various studies emphasized the importance of understanding the larger meanings in the selection and of seeing their pattern of relationship. Outlining, relating the material to one's interests, and a brief review at the end of a reading session were shown to help with this understanding. Still other experiments showed the value of distribution of effort in studying.

The creation of a study skill that uses these findings, that satisfies the demands of school study, and that pleases the student with its efficiency is a challenge to the reading specialist. The student wants any suggested method to help him (1) select what he is expected to know, (2) comprehend these ideas rapidly, (3) fix them in memory, and later (4) review efficiently for examinations. The method must be more efficient and less time consuming than rereading lessons; and it should not be difficult to learn.

For years this writer has had students try out various methods that such experiments have suggested; such trials have led to further refinements and suggestions. One method has finally been devised that fits the criteria above. Further research may show other possible refinements, but it is felt that this now represents a higher-level skill of great effectiveness for schoolwork. The material that follows is devoted to a description of this study technique and to exercises directed toward developing such skill.

STEPS IN THE SQ3R METHOD

The title for this new higher-level study skill is abbreviated to make it easier to remember and to make reference to it more simple. The abbreviation SQ3R stands for the steps that the student follows in using the method. A description of each of these steps is given below.

Survey 1. Glance over the headings in the chapter to see the few big points that will be developed. Also read the final summary paragraph if the chapter has one. This survey should not take more than a minute and will show the three to six core ideas around which the discussion will cluster. This orientation will help you organize the ideas as you read them later.

Question   2.   Now begin to work. Turn the first heading into a question. This will arouse your curiosity and thereby increase comprehension. It will bring to mind information already known, thus helping you to understand that section more quickly. The question also will make important points stand out at the same time that explanatory detail is recognized as such. Turning a heading into a question can be done at the instant of reading the heading, but it demands a conscious effort on your part.

Read   3.   Read to answer that question, *i.e.,* to the end of the first headed section. This is not a passive plodding along each line, but an active search for the answer.

Recite   4.   Having read the first section, look away from the book and try briefly to recite the answer to your question. Use your own words and cite an example. If you can do this you know what is in the book; if you cannot, glance over the section again. An excellent way to do this reciting from memory is to jot down brief cue phrases in outline form on a sheet of paper.

Now repeat steps 2, 3, and 4 with each successive headed section: that is, turn the next heading into a question, read to answer that question, and recite the answer by jotting down cue phrases in your outline. Read in this way until the entire lesson is completed.

Review   5.   When the lesson has been read through in this way, look over your notes to get a bird's-eye view of the points and their relationship and check your memory as to the content by reciting the major subpoints under each heading. This checking of memory can be done by covering up the notes and trying to recall the main points. Then expose each major point and try to recall the subpoints listed under it.

These five steps of the SQ3R method—survey, question, read, recite, and review—when polished into a smooth and efficient method should result in faster reading, picking out the important points, and fixing them in memory. The student will find one other worthwhile outcome: Quiz questions will seem familiar because the headings turned into questions are usually the points emphasized in quizzes. By predicting actual quiz questions and looking up the answers beforehand the student feels that he is effectively studying what is considered important in a course.

EFFECTIVENESS OF THE SQ3R METHOD

Evidence of the success of this method has been obtained from several studies. In one experiment several sections of a how-to-study class measured their reading ability (reading rate and comprehension accuracy) on a test that dealt with the history of Canada; they were then given practice in the use of the SQ3R method for several days, after which they took another comparable reading test. Before training, the average rate of reading for the sections was at the 34th percentile and after training it was at the 56th percentile; before training the average accuracy of comprehension was at the 43rd percentile; after training it was at the 53rd percentile. In another experiment an attempt was made to measure the effectiveness of this method for examination preparation. Two quizzes of equal difficulty were prepared; for the first quiz the students were permitted to study in their own way, but for the second quiz they were shown how to predict questions. The average number of errors on the first quiz was 15, but on the second quiz the average was only 6. One of the most convincing arguments for the method has been the comments of students who have tried the method and found that it works. Students have walked into class and said, "I predicted 15 of the 20 questions he asked" or "Boy, oh boy, I've been getting Ds in chemistry but I got a B yesterday" or "It looked as if he had picked the quiz questions from my list."

FURTHER DETAILS OF THE METHOD

A description that is an over-all picture of the method has been given. Experience in teaching its use, however, shows that certain typical errors may occur, usually because old study methods interfere (427). An indication of certain critical points, so the student can be particularly careful concerning them, is helpful in learning a skill. These cautions are arranged according to the steps in the method:

1. Survey.   A survey of headings in a lesson should take only a minute. Some students are so in the habit of reading on once they start that, until they have learned how, they need to make a conscious effort to look just at the headings and then to estimate what the lesson is about. It is worthwhile to practice this skill. Take some reading material on topics with which you are familiar, *e.g.*, newspapers, digest magazines, previously read textbooks, and so on. Glance at the headings in an article or a chapter and then make guesses as to what the material will actually say. Check to see how well you have done.

2 and 3. Reading to answer questions.   Changing a heading into a question should be a conscious effort to orient yourself actively toward the material to be read. You definitely should have in mind what you want to learn as you read each section and not read it passively line by line. Habits accumulated from reading fiction often make textbook reading difficult, for it has been found that most people read fiction in order to forget their troubles and not to remember what is in the book. Such an attitude of comprehending for the moment, when carried over into textbook reading, gives rise to a delusion that since the ideas are comprehended as they are read, they will, of course, be remembered and unconsciously organized as answers to questions. This is far from the truth. Reading a textbook is work; you must know what you are looking for, look for it, and then organize your thinking concerning the topic you have been reading about.

The SQ3R method of studying   33

4. Reciting.   The tendency in reading is to keep going, but you should stop at the end of each headed section to see if you can answer the question asked at the start of the section. As indicated before, this procedure tends to act as a check on whether you have comprehended the material, and the recitation fixes the ideas in your memory. Furthermore, this insistence on answering the question makes it easier to force yourself to read with an active, inquiring attitude.

Self-recitation may consist of mentally reviewing the answer or of writing it out. The latter is more effective, since it forces the reader actually to verbalize the answer, whereas a mental review often may fool a reader into believing that a vague feeling of comprehension represents mastery. Furthermore, the more sensory channels are used in learning, the more effective they are; for example, in writing notes one receives visual and kinesthetic (muscle) cues as well as verbal imagery in thinking about the material.

It is very important that this note-taking require little time and energy; the notes should be exceedingly brief. It is at this stage, in fact, that many students have much difficulty with the SQ3R method. Some think they should use old habits of lengthy note-taking, in which all details are copied from the book, usually as complete sentences. This technique so disrupts the progress of reading that the train of thought is lost. Other students, when they see something important, are in the habit of stopping to copy it into their notes—with one finger marking each phrase as they look back and forth between book and notes. It truthfully can be said that many students copy a sentence into their notes without ever having read it for meaning.

The student will have to practice taking the type of "working notes," as they are called, recommended here. First, no notes should be written until the whole headed section is completely read. Second, the notes should be jotted down from memory and not from the book. And third, the notes should be taken in the student's own words and should be brief, *i.e.*, little more than a word or phrase. Just as a public speaker's notes usually consist of a list of topics as reminders of what to talk about, so the student's notes should include only cue words and phrases to demonstrate to his own satisfaction that he knows what points are included. The student, knowing a topic, can then easily supply an explanation of it. Such brief wording also keeps the notes in compact form so that they can be easily visualized later in review.

The following sample of working notes based on the preceding section shows how indentation makes points stand out and how brief wording makes visualization of the subpoints easier. The brief wording will not convey full meaning to a stranger—he should read the article—but to the student who made the notes, the cue phrases are sufficient reminders about what is in the article.

Notes on Previous Sections

A. Discovering new study methods
   1. To select what is important

34   *Higher-level work skills*

a. Quick preview helps rate
b. Previous questions help
  1. When?
    (a) Before whole lesson
    (b) Before each section
  2. Headings give questions
c. Outlining
  1. Little value first trial
  2. Work notes help if trained

2. To retard forgetting
  a. Not a wearing away
  b. Helped by
    1. Interest and intent to remember
    2. Selecting major points
    3. Recitation
      (a) Remember 80 vs. 20% after 2 weeks
      (b) Immediate recitation better
      (c) Best: brief note from memory after a section
    4. Distributed study

It is difficult to maintain an attitude of active attack on any type of work over a long period of time. In industry it has been found more efficient to alternate periods of working at different activities; the change of activity is less boring and one can start each new period with zest. In studying, an alternation of reading and note-taking makes it easier for the student to keep studying his lessons and to maintain an attitude of active searching for ideas. It is easier to keep reading until a headed section is finished than it is to complete the whole lesson. Therefore, breaks in attention are apt to come at logical places in the reading material and so do not disrupt the student's thinking too much. This alternation of tasks, in fact, helps make concentration much easier in studying lessons.

5. Review. Review immediately after reading should be brief; probably not more than five minutes will be needed. This is certainly much faster than rereading the lesson. The total outline should be looked over to get an over-all, easily visualized picture, but the review should not be limited to this. As indicated earlier, self-recitation should be used to make sure that the material is fixed better in your memory. A good way to do this is to cover the notes, recite on the main points, and then check to see if you are correct. Then, cover up the notes again, recite on the subpoints under the first main point, and again check for accuracy. This system should be repeated with each major point. This method will help you to see the organization that exists between the various ideas, will help to indicate what is not yet mastered, and will help to fix known ideas more clearly in mind so they are forgotten more slowly.

Later reviews are also worthwhile because of the forgetting that takes place. The factors influencing the efficiency of these delayed reviews will be discussed in the next chapter.

The SQ3R method of studying   35

Now answer the following questions without looking back to see how well you surveyed the chapter.

1. Based on the length of the reading selection, how long will it take you to read it? _____

2. What is the title of the chapter? _____

_____

3. How many steps are there in the SQ3R method? _____

4. Name the three main headings of the selection. Your wording does not have to be exactly the same. _____

_____

_____

_____

5. Are there any study aids in the chapter? _____

6. What do you think the chapter will cover? _____

_____

_____

7. What questions do you have that you can focus on when you study-read the chapter? _____

_____

_____

_____

8. What do you now know about the chapter that you did not know before surveying it? _____

_____

_____

_____

Drill A-2: A STUDY STRATEGY: THE SQ3R METHOD

Directions: This drill has a twofold purpose. The first is to read the selection you just surveyed in Drill A-1 on page 107. The second is to teach you the SQ3R study method by having you read it just as you would an assignment you know you will be tested on later. Return now to Drill A-1 and read "Development of SQ3R Method." When finished, return to the following questions and try to answer them without looking back.

Comprehension Questions

1. List the steps in the SQ3R method: _____

   _____

   _____

   _____

   _____

   _____

2. How can you be certain of the effectiveness of the SQ3R method? _____

   _____

3. Making a preview of the headings in the chapter should take less than a

   _____ .

4. Which is correct? (a) notes are written in your own words from memory; or (b) notes are written by jotting down important phrases and sentences from the

   chapter. _____

5. At what point in your reading should you take notes? _____

   _____

6. Why should you stop reading and recite at the end of each heading?

   _____

   _____

7. When should you review a chapter you have finished reading? _____

   _____

Drill A-3: APPLYING SQ3R TO A PSYCHOLOGY TEXTBOOK CHAPTER

Directions: The following is a portion of a chapter from *Introduction to Psychology: Exploration and Application*, 3rd edition, by Dennis Coon. The point of this drill is to apply the SQ3R technique to the selection to make certain you understand how to apply what you just read. If you need to, review the information on SQ3R in Drill A-2. Then apply all five steps to the passage.

Altered States of Consciousness

Just about everyone distinguishes ordinary waking consciousness from at least a few altered states, such as dreaming, dreamless sleep, and daydreaming. Depending on personal experience and cultural training, a person may add drunkenness, drug "highs," meditation, and the like, to his or her personal list of states of consciousness.

Question: There must be many altered states of consciousness; how are they distinguished from normal consciousness?

An **altered state of consciousness** (ASC) represents a distinct change in the *quality* and *pattern* of mental functioning. ASCs typically differ from normal waking consciousness with regard to: sense impressions, body image, intensity of emotion, memory (gaps, loss, or enhancement), time sense, feeling of personal identity, patterns of thought, feelings of self-control, suggestibility, and the meaning attached to events (Tart, 1975). Definitions aside, most people have little difficulty recognizing that they have experienced an ASC.

Question: Aside from drugs, what causes ASCs?

The list of causes is practically endless. In addition to drugs, sleep, dreaming, and meditation, we could add: sensory overload (for example, a light show, Mardi Gras crowd, or disco), monotonous stimulation ("highway hypnotism" on long drives is a good example), religious and mystical experiences (revivals and religious conversions), unusual physical conditions (high fever, hyperventilation, dehydration, sleep deprivation), long-distance running, music, and too many other possibilities to mention.

To get right to the questions raised by the "Chapter Preview," let's begin with psychic phenomena, including ESP, which is the most controversial of the altered states.

Psychic Phenomena— Beyond Normal Awareness?

Parapsychology is the study of *psychic* phenomena (also known as **psi** phenomena). Psi events are those that lie outside normal experience and seem to defy accepted scientific laws. Modern parapsychologists are seeking answers to the questions raised by psi phenomena. Four major areas of investigation are:

1. Clairvoyance. The ability to perceive events or gain information in ways that appear unaffected by distance or normal physical barriers.
2. Telepathy. Extrasensory perception of another person's thoughts, or more simply, an ability to read someone else's mind.
3. Precognition. The ability to perceive or accurately predict future events. Precognition may take the form of *prophetic dreams* that foretell the future.
4. Psychokinesis. The ability to exert influence over inanimate objects by will power ("mind over matter"). If you are able to influence which face of a flipped coin comes up or move an object without touching it, then you have demonstrated psychokinesis.

Question: Do psychologists believe in ESP?

American psychologists as a group remain skeptical about ESP and other psi abilities, a skepticism not fully shared by the general public. A recent Gallup poll found that about half of those interviewed believe in ESP. If you are in the half that doubts ESP, then you should know that there have been some carefully run experiments supporting its existence. If you are among those who believe in ESP, then you should know why the scientific community doubts its existence!

Coincidence Anyone who has ever had a clairvoyant or telepathic experience will find it hard to question the existence of ESP. But the difficulty of excluding *coincidence* makes natural ESP occurrences less conclusive than they might seem. For example, consider this typical psychic experience: During the middle of the night, a woman away for a weekend visit suddenly had a strong impulse to return home. When she arrived she found the house on fire with her husband asleep inside (Rhine, 1953). An experience like this is striking, but it does not *prove* the existence of ESP. If, by coincidence, a "hunch" turns out to be correct, it may be *reinterpreted* as a premonition or case of clairvoyance (Marks and Kammann, 1979). If it is not confirmed, it will simply be forgotten.*

The formal study of psi events owes much to the late J. B. Rhine. Rhine established the first parapsychological laboratory at Duke University and spent the rest of his life

*A related error in logic (no offense, dolphin-lovers) is the conclusion that dolphins try to save drowning humans. We can never be sure about this because it is not too likely that we will ever hear from drowning swimmers who get carried out to sea by "helpful" dolphins.

130   Foundations of Human Consciousness

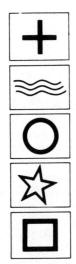

Fig. 6-1   *ESP cards used by J. B. Rhine, an early experimenter in parapsychology.*

trying to document ESP. To avoid problems of coincidence and after-the-fact interpretation of "natural" ESP events, Rhine tried to study ESP more objectively. Many of his early experiments made use of the **Zener cards** (see Fig. 6-1). In a typical clairvoyance test, subjects tried to guess the symbols on the cards as they were turned up from a shuffled deck. Pure guessing in this test will produce an average score of 5 "hits" out of 25 cards. A person who consistently scores above this chance level is credited with ESP. Telepathy is tested when one person (the "sender") concentrates on a card and another person (the "receiver") tries to "read the mind" of the sender.

Unfortunately, some of Rhine's most dramatic early experiments used badly printed Zener cards on which a faint outline of the symbol showed through the back. In other experiments, there is evidence that the experimenter knew which card was correct, and unconsciously gave subjects cues with his eyes, facial gestures, or lip movements.

Modern parapsychologists are now well aware of the need for double-blind experiments, maximum security and accuracy in record-keeping, meticulous experimental control, and repeatability of experiments (Rhine, 1974a). In the last 10 years, hundreds of experiments have been reported in parapsychological journals. Many appear to support the existence of psi abilities. Parapsychologist John Palmer recently analyzed over 700 such reports and found that spontaneous guessing, a good emotional adjustment, a positive attitude toward ESP, and altered states of consciousness all improved ESP scores (Hyman, 1979).

Question: Then why do most psychologists remain skeptical about psi abilities?

Statistics and Chance   Most criticisms of psychic research focus on the inconsistency of psi abilities. For every study with positive results, there are others that fail (Hansel, 1980). It is rare for a subject to maintain psi ability over any sustained period of time (Schmeidler, 1977). ESP researchers consider this fact an indication that parapsychological skills are very fragile and unpredictable (Rhine, 1977). But critics argue that subjects who only temporarily score above chance have just received credit for a **run of luck.** When the run is over, it is not fair to assume that ESP is temporarily gone. We must count *all* attempts.

Question: What if a researcher does count all attempts, and finds that the results could occur by chance only one time in a million?

Just such results are reported in many parapsychology experiments. They are, however, still open to the run-of-luck criticism. Suppose an experimenter tests 100 students for psi abilities and finds one who scores well above chance on 200 trials of card-guessing. Even if the experimenter includes all "trial runs," "days when the subject couldn't concentrate," and the scores of the other 99 subjects, a true estimate of the odds against the "psychic" subject's score have not been figured. Why? Because the experimenter can never include all the thousands of trials run in hundreds of other experiments, trials that were *never reported* because no psi effect was found.

Research Methods   Unfortunately, the most spectacular findings in parapsychology are those least often repeated (Gardner, 1977; Hyman, 1977). More importantly, improvements in research methods usually result in fewer positive results. But believers in ESP, such as ex-astronaut Edgar Mitchell, believe other factors explain negative results in ESP tests: "The scientist has to recognize that his own mental processes may influence the phenomenon he's observing. If he's really a total skeptic, the scientist may well turn off the psychic subject" (*Newsweek,* March 4, 1974).

Skeptics and serious researchers in ESP both agree on one point. If psychic phenomena do occur, they cannot be controlled well enough to be used by entertainers. Stage ESP (like stage magic) is based upon a combination of sleight of hand, deception, and patented gadgets. A case in point is Uri Geller, a former nightclub magician who "astounded" audiences from coast to coast with apparent feats of telepathy, psychokinesis, and precognition. Geller's performance in tests at Stanford Research Institute is de-

131   Altered States of Consciousness

scribed in the preview of this chapter. Not mentioned is what University of Oregon Professor Ray Hyman calls an "incredible sloppiness" in performance of these tests. As one example, it has since been shown that needles and laboratory scales placed in jars can be deflected by static electricity transferred to the jar by the "psychic's" hands (Balanovski and Taylor, 1978). Geller's reproductions of sealed drawings, it turns out, were done in a room next to the one where the drawings were made. Original reports of Geller's alleged "ability" failed to mention that there was a hole in the wall between the two rooms. Also unreported in the "die in the box" tests was the fact that Geller was allowed to hold the box and shake it. He is even reported to have been the one to open the box (Wilhelm, 1976; Randi, 1980).

It is important to recognize that criticism of psi research runs deeper than unmasking frauds such as Geller. A first-hand look at psi experiments often reveals serious problems (Marks and Kammann, 1979). For example, para-psychologists Russell Targ and Harold Puthoff (1977) reported a seemingly sensational experiment in "remote viewing." In the experiment, a psychic remained in the lab, while a "sender" went to remote locations. At each location, the sender gave his or her impressions of the spot, which were tape-recorded. At the same time, the psychic taped the impressions he was receiving from the sender. Later, judges tried to match transcripts from the sender and the psychic. Targ and Puthoff claim that an independent judge matched the descriptions at far above chance level. However, critics later discovered that the list of targets was arranged in the order of the visits, and that the judge knew it. Also, the sender's descriptions contained all sorts of clues to targets already visited and the number of tests already performed (Randi, 1980). Thus, *any* judge could easily match targets with the psychic's descriptions from the clues they contained. In fact, when these clues were removed from the transcripts, other judges were unable to successfully match them (Marks and Kammann, 1979).

A good summary of the overall status of parapsychological research is provided by the remarks of Wayne Sage (1972): "Forty years of experiments in the telepathic, clairvoyant, and precognitive capacities of the human mind have left us no more certain, or uncertain, that such abilities even exist." Perhaps exciting discoveries in this realm of consciousness still await us. But, for now, it would seem that the best attitude toward ESP is to maintain an open mind while being carefully skeptical of evidence reported in the popular press or by researchers who are "true believers."

Learning Check

Before reading on, answer the following questions about what you just read.

1. List four major types of psychic phenomena under investigation by parapsychologists.

   _____   _____

   _____   _____

2. Dreaming and dreamless sleep are considered ASCs. T or F?

3. The _____ cards were used as an early test of ESP.

   a. Rhine   *b.* Zener   *c.* Geller   *d.* psi

4. Critics attribute positive results in psi experiments to statistical runs of luck. T or F?

Answers: 1. clairvoyance, telepathy, precognition, psychokinesis   2. T   3. b   4. T

Now answer the following questions without looking back.

1. What is the title of the chapter? _____

   _____

2. To what does ASC refer? _____

   _____

3. List four major types of psychic phenomena under investigation by para-

   psychologists: (a) _____

   (b) _____ (c) _____

   (d) _____

4. What are Zener Cards? _____

   _____

5. Do psychologists as a group believe in ESP? _____

   Why? _____

   _____

6. Why are psychologists concerned with the research methods used to support

   or refute psi? _____

   _____

7. The best attitude toward parapsychology at this time is _____

   _____

8. What study aids are provided in the chapter? _____
   _____
   _____

If you have any problems answering these questions, discuss them with your instructor. Make certain you fully understand the SQ3R method before going on to the next drill.

Drill A-4: MODIFYING THE SQ3R METHOD—A BIOLOGY TEXTBOOK PASSAGE

Directions: Some textbook passages do not have many study aids such as headings, subheadings, learning checks, and the like. For such books you may need to modify the SQ3R method to fit the text. The following passage is from *Invitation to Biology*, 3rd edition, by Helena Curtis and N. Sue Barnes. There are no headings to survey or turn into questions. When such passages occur in your study-reading, form your questions by skimming the paragraphs, looking for italicized or boldface typed words or phrases, or the topic sentence of the paragraphs.

Remember these steps as you work on the following passage:

1. *Survey* the selection, noticing the title and skimming each paragraph to get a general overview of the contents. Don't worry about what you don't understand.

2. Form *questions* based on what you skimmed. For instance, the title is "Cro-Magnon Man." A question might be "What is a Cro-Magnon man?" In the first paragraph the term *Upper Pleistocene man* is used. Another question might be, "What is Upper Pleistocene man?" In other words, make questions based on what you need to clarify in order to understand the passage.

3. When you have finished surveying and forming questions, you are ready to *read.* Since there are no headings, you will have to decide how much you should read before stopping to recite. You may need to stop after each paragraph or two. It depends on your needs.

4. *Reciting,* remember, can serve as an oral quiz. Cover up the passage and answer your questions or written notes. The main thing is to make certain you understand what you are reading as you go along.

5. *Review* the passage when you have finished, making sure you have answered all your questions or any new ones that came up as you were reading.

Use what you learned in previous chapters about vocabulary in context and finding main ideas and supporting details.

Cro-Magnon Man

About 30,000 to 40,000 years ago, specimens of Neanderthal man disappear abruptly from the fossil record and are replaced by what is known as Cro-Magnon man, or sometimes as Upper Pleistocene man, who is physically indistinguishable from modern *Homo sapiens.* We do not know what became of the Neanderthals. Perhaps they were exterminated in warfare, although there is no evidence of this. Perhaps they were simply unable to compete for

From Helena Curtis and N. Sue Barnes, *Invitation to Biology,* Third Edition, Worth Publishers, 1981, pp. 629–630.

food and living space with the better-equipped Cro-Magnon type. Perhaps they interbred, although there are no clear traces of intermediate forms. Some have suggested that Cro-Magnon men brought with them some disease to which they themselves were resistant and the Neanderthals were not. In any case, soon after the appearance of Cro-Magnon man, there were no other hominids in Europe, and within the course of 10,000 to 20,000 years, this new variety of primate had spread over the face of the planet.

Cro-Magnon man, when he first appeared in Europe, came bearing a new, quite different, and far better tool kit (Figure 42–18). The stone tools were essentially flakes—which, of course, had been in use for more than 2½ million years—but they were struck from a carefully prepared core with the aid of a punch (a tool made to make another tool). These flakes, usually referred to as blades, were smaller, flatter, and narrower, and, most important, they could be and were shaped in a large variety of ways. From the beginning they included various scraping and piercing tools, flat-backed knives, awls, chisels, and a number of different engraving tools. Using these tools to work other materials, especially bone and ivory, Cro-Magnon man made a variety of projectile points, barbed points for spears and harpoons, fishing hooks, and needles. Thus, although Cro-Magnon man lived much the same sort of existence as that of his forebears, he apparently lived it with more possessions, more comfort, and more style.

Perhaps our closest emotional links to this most immediate ancestor are the cave paintings of western Spain and southern France (Figure 42–19). The examples that remain to us, many surprisingly untouched by time, clearly form a part of a rich artistic tradition that endured for at least 10,000 years. The cave drawings are almost entirely of animals, nearly all game animals, and they are deep within the caves, so they must have been viewed (as they must have been painted) by the light of crude lamps or torches.

The meaning of these drawings and paintings has long been a matter of debate. Some of the animals are marked with darts or wounds (although very few appear to be seriously injured or dying). Such markings have led to the suggestion that the figures are examples of sympathetic magic, in which there is the notion that one can do harm to one's enemy by sticking needles in his image. The fact that many of the animals appear to be pregnant suggests that they may symbolize fertility. Many appear also to be in motion. Perhaps these animals, so vital to the hunters' welfare, were migratory in these areas, and they may have seemed to vanish at certain times in the year, mysteriously returning, heavy with young, in the springtime. This return of the animals might have been an event to be solicited or celebrated in much the same spirit as the rites of spring of more recent peoples or Easter are celebrated.

Cave art came to an end perhaps 8,000 or 10,000 years ago. Not only were the tools and pigments laid aside, but the sacred places—for such they seem to have been—were no longer visited. New forces were at work to mold the course of human existence, and the end of this first great era in human art is our clearest line of demarcation between the old life of the hunter and the new life that was to come.

Now answer these questions without looking back.

1. Write in the questions you formed after your survey: _____

    _____

    _____

    _____

2. What is the main idea of the passage? _____

    _____

3. What is an Upper Pleistocene man? _____

    _____

4. When did Cro-Magnon man appear? _____

    _____

5. What happened to the Neanderthals? _____

    _____

6. How did Cro-Magnon man's "tool kit" differ from that of his ancestors? ___

    _____

    _____

7. What are our closest "emotional links" to the Cro-Magnon? _____

    _____

8. What are some meanings of the cave drawings and paintings? _____

    _____

    _____

    _____

9. Cave art came to an end perhaps _____ years ago.
10. Discuss why you were or were not able to answer most of the questions

    above. _____

    _____

    _____

    _____

    _____

B. Marking and Underlining Textbooks

In Part A you learned that reciting is one of the three Rs in the SQ3R study method. While oral recitation was described, it was recommended that you take some form of notes during the Read-Recite cycle. It is strongly suggested that you use one of the methods described here and in the next section.

Basically, there are two ways to take notes as you read: (1) you can mark in your book, using the margins for your own remarks and underlining and circling important words and phrases; or (2) you can take notes from the text in a notebook. Section C will cover taking notes in a notebook. This section deals with marking and underlining correctly.

Take a look at the following passage and how it is marked:

It is now believed that the earth's outer layer of rock, called the lithosphere, is divided into large, rigid plates that fit together like pieces of a huge jigsaw puzzle. There are twelve major plates (and numerous subplates), each about sixty miles thick and some almost as wide as the Pacific Ocean. They float on a layer of dense, viscous rock called the asthenosphere, which, in turn, surrounds the earth's hot core.

How helpful are all those markings going to be when you review for a test a month later? What do they mean? The act of underlining is not in itself a helpful comprehension or recall device.

Notice the same passage marked in a more sensible way:

lithosphere, outer layer

asthenosphere, inner layer

It is now believed that the earth's outer layer of rock, called the lithosphere, is divided into large, rigid plates that fit together like pieces of a huge jigsaw puzzle. There are twelve major plates (and numerous subplates), each about sixty miles thick and almost as wide as the Pacific Ocean. They float on a layer of dense, viscous rock called the asthenosphere, which in turn, surrounds the earth's hot core.

Here only the key points are highlighted. The student used what was learned about finding main ideas and supporting details. Thought went into what was to be marked for later review as well as what would be helpful for understanding the passage during the Read-Recite portion of SQ3R.

While there is no particular way to mark or underline, good notetakers seem to follow two basic principles: (1) mark only the main points and (2) be consistent in the way you mark. Here are some suggestions for marking and underlining:

1. Use pen, not pencil. Pencil marks will fade and smear in time.
2. Underline main ideas and circle important words or phrases. Studies show that when students were allowed to underline only one sentence in a paragraph, they took more time and underlined only important sentences, which produced better comprehension and recall.
3. Underline minor yet important, points with broken lines. Later, during a review, such markings will make it easy for you to distinguish between main and minor ideas, but relevant ones nonetheless.
4. Use numbers in the margins to indicate a series of points or items being discussed.
5. Use the margins to write in what you feel is important, questions you have for the instructor, or notes to yourself.
6. Draw rectangles around names or places that might be used in a test or quiz.

Remember that these are just suggestions. You may want to use your own type of marking. That's fine, as long as it is consistent and meaningful to you as you are marking and helps you later during reviews.

Marking and underlining are not as efficient as notetaking *unless* you take the time to study what to underline and later review what you underlined. Underlining and marking are faster than notetaking, but it doesn't do you any good to underline if you don't actually study-read as you do it.

Drill   B-1: MARKING AND UNDERLINING

Directions: Apply the SQ3R study strategy to the following textbook passage, marking and underlining as described above when you get to the Read-Recite portion.

Nicotine   Nicotine is a natural stimulant found mainly in tobacco. Next to caffeine, it is the most widely used psychoactive drug (Julien, 1978).

Question: How does nicotine compare to other stimulants?

Nicotine is a potent drug. In large doses it causes stomach pain, vomiting and diarrhea, cold sweats, dizziness, confusion, and tremors. In very large doses, nicotine may cause convulsions, respiratory failure, and death (Levitt, 1977). For a nonsmoker, 50–75 milligrams of nicotine could be lethal (smoking about 17 to 25 cigarettes will produce this dosage). Most beginning smokers get sick on one or two cigarettes. In contrast, a heavy smoker may consume 40 cigarettes a day without feeling ill. This difference indicates that regular smokers build a tolerance for nicotine (Levitt, 1977).

Question: Is it true that nicotine can be addicting?

There is growing evidence that for some smokers nicotine is addicting. For many, withdrawal from nicotine causes headache, sweating, cramps, insomnia, digestive upset, irritability, and a sharp craving for cigarettes (Shiffman, 1980).

Question: How serious are the health risks of smoking?

A burning cigarette releases more than 6800 different chemicals. Many of these are potent **carcinogens** (cancer-causing substances). In addition, nicotine itself may be cancer-causing (Bock, 1980). Lung cancer and other cancers caused by smoking are now considered the single most preventable cause of death in the United States. Among men, 97 percent of lung cancers are due to smok-ing. For women, 74 percent of all lung cancers are due to smoking, a rate that has risen sharply in recent years. Altogether, smoking is responsible for about 30 percent of all cancer deaths in the United States (Reif, 1981). If you think smoking is harmless, or the link between smoking and cancer is unproven, you're kidding yourself. As one expert says, "The scientific link between tobacco smoking and cancer is now as firmly established as any link between cause and effect in a human disease is likely to be" (Reif, 1981). As if this weren't enough, smoking is also linked to heart disease, emphysema, and birth defects (Schwartz *et al.,* 1980). An estimated 340,000 Americans die yearly of smoking-related diseases.

Smokers, unless they have a death wish, must be getting something out of smoking. Most claim that smoking helps them concentrate, makes them feel sociable, or that it calms them. However, psychologist Stanley Schachter asserts, "The heavy smoker gets nothing out of smoking. He smokes only to prevent withdrawal" (Schachter, 1978). Undoubtedly, people smoke for many reasons. But Schachter has shown that smoking does not improve the mood or the performance of heavy smokers in comparison to non-smokers. On the other hand, heavy smokers who are *deprived* of nicotine feel worse and perform worse than non-smokers. Schachter has also shown that heavy smokers adjust their smoking to keep bodily levels of nicotine constant. Thus, when smokers are given lighter cigarettes, they smoke more. Also, if they are under stress (which speeds the removal of nicotine from the body), they smoke more (Schachter, 1978). The connection between stress and nicotine probably explains why students smoke more during stressful periods, such as final exams, or at parties, which are also quite stressful.

In the spaces provided, explain what you did for each step of the SQ3R:

1. *Survey:*

2. *Question:*

3. *Read:*

4. *Recite:*

5. *Review:*

Drill B-2: MORE MARKING AND UNDERLINING

Directions: Follow the same directions as for Drill B-1 in the reading selection
following on the next page.

Westward March of Empire

The deeply rooted racial prejudice of the Anglo-white Americans against the Red Indians, virtually a national psychosis, is one of the strangest and most terrifying phenomena in all history. It has no parallel throughout the Western Hemisphere. The hot-blooded Spanish and Portuguese freebooters had achieved the conquests of Mexico, Central America, and South America in the name of the crown and the cross. Yet for all their cruelties they had no racial prejudice. From the start they intermarried lawfully with subjected Indians, creating a new race, the *mestizo*. In Canada and the United States the French also mixed blood with the Indians, and the Germans everywhere allied themselves as colonists with the native peoples.

The Anglo-Protestants were the direct antithesis of these other Euro-Americans. Cold-blooded, deeply inhibited, and bound by their Puritan traditions, they began a program of complete extermination of all Indians almost from the day they landed on Plymouth Rock.

The precedent was set by a Pequot massacre shortly after the *Mayflower* arrived. Of this Cotton Mather wrote proudly, "The woods were almost cleared of those pernicious creatures, to make room for a better growth." A century and a half later Benjamin Franklin echoed this opinion when he wrote of "the design of Providence to extirpate those savages in order to make room for the cultivators of the earth." Still later, in Lincoln's boyhood, the "natural and kindly fraternization of the Frenchmen with the Indians was a cause of wonder to the Americans. This friendly intercourse between them, and their occasional intermarriages, seemed little short of monstrous to the ferocious exclusiveness of the Anglo-Saxon."* This horror of miscegenation and the self-righteous slaughtering of Indians were the banners under which the new conquerors marched westward through the Alleghenies, across the Great Plains, and over the Rockies.

As early as 1641, New Netherlands began offering bounties for Indian scalps. The practice was adopted in 1704 by Connecticut, and then by Massachusetts, where the Reverend Solomon Stoddard of Northampton urged settlers to hunt Indians with dogs as they did bears. Virginia and Pennsylvania followed suit, the latter in 1764 offering rewards for scalps of Indian bucks, squaws, and boys under ten years of age.

In 1814 a fifty-dollar reward for Indian scalps was proclaimed by the Territory of Indiana. In Colorado, legislation was offered placing bounties for the "destruction of Indians and skunks." By 1876, in Deadwood, Dakota Territory, the price of scalps had jumped to two hundred dollars. In Oregon a bounty was placed on Indians and coyotes. Indians were trailed with hounds, their springs poisoned. Women were clubbed to death, and children had their brains knocked out against trees to save the expense of lead and powder.

Massacres of entire tribes and villages, such as that of Sand Creek, Colorado, in 1864, were not uncommon. Here a village of Cheyennes and

*Cary McWilliams. *Brothers under the Skin.* 1943.

Arapahoes were asleep in their lodges when the Reverend J. M. Chivington, a minister of the Methodist Church and a presiding elder in Denver, rode up with a troop of volunteers. "Kill and scalp all Indians, big and little," he ordered, "since nits make lice." Without warning, every Indian was killed—75 men, 225 old people, women, and children. Scalps were then taken to Denver and exhibited on the stage of a theater.

Wholesale removal of whole tribes from reservations granted them by solemn treaties was in order whenever their land was found to be valuable. The Cherokee Nation was the largest of the Iroquois tribes; its people had invented an alphabet and had written a constitution, establishing a legislature, a judiciary, and executive branch. In 1794, in accordance with a treaty made with the United States, the Cherokees were confined to seven million acres of mountain country in Georgia, North Carolina, and Tennessee. In 1828 gold was discovered on their land. The Georgia legislature passed an act confiscating all Cherokee lands, declaring all laws of the Cherokee Nation to be null and void, and forbidding Indians to testify in court against whites. The confiscated lands were distributed by lottery to whites.

The case of the Cherokee Nation came up before the Supreme Court. The Chief Justice rendered his decision, upholding the Cherokees' rights to their land. Retorted President Jackson, "John Marshall has rendered his decision; now let him enforce it."

What was enforced was a fictional treaty whereby the Cherokees agreed to give up their remaining seven million acres for $4,500,000 to be deposited to their credit in the United States treasury. General Winfield Scott with seven thousand troops then enforced their removal west of the Mississippi.

Of the fourteen to seventeen thousand Cherokees who started on the "Trail of Tears," some four thousand died on the way. The financial costs of their removal were promptly charged against the funds credited to them. And when it was over, President Van Buren in December 1838 proudly informed Congress, "The measures by Congress at its last session have had the happiest effects. . . . The Cherokees have emigrated without any apparent reluctance."

The legality of this procedure was upheld again on the seven-million-acre Sioux Reservation in the Black Hills of Dakota. To this land the Sioux Nation had been granted "absolute and undisturbed" possession by a solemn United States treaty ratified by the Senate in 1868. But when in 1874 gold was found in the region, General Custer was sent with United States troops to protect white prospectors. After the massacre of his troops the full force of the Army was summoned to eject the Sioux and throw the reservation open to whites. The United States Court of Claims subsequently upheld the legality of the procedure.

Commissioner of Indian Affairs Francis C. Walker gave voice to public sentiment when in 1871 he stated that he would prefer to see the Indians exterminated rather than an amalgamation of the two races, asserting, "When dealing with savage men, as with savage beasts, no question of national honor can arise. Whether to fight, to run away, or to employ a ruse, is solely a question of expediency."

So mile by mile westward, and year by year through the "Century of Dishonor," the United States pursued on all levels its policy of virtual extermination of Indians, accompanied by a folk saying that served as a national motto: "The only good Indian is a dead Indian." A racial prejudice that became an *idée fixe*, a national psychosis sanctioning the wanton killing of

Indians, is still the theme of America's only truly indigenous morality play—the cowboy-Indian movie thriller.

This, then, was a great motif of the westward expansion of an Anglo-white nation whose existence and growth was predicated upon the primary sanctity of property rights. In the shadow cast by the death of a race, the tragedy of a continent, we can discern the justified fears of the peaceful, religious Hopis that the approaching Americans were not their long-lost brothers the white Pahánas.

Now answer the following questions in the spaces provided. Try not to look back at the reading selection.

1. Briefly describe the difference in attitude the Spanish, Portuguese, and French had toward the Indian with that of the Anglo-Protestants.

2. Discuss the various types of bounties placed on Indians as described in this passage.

3. What was the Sand Creek massacre?

4. Discuss the case of the Cherokee Nation.

5. What was the "Trail of Tears"?

6. What is meant by the "Century of Dishonor"?

If you had problems answering any of these questions, reread the sections of the passage that provide the answers. Make certain you are applying the SQ3R method properly and that your markings and underlining techniques are benefiting you. You may need to consult with your instructor. If you did well, go on to the next section.

C. Taking Reading Notes

Some students don't want to mark or underline their textbooks because they want to sell them when the class is over. This is understandable considering the cost of textbooks these days. Still, marking and underlining, if done correctly, are preferable to taking notes for the reasons described in the previous section. But there are times when you use books that are not yours, so a method for taking notes is needed.

The main thing to remember about taking reading notes is not to copy word for word from the book. Rephrase what the author says in your own words as much as possible. Many students make the mistake of copying right from the book, thinking that they are doing a good job of studying. Such action usually produces no results. The purpose of taking notes is to make certain that you understand what you are reading at the time and to record it for later review.

As with marking and underlining, there is no one way. But here are some guidelines for you to follow:

1. At the top of the notebook page, always write down the title of the book, the chapter title, and the pages your notes cover. There may be a time in the future when your notes aren't as helpful as you thought and you need to refer back to the book. This information will help you find the material in the book quickly.
2. Write the main ideas of the passage as your own heading, then list the supporting details under this heading. In effect, you are summarizing main ideas and supporting details just as you did in Chapter 2 with paragraphs and essays.
3. Don't write anything down until you have studied a short passage and understood it. Let the writing patterns discussed in the last chapter help you sort out the key points. If an author is defining a term or concept, make certain your notes contain the definition. If the author is comparing or contrasting two items, make certain your notes reflect the comparison, contrast, and so on.
4. Remember, don't use the same words as the author unless they are necessary. If you do use the author's own words, make certain you know their meanings.
5. Keep track of words you need to look up. If the vocabulary is difficult, you may need to look up words in the glossary or in a dictionary before you can take notes.
6. Write down questions that you can't answer or that give you trouble so that you can ask your instructor about them at the next class meeting.

Feel free to modify these suggestions. Just make certain that you are not going through the motions of taking notes without really understanding what you are writing down.

Drill   C-1: TAKING NOTES FROM A POLITICAL SCIENCE TEXT

Directions: Read the following short passage from a political science textbook.
In the space following the reading selection write your notes.

Chapter 7

The Conservative and Labor Programs

Against the background of economic depression, British domestic politics during the twenty years' truce displayed a fairly clear class basis. The Conservatives, still often called Tories, tended to get the support of aristocrats and of middle-class people who wanted to attack new problems with traditional methods and with a minimum of government intervention. The Labor party tended to get the support of trade unionists and of intellectuals from all classes who demanded that the government intervene more vigorously in the economic field. We must not oversimplify, however; not every reformer necessarily voted Labor nor every stand-patter Tory. Yet economic issues did sharpen the difference between the two major British parties.

Both Conservatives and Labor realized the underlying difficulties of Britain's position. Both were fully aware that twentieth-century Britain had to sell enough goods and services abroad—enough manufactured goods and shipping, insurance, banking, and tourist services—so that the income from them would buy food for her people and much of the raw materials for her factories. But the parties were not agreed on how to achieve this necessary task. Broadly speaking, the Conservatives wanted to retain private industry, with government and other technical experts helping to make it efficient. But they were thwarted by high tariffs in the United States and elsewhere, by the drive to economic self-sufficiency all over the world, and by the difficulties of trade with communist Russia.

From Brinton, Christopher, and Wolff, *A History of Civilization*, Vol. 2, 1715 to Present, 2nd ed., 1960, p. 506.
Reprinted by permission of Prentice-Hall, Inc., Englewood Cliffs, N.J.

Compare your notes with these. Wording will vary, but yours should be somewhat similar.

Do your notes contain book and chapter titles? Page reference?

Brinton, Christopher, and Wolff, A History of Civilization
"Chapter 7: The Conservative and Labor Programs," p. 506

Did you notice that the author was using comparison/contrast to make the key point?

Compares and contrasts Conservatives and Labor Party:
Conservatives (Tories) = aristocrats
*   vs.   middle class*
Labor Party = union and intellectuals of all
*   classes—wanted governmental*
*   help*

Do your notes reflect the major differences of the two parties?

Biggest difference = economic issues
—Both parties wanted to sell abroad to buy
* food and raw goods*
—Differed on how to
—Conservatives wanted private industry
—Labor wanted govern. controls

Did you write down unfamiliar words to look up? Questions for the instructor?

Look up: thwarted
Is it this way today?

Drill   C-2: TAKING READING NOTES FROM A SOCIAL SCIENCE TEXT

Directions: Read the following passage from a social science textbook and take notes in the space on the following page.

The Nature of Democratic Government: Democracy—like liberty, equality, and justice—is hard to define precisely. The term has come to mean so many different things and has won such great popularity that even the communists have tried to take it over; communist-controlled eastern Germany, for example, is called the German Democratic Republic. The word itself is made up of two Greek roots—*demos,* the people, and *kratia,* authority—and was used by the Greeks to mean government by the many, as contrasted with government by the few (oligarchy), or by one (autocracy). The word came into English usage in the seventeenth century and was originally used to denote only *direct* democracy, the kind of government that existed in Athens and other Greek city-states, where all enfranchised citizens came together to discuss and pass laws.

The term democratic government, like the term democracy, can be ambiguous and confusing. Some writers distinguish between *democratic* and *republican* governments, the former meaning governments in which decisions are made *directly* by a majority of the people—as in a New England town meeting—and the latter meaning governments in which the people's wishes are filtered through a series of *representative bodies,* such as Congress. But in this book we shall use the term democratic government to mean a representative democracy and shall use democratic and republican governments interchangeably to mean any government in which those who do the actual governing acquire their power to do so by means of a *fair, free,* and *competitive contest for the people's votes.* Or to paraphrase a definition by James Madison, a government in which the persons making and carrying out public policies are chosen directly or indirectly by the voters at free and periodic elections.

From James MacGregor Burns and Jack Walter Peltason, *Government by the People: The Dynamics of American National, State, and Local Government,* 5th ed., 1963, p. 19. Reprinted by permission of Prentice-Hall, Inc., Englewood Cliffs, N.J.

Write your notes in the space below.

Drill   C-3: MAPPING—ANOTHER TYPE OF NOTETAKING

Directions: Mapping, a technique developed by an educator named M. Buckley Hanf, is a way to get your notes for an entire chapter on one or two notebook pages. The technique forces you to see a chapter as a whole rather than in pieces and helps you store what you read in your long-term memory. As with any study device, it is only as good as you make it.

Mapping works well with the SQ3R. This drill will show you how to map a chapter as well as have you do some of it. Since you now know how to use SQ3R, learning how and why to map a chapter should make sense and prove to be another alternative for good studying.

Part A

First, survey the following passage adapted from a communications textbook. As you carefully read the title and headings and look for study aids, count the number of major headings that divide the chapter. When you are finished with your survey, go to Part B, which follows the textbook passage.

1
Assertiveness: What and Why

What kind of people want to gain confidence in communication? Here are the stories of some typical students enrolled in assertiveness training classes. See if you recognize yourself in any of their experiences:

—Pat was a bright student, but his grades suffered because he couldn't bring himself to ask questions or volunteer ideas in class. "I'm always afraid I'll sound stupid," he confessed. "Later it turns out that everybody else was wondering about the same thing. I wish I had the nerve to speak up."

—Beth often felt uncomfortable saying "no," and because of this found herself accepting many social invitations that sounded (and usually were) boring. These dull events left her less time to spend with her friends and family, who did matter to her.

—Leslie found it difficult to carry on a conversation with anyone but her closest friends and family. She said, "At parties I run out of things to say after a few minutes and then spend the rest of the time making small talk and feeling like an idiot. It's gotten to the point that I don't go out much anymore so I won't have to feel uncomfortable."

3

4 Background on Assertion

—Frank was a happily married father of three. He deeply loved his wife and children, yet found it impossible to tell them just how much he cared. "They probably know anyhow," he said, "but sometimes I want to tell them how much they mean to me, and I can't get out the words."

—Jerry was married to Susan, a gregarious woman who dominated every conversation with her stories and jokes. Whenever Jerry would join in, Sue would interrupt to correct him or change the subject. This left Jerry feeling like a spectator, angry at being cut off. He wanted to share his feelings with Sue but didn't know how to do so without making her defensive and starting another round of criticism.

ASSUMPTIONS OF THIS BOOK

These accounts represent literally hundreds of stories that students have shared with my colleagues and me in an effort to improve the quality of their communication. Over the past few decades social scientists have developed a number of methods designed to help people handle themselves in situations like these. This group of techniques goes by several names: Social skills training, social effectiveness training, personal effectiveness training, expressive training, and the term used in this book, assertiveness training.

Assertiveness training is based on the idea that verbal and nonverbal self-expression are *skills*, similar in many ways to other skills, such as playing a musical instrument, participating in a sport, or writing a clear sentence. Like these other skills, the ability to communicate can be learned. This is good news, for it means that effective self-expression is not a trait possessed by only a few fortunate people; rather, it is a set of behaviors that can be learned by any person who is willing to invest sufficient time and effort. Helping you to define and then to master these behaviors is the major goal of this book. As you read it and carry out the exercises, you'll not only learn a great deal of information about effective communication—you should actually start to *behave* in new, more satisfying ways.

The path to assertive communication is based on three assumptions, each of which is supported by extensive research. Because these assumptions are basic to everything that follows, it is important to state them here.

1. You Can Change This statement may sound obvious, but many people fail to accept it, and thus commit themselves to a lifetime of unsatisfying relationships. The tendency to explain unassertiveness by saying "That's the way I am" is common, as the case of Margaret illustrates. Margaret was an intelligent, attractive woman whose life was made miserable by a domineering great-aunt who had filled the role of a mother since Margaret's parents were killed in an automobile crash when she was a child. The aunt was a critical woman who found fault with most everything her niece did,

5 Assertiveness: What and Why

in spite of the fact that Margaret had almost single-handedly raised three well adjusted sons since a divorce several years earlier. The aunt's complaints ranged from small to large: The boys' hair was too long. The house always (in her estimation) needed cleaning. Margaret was not a decent provider. She owed it to her sons to remarry in order to give them a father. And so it went almost endlessly, according to Margaret's account. When asked why she put up with such constant negativity Margaret replied that asserting herself was out of the question. The aunt was such a strong woman that there was no chance of standing up to her. Besides, the aunt had always helped out financially during hard times, and it would be ungrateful to bite the hand that sometimes fed her family. And finally, the aunt had known and raised her for years, so perhaps her criticisms were right. A course in assertiveness training convinced Margaret that what looked like a lifetime sentence of deference and quiet resentment was not the only alternative open to her. After instruction and practice in the principles that follow, Margaret reported an astonishing change in her relationship with the aunt. Where she had meekly accepted and even agreed with her aunt's remarks, she now expressed her own reasons for living as she did. And as she grew more confident in the validity of these reasons and more skillful in expressing them, the aunt's complaints fell off sharply. "I suppose I could have stood up for myself all along," Margaret confessed, "but I always figured that she was she and I was I and that's the way it always would be."

The lesson in Margaret's story is that change *is* possible, even in situations that seem hopeless. Each of the accounts that opened this chapter had successful endings, and the chances are good that most communication difficulties of this type can also be resolved.

2. Change Can Be Relatively Quick and Permanent As the previous account illustrates, it's not necessary to spend the entire second half of one's life unlearning the unassertive behaviors developed during the first half. People often assume that any worthwhile change takes an extended time—perhaps measurable in years. While this may sometimes be the case, when it comes to improving communication and other social skills it is not necessarily so. You will find that many of the principles of assertive communication are surprisingly simple to learn and to put into action. Most readers will begin to notice changes in their behavior by the time they have finished Chapter 3.

On the other hand, the fact that you can expect to *begin* changing quickly does not mean that this or any book can guarantee instant attainment of your goals. As you will read over and over again, the principle of change stressed in this book is that of gradual but steady progress. As you define each goal, the methods outlined will show you how to begin adding that way of behaving to your life. The advantage to this steady progress is that the changes which result usually last. Unlike New Years' resolutions,

6 Background on Assertion

which are rarely permanent, the assertive behaviors you develop here will
become genuine parts of your personality, so that after an initial period of
concentration and practice, they will occur naturally and effortlessly.

3. Change Comes from Doing As its name implies, assertiveness *training*
is an active process. While you might learn a great deal intellectually just
from reading this book, such an approach is unlikely to help change the
way you act toward others. In order actually to bring about a difference in
the way you communicate, it will be necessary for you to actively practice
the concepts introduced here. To help you with this practice, there are a
number of exercises scattered through the following pages. It is absolutely
essential that you carry out each exercise as you come to it. In doing so you
will begin to put into practice the concepts that will improve your assertive
skills. While the exercises may sometimes seem artificial, they will help
bridge the gap between your present unfamiliarity with assertive behavior
and the moment when you will actually use these skills in the everyday
world. Just as a pianist must run through scales before performing in concert, it will be necessary for you to practice the assertive exercises. Remember: *No exercises, no change.*

Part B

Now answer these questions.

1. What is the title of the chapter? _____

_____

2. How many headings does the chapter contain? _____

List them: _____

_____

_____

_____

3. What do you think the chapter will cover? _____

_____

_____

Here is how you use your survey information to begin a map of the chapter.
Using a regular 8½ × 11 page in your notebook, plot out a general outline of the
total chapter by placing the title in the middle of the page. Then draw some type of
design around it based on the number of divisions in the chapter. In this case there

are four major headings, so a rectangle is used. Each corner of the rectangle then has a line or a branch drawn from it with the title of a heading written on it as you see in the following drawing.

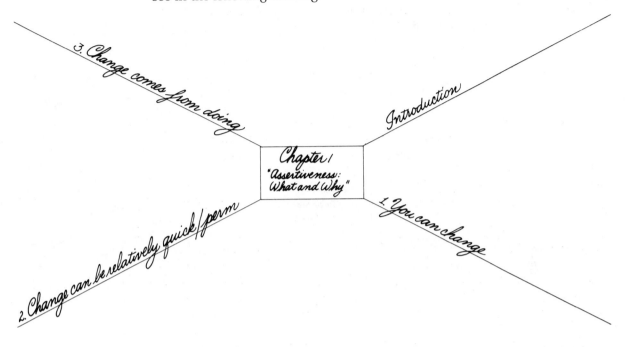

Part C

Once you have an overview of the chapter, you are ready to turn each heading into a question, the second step in SQ3R. You then read from one heading to the next, looking for the answer(s) to your question(s). Return to the textbook passage again, this time study-reading from the first heading to the second. When you get to the second heading, return here and answer the questions below.

1. Record your question and the answer you found. _____

   Question: _____

   Answer: _____

   _____

2. What is the main idea of the passage under the first heading? _____

   _____

3. What are some other important points you want in your notes from this

   section? _____

   _____

   _____

Now look at the following figure and notice the information that has been written in on the branches of the map for the first heading. Compare the answers to your questions above with the notes written on the branch. Your wording may be different, but the main points should be expressed similarly. Notice that the titles of the headings are written on the top of the drawn lines. This is so you will have room to write your notes *under* the headings. Notice that all writing is done so the map can be read without twisting the page around. Design your maps the same way.

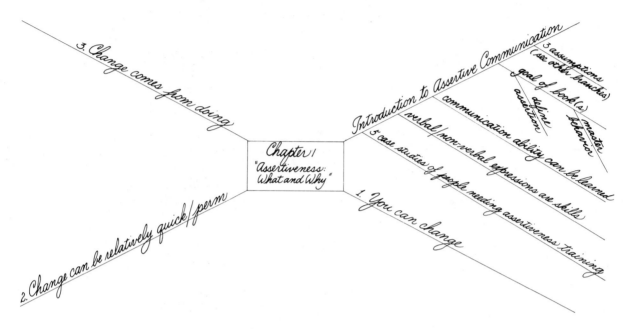

Part D

From this point on, you are on your own. Complete the SQ3R cycle, reading from the second heading to the next, stopping to complete that portion of the unfinished map above. Then go on to the next section, repeating these steps until you have completed the map of the chapter. Save your map, as you will need it in the next section of this chapter.

Drill C-4: MORE MAPPING PRACTICE

Directions: There are four parts to this drill. Do them in order.

Part A

First, take just a minute or two and survey the following passage from a logic textbook. As you carefully read the title and headings, count the number of major headings that divide the chapter. When you are finished with your survey, go to Part B, which follows the textbook passage.

RECOGNIZING ERRORS IN REASONING

Vincent Ryan Ruggiero

The ten reasoning errors we will discuss in this chapter are not the only ones you will find in dialogues, but they are the most common ones. By becoming familiar with them you will be able to identify where most arguments go wrong and determine how to set them right again.

EITHER-OR THINKING

The error in either-or thinking consists of viewing a particular reality solely in terms of opposing extremes when, in fact, other views are possible. It is often accompanied by the demand that people choose between the two extremes and the clear, if often unstated, suggestion that no third choice is possible. Here is an example of either-or thinking.

> GERTRUDE: The real aim of religion is perfecting one's self. Nothing else but that matters.

> HEATHCLIFF: That's not true. The real aim is loving one's neighbor. If your focus is in yourself, you simply aren't a religious person.

Now it may be that one or the other of these aims is the "real" aim of religion. But it may also be that religion has two or three or eighteen important aims. To discount that possibility even before considering it is unreasonable. Whenever you encounter either-or thinking, ask, "Why must it be one or the other? Why not both (or neither)?"

STEREOTYPING

Stereotyping is ignoring someone's or something's individuality and focusing instead on some preconceived notion about the person or thing. (It is one of the central features of prejudice.) There are stereotyped notions about Jews and blacks and atheists and political parties—in short, about many things. Here is an example:

> GERTRUDE: Are you going to that public lecture tonight, the one about the effects of exercise on stress? The local tennis coach is delivering it.

> HEATHCLIFF: I wouldn't waste my time listening to some dumb jock's simple-minded muttering.

Is the coach an authority on the subject he is lecturing on? Has he done research? Has he written articles or books? These are reasonable matters to inquire about. But Heathcliff's negative stereotyping smothers his curiosity and makes fair judgment impossible. Whenever you encounter such prefabricated assessments of an entire class of people or things, ask, "What evidence is offered that the assessment fits the individual in question?"

ATTACKING THE PERSON

Another error consists of disposing of an argument by attacking the person who advances it. It is not a reasonable approach because an argument's validity does not

From *Enter the Dialogue* by Vincent Ryan Ruggiero © 1985 by Wadsworth, Inc. Reprinted by permission of the publisher.

depend on the character of its advocates. A scoundrel may, on occasion, support a valid argument, and a saint an invalid one. Here is an example of attacking the person.

> GERTRUDE: Arthur Dean is organizing a group to protest the tearing down of the Hastings Mansion. He believes its historic value is too great to let it be sacrificed for a shopping center. I'm going to join.

> HEATHCLIFF: You're crazy to join. Dean is a real lowlife. He runs around with other girls behind his fiancé's back and uses his roommate's things without permission. Besides, he sponges off everyone.

Everything Heathcliff says about Dean may be accurate. And yet it sheds no light on whether the protest Dean is organizing is worthy of support. Whenever you find an attack on a person in a dialogue, ask, "Are the charges being made against the person relevant to the issue under discussion?" If they are not, refuse to consider them in your analysis.

CONTRADICTION

Contradiction occurs when a person makes two assertions that are logically inconsistent with each other. It is an error that occurs more often in long dialogues than in short ones and is more difficult to detect than other errors because the conflicting assertions seldom appear together. To detect contradiction you must remember each dialoguer's early assertions and recognize their relationship to later assertions. Here is an example of a contradiction dialogue:

> GERTRUDE: Morally, our nation is in big trouble. Let me give you an example. For centuries, the taking of a life was regarded as wrong. That's as it should be. No one is ever justified in taking a human life. Yet today books and articles are written defending so-called mercy killing and giving directions on how to commit suicide.

> [Later in the dialogue, after several exchanges with Heathcliff, Gertrude speaks again.]

> GERTRUDE: I still say we've grown too casual about human life. The only situation in which the taking of a life is ever justified is self-defense.

First Gertrude says the taking of a human life is never justified. Then she says there is a situation where it is justified. That is a contradiction. Whenever you encounter a contradiction in a person's argument, ask, "Does the contradiction invalidate the person's entire argument or only a part of it? And if a part, which part?" A note of caution is in order here. Careful inspection of what at first glance appear to be contradictions will often reveal they are not contradictions at all. If, for example, Gertrude had said, "No one should ever be applauded for taking a human life," instead of "No one is ever justified in taking a human life," she could not fairly be charged with contradicting herself, at least until you knew what she meant by "applauded."

FAULTY ANALOGY

Analogy is a line of reasoning suggesting that things alike in one respect are also alike in other respects. Analogy is a very common kind of reasoning and there is nothing wrong with it as long as the similarities that are claimed are real. An analogy is faulty when they are not real.

Here is an example of faulty analogy:

> GERTRUDE: I hear the government is requiring that stronger warnings be placed on cigarette packages and in advertisements.

HEATHCLIFF: Putting warnings on cigarette packages is as foolish as putting "Warning! Eating too much of this product may make you a fat slob!" on packages of spaghetti or "Warning! Careless use of this instrument may smash your fingers" on hammers.

Heathcliff's analogies are vivid, but faulty. Eating spaghetti is good for people, if done in moderation; it provides nutrition. Smoking cigarettes does no comparable good. Similarly, the hammer can do harm if used carelessly. But cigarettes have been shown to do harm no matter how carefully they are used. Whenever you encounter any analogy, say, "Granted, these two things may be similar in certain respects, but are there any respects in which they are dissimilar?"

FAULTY CAUSATION

Faulty causation may take either of two forms. The first is concluding that one thing caused another merely because of their proximity in time or space. For example, shortly after a black cat crosses someone's path, an accident befalls her, so she concludes that the cat's crossing her path caused her misfortune. This error occurs not only in everyday reasoning, but in formal reasoning as well. For many years the prevailing medical opinion was that damp night air causes malaria simply because the onset of the disease occurred after exposure to night air. (The real cause, mosquitoes, which happened to be more active in evening hours, was discovered much later.)

The other form taken by faulty causation is concluding that learning why people are interested in an issue is the same as evaluating their thinking about the issue. "Find the motivation," goes this reasoning, "and you have determined whether that argument is valid." This line of reasoning, which resembles attacking the person, is erroneous for a similar reason. A person's motivation for advancing an argument is never sufficient reason for approving or rejecting an argument. Noble motives may underlie bad arguments and ignoble motives good ones. Here is an example of this form of faulty causation:

GERTRUDE: Professor McCready told my class today he believes the way student evaluations are used on this campus doesn't provide effective evaluations of the quality of teaching. He said the questions themselves are OK, but the evaluation should be made at the end of the semester instead of during the tenth week. He blasted the administration, saying they are more concerned with suiting their schedules than getting meaningful input from students. He made a lot of sense.

HEATHCLIFF: Sometimes you're really naive, Gertie. Didn't you even wonder why he attacked the testing procedure? If you had done so, you'd know. It must be he got scorched by students on the evaluation last semester. If he'd received a good rating, he'd be praising the evaluation process. So much for his "sensible argument."

Perhaps Heathcliff is correct in what he says about the professor. Perhaps he did get a poor evaluation last semester. And perhaps that's what prompted him to take a critical look at the evaluation procedure. So what? That would be a normal reaction, yet it has no bearing on the validity of his argument about student evaluation of teachers. That argument can be appraised only by examining the evidence that supports or challenges it.

Whenever you encounter an assertion that one thing has caused another, ask, "Is the proximity in time or space evidence of a true cause/effect relationship or merely a coincidence?" Whenever you find an argument being approved or rejected because of a person's motivation, remember that motivation is irrelevant and test the argument against the evidence.

IRRATIONAL APPEAL

There are four common kinds of irrational appeal: appeals to emotion, to tradition or faith, to moderation, and to authority. Each of these is a misuse of a rational appeal and may be identified as follows:

An *appeal to emotion* is rational when it accompanies thought and analysis, and irrational when it substitutes for them.

An *appeal to tradition or faith* is rational when the particular practice or belief is regarded in light of the present circumstances, and irrational when it means "Let's continue to do (believe) as we have done merely because we have always done so."

An *appeal to moderation* is rational when the moderate approach is offered as the best solution to the problem or issue, and irrational when moderation is merely a convenient way to avoid offending someone or to evade the responsibility of judging.

An *appeal to authority* is rational when it acknowledges the fallibility of people and their institutions and the possibility of differing interpretations, and irrational when it disallows reasonable questions and challenges. (As used here, *authority* means not only eminent people, but also eminent books and documents, such as the *Bible* and the U.S. Constitution, and eminent agencies, such as the Supreme Court.)

Here are some examples of irrational appeals:

GERTRUDE: I can't understand how any sensitive person can be opposed to the control of handguns.

HEATHCLIFF: To begin with, Americans have always been free to bear arms. It's a part of our heritage to do so if we wish. But if you need more proof than that, consider the Constitution. It specifically refers to the freedom to bear arms as a right of every citizen.

GERTRUDE: But the framers of the Constitution couldn't have envisioned the problems of modern society when they were writing. Therefore their meaning . . .

HEATHCLIFF: It's the responsibility of loyal Americans to defend the Constitution, not to question it.

Both of Heathcliff's arguments are irrational. The first, that Americans should be free to bear arms because they have been free to do so in the past, is an irrational appeal to tradition. The second, that it is an act of disloyalty to question the Constitution, is an irrational appeal to authority.

HASTY CONCLUSION

A hasty conclusion is one that is drawn without appropriate evidence. In other words, it is a conclusion chosen without sufficient reason from two or more possible conclusions. Hasty conclusions are especially tempting in situations where prior opinions compromise objectivity. These opinions make a person wish for a particular conclusion to be so, and wishing leads to uncritical acceptance. Here is an example of a hasty conclusion:

GERTRUDE: How did you make out with that part-time job you were applying for?

HEATHCLIFF: I didn't get it, and I know very well why too. It's because I'm not black or Hispanic and I'm not a woman.

GERTRUDE: How do you know that was the reason?

HEATHCLIFF: Come on, Gertie. You know perfectly well that minorities have an advantage in today's job market.

Even if Heathcliff were right about minorities' having an advantage in the job market (and considerable evidence challenges that view), his conclusion about his failure to get the job is hasty. The fact that something is generally true is not sufficient evidence that it is true in a particular case. It is possible that Heathcliff was passed over because of lack of experience or a bad attitude or some other reason. Whenever you encounter any conclusion, ask whether the evidence is sufficient to warrant choosing it over other possible conclusions.

OVERGENERALIZATION

A generalization is a judgment about a class of people or things made after observation of a number of members of that class. Overgeneralization is generalization based upon insufficient observation. One of the most common errors in argument, overgeneralization may be explained by the natural human tendency to classify sensory data tidily, and by the difficulty of determining what, in any given situation, constitutes "sufficient evidence." Accordingly, people are often found making careless assertions about whole groups of people and things. Here are some examples:

GERTRUDE: Ever since I arrived on campus last month, I've been appalled by the manners of the students here. They're unbelievably boorish.

HEATHCLIFF: Yes, and the townspeople are so unfriendly, too. I don't know why I ever picked this college.

GERTRUDE: Oh, I'm not sorry I came here. The professors are very helpful and encouraging. They go out of their way to explain things.

We don't know how many students are enrolled in the college, what the population of the town is, or how many professors are on the college staff. But however small the college and the town are, it is unlikely that Gertrude and Heathcliff have had enough contact with people to justify their level of generalization. Whenever you encounter a statement about entire groups of people or things, look for evidence that the observations have been sufficient in number and that the person has demonstrated that what was observed is typical of the group in general. If that evidence is lacking in the dialogue, and your own experience does not provide it, you may conclude that you are dealing with an overgeneralization.

OVERSIMPLIFICATION

It is natural to want to simplify matters; simplification aids understanding and communication. For that reason, simplification is legitimate—as long as it does not distort the reality it describes. When it does that, it becomes oversimplification. The most frequent kind of oversimplification that occurs in dialogues is the presentation of only one side of a two-sided (or three- or four-sided) reality. Here is an example of such oversimplification:

GERTRUDE: I'm really looking forward to being a high school teacher some day. I only hope I can meet the demands of the profession.

HEATHCLIFF: Demands? High school teachers have it made. They're through at three o'clock every day and only work nine months of the year. The only cushier job I know of is the job of a college professor.

There is some truth in what Heathcliff says. The high school class schedule usually ends at 3:00 P.M. and the official work year, with holidays and summer vacation time considered, is nine months. But that is only part of the complex reality of high school teaching. Many teachers are responsible for five different classes each day, each of which requires preparation for lectures and discussions, and for the grading of homework. All that work must be done after 3:00 P.M. In addition, teachers are often expected to chaperone after-school activities and advise clubs and organizations. Finally, they are required to extend their knowledge of the subject matter they teach by pursuing graduate degrees in their spare time. To ignore all these duties is to over-simplify the reality of high school teaching.

There is no easy formula for detecting oversimplification. Your best approach is to be suspicious of any brief description of a complex reality. When you encounter one, ask, "Is it really this neat and simple? Is there another side to the reality that is not represented here?"

Part B

If you have finished your survey, answer the following questions:

1. What is the title of the chapter? _____

   _____

2. How many headings does the chapter have? _____
   List them (you may look back):

   _____

   _____

   _____

   _____

   _____

   _____

   _____

   _____

3. What do you think the chapter will cover? _____

   _____

   _____

Using this survey information, on a regular 8½" × 11" page in your notebook, place the title of the chapter in the middle of the page. Since there are ten headings to this chapter, you may want to draw a circle around the title. Draw a line out from the circle and write in the title of the first heading so that your map will look like this:

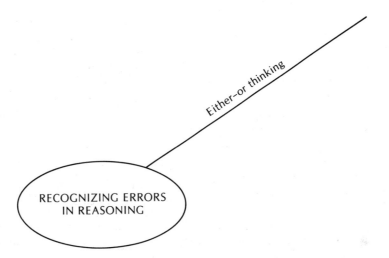

Note: Sometimes it is necessary to divide a chapter into two or more parts, depending on the length and number of headings. For instance, if you discover you need more room for notes, you might list only five headings on one map page and five on another.

Part C

You are now ready to turn each heading into a question, the second step in the SQ3R method. The first heading is "Either-or Thinking." Turn the heading into a question, such as, "What is either-or thinking?" Then read until you get to the second heading. When you come to the second heading, come back here and answer the following questions.

1. What is "either-or thinking"? _____

    _____

    _____

2. What is the main idea of the passage under the first heading? _____

    _____

    _____

    _____

3. What are some important supporting points you want in your notes from this

    section? _____

    _____

    _____

Now look at the following partial map and notice the information that has been written in on the branch for the first heading. Your wording may be different, but the main points should be the same.

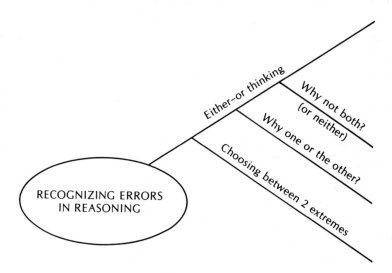

Part D

Now read from the second heading, "Stereotyping," to the third heading, then stop. Repeat the same process: draw another line or branch from the center of your map, writing in the heading on the top of the line. List under that branch what you think are the key supporting points about stereotyping. Continue this process until you have read the entire chapter. Save your map; you will need it later.

D. Test-Taking Strategies

When taking tests, it is important that you are able to read and interpret the questions correctly. It doesn't matter how well you studied if you can't show what you learned on a test.

Tests are usually classified as either *objective* or *subjective*. *Objective exams* include true-false, multiple-choice, matching and completion, or fill-in type questions. Your job on an objective exam is to choose the best answer from those provided. You may be asked to select a word or phrase that correctly completes a statement. Or, you may need to recall on your own some fact, date, or figure to fill in a blank. Objective tests can be scored with an answer key and frequently are machine scored. *Subjective exams*, on the other hand, usually require short to long written answers, usually called essay tests. Rather than a simple statement of fact, essay exams usually require that you demonstrate an understanding of the ideas learned rather than just a recall of facts and figures. Frequently, writing well is as important as knowing the answer in subjective tests.

In a recent research study, instructors were asked to list what they found to be the most common reasons students do poorly on tests. Here's what they listed in order of importance:

1. Most students don't know how to reason correctly.
2. Students cannot express themselves clearly in written responses.
3. Answers were not organized or stated logically.
4. Students misinterpret the questions, or don't read them carefully enough.
5. Students don't know the information needed.

Many students read the assignments, listen in class, take good notes, but can't put what they learned together for an exam. Here are some pointers to help you do better on tests.

PREPARING FOR EXAMS

As almost any study skills book will tell you, preparing for exams begins the first day of class. Surveying your textbooks, using the SQ3R study method, taking lecture and reading notes, mapping, attending classes, and reviewing your notes frequently are all part of preparing for an exam. Unfortunately, too many students wait until a few days before a test to get serious about it. This usually results in skipping other classes to devote time to finally studying for the test. Students then try to cram into a few hours what they think is important to memorize for the test. Cramming may get you by, but you'll soon forget whatever you memorized once the test is over—not what can be called an intelligent way to get an education. Studies show that without frequent study review sessions we forget over 80 percent of what we read in less than two weeks.

Here are a few guidelines for more efficient use of time in preparing for exams:

1. *Ask the instructor what type of exam you will be taking.* Knowing this can help you prepare better. If it will be an objective test, you will need to memorize a certain amount of material. If it's an essay test, you can practice writing some answers to the types of questions you think the instructor might ask. Find out if you can bring a dictionary or if the exam will be "open book," meaning you can use your text when writing the exam. Will the teacher provide paper or will you need to? Should the exam be done on a special form? Should you bring a "blue book" (exam booklet)? Should the exam be done in ink or pencil? Such things may seem

trivial, but they aren't. They are things you should prepare for before coming to take the test.

It's also a good idea to go see your instructor during his or her office hours. Some instructors are willing to give you copies of old tests so that you can see what you will be asked to do. But even if they aren't, your face and name will be more familiar to them if they meet you personally. This can work to your advantage when grades are being determined.

2. *Review what has been covered in some methodical manner.* If you have good maps or notes of the chapters that will be covered in the exam, review them. Skim over the assigned chapters in your textbook, making certain the headings make sense. Reread any sections that you may have forgotten. See if you can define any words in bold type or italics. Answer, either in writing or in your head, any questions that appear at the end of a chapter. If you have trouble answering any of them, reread the section of the chapter that discusses the question.

The index of your text is a good study tool. If you are going to have a test on pages 32–187, let's say, then turn to the index in the back of the book and look down the columns for any listings under those pages. If you don't remember the name or event of any items listed under those pages, then turn to the page in the book and reread that section.

If there is a glossary in the book, look for any words or phrases that you read about and make certain you can define those words. Frequently, objective tests are based on definitions given in the glossary.

Form a study group composed of students who are willing to hold one or two study sessions. Each person in the group should be assigned a particular section of the material to be covered and either present a summary of the key points and supporting details, and/or make up possible test questions to form a basis for group discussion of the test material.

3. *Study for shorter but frequent periods of time.* Research has shown that it's better to study for short periods of time rather than in long blocks. Long study periods may give you the feeling you are studying diligently, but the results will be an overload. Many study skills experts even recommend that you don't study the night before a test. If you have been preparing all along, a rested mind on the day of the exam will function better than a tired one.

SCORING WELL ON OBJECTIVE TESTS

When the day of the big event arrives, here are some things to keep in mind:

1. *Schedule your time properly.* Look over the entire exam before you begin to answer any questions. How long is it? How many parts are there? Is there a point system that reflects one section is more important than another? Some students plunge into one section of a test and spend more time on it than they should. Time runs out before there's a chance to answer other questions that may have given them more points for a higher grade.

2. *Answer the easy questions first.* By answering first the questions you know, you help refresh and stimulate your memory. When you finish the easy ones, go back and look again at the others. Chances are that by answering the ones you did know, you will be able to remember answers to the more difficult ones. Don't spend too much time on a question. You may want to leave some kind of mark by the tough ones and come back to them later if you have time.

3. *Look for clue words that will help you interpret the question.* In objective tests especially, there are clue words that can make a question absolutely false or absolutely correct. The following words frequently make a statement false:

    all   (All objective tests are easier than essay exams.)
    every   (Every objective test is difficult.)
    always (Objective tests are always difficult.)

never   (Objective tests are never easy.)
best   (Objective tests are the best kind.)
worst   (Objective tests are the worst kind.)
none   (None of the tests are easy.)

When you see these words on test questions, read them very carefully to see what they are modifying. More often than not, these words produce a false answer.

Clue words that tend to make a question frequently true are

some   (Some objective tests are easier than essay exams.)
often   (Often objective tests are easier than essay exams.
many   (Many essay exams are easier than objective ones.)
sometimes   (Sometimes essay tests are easy.)

There are clue words that can make an answer true or false depending on the point of the question. Read especially carefully questions that contain these words:

generally   (Generally speaking, essay tests are more difficult than others.)
few   (Few tests are more difficult than essay tests.)
only   (Only subjective tests should be given.)

Of course, just recognizing these clue words in a question will not automatically help you correctly answer it, but knowing how they work can give you an edge.

4. *If you don't know an answer, guess—intelligently.* Unless the test directions say that you will be penalized for wrong answers, don't be afraid to guess at an answer. Here are some clues to intelligent guessing:

a. Usually, true-false tests will contain more true answers than false ones. (That's *usually*, not always!)

b. Long statements tend to be false, because in order for a question to be true everything in it must be true. The longer the question, the more chance of a false statement. However, in multiple-choice answers, long statements tend to be the correct answer.

c. Don't change an answer unless you are absolutely sure you were wrong the first time you marked it.

d. With multiple-choice questions, "all of the above" tends to be a correct answer.

e. When answers to multiple-choice questions require a number, it's best to disregard the highest and lowest numbers and go for something in between.

f. If you are in doubt about an answer, think of your instructor. What would she or he probably want as an answer based on what has been said in class?

g. If a question uses double negatives, remove the negatives to see how the question reads. For example, take out the negatives in this statement.

It is not unadvisable to guess when you don't know an answer on a test.

The statement then reads:

It is advisable to guess when you don't know an answer on a test.

This makes the statement true.

h. When taking a matching test with two columns, read both columns before marking any answers. Make a mark by the answers you use so that you don't use them twice.

Remember, these suggestions are not always going to work in your favor. But if you have studied carefully, chances are they can help you gain a better grade.

Drill   D-1: PREPARING FOR OBJECTIVE TESTS

Directions: Apply what you have just read about preparing for and taking objective tests to the following questions.

1. A recent study showed that the most common reason for students doing poorly, according to instructors, is that they know the information needed.
    a.   True

    b.   False because _____

2. Studies show that when we don't review on a frequent basis, we tend to

    forget _____ of what we study.
    a.   60 percent
    b.   70 percent
    c.   80 percent
    d.   90 percent

3. Which of the following is recommended that you do before taking an exam?
    a.   ask the instructor what type of exam it will be
    b.   review what has been assigned in a methodical manner
    c.   study for shorter but more frequent periods of time
    d.   all of the above

4. Frequently, objective tests are based on _____
    given in the glossary.

5. It is never a good idea not to answer the easy questions first.
    a.   True

    b.   False because _____

6. List at least four clue words that frequently make a true-false question false.

    _____

7. List three clue words that frequently are used to make a true-false statement

    true. _____

8. In true-false tests, long statements tend to be true whereas the opposite is true of multiple-choice answers.
    a.   True

    b.   False because _____

9. Which of the following is not recommended as a method to review for a test?
    a.   using the textbook's index
    b.   using the textbook's glossary
    c.   forming study groups with responsibilities for each member
    d.   cramming

10. Subjective exams are best described as those which require _____

    _____.

Drill D-2: ANALYZING OBJECTIVE TEST QUESTIONS

Directions: In the spaces provided, explain what clues appear in each of the questions in Drill D-1 that would help you guess more intelligently at the answer if you didn't know it. The first one has been done for you.

1. *Read the questions carefully. If the information is known, chances are they won't do poorly.*

2. _____

3. _____

4. _____

5. _____

6. _____

7. _____

8. _____

9. _____

10. _____

SCORING WELL ON ESSAY TESTS

Preparing for an essay test is not much different from preparing for an objective test. The big difference has less to do with how much you know and more with how well you can organize and write an answer. If writing itself is not one of your strong points, the best approach you can take is to write some answers to questions you think might be on the exam.

There are at least three good sources to use in preparing for essay exam questions. As mentioned earlier, some instructors will share previous test questions. Don't be afraid to ask if any are available. Seeing what type of questions will be asked can help you anticipate probable questions the instructor might ask. Another source for possible essay questions is the text itself. Frequently, instructors base their questions on those at the beginning or end of chapters in the course textbook. Chances are that if you practice writing answers to those, you'll gain the information needed for the instructor's questions. A third source is the course syllabus. Students are often provided with handouts at the beginning of a course that list the objectives, assignments, and contain study-guide questions. These are often shoved into a notebook and never referred to again. Exam time is a good time to look again at such handouts.

Here are some guidelines for writing answers to essay questions:

1. *Read the questions carefully.* This seems obvious, but frequently students get involved in writing an answer to a question without regard for the total test. If directions aren't clear, ask the instructor to explain. Look for the following clue words that appear in essay exams and make certain your answer states what is called for:

analyze	state the main ideas and show how they are related and why they are important
comment on	discuss, criticize, or explain (ask instructor for more specifics on this one)
compare	show both similarities and differences, but your instructor may only want similarities
contrast	show differences
criticize	give your judgment or reasoned opinion, showing good and bad points
define	give a formal meaning or elaborate definition with supporting details
describe	give a detailed account or verbal picture in an organized or logical sequence
discuss	give details, discuss pros and cons
enumerate	list main ideas one by one and number them
evaluate	give your opinion, showing advantages and disadvantages
illustrate	explain by giving concrete details, examples, or analogies
interpret	use examples to explain or give meaning through personal comments or judgments
justify	give proof or reasons
list	list, usually by number, without details
outline	give a general summary using main ideas and skipping minor details
prove	use argument or logic to explain
relate	show the connection between one thing and another
review	give a summary or survey
state	provide the main points in precise terms
summarize	give a brief account of the main ideas
trace	show in chronology the progress of history

Students often ignore these clue words and end up writing answers that are only partially correct or even totally miss the answer the instructor wants.

2. *Answer the easy questions first.* Usually you don't have to answer essay questions in their order on the test as long as you identify which questions you are answering. By writing an answer to the easier questions first, you gain confidence and begin to call from memory other points you have studied.

3. *Write out a brief outline before you begin your essay answer.* Think

through what you want to say before you begin writing your answer by making some type of outline. If you are writing answers in a "blue book," it is recommended that you use the inside and back of the cover for your outlines. That way, if you run out of time, you can refer your instructor to your outline that will contain parts of the answer you didn't complete, and show that had you the time you would have covered those areas on the outline.

Making an outline may seem to take more time, but actually it is worth it to make certain your ideas are organized before you begin writing. It also helps you recall what you learned before trying to write it down in essay form.

4.   *Get right to the question.* Don't waste time getting to the question. Let's say one of your essay questions is "Discuss the role Thomas Jefferson played in the development of American higher education." Don't waste time rewriting the question. Rather, turn the question into your first sentence:

> Thomas Jefferson played an important role in the development of American higher education in three important ways. One, . . .

Then take each of the three important ways and discuss how he helped.

5.   *As you write your answers, leave room for changes you may make.* It's best to use only one side of a sheet of paper. Leave margins and skip every other line in case you need to add or make changes. If you misspell a word, don't write over it; scratch through it and write it correctly in the space above the word.

Remember that your instructor is going to be reading class sets of essay answers. A neat, clearly written essay will stand out. The easier you make it for the instructor the better impression and the better the chances for a higher grade.

6.   *Combat exam panic.* Sweaty palms, fast heartbeat, a sick feeling in the stomach, flushed face—all of these are common feelings at exam time. What can you do? Relax. Take a moment to sit up straight, close your eyes, and take some deep breaths. Let the tension out of your body. Slowly relax various parts of your body, working down from the head to the neck, to the shoulders, to your arms, upper torso, and so on down to your feet. Concentrate on your breathing; draw in a deep breath and then exhale slowly as you tell yourself you are forcing tension out of your body. Do this whenever you begin to feel tension building.

Some students have success with *imaging.* They close their eyes and see themselves taking the test and writing excellent answers to the questions. They see themselves confident and prepared. Once they see this image of themselves at work, they open their eyes and apply the confidence they saw.

Success in exams depends on accepting those anxious feelings and learning to control them. It may take several practice sessions before you master your feelings.

Drill   D-3: CLUE WORDS IN ESSAY TESTS

Directions: Define the following clue words frequently used in essay exam questions.

1.   discuss _____

_____

2.   contrast _____

_____

   3. define _____

   _____

   4. describe _____

   _____

   5. list _____

   _____

   6. evaluate _____

   _____

   7. enumerate _____

   _____

   8. compare _____

   _____

Drill D-4: PRACTICING ESSAY QUESTION ANSWERS

Directions: Answer each of the following questions.

   1. An essay question reads: "List the four major causes of the Civil War." Read the following beginning answer to this question and in the space provided evaluate how well it starts.

>   During the period prior to 1860, there were many problems confronting the North and the South. It began to look as though there were unresolved problems that could bring the country to a civil war.....

2. Discuss the difference between objective and subjective tests.

3. Summarize the main points discussed in this section on scoring well on essay exams.

E. Putting It All Together

The following practices are provided to help you put all the information in this chapter to work. First, you will be asked to review your notes and maps from previous exercises in this chapter as a way to study for the tests in this section. Then you will be asked to apply the SQ3R technique to a chapter from a history textbook using some form of marking, mapping, or notetaking. You will then be given both objective and subjective tests on the chapter.

Drill   E-1

Directions: Review page 107 on "The Development of SQ3R Method," which you read earlier. Then look over your answers to Drill A-2 on page 113. Once finished, answer the following questions without looking back.

COMPREHENSION CHECK

1. The S in the SQ3R study method stands for
   a. selectively read   c. sample
   b. search   d. none of the above

2. The Q in the SQ3R study method stands for _____.
3. The correct order for the 3R portion of the SQ3R method is
   a. recite, read, review
   b. read, recite, review
   c. review, read, recite
   d. none of the above
4. One of the reasons the SQ3R method is effective if done correctly is that it
   a. results in faster reading
   b. helps pick out important points
   c. aids memory of what is read
   d. all of the above
5. Research does not prove that the SQ3R method works if done incorrectly.
   a. True

   b. False because _____
6. The S portion of the SQ3R method should only take a minute or so.
   a. True

   b. False because _____
7. Changing a heading into a question takes a conscious effort on your part to become
   a. actively involved in the reading material
   b. passively involved in the reading material
   c. both of the above
   d. none of the above
8. You should stop after reading from heading to heading and question yourself on what you just read.
   a. True

   b. False because _____

9. The reciting part of the SQ3R study method can consist of mentally reviewing what was read or writing out notes. Which one is most recommended?

_____

10. Reviewing should be done
    a. immediately after reading
    b. at a later period
    c. neither times
    d. both a and b

Number correct: _____

VOCABULARY CHECK

Directions: Define the following underlined words or phrases as they appear in context.

1. speeded up reading and aided <u>retention</u>

_____

2. slowed by the simple <u>expedient</u> of forcing oneself to recite

_____

3. try to recall the <u>subpoints</u> listed under it

_____

4. took another <u>comparable</u> reading test

_____

5. at the 34th <u>percentile</u>

_____

6. habits <u>accumulated</u> from reading fiction

_____

7. one receives visual and <u>kinesthetic</u> cues as well

_____

8. on the <u>preceding</u> section

_____

9. <u>self-recitation</u> should be used to make certain

_____

10. this <u>alternation</u> of tasks works

_____

Number correct: _____

Record the results of the checks on the record chart on page 495.

Drill E-2

Directions: On another sheet of paper to be turned in to your instructor, write an essay answer to the following question: "Discuss the main points of the SQ3R method."

Drill E-3

Directions: Use the SQ3R method of study-reading on the following textbook chapter from a history textbook. Make a map of the chapter in the space provided on page 168. Then answer the questions that follow the reading selection.

Chapter 6

The Black Man in Early British Colonies

Chronology

Here are a few of the major events which occurred during the time span discussed in this chapter.

1300	High Point of West African Development
1400	Decline of West African Kingdoms
1440–1498	Portuguese Exploration, Start of Slave Trade
1505	Slavery in the West Indies
1619	First Africans Brought to English Colonies
1690–1713	Slavery Established in English Colonies
1713	Treaty of Utrecht Gives British South Sea Company the Right to Import 4,800 Blacks a Year for 30 Years and to Send British Trading Ships to Spanish Territory.
1739	Stono Slave Uprising in South Carolina
1775	Blacks Make Up Nearly 10 Percent of the Total Colonial Population

Your purpose in reading this chapter is to become aware of the following points in more detail:

1. Early Negroes in America came as explorers, servants, and slaves, traveling with men such as Balboa, Cortés, Pizarro, and with the French in the exploration of Canada.

2. The Africans brought to America as slaves had a rich and varied cultural background. The richness of African history is only now being widely publicized.

62

From *From Columbus to Aquarius: An Interpretive History*, Vol. 1, by George E. Frakes and W. Royce Adams. Copyright © 1976 by the Dryden Press. A Division of Holt, Rinehart and Winston, Inc. Reprinted by permission of Holt, Rinehart and Winston, Inc.

3. The European practice of African slave trade began with the Portuguese in the 1400s.

4. Among the many reasons for the early practice of slavery, the most important is probably economic gain.

5. Racial attitudes in America can be traced, in part, back to European attitudes.

6. Colonial slave practices are at the root of many of our modern racial problems.

Concentrate on the following questions as you read:

1. What role did the Black man play in early America?

2. How and why did the European slave trade develop?

3. When and why did slavery get started in America?

4. Why did the white man develop a superior attitude toward the Black man?

5. Who was Gustavas Vassa?

6. What relationship is there between the early treatment of the Negro in the New World and the racial problems of today?

Suggestion: Remember that events of the past often create problems for the present. As you read this chapter, try to determine how your own feelings and opinions have been formed or shaped by historical events.

Like the first English immigrants, the first Africans came to America in the seventeenth century. Unlike the Europeans, however, the Africans did not come here voluntarily. From the time the first Blacks were brought as slaves, their numbers increased. By 1775, nearly one-sixth of the population of the British colonies was of African background. The large number of Afro-Americans was to have a strong effect upon economic development, social attitudes, and colonial culture in general. The presence of Blacks indirectly influenced laws, religion, military defense, and education in America. The African, as well as the Indian and the European, directly and indirectly helped shape the history of the American continent.

The Negro Slave Heritage

The term Negro is thought to come from the Spanish and Portuguese word *negro* which means black. Most Africans were brought to America from a 3,000-mile area which stretched from the Senegal River in the bulge of Africa to the southern part of what is now Angola (see Figure 6-1). Many of the stories of darkest Africa—with emphasis on the barbarianism and the savagery of the African tribes—are myths created by whites who did not bother to learn or to understand the African cultures. Until very recently, most people thought Africa was similar to what they saw in Tarzan movies. In this

64   EARLY AMERICA

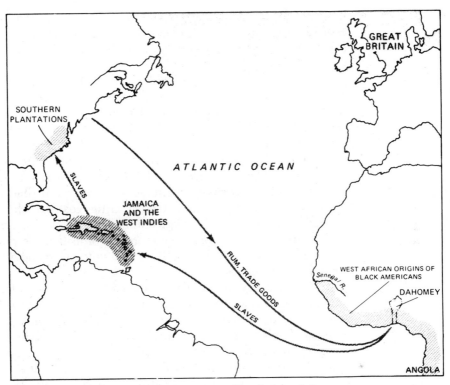

Figure 6-1 *Slave trade on the Atlantic during the colonial period*

area of Western Africa there were many types of people, with different languages and cultures. Black Africa, as it was in 1500, contained some people who were politically, agriculturally, and artistically very advanced, as well as some primitive tribes. Much of the historical richness of this area has been rediscovered in recent years by anthropologists and historians.

Dahomey, an Example of an Advanced African Culture

Before the white man arrived, the country of Dahomey (see Figure 6-1) along the west African coast had a well-developed culture. With no written language, the people of Dahomey kept an oral account of births, deaths, and marriages. Records of political and economic concerns, such as trade exchanges, political activities, slave trade, and even a military draft system of sorts were kept by memory. In spite of the lack of a written language, this country controlled surrounding areas and prospered until the white man arrived. The people of Dahomey were not naked savages running around the jungles, but a sophisticated people.

Tribe, Family, and Religion

Because there were so many African cultures, it is not easy to describe all of them or to classify them into types, but three basic patterns can be found. The tribe was the most important political and social unit. Each tribe was comprised of several families of many generations. The family group was the basic means for passing knowledge from generation to generation.

65   THE BLACK MAN IN EARLY BRITISH COLONIES

In addition, religion was of great importance to the African. Religion was usually a tribal activity, with special beliefs and practices among different tribes. Most tribes believed in a single god who, they thought, had set the world moving.

Influence of Religion

The influence of religion can be seen in African art. Statues, masks, and other artifacts made of bronze, ivory, and wood were used in ceremonies combining religion and magic. Besides the religious purpose, most art work was functional and part of daily life. The wedding of art and daily experience is shown in ceremonial dances for marriages, births, deaths, hunting expeditions, and so on. Each piece of art served a specific purpose.

Like the American Indians discussed in Chapter 1, African cultures were shaped by their environment. For example, river tribes were fishermen, while tribes on the grasslands tended cattle, goats, or sheep. Each village generally had its weavers, blacksmiths, shoemakers, or craftsmen. Many African art objects of ivory, wood, bronze, or leather are considered collector's items today. Trade among tribes was widespread and often consisted of a monetary system based on shells.

Life in Tribal Towns

Most West Africans lived in settled towns, some in large cities. Most of their food was grown in nearby fields, the men doing the heavy plowing and clearing of the fields, the women caring for the crops. As in most advanced cultures, men were not afraid of work. Once the field work was well along, men developed crafts and skills. In addition, Africans were not unfamiliar with slavery and lived with the awareness that any man might become a slave under certain conditions. In fact, some African tribes were slaveholders themselves.

The Arrival of the White Man in Africa

These tribal communities were doing well before the arrival of the Europeans. Shortly after 1400, the Portuguese, under the direction of Prince Henry the Navigator, began to explore the West African coast. The aim was to expand trade by finding a water route to India. In 1441, a ship captain, Antam Goncalvez, brought ten natives back to Portugal to prove he had sailed beyond North Africa. Within ten years, Lisbon, the capital of Portugal, became the center for trade in African products, including slaves.

The Portuguese, profiting not only from the slave trade, but from trade in gold, pepper, and ivory, wanted to keep African trade for themselves. For about one hundred years they succeeded, but by the late 1500s, Swedes, Danes, French, German, Dutch, and English were all trading with Africa.

In the sixteenth century, the Moslems from North Africa began a series of attacks on what is now Nigeria, Ghana, and surrounding regions (see Figure 6-1). One result of these attacks was the development of the African slave trade. This, combined with the growing European slave trade, helped bring about the decline of many African cultures.

The slave-trading operations of all these countries followed the Por-

66   EARLY AMERICA

Slave Trading Operations

tuguese pattern. The first task of a slave trader was to obtain a charter from his king. The trading company would then fill its ships with notions, textiles, guns, metalware, and rum. The slave-ship captain would sail to one of the trading ports or forts established on the coast of West Africa. The traders obtained slaves from the native chief in that area, who captured people of other tribes.

The Effect of Slave-Trading on African Culture

The practice of slavery had existed in Africa for centuries before the white man came. However, in pre-European Africa, the status of a slave was greatly different from his status in the New World. In Africa, a slave often was able to rise to a position of trust, honor, and sometimes authority. With the coming of the Europeans, African slavetaking increased rapidly in numbers, often destroying whole tribes. The African kings who dealt in slave trade with the Europeans were not aware of the eventual outcome of this trade. Within 350 years, Africa lost from 18 million to 24 million of its best people. The Europeans felt superior to the African, who seemed backward and less advanced to the Europeans. They classified the African as a *natural* slave and created a myth that was to be a cancer that remains even today.

Those Africans engaged in the slave trade were very shrewd. They insisted on being given gifts before they even began bargaining. The average healthy African male brought about sixty dollars in trade goods. Indeed, certain Africans profited by thousands of dollars from the sale of a single shipload of their Black brothers to white men.

The Middle Passage

The journey across the Atlantic to the West Indies, often called the *middle passage,* was one of hardship. Disease, mostly smallpox, took many lives. Food and water supplies often ran out. The crews had to constantly watch for mutinies and for slaves who would rather throw themselves overboard than lose their freedom.

Once the slave ships arrived in the West Indies, the Africans were sold to sugar planters in the English island colonies. Usually this was a conditioning period before the Africans were shipped to the mainland. While waiting to be transferred, the natives were trained in the routines of slavery. They were forced to work hard in the fields, where the food was often poor and the hours long. If the slave survived a seasoning period, he was considered ready to be sold again, usually for a profit. By 1700, the Atlantic coastal colonies were ready and willing to bring in slaves.

Gustavas Vassa: A Case Study

Olaudah Equino, who later changed his name to Gustavas Vassa, was born in Benin, in West Africa, in 1745. When he was eleven, he was captured by a neighboring African tribe and sold into slavery. A few years later he was resold to a group of European traders and put aboard a slave ship headed for America.

In his autobiography, *The Interesting Narrative of the Life of Olaudah Equino, or Gustavas Vassa, the African* (1791), he describes his voyage on the slave ship and his life as a slave. Here is a short passage from his autobiography that describes his experience:

> ... the blacks who brought me on board went off, and left me abandoned to despair. I now saw myself deprived of all chance of returning to my native country, or even the least glimpse of hope of gaining the shore, which I now considered as friendly; and I even wished for my former slavery in preference to my present situation, which was filled with horrors of every kind, still heightened by my ignorance of what I was to undergo.
> ... I was soon put down under the decks, and there I received such a salutation in my nostrils as I had never experienced in my life: so that with the loathsomeness of the stench and crying together, I became so sick and low that I was not able to eat, nor had I the least desire to taste anything.
> I now wished for the last friend, death, to relieve me; but soon, to my grief, two of the white men offered me eatables, and, on my refusing to eat, one of them held me fast by the hands, and laid me across, I think, the windlass, and tied my feet, while the other flogged me severely.
> I had never experienced anything of this kind before; and although, not being used to the water, I naturally feared that element the first time I saw it, yet nevertheless, could I have got over the nettings, I would have jumped over the side.

Gustavas Vassa's experience was typical of the horrors of the middle passage, but to white slave masters, Africans were considered only a piece of property to be sold. Later, when the ship reached the mainland, Vassa was sold to a Virginia planter, then to a British naval officer, and finally to a Philadelphia merchant. Shortly after this third sale, he was given a chance to buy his freedom, a rare opportunity for a slave.

Unlike many slaves who were confined to a plantation, Gustavas Vassa had the opportunity to travel widely as a ship's steward. This brought him in contact with many types of people. As a result of his experiences he became a forceful, self-educated man. Vassa spent the last years of his life trying to end the slave trade.

Early Negro Arrivals in America

Gustavas Vassa's experience shows how most, but not all, Black men came to colonial Anglo-America. Others before him came to the New World not as slaves, but as explorers and servants. Some historians believe there was a Black crew member on one of Columbus's ships. But even if this is not true, it is known that Balboa, discoverer of the Pacific Ocean, had as many as thirty Blacks on his expedition through Panama. Cortés had Black soldiers with him in Mexico and so did Pizarro, when he conquered Peru. A member of an early exploring group in the southern United States was Esteban, sometimes called Estevanico (Little Stephen), an Afro-American. (He was mentioned in Chapter 3.) Formerly a slave, he was captured by Indians in the sixteenth century and later escaped to the Spanish settlements in Mexico.

The reports of his discoveries helped stimulate later Spanish exploration. Esteban then became a guide and leader of later expeditions to the Southwest. The French were known to have Negroes with them when they explored Canada. In fact, one of the founders of Chicago was a Black, French-speaking pioneer, du Sable. The Blacks in early America were not all slaves.

Blacks in the British Colonies

The First Selling of Slaves

In August, 1619, the year before the *Mayflower* sailed, a Dutch ship captain reported he had sold "twenty Negars" at Jamestown, Virginia. Yet slavery, as Gustavas Vassa knew it, did not begin at this time. It was nearly forty years before colonies began the real business of slavery and almost sixty years before the British government established slavery in America. In fact, as late as 1700, most colonial farmers had no slaves. According to population reports, Negroes made up less than 5 percent of the people of such states as Virginia and South Carolina. This was to change drastically within fifty years.

During the 1600s, the southern colonies were mostly frontier colonies. Small, independent farmers, trappers and traders had no need for slaves. There were a few large-scale planters with large numbers of permanent indentured servants or slaves, but Blacks were treated more like servants than slaves.

Treatment of Early Black Man

Although Black men living in the colonies in the 1600s were more favorably treated than in later years, their situation was far from equal to that of white servants. Black women servants were not given the same legal protection that white women servants were. While white indentured servants were given freedom after working out their contract time, Blacks often were not given their freedom.

Reasons for the Treatment of the Blacks

The bias or prejudice toward the Black was an attitude brought to the New World from the Old World. Numerous causes can be suggested for this prejudice. Some authorities believe that the color black has always been unfavorable to white men. Black is often used to represent darkness, the unknown, something dirty or evil. Another reason for white prejudice is the fact that, unlike the Spaniards and the Portuguese, the first contact the English had with people of color was with Blacks who were a defeated, servant-class people. At a time in history when the English were conquering other men, they naturally tended to look down on people they defeated, especially people very different from themselves.

Economic Causes of Slavery

Perhaps the most important cause for the growing practice of making Black men slaves was economic. The English settlements, like the older Spanish colonies, were started with the hope of sending wealth back to the king and the wealthy men whose money backed the colonies. England sometimes sent white prisoners or poor persons to the colonies to serve as servants and to work cheaply, but this system did not succeed. Many of these servants would not put up with poor conditions and brought their cases to court. Others ran away to the frontier, where they could lose their servant identity.

Indentured Servants, a Form of White Slavery

69   THE BLACK MAN IN EARLY BRITISH COLONIES

Some served their time and became free men, requiring their former owners to look for help elsewhere.

Blacks were easier to keep than white indentured servants: Because of their color, they could be easily recognized and caught if they ran away, and their owners did not have to worry about freeing them after a few years of service. Since they often could not speak English and had different customs, they were falsely considered ignorant people who deserved to be slaves. A myth of white superiority developed in colonial America. The British colonial slave masters, some of whom were educated in classical subjects (Greek and Latin), used the existence of slavery during the golden days of Greece and Rome as a justification for their own use of slaves in the 1700s.

The Church, Slavery, and Discrimination

Even though few of the early British colonies had many slaves, racial and religious discrimination existed in most of the English-speaking world. One might wonder why the churches in England, the chief influence on the moral attitudes of the day, did not speak out more often against slavery and discrimination. The Church of England and other Protestant denominations, unlike the Catholic church, were not particularly missionary-oriented. That is, the Protestant churches were not always overly interested in converting "savages" to Christianity. The English Society for the Propagation of the Gospel (SPG) never had much financial backing. Since the churches could not afford to send many missionaries to the New World, they frequently confined themselves to developing churches for white settlers only.

It was not just the Black man the English discriminated against. Indians were captured by Englishmen and sold as slaves. In Ireland, the Catholic Irish were treated as brutally as the Black would be treated later. Indeed, it was fashionable for certain Englishmen to refer to the Irish as slaves even before 1607.

While the Protestant churches did not discriminate against the Blacks, they were more or less ignored, just as the American Indian and his problems were ignored. While occasional attempts were made to convert Blacks to Christianity, most slave owners were against the idea because they feared any influence that might reduce their control over their slaves. No wealthy slave owner wanted to lose his possessions.

American Slavery, an Outgrowth of British Attitudes

The tragic experience of the Black American, starting in the 1600s, is an outgrowth of discrimination already present in England prior to colonization. British attitudes toward conquered people in Ireland and toward the Spaniards reflected British feelings of superiority. These beliefs were reinforced in the 1700s. Southerners accepted and further developed these attitudes toward Blacks because the large plantation owner derived great profits from the cheap slave labor.

Slavery Legalized in British Empire

The wealth derived from slavery, plus the discriminatory attitude of some whites, were the basic reasons for the chain of events which led to slavery in the United States. The Black population changed rapidly after 1700. Africans began to arrive in larger numbers after the British won the right to monopolize the slave trade of North and South America in the Treaty of Utrecht in 1713. The British Board of Trade established Negro slavery

70   EARLY AMERICA

So-called Reasons
for Slave Codes

throughout the empire. Although some Blacks retained their land and earlier status as freemen, the percentage of free men declined rapidly and in a short time nearly all Black men and women in the British Empire became slaves.

Like the indentured servants, very early African slaves sometimes earned their freedom. They were allowed to own property in some cases. However, there is evidence that as early as 1630 Virginia and Maryland were discriminating against Negroes. They were denied the right to carry guns in Virginia in 1640 and in Maryland in 1648. There are also cases which reveal harsh treatment of runaway Negroes. In the late 1600s, colonists from the West Indies, Bermuda, and the Bahamas introduced their restrictive and brutal slave codes into some of the mainland colonies, particularly in South Carolina. The reasoning behind these laws was that "the Negroes and other slaves brought into the people of this province . . . are of barbarous, wild, savage natives, and such as renders them wholly unqualified to be governed by the laws, customs, and practices of this province. . . ."

Restrictive Laws

Other colonies from Massachusetts to the West Indies passed laws against *miscegenation* (marriage between two people of different races). Other laws were developed to control the Negroes on plantations, to deny them ownership of land, and to restrict their freedoms, which made Blacks appear inferior to whites. With each such law, the faulty logic of white supremacy and Black inferiority became more and more a part of the heritage of the American people.

By the time of the American independence, it appeared to many whites that the Black man, slavery, and southern wealth were woven from the same cloth. Most whites came to believe slavery was the natural state for Black men and women. The several decades of colonial slavery gave birth to the racial problems of modern America.

Interesting Reading

NONFICTION

Cuban, Larry. *The Negro in America.* Glenview, Ill.: Scott, Foresman, 1964.

Franklin, John Hope. *From Slavery to Freedom.* New York: Knopf, 1956.

Hughes, Langston and Milton Meltzer. *A Pictorial History of the Negro in America.* New York: Crown, 1963.

Jordan, Winthrop D. *White Over Black.* Chapel Hill: University of North Carolina Press, 1968.

Litwack, Leon F. *North of Slavery.* Chicago: University of Chicago Press, 1961.

Meltzer, Milton. *In Their Own Words: A History of the American Negro.* New York: Thomas Y. Crowell, 1964.

Redding, J. Saunders. *They Came in Chains.* Philadelphia: Lippincott, 1950.

Reimers, David M. *Racism in the United States.* Hinsdale, Ill.: Dryden Press, 1972.

Stampp, Kenneth M. *The Peculiar Institution.* New York: Vintage Books, 1964.

In the space below, map the chapter you just read on "The Black Man in Early British Colonies."

Now answer the following questions.

COMPREHENSION CHECK

Part A

Directions: Answer the following questions without looking back. If you feel it necessary, review your notes before answering the questions.

1.   Which of the following study aids is provided in the history chapter you just read?
     a.   a chronology
     b.   purposes for reading the chapter
     c.   questions to look for as you read
     d.   headings and marginal notes
     e.   all of the above

2.   Early blacks in American history came as explorers, servants, and slaves, traveling with men such as Balboa, Cortes, and Pizarro.
     a.   True
     b.   False

3.   The Africans brought to America as slaves did not have a rich or varied cultural background.
     a.   True
     b.   False

4.   The European practice of African slave trade began with the Portuguese around
     a.   1350
     b.   1400
     c.   1500
     d.   not known

5.   Among the many reasons for the early practice of slavery, the most important

     is probably _____.

6.   Colonial slave practices are at the root of many of our modern racial problems.
     a.   True
     b.   False

7.   The term "middle passage" refers to
     a.   the slave journey traders made across the Pacific to the East Indies
     b.   the slave journey traders made across the Atlantic to the West Indies
     c.   the harsh journey made by the slaves.
     d.   crossing the Atlantic near the equator or middle of the map.

8.   Who was Gustavas Vassa?
     a.   a Portuguese ship captain who began the African slave trade
     b.   an author who wrote about the agonies of slaves
     c.   an African sold into slavery who wrote an autobiography describing the horrors of slavery
     d.   a fictional character in a book on slavery

9.   Blacks were easier to keep as slaves than were whites because _____

     _____

10.   Some people tried to abolish slavery in the British colonies by pointing out that during the golden days of Greece and Rome slavery was an unaccepted way of life.
      a.   True
      b.   False

Part B

Directions: Pick one of the following essay questions and on another sheet of paper, answer it as completely as you can.

1.   Discuss when and why slavery got started in early America.
2.   Compare the myths created by early slave traders regarding African lifestyles with the realities that existed at the time.

Turn in your written answer to your instructor.

VOCABULARY CHECK

Directions: Define the following words from the textbook chapter you just read.

1.   anthropologists

_____

2.   a generation

_____

3.   functional

_____

4.   monetary

_____

5.   middle passage

_____

6.   indentured servants

_____

7.   denominations

_____

8.   derived

_____

9.   renders

_____

10.   miscegenation

_____

Once your answers have been checked and you understand any errors or problems you may have had, record the results of both the comprehension and vocabulary checks on the Student Record Chart on page 495.

A FINAL WORD: FROM HERE TO THERE

The study-reading skills presented in this chapter are only as good as you make them. In order to make the techniques work well for you, you must practice. As with any new skill you wish to develop, whether it's in tennis, skiing, reading, or whatever, it can seem awkward and uncomfortable at first. But the more you practice, the easier and better that skill becomes.

It is very important that you apply the skills of this book to other reading and studying activities. It does you no good to do well on the drills here and then not use them elsewhere. Be patient with yourself as you try these skills in your daily reading and studying. When things don't work well, consult your instructor for aid or more instruction. Many students have benefited from these techniques; there's no reason you can't. So, go from here to...there—those readings you do outside this text.

CHAPTER 4

Developing Skimming and Scanning Skills

Skimming and scanning are terms sometimes used interchangeably. In this book, however, *skimming* is defined as the ability to identify *main ideas* while very rapidly and selectively skipping over the reading material. *Scanning*, in contrast, is defined as the ability to locate *specific information or facts* as rapidly as possible. Generally when you scan for information you know what you are looking for before you begin.

Skimming and scanning are both very rapid reading techniques. But skimming is a technique used to find out how a news story, magazine article, or textbook chapter is organized and what it is generally about without having to read the entire selection. You did a form of skimming in the last chapter during the survey portions of the SQ3R method when you looked over textbook passages before reading them. You will have more practice in skimming textbook selections in this chapter.

Contrary to what many readers think, skimming is not a sloppy hit-or-miss technique. To skim correctly, it is necessary to know the various organizational patterns of writing. News stories, for instance, usually are printed so that each sentence or two is a paragraph in itself. This style prevents paragraphs from looking too long in the narrow columns that newspapers often use. The opening sentence to a news story tries to cover *who, what, where, when,* and sometimes *why.* At the very least, most stories tell *who* and *what* in the opening line. Thus, when skimming a newspaper story, it is always advisable to concentrate on the opening sentence.

A magazine article or essay has a different organization. Titles are more reliable than newspaper stories, which tend to be misleading. Magazine titles tend to reveal a subject and sometimes a thesis or the author's attitude. This is an aid in skimming. For instance, if the title of a magazine article reads "Lake Havasu: A Fisherman's Paradise," you already have a clue to the article's content and the author's attitude or point of view. As you skim, you would then look for reasons the author feels the lake is a "paradise" for a fisherman.

Some magazine articles are set up the same way as most textbook chapters. In addition to helpful titles, most contain headings and subheadings to alert the reader that a new idea related to the subject is beginning. The word *alert* is the key to being a good skim reader.

Here is what to be alert to when you skim magazine articles:

1. Read the title and scan the opening paragraph or two, looking for the subject of the article and the author's thesis or point of view about the subject.
2. Read the first sentence or parts of the first sentence of each following paragraph, looking for ideas related to or supporting the author's thesis.
3. Read the last paragraph (or last two, depending on the article), looking for a summary or conclusion about the subject.

This approach or a modification of it will help you get an overview of an article's contents. At least you will know whether you want or need to read the article more closely.

Skimming a textbook chapter may seem a sin to some students. However, there are two appropriate times to skim a chapter: before reading it carefully and when reviewing for a test. Some good rules of thumb for skimming a chapter in a textbook are

1. Check to see how long the chapter is. If it can't be read in one sitting, you may want to mark a place to stop.
2. Read the title, the opening paragraph, and the summary, if there is one.
3. If there are questions at the end of the chapter, read them and scan for the answers.
4. Find the major idea related to each heading or subheading of the chapter.

How closely you skim depends on whether you are skimming to prepare to read or whether you are skimming for review. Whereas skimming should seldom, if ever, be used to replace close, careful reading, a proper application of skimming can save you many hours of slow, plodding reading when it isn't necessary.

Scanning is what you do when you look for a friend's telephone number in the phone book. It is the technique used when locating a word in the dictionary, when seeking a page number in the index, or when checking to see what television programs are offered at eight o'clock. In all of these examples, you know what you are looking for before you begin to read. You have to use guides and aids to find what you want rather than reading everything on the page. Good scanning ability, then, depends on knowing what you want to find and knowing the organization of the material to be read.

Scanning is something you already know how to do, but you may or may not be very proficient at it. In either case, the drills in this chapter will help you increase your scanning speed and become more aware of the organizational patterns in materials where scanning is best utilized.

This chapter is divided into four sections. Part A provides some rapid word and phrase recognition drills. Since skimming and scanning require fast and correct recognition of words and phrases, it is necessary to develop your perception skills. Part B builds on the survey portion of the SQ3R method by having you skim and scan textbook material. Part C offers practice in skimming and scanning reference materials. The last section, Part D, again offers two reading selections with comprehension and vocabulary checks.

As you do these drills, try finding a skimming and scanning technique that works well for you. Remember that you are not reading in the normal sense of the word; you are learning to develop a skill. Feel free to experiment and don't worry about mistakes. This is the place to make mistakes and to learn from them.

A. Rapid Word and Phrase Recognition

How fast we can read and understand the material being read depends on many variables: our visual skills, perceptual skills, vocabulary power, our purpose for reading, intelligence, past experience, familiarity with the material being read and many other things, including our state of mind. Reading is a very complex process involving many physical, intellectual, and often emotional reactions.

The exercises in this section are concerned with a basic skill necessary for developing reading flexibility—visual perception. If properly done, the drills here should develop speed of eye movement, improve visual perception of words and phrases, and help eliminate the tendency to vocalize or pronounce words orally or silently as you read. More will be said about this in the next chapter.

All of the following drills should be timed.

Drill A-1: RAPID VISUAL PERCEPTION OF WORDS

Set 1

Directions: Moving your eyes rapidly across each line, quickly underline the numbered word each time it appears on the same line. Example:

1. shirt shirk <u>shirt</u> shirk shrink <u>shirt</u>
2. utter udder until <u>utter</u> <u>utter</u> unless

The purpose of the drills is to help you speed up your perception of words. Do not look back on any line. Work as rapidly as you can. Don't stop to change your markings. Time yourself or have someone time you. Try to finish the drill in less than 30 seconds.

Begin timing.

1. laugh tough laugh tough tough tough laugh
2. cough cough rough rough rough cough rough
3. phrase phase phase phrase phase phase phase
4. right right right night night night night
5. night might might might might night might
6. sought sought fought sought fought sought fought
7. freight weight weight weight freight weight weight
8. fight tight tight fight fight tight tight
9. sliver silver silver silver silver sliver silver
10. chrome chrome chronic chrome chronic chronic chrome
11. bough dough bough dough dough dough bough
12. whale while while while while while while
13. udder udder utter utmost udder utter until
14. think thank think think thank thank thank
15. minks sinks minks minks sinks sinks sink

Time: _____ **seconds. Check each line carefully for mistakes.**

Number of lines correct: _____

Note: Item 12 purposely does not include the key word at all in the right-hand group. Do not waste time looking back on any line; either you will see the key word the first time or you missed it, so go right on to the next item.

Set 2

Directions: Follow the same directions; moving your eyes quickly from left to right, mark the word by the number every time it appears. Don't stop to change any marks; don't worry about any mistakes you know you make; and don't look back on any line. Do this for each of the following sets.

Begin timing.

1.	cereal	serial cereal cereal serial cereal serial
2.	cheerful	cheerful careful careful careful careful
3.	whirl	whirr whim whirl whim whirr
4.	rinsed	raised raised raised rinsed rinsed
5.	shift	shirt shirt shift shirt shift
6.	blush	brush blush brush blush brush
7.	breath	breathe breathe breathe breath breathe
8.	altar	alter alter alter altar altar
9.	course	coarse course course coarse coarse
10.	bathe	bathe bath bathe bath bath
11.	statue	status status statue status statue
12.	peach	peach peace peace peace peach
13.	pester	pastor pastor pastor pastor pester
14.	wares	wars wars wares wares wars
15.	twist	twins twist twins twins twins

Time: _____ seconds. Check each line carefully for mistakes.

Number of lines correct: _____

Set 3

Begin timing.

1.	ponder	pander pander ponder pander ponder
2.	shudder	shutter shutter shudder shutter shutter
3.	possible	passable possible passable passable possible
4.	mental	mantle mental mantle mental mantle
5.	atheist	atheism atheism atheism atheism atheist
6.	forces	forces faces faces forces faces
7.	porpoise	purpose purpose porpoise porpoise purpose
8.	egotistic	egoistic egoistic egotistic egotistic egoistic
9.	bigamy	biology biology biology biology bigamy
10.	monopoly	monarchy monopoly monarchy monopoly monarchy
11.	effect	effete effect effete effete effete
12.	curtain	certain certain certain curtain certain
13.	plain	plane plain plane plain plane plain
14.	maniac	mania maniac maniac mania mania
15.	psychology	psychologist psychology psychology psychologist

Time: _____ seconds. Check each line carefully for mistakes.

Number of lines correct: _____

Set 4

Begin timing.

1.	factual	factual factors factual factors factors
2.	simile	smile simile simile smile simile
3.	uniform	unicorn unicorn uniform unicorn uniform
4.	fiction	fiction fiction fraction fraction fiction
5.	filed	field field filed field filed
6.	crutch	crutch catch crutch crutch catch
7.	tried	tired tired tired tried tried
8.	farthest	farthest fastest fastest fastest farthest
9.	underneath	underground underground underneath underground
10.	exploded	exploded explored exploded explored explored
11.	wrath	worth worth worth wrath wrath
12.	parson	person parson parson parson person
13.	quantity	quantity quality quantity quality quality
14.	flavor	favor flavor flavor favor flavor
15.	precious	precious precise precise precise precious

Time: _____ seconds. Check each line carefully for mistakes.

Number of lines correct: _____

Set 5

Begin timing.

1.	sweat	sweet sweat sweat sweet sweet
2.	volunteer	voluntary voluntary voluntary volunteer
3.	unison	unique unison unique unison unique
4.	telegraph	telegraph telegraph telephone telegraph
5.	tricycle	trilogy tricycle trilogy trilogy tricycle
6.	triplets	triplets triplets triple triple triplets
7.	optical	optician optician optical optician optical
8.	nostalgia	nostalgic nostalgia nostalgia nostalgic
9.	monotone	monotonous monotonous monotone monotone
10.	graphite	graphite graphite graphic graphic graphite
11.	benediction	benevolent benevolent benevolent benediction
12.	geology	geography geography geography geology geology
13.	crass	class crass crass class crass
14.	diction	diction diction dictate dictate dictate
15.	broker	broken broken broker broker broker

Time: _____ seconds. Check each line carefully for mistakes.

Number of lines correct: _____

Drill A-2: WORD KNOWLEDGE CHECK

Directions: Define or use in a sentence the following words taken from the first five exercises. Make vocabulary cards for any words you need to overlearn.

   1. bough _____

   2. udder _____

   3. utter _____

   4. breath _____

   5. breathe _____

   6. course _____

   7. coarse _____

   8. ponder _____

   9. pander _____

  10. egotistic _____

  11. egoistic _____

  12. monopoly _____

  13. mania _____

  14. simile _____

  15. wrath _____

  16. crass _____

  17. unison _____

  18. benevolent _____

  19. benediction _____

  20. monotone _____

Drill A-3: RAPID VISUAL PERCEPTION OF PHRASES

Directions: For the following drills, move your eyes down the columns, looking for the key phrase. Every time the key phrase appears, make a mark by it. Do not use one word in the phrase as a clue to identification. Read the whole phrase. Work quickly. Try to finish the drill in less than 15 seconds.

Set 1

Key phrase: **fast and efficient**

Begin timing.

fat and efficient	fronded with moss	fill the air
far and wide	fifth avenue museums	fast and efficient
fast and efficient	fantastically rich	fantastically rich
friendly or not	fast and efficient	full of color
fantastic person	fine log fires	furniture from France
furniture from France	full of color	frantic with terror
flourish for now	fill the air	fast and efficient
fashionable one	fifty to nothing	flourish for now
festival in honor	fast and efficient	full of color
fast and efficient	fourteen for one	fill the air
flowering with trees	flowering with trees	fronded with moss
fat and efficient	fat and efficient	fast and efficient
fill the air	fashionable one	fifth avenue museums
		festival in honor

Time: _____ 11 _____ seconds

The key phrase appears seven times. Check your responses.

Number of key phrases you marked: _____ 7 _____ out of 7

Set 2

Key phrase: **success in something**

Begin timing.

sharp as though	seems to me	shadow once more
standing in shade	sinks far ahead	suddenly you see
still stands there	semblance of speed	something just beyond
success in something	suddenly you see	success in something
suspected of containing	success in something	sell for someone
sell to someone	shadow once more	suspected of containing
should again build	something just beyond	still stands there
seems to me	seems to me	success in something
smile at you	success in something	sharp as though
success in something	sinks far ahead	smile at you
same bright hazel	success in everything	success in everything
something for success	semblance of speed	sharp as though
still stands there	success in something	success in something
		seems to me

Time: _____ 12 _____ seconds

The key phrase appears eight times. Check your responses.

Number of key phrases you marked: _____ 7 _____ out of 8

Set 3

Key phrase: **continually surprised**

Begin timing.

center of town	center of town	consciously ignoring him
come into town	communication between	containing the lake
continually surprised	containing the lake	communication between
climbing and winding	continually surprised	climbing and winding
confident and wild	catch the words	continually surprised
communication between	classes in country	center of town
cries of birds	compulsory games	cries of birds
containing the lake	confident and wild	constantly surprised
confident and wild	continually surprised	consciously ignoring him
catch in it	containing the lake	climbing and winding
constantly surprised	communication between	constantly surprised
consciously ignoring him	center of town	center of town
continually surprised	continually surprised	continually surprised
		cries of birds

Time: _____ // _____ seconds

The key phrase appears seven times. Check your responses.

Number of key phrases you marked: _____ 6 _____ out of 7

Set 4

Key phrase: **virtually every city**

Begin timing.

very hopeful affair	various calm colors	vainly look for
various calm colors	very hopeful affair	villains also possess
vainly look for	virtually every town	violent about sin
virtually every city	villains also possess	virtually every city
violent about sin	vainly look for	vitally important thing
villains also possess	virtually every city	very hopeful affair
virtually every city	virtually every place	vainly look for
vainly look for	villains also possess	violent about sin
very hopeful affair	violent about sin	villains also possess
various calm colors	virtually every city	virtually every city
virtually every town	vainly look for	very hopeful affair
violent about sin	very hopeful affair	virtually every town
vainly look for	virtually every town	vitally important thing
		virtually every place

Time: _____ 12 _____ seconds

The key phrase appears six times. Check your responses.

Number of key phrases you marked: _____ 5 _____ out of 6

Set 5

Key phrase: **one is likely**

Begin timing.

ought to go	one could call	one is likely
one is likely	one is likely	one could call
obligated to go	obligated to go	ought to do
over the edge	over the edge	occurs to him
occurs to him	occurs to him	one is likely
one is likely	only the box	over the edge
only the box	one could call	only the box
ought to do	ought to do	one is likely
obligated to go	obligated to go	one could call
one is likely	one is likely	ought to do
over the edge	over the edge	one is likely
occurs to him	only the box	over the edge
only the box	occurs to him	one could call
		one is likely

Time: _____ 10 _____ seconds

The key phrase appears ten times. Check your responses.

Number of key phrases you marked: _____ 10 _____ out of 10

Set 6

Key phrase: **everything must work**

Begin timing.

east and west	east and west	everything must be
everything must work	everything must work	east and west
evidence for us	evidence for us	everything must work
eye to eye	even among things	elude its hostility
even to ask	eye to eye	eye to eye
even among things	even to ask	enrich his activities
everything must work	even the most	even to ask
even the most	elude its hostility	everything must be
east and west	east and west	east and west
evidence for us	enrich his activities	enrich his activities
eye to eye	everything must work	everything must work
even to ask	eye to eye	elude its hostility
everything must go	even to ask	eye to eye
		even to ask

Time: _____ 10 _____ seconds

The key phrase appears six times. Check your responses.

Number of key phrases you marked: _____ 5 _____ out of 6

Directions: In the following four drills, mark the key phrase every time it appears in the groups of unrelated phrases. Read from left to right just as you normally would read a paragraph. Try to finish in 25 seconds or less.

Set 7

Key phrase: **expect to win**

Begin timing.

should not have   music should be   down here on the ground   expect to win
over the ground   not displeased   except the winner   expect to lose   paint-
smeared jeans   expect the unexpected   vulgar of me   expect the unexpected
enjoyed the idea   expect to win   the idea of   rather enjoyed it   on one stage
expect to win   men must be tall   expect to win   nor can I   expect to win
look at   uncombed hair   struggle to win   expect to win   the great hotels
tons of makeup   expect to lose   expect to win   much of the lure   in all those
areas   compared to what   heard it before   expect to win   to test your luck
within the limit   almost too much   not now

Time: _____ 20 _____ seconds

The key phrase appears eight times. Check your responses.

Number of key phrases you marked: _____ 8 _____ out of 8

Set 8

Key phrase: **a showgirl's smile**

Begin timing.

hit the right note   a showman's dream   not on your life   a showgirl's smile
over the hill   on the market   the current passion   a showgirl's smile   was a
spectacle   to look upon   not now or ever   we were told   a showgirl's smile
cost the management   a showcase of beauty   never you mind   a showgirl's
smile   a showgirl's mother   once in a lifetime   call me mister   a showgirl's
smile   the struggle is on   forever and ever   what I wanted   a showgirl's smile
nice and easy   its own reward   not from me   trouble and expense
a showgirl's smile   in our society   when we were young   a showgirl's smile
boggles the mind   inherent in us   a show to remember   a showgirl's smile
never on time

Time: _____ 16 _____ seconds

The key phrase appears nine times. Check your responses.

Number of key phrases you marked: _____ 9 _____ out of 9

Set 9

Key phrase: **endless flirtation**

Begin timing.

enjoyed the idea   to look at   rather enjoyed it   endless flirtation   tons of
makeup   compared to what   should not have   endless flirtation   heard it
before   not on your life   endless flirtation   nor can I   the current passion
to look at   endless trouble   enjoyed it some   endless flirtation   compared to
what   enjoyed the idea   should not have   endless flirtation   in all those areas
endless trouble   on the way   almost too much   over the hill   endless
flirtation   what I wanted   to look at   compared to what   to fill the bottle
endless flirtation   now or never   something just beyond   endless remarks
on the way   to look at   endless flirtation   heard it before

Time: _____ seconds

The key phrase appears eight times. Check your responses.

Number of key phrases you marked: _____ out of 8

Set 10

Key phrase: **may be vulgar**

Begin timing.

music should be   compared to what   vulgar of me   to test your luck   may be
vulgar   nor can I   expect to lose   within the limit   almost too much   may be
good   over the hill   may be vulgar   like no other   to come here   vulgar of me
one is likely   over the edge   ought to do   may be vulgar   seems to me   still
stands there   may be right   a better way   may be vulgar   a chief reason
vulgar of me   to test your luck   may be vulgar   compared to what   may be
right   a class conflict   struggle to see   may be vulgar   almost too much
better way   in all those areas   within the limit   may be vulgar   heard it before
may be wrong   a class conflict

Time: _____ seconds

The key phrase appears seven times. Check your responses.

Number of key phrases you marked: _____ out of 7

Drill A-4: RAPID WORD MEANING RECOGNITION

Directions: Note the numbered definition; then move your eyes quickly across the line of words and underline the word that best fits the definition. For example:

1. dwelling place   record culture suffrage <u>habitat</u> jungle
2. male honeybee   deter angle <u>drone</u> queen entail

Work as rapidly as you can. Try to finish each drill in less than 40 seconds.

Set 1

Begin timing.

1. agree to — usually ascend consent deliver rustic
2. not straightforward — brevity devious cite awkward seamy
3. shortness, briefness — height renown discussion brevity length
4. pity, sympathy — commit compassion scornful attribute verify
5. guess, deduce, conclude — infer question refuse delay direction
6. a selected passage — record secret excerpt pursue avoid
7. easily deceived — gentle deceptive false sincere gullible
8. frank, straightforward — unplanned unexpected serious tired candid
9. not similar, unlike — unusual qualm trick dissimilar locate
10. required, needed — refill requisite strategy cull trivial
11. producing abundantly — ornate flush comfortable expensive luxurious
12. helpful, favorable — conducive exalt impulsive unhappy conquer
13. similar, alike — check disparate uniform argument mirror
14. violent, stormy — stanch bland turbulent revel relax
15. sleeping, inactive — restless agitated active dormant awake

Time: _____ seconds

Number correct: _____ Check your answers on page 186.

Set 2

Begin timing.

1. calmness, quietness — obstinate composure idle trivial expire
2. lunge forward — recharge hesitant agree surge locate
3. forgive, overlook — condone notice frequent elect foresight
4. reflect, consider — compile occupy speculate enlarge direct
5. not steady, irregular — erratic exploit resist defeat extinct
6. come out — conceal strength deface emerge event
7. tightly drawn — calm taut nervous hinder weak
8. absolutely clean — spacious varied airy clear immaculate
9. a solemn ceremony — chapel stage rite control atmosphere
10. authority, power — agreement method jurisdiction govern rules
11. of the night — nocturnal enhance deplete serenity result
12. fill again — resist reenter replenish direct destroy
13. rob with violence — collect pillage rage terror extinct
14. peculiarity — foreign menace unknown mannerism deadly
15. party, group, clique — faction cave maze survey mob

Time: _____ seconds

Number correct: _____ Check your answers on page 186.

Set 3

Begin timing.

1.	stroll	gait run saunter gallop crawl
2.	rejoicing, exulting	solemn jubilant giddy disloyal dedicate
3.	prepare, make up	concoct conject commit carve avoid
4.	annul, repeal	consider annihilate nullify aid consent
5.	at ease in talking	alert polite beautiful affable courageous
6.	examine and check	empty error audit asset discharge
7.	distorting	mask suggestive contortion creation plan
8.	speaking two languages	rhythmic bilingual discover hearty whole
9.	heavenly, of the sky	brilliant extreme pleasant celestial far
10.	rise and fall	equal attribute limit accuse fluctuate
11.	agreeable, suitable	congenial puncture peasant enjoy flavor
12.	criminal	thwart commit felon collect lawful
13.	seasoning	serve taste condiment digestible flavor
14.	funny, joking	silly bland consent favor jocular
15.	appetizing, tasty	menu savory dining hungry flavor

Time: _____ seconds

Number correct: _____ Check your answers on page 186.

Set 4

Begin timing.

1.	diverge, digress	article deviate repel progress repeat
2.	free from error	visible broken peculiar peaceful infallible
3.	fight, struggle	ramble destroy content defeat victory
4.	hearty enjoyment	moist gusto relax pleasant leisure
5.	widespread, scattered	enclosed gather diffuse abundant clear
6.	very bright, shining	removal migrate clean pure resplendent
7.	width, breadth, size	occupy amplitude neglect brief asset
8.	occupy wholly	spacious doubt engross divide inform
9.	doubtful, uncertain	odd ornate guilty dubious envious
10.	odd, queer, fantastic	bizarre knoll judge finish previous
11.	worship of idols	scorn false idolatry notorious liability
12.	notorious, wicked	infamous punish forgive ugly mislead
13.	contemptuous, scornful	trivial expire disdainful opening nervous
14.	small, rounded hill	valley gorge apse knoll cave
15.	causing death	strong lethal poisonous immortal invoke

Time: _____ seconds

Number correct: _____ Check your answers on page 186.

Set 5

Begin timing.

1.	historical records	strategy direct include annals ancestry
2.	not movable	unsteady immobile moving changing unstable
3.	ancestry	continue consult lineage rule language
4.	distinguished, exalted	eminent heritage dominant contrast extend
5.	pause	sensation endurance agree cessation appall
6.	consent, assent	sentiment realize concur confine final
7.	deadly	obscure lethal condense inanimate refer
8.	very hot	dense torrid ferocious increase reduce
9.	false idea	fallacy floral fiction untidy weak
10.	boil, bubble	relax alert melt seethe float
11.	thwart, baffle	division frustrate change fierce quiet
12.	foam, lather	smooth quick froth natural strain
13.	deaden, stun	dissolve stupefy deceive sincere restore
14.	smooth-tongued	arrange glib recruit inspire hesitate
15.	cut into pieces	model explode impair dissect lose

Time: _____ seconds

Number correct: _____ Check your answers with these:

Drill A-4

Set 1

1. consent 2. devious 3. brevity 4. compassion 5. infer 6. excerpt 7. gullible
8. candid 9. dissimilar 10. requisite 11. luxurious 12. conducive 13. uniform
14. turbulent 15. dormant

Set 2

1. composure 2. surge 3. condone 4. speculate 5. erratic 6. emerge 7. taut
8. immaculate 9. rite 10. jurisdiction 11. nocturnal 12. replenish 13. pillage
14. mannerism 15. faction

Set 3

1. saunter 2. jubilant 3. concoct 4. nullify 5. affable 6. audit 7. contortion
8. bilingual 9. celestial 10. fluctuate 11. congenial 12. felon 13. condiment
14. jocular 15. savory

Set 4

1. deviate 2. infallible 3. contend 4. gusto 5. diffuse 6. resplendent 7. amplitude
8. engross 9. dubious 10. bizarre 11. idolatry 12. infamous 13. disdainful
14. knoll 15. lethal

Set 5

1. annals 2. immobile 3. lineage 4. eminent 5. cessation 6. concur 7. lethal
8. torrid 9. fallacy 10. seethe 11. frustrate 12. froth 13. stupefy
14. glib 15. dissect

Drill A-5: QUICK VOCABULARY QUIZ

Part 1

Directions: Use the following words taken from the last five drills in sentences that contextually reflect or hint at their meanings.

1. devious _____

_____

2. brevity _____

_____

3. conducive _____

_____

4. dormant _____

_____

5. composure _____

_____

6. erratic _____

_____

7. nocturnal _____

_____

8. pillage _____

_____

9. concoct _____

_____

10. taut _____

_____

Go on to the next page.

Part 2

Directions: Write the letter of the word that best fits the definition in the blank before that word.

_____ **11.** foam lather   **a.** annals

_____ **12.** deadly   **b.** infallible

_____ **13.** historical records   **c.** froth

_____ **14.** doubtful, uncertain   **d.** affable

_____ **15.** free from error   **e.** infamous

_____ **16.** notorious, wicked   **f.** lethal

_____ **17.** easy to talk to, friendly   **g.** candid

_____ **18.** easily deceived   **h.** dubious

_____ **19.** frank, straightforward   **i.** resplendent

_____ **20.** very bright, shining   **j.** gullible

Make vocabulary cards or use whatever method you have selected to learn the words you missed or had trouble with.

NAME _____ SECTION _____ DATE _____

B. Skimming and Scanning Textbook Material

In Chapter 3, "Developing Study-Reading Skills," we discussed briefly the need to survey textbooks in order to know what study aids are provided. You were also shown how and why the SQ3R method of study was worth using. Since the survey step in SQ3R is in a sense a skimming/scanning technique, it is important that you understand how to do this step efficiently. In this section, material from a science textbook is used for practice.

Drill   B-1: SKIMMING

Directions: The following passage is from the textbook *Conceptual Physics: A New Introduction to Your Environment,* by Paul G. Hewitt. As you skim the chapter, do the following:

1.   Read the title carefully.
2.   Read the first paragraph and skim over the second paragraph.
3.   Read each heading carefully. Skim from heading to heading to get a general idea of what is covered.
4.   Look for any visual aids.
5.   If there is a summary, read it. If not, read the last paragraph.

Try to do this in two minutes or less.

1
About Science

Science is the body of knowledge about nature that represents the collective efforts, insights, findings, and wisdom of the human race. Science is not something new but had its beginnings before recorded history when humans first discovered reoccurring relationships around them. Through careful observations of these relationships, they began to know nature and, because of nature's dependability, found they could make predictions to enable some control over their surroundings.

Science made its greatest headway in the sixteenth century when people began asking answerable questions about nature—when they began replacing superstition by a systematic search for order—when experiment in addition to logic was used to test ideas. Where people once tried to influence natural events with magic and supernatural forces, they now had science to guide them. Advance was slow, however, because of the powerful opposition to scientific methods and ideas.

From Paul G. Hewitt, *Conceptual Physics: A New Introduction to Your Environment,* 4th ed., pp. 1–5, Copyright © 1981 by Paul G. Hewitt. Reprinted by permission of Little, Brown and Company.

2 Conceptual Physics

In about 1510 Copernicus suggested that the sun was stationary and that the earth revolved about the sun. He refuted the idea that the earth was the center of the universe. After years of hesitation, he published his findings but died before his book was circulated. His book was considered heretical and dangerous and was banned by the Church for 200 years. A century after Copernicus, the mathematician Bruno was burned at the stake—largely for supporting Copernicus, suggesting the sun to be a star, and suggesting that space was infinite. Galileo was imprisoned for popularizing the Copernican theory and for his other contributions to scientific thought. Yet a couple of centuries later, Copernican advocates seemed harmless.

This happens age after age. In the early 1800s geologists met with violent condemnation because they differed with the Genesis account of creation. Later in the same century, geology was safe, but theories of evolution were condemned and the teaching of them forbidden. This most likely continues. "At every crossway on the road that leads to the future, each progressive spirit is opposed by a thousand men appointed to guard the past."* Every age has one or more groups of intellectual rebels who are persecuted, condemned, or suppressed at the time; but to a later age, they seem harmless and often essential to the elevation of human conditions.

The Scientific Attitude

The enormous success of science has led to the general belief that scientists have developed and are employing a "method"—a method that is extremely effective in gaining, organizing, and applying new knowledge. Galileo, famous scientist of the 1600s, is usually credited with being the "Father of the Scientific Method." His method is essentially as follows:

1. Recognize a problem.
2. Guess an answer.
3. Predict the consequences of the guess.
4. Perform experiments to test predictions.
5. Formulate the simplest theory that organizes the three main ingredients: guess, prediction, experimental outcome.

Although this cookbook method has a certain appeal, it has not been the key to most of the breakthroughs and discoveries in science. Trial and error, experimentation without guessing, accidental discovery, and other methods account for much of the progress in science. Rather than a particular method, the success of science has more to do with an attitude common to scientists. This attitude is essentially one of inquiry, experimentation, and humility before the facts. If a scientist holds an idea to be true and finds any counterevidence whatever, the idea is either modified or abandoned. In the scientific spirit, the idea must be modified or abandoned in spite of the reputation of the person advocating it. As an example, the greatly respected Greek philosopher Aristotle said that falling bodies fall at a speed proportional to their weight. This false idea was held to be true for more than 2000 years because of Aristotle's compelling authority. In the scientific spirit, however, a single verifiable experiment to the contrary outweighs any authority, regardless of reputation or the number of followers and advocates.

Scientists must accept facts even when they would like them to be different. They must strive to distinguish between what they see and what they wish to see—for humanity's capacity for self-deception is vast. People have traditionally tended to adopt general rules, beliefs, creeds, theories, and ideas without thoroughly questioning their validity and to retain them long

*From "Our Social Duty," by Count Maurice Maeterlinck.

after they have been shown to be meaningless, false, or at least questionable. The most widespread assumptions are the least questioned. Most often, when an idea is adopted, particular attention is given to cases that seem to support it, while cases that seem to refute it are distorted, belittled, or ignored. We feel deeply that it is a sign of weakness to "change our minds." Competent scientists, however, must be expert at changing their minds. This is because science seeks not to defend our beliefs but to improve them. Better theories are made by those who are not hung up on prevailing ones.

Away from their profession, scientists are inherently no more honest or ethical than other people. But in their profession they work in an arena that puts a high premium on honesty. The cardinal rule in science is that all claims must be testable—they must be capable, at least in principle, of being proved wrong. For example, if someone claims that a certain procedure has a certain result, it must in principle be possible to perform a procedure that will either confirm or contradict the claim. If confirmed, then the claim is regarded as useful and a stepping-stone to further knowledge. None of us has the time or energy or resources to test every claim, so most of the time we must take somebody's word. However, we must have some criterion for deciding whether one person's word is as good as another's and whether one claim is as good as another. The criterion, again, is that the claim must be testable. To reduce the likelihood of error, scientists accept the word only of those whose ideas, theories, and findings are testable—if not in practice then at least in principle. Speculations that cannot be tested are regarded as "unscientific." This has the long-run effect of *compelling* honesty—findings widely publicized among fellow scientists are generally subjected to further testing. Sooner or later, mistakes (and lies) are bound to be found out; wishful thinking is bound to be exposed. The honesty so important to the progress of science thus becomes a matter of self-interest to scientists. There is relatively little bluffing in a game where all bets are called. In fields of study where right and wrong are not so easily established, the pressure to be honest is considerably less.

The ideas and concepts most important to our everday lives are largely unscientific; their correctness or incorrectness cannot be determined in the laboratory. Interestingly enough, it seems that everybody honestly believes his own ideas about the rightness or wrongness of things are correct, and almost everybody is acquainted with people who hold completely opposite views—so the ideas of some (or all) must be incorrect. How do you know whether or not *you* are one of those holding erroneous beliefs? There is a test: Before you can be reasonably convinced that you are right about a particular idea, you should be sure that you understand the objections and the positions of your most articulate antagonists. You must find out whether your views are supported by a sound knowledge of opposing ideas or by your *misconceptions* of opposing ideas. You make this distinction by seeing whether or not you can state the objections and positions of your opposition to *their* satisfaction. Even if you can successfully do this, you cannot be absolutely certain of being right about your own ideas, but the probability of being right is considerably higher than if you can't pass this test. The person who can state his antagonist's point of view to the satisfaction of his antagonist is more likely to be correct in his own beliefs than the person who cannot.

Although this seems reasonable to most thinking people, just the opposite—shielding oneself and others from opposing ideas—has been more widely practiced. We have been taught to discredit unpopular ideas without understanding them in proper context. From the $^{20}/_{20}$ vision of hindsight we can see that many of the "deep truths" that were the cornerstones of whole civilizations were shallow reflections of the prevailing ignorance of the time.

4 Conceptual Physics

Many of the problems that have plagued societies stemmed from this ignorance and the resulting misconceptions; much of what they held to be true simply wasn't true. Are we different today?

Science and Technology

There is a difference between science and technology. Science is a method of answering theoretical questions; technology is a method of solving practical problems (and sometimes creating new problems out of the "solutions"). Science has to do with discovering the facts and relationships between observable phenomena in nature and with establishing theories that serve to organize these facts and relationships; technology has to do with tools, techniques, and procedures for implementing the findings of science. Another distinction between science and technology has to do with the progress in each.

Progress in science excludes the human factor. And this is justly so. Scientists, who seek to comprehend the universe and know the truth within the highest degree of accuracy and certainty, cannot pay heed to their own or other people's likes or dislikes or to popular ideas about the fitness of things. What scientists discover may shock or anger people—as did Darwin's theory of evolution. But even an unpleasant truth is more than likely to be useful; besides, we have the option of refusing to believe it! But hardly so with technology; we do not have the option of refusing to hear the sonic boom produced by a supersonic aircraft flying overhead; we do not have the option of refusing to breathe polluted air; and we do not have the option of living in a nonatomic age. Unlike science, progress in technology *must* be measured in terms of the human factor. Technology must be our slave and not the reverse. The legitimate purpose of technology is to serve people— people in general, not merely some people; and future generations, not merely those who presently wish to gain advantage for themselves. Technology must be humanistic if it is to lead to a better world.

We are all familiar with the abuses of technology. Many people blame technology itself for widespread pollution, resource depletion and even social decay in general—so much so that the promise of technology is obscured. That promise is a cleaner and healthier world. If wise applications of science and technology do not lead to a better world, what else will?

Pioneers in technology such as Buckminster Fuller see the extension of science and technology in our spacefaring activities of the last 2 decades as marking a major stage in our evolution. As little Jenny suggests in the photo at the beginning of this chapter, perhaps we are like the hatching chicken who has exhausted the resources of its inner egg environment and is about to break through to a whole new range of possibilities. This is an exciting time.

Physics—The Basic Science

Science first branches into the study of living things and nonliving things: the life sciences and the physical sciences. Life science branches into such areas as biology, zoology, and botany. Physical science diverges into such areas as astronomy, chemistry, and physics. But physics is more than a part of the physical sciences. Physics is the most fundamental and all-inclusive of the sciences, both life and physical. Physics, essentially the study of matter and energy, is at the root of every field of science and underlies all phenomena. Physics is the present-day equivalent of what used to be called *natural philosophy,* from which most of present-day science arose.

1 About Science 5

The following chapters represent the findings of those who answered the compelling call to adventure—the expedition in search of the hows and whys of the physical world. Their findings are our legacy. In these chapters we will attempt to develop a conceptual understanding of this legacy as it relates to the phenomena of motion, force, energy, matter, sound, electricity, magnetism, light, and the atom and its nucleus. The analysis of these topics makes up what we call physics, the knowledge of which opens new doors of perception. Our environment is far richer when we are aware of the beauty, harmony, and interplay of the laws of physics around us.

Suggested Reading

Florman, Samuel C., *The Existential Pleasures of Engineering*, New York, St. Martin's Press, 1976.

Pirsig, Robert M., *Zen and the Art of Motorcycle Maintenance: An Inquiry into Values*, New York, Morrow, 1974.

Zukav, Gary, *The Dancing Wu Li Masters: An Overview of The New Physics*, New York, Morrow, 1979.

Now answer the following questions without looking back.

1.   What is the title of the chapter? *About Science*

2.   How many headings divide the chapter? *3*

3.   Based on the headings, what will the chapter cover? *all Sciences*

4.   Are there any visual aids? *No*

5.   Is there a summary? *No*

6.   What will the rest of the chapters in the book cover?

7. Jot down anything you remember noticing in your skimming survey. Your notes don't have to be in any order or make sense at this point. It's just a matter of recalling words, phrases, or ideas. _____

_____

_____

_____

_____

8. What questions do you have after doing your skimming survey that would help you read the chapter if you were required to do so? _____

_____

_____

Drill   B-2: SCANNING

Directions: It is not always necessary to study-read a chapter closely. Some instructors will tell you to "look over" a particular chapter or give you study-guide questions to use so that you don't spend too much time on a chapter that is less important than others. Below are some study-guide questions. Scan the chapter you just skimmed in the previous drill for the answers. Use the key words in the questions as clues, just as you did in the rapid word and phrase recognition drills in Part A.

1. Who is considered the "Father of the Scientific Method"? *Galileo*

_____

2. What is the cardinal rule of all scientific claims? _____
    all claims must be testable

3. What is the difference between science and technology? *Science answers theoretical questions, technology solves practical problems*

4. According to the author, how might the wise application of science change man's relationship with man for the better? *technology must serve man.*

5. Why is physics considered the most basic of the sciences? _____
    the study of matter + energy from which all other sciences evolve.

6. Physics is the present-day equivalent of what used to be called _____

   natural philosophy. _____.

7. For what discovery is Copernicus best known? *the earth*

   revolves around the sun _____

8. What false idea of Aristotle's was held to be true for more than 2,000 years?

   falling bodies fall at a rate proportional to

   their weight. _____

C. Scanning Reference Materials

One of the most widely used library references is the *Reader's Guide to Periodical Literature*, which provides a bibliography by subject matter of current and past articles appearing in many magazines and periodicals. Below is a list of the abbreviations the *Reader's Guide* uses in its listings to save space, with a sample entry and explanation. Take a few minutes to study the abbreviations and sample entry explanation. Your next drill will require you to use this information.

ABBREVIATIONS

*	following name entry, a printer's device	ed	edited, edition, editor	por	portrait
+	continued on later pages of same issue			pseud	pseudonym
		F	February	pt	part
Abp	archbishop			pub	published, publisher, publishing
abr	abridged	Hon	Honorable		
Ag	August				
Ap	April	il	illustrated, illustration, illustrator	q	quarterly
arch	architect				
assn	association	inc	incorporated	rev	revised
Aut	Autumn	introd	introduction, introductory		
ave	avenue			S	September
				sec	section
				semi-m	semimonthly
bart	baronet	Ja	January	soc	society
bibl	bibliography	Je	June	Spr	Spring
bibl f	bibliographical footnotes	Jl	July	sq	square
		Jr	junior	Sr	senior
bi-m	bimonthly	jt auth	joint author	st	street
bi-w	biweekly			Summ	Summer
bldg	building			supp	supplement
Bp	bishop	ltd	limited	supt	superintendent
co	company	m	monthly	tr	translated, translation, translator
comp	compiled, compiler	Mr	March		
cond	condensed	My	May		
cont	continued			v	volume
corp	corporation	N	November		
		no	number	w	weekly
				Wint	Winter
D	December				
dept	department	O	October	yr	year

For those unfamiliar with form of reference used in the entries, the following explanation is given.

Sample entry: OIL well drilling
Striking it rich—oil in your own back yard.
J. M. Liston. il Pop Mech 145:84-5+ Ja '76

An illustrated article on the subject OIL well drilling entitled "Striking it rich—oil in your own back yard," by J. M. Liston, will be found in volume 145 of Popular Mechanics, pages 84-5 (continued on later pages of the same issue), the January 1976 number.

Reader's Guide to Periodical Literature, Volume 41, Copyright © 1981, 1982 by The H. W. Wilson Company.

WOMEN artists—See also—*Continued*
McAfee, Ila
Mcpherson, Sarah Freedman
Marisol (artist)
Mitchell, Joan
Morton, Ree
O'Keeffe, Georgia
Parker, Judith Exner
Pfaff, Judy
Pratt, Mary
Putterman, Florence
Rankaitis, Susan
Robineau, Adelaide (Alsop)
Rothenberg, Susan
Salomon, Charlotte
Sato, Norie
Scatuccio, Maria
Schapiro, Miriam
Schwarcz, June
Shaw-Sutton, Carol
Sherman, Maggie
Smith, Alexis (artist)
Stack, Gael
Stone, Sylvia
Vezelay, Paule
Wheeler, Irene
Wieland, Joyce
Zeisler, Claire

Keep your eye on: American women in sculpture. J. Shaw-Eagle. il Harp Baz 114:162-3+ Ag '81

WOMEN astronauts
See also
Fisher, Anna
Seddon, Rhea

WOMEN astronomers
See also
Burbidge, Margaret (Peachey)
Mitchell, Maria

WOMEN athletes
See also
Automobile racing drivers
Sports for women
also names of women athletes, e.g. Ashford, Evelyn

Getting him to respect you in your cleats... an athlete's feat [teenage girls] P. Filichia. Seventeen 40:79 My '81
In sports, lions vs. tigers [sex differences] E. Gelman. il Newsweek 97:75 My 18 '81
So you want to be a pro athlete? C. Leerhsen. il Seventeen 40:76 Jl '81
Women's fascination with strength, competition, aggressiveness—femininity. G. Lichtenstein. il Vogue 171:458-9+ N '81
Wooing of women athletes [college recruiting] G. Lichtenstein. il N Y Times Mag p26-7+ F 8 '81

Health and hygiene

Frailty, thy name's been changed: what sports medicine is discovering about women's bodies. G. Selden. il Ms 10:51-3+ Jl '81
How women athletes can avoid injuries. A. Canby. il McCalls 108:43 S '81
Right approach to weekend athletics. J. Kaplan. il Vogue 171:163+ Je '81
Weekend athlete. S. Q. Merritt. il Work Wom 6:82+ Jl '81

Psychology

See Sports—Psychological aspects

Sexual behavior

Case of Billie Jean King. P. Axthelm. il Newsweek 97:133 My 18 '81
Facing up to Billie Jean's revelations [lesbian relationships] J. Kirshenbaum. Sports Illus 54:13+ My 11 '81
Sex and the female athlete. G. Lichtenstein. Vogue 171:100 Ag '81

WOMEN authors
See also
Alther, Lisa
Bainbridge, Beryl
Bombal, Maria Luisa
Brittain, Vera
Brodie, Fawn
Brody, Jane
Cartland, Barbara Hamilton
Charles-Roux, Edmonde
Clothing and dress—Authors
Dailey, Janet
Eliot, George, pseud
Fielding, Joy
Gilman, Charlotte (Perkins)
Gordimer, Nadine
Gordon, Mary
Holtby, Winifred
Jaffe, Rona
Janowitz, Tama
Jones, Gayl
Kaye, Mary Margaret
Kerouac, Jan
Kerr, Jean
King, Tabitha (Spruce)

Lebowitz, Fran
Le Guin, Ursula Kroeber
McCarthy, Mary
McCullough, Colleen
Metalious, Grace
Mitchell, Margaret
Morrison, Toni
Murdoch, Iris
Penney, Alexandra
Schreiner, Olive
Sontag, Susan
Stein, Gertrude
Uhnak, Dorothy
Vorse, Mary Marvin (Heaton)
Wallach, Anne Tolstoi
Weldon, Fay
Wharton, Edith Newbold (Jones)
Woolf, Virginia (Stephen)
Yourcenar, Marguerite

Latin American women writers—the power of the pen. M. Kort. Ms 10:19 O '81
Why is your writing so violent? J. C. Oates. N Y Times Bk R 86:15+ Mr 29 '81

WOMEN authors and editors. See Authors and editors

WOMEN automobile drivers. See Automobile drivers

WOMEN automobile racing drivers. See Automobile racing drivers

WOMEN aviation workers
See also
Women air pilots

WOMEN backpackers. See Backpacks and backpacking

WOMEN baseball players. See Baseball players

WOMEN body builders. See Body building

WOMEN bowlers. See Bowling

WOMEN brokers
Women on Wall Street [views of N. Crisp] il USA Today 109:12 F '81

WOMEN business consultants. See Business consultants

WOMEN caterers and catering. See Caterers and catering

WOMEN chemists
See also
Askins, Barbara S.
Silbergeld, Ellen K.

WOMEN clergy
See also
Ordination of women

First for UCC woman [M. C. Leysath elected conference minister] Chr Cent 98:408 Ap 15 '81
Guards patrol Maryland church rent by controversy [disagreement at Babcock Memorial Church in Towson, Md. over secession from United Presbyterian Church in the U.S.A.] R. Clapp. il Chr Today 25:37-8 Ap 24 '81
In the male domain of pastoring, women find success in the pulpit [black women ministers] L. Norment. il Ebony 37:99-100+ N '81
Passages of a pathfinder [D. Barnes] G. Sheehy. Ladies Home J 98:87+ S '81
Women clergy survey [study by Ford Foundation, Men and women of the cloth: comparative study of parish clergy] Chr Cent 99:9 Ja 6-13 '82

WOMEN clowns
Funny face. J. Ashworth. il pors Seventeen 40:108 My '81

WOMEN coal miners
Day in the life of a woman miner [P. Estrada] S. Crute. il pors Ms 9:54-8 Je '81

WOMEN college graduates
See also
Business schools and colleges—Graduates

Reunions: when college never ends [Smith College reunion of women graduates] G. Steinem. Ms 10:30+ S '81

WOMEN college students
See also
College sororities
Sex discrimination in education

Campus queens [black colleges] il Ebony 36:150-2+ Ap '81
Is your campus good for your health? F. Howe. Ms 10:108 S '81
Mother/daughter factor. E. Sweet. bibl il Ms 10:45+ S '81
Ms. gazette [aid programs] G. Jacobs and E. Hess. bibl Ms 9:81-4 Mr '81
Teacher's pet: when students and professors fall in love. K. Kormendi. Mademoiselle 87:176-8 S '81
Top ten college women '81. il Glamour 79:232-5+ Ag '81

Attitudes

What do women want? [views of students at Smith College on feminism] B. G. Harrison. il Harpers 263:39-48+ O '81

Drill   C-1: READER'S GUIDE

Directions: First, take a minute to look over the entry on the opposite page from the *Reader's Guide*. Then find the answers to the following questions by scanning the entry. Write your answers in the blanks provided. If you need to, refer to the list of abbreviations on page 196. You should finish in less than four minutes.

Begin timing.

1.   What general category does the listing on the opposite page cover? _____

Women

2.   Under the subhead "Health and hygiene" how many articles are listed?

4

3.   Under the heading "WOMEN athletes," there is an article listed that appears

in the *New York Times* magazine. Is it illustrated? *Yes*

4.   On what pages of *Ebony* magazine does the article about black women

ministers appear? *37:99*

5.   If you wanted more information about women athletes than is given here, under what other heading in the *Reader's Guide* are you directed to look?

Sports for Women

6.   Who is the author of the article "Is Your Campus Good for Your Health?

F. Howe

7.   No reference is listed under the heading "WOMEN business consultants."

Where are you directed to look? *Business Consultants*

8.   On what page in *Ms.* does the article "Latin American Women Writers—the

Power of the Pen" begin? (Clue: look under "WOMEN authors.") *10*

9.   Under the heading "Health and hygiene" there is a reference to an article

entitled "Weekend Athlete." In what magazine does it appear? _____

Working Woman

10.   Where should you look to find information on women astronauts? _____

Look up their Names

Time: _____

Number correct: _____

Drill C-2: CHARTS

Directions: First take a minute to look at the chart below. Then scan the chart for the answers to the questions under the chart. Write your answers in the blanks provided. You should finish in less than three minutes.

CALORIES USED PER HOUR

	Body Size		
	120 Pounds	150 Pounds	175 Pounds
Calisthenics	235–285	270–300	285–335
Running	550–660	625–700	660–775
Walking	235–285	270–330	285–335
Bowling	150–180	170–190	180–210
Swimming	425–510	480–540	510–600
Bicycling	325–395	370–415	395–460
Tennis	335–405	380–425	405–470
Golf	260–315	295–335	315–370

HOURS/MINUTES PER WEEK TO BURN 1,500 CALORIES

	Body Size		
	120 Pounds	150 Pounds	175 Pounds
Calisthenics	5:16–6:23	5:00–5:33	4:29–5:16
Running	2:16–2:44	2:09–2:25	1:56–2:16
Walking	5:16–6:23	5:00–5:33	4:29–5:16
Bowling	8:20–10:00	7:54–8:49	7:09–8:20
Swimming	2:56–3:32	2:47–3:08	2:30–2:56
Bicycling	3:48–4:37	3:37–4:03	3:16–3:48
Tennis	3:42–4:29	3:32–3:57	3:11–3:42
Golf	4:46–5:46	4:29–5:05	4:03–4:46

Begin timing.

1. If you weigh about 120 pounds, what form of exercise burns the most calories? _____

2. If you weigh about 150 pounds, will you burn more calories if you swim or if you run? _____

3. If you weigh about 175 pounds, how long will it take you to burn 1500 calories per week by walking? _____

4. What activity on the chart is the slowest way to burn calories at any weight? _____

5. If you want to burn as many calories as you can in order to lose weight, what activity should you do? _____

6. If you don't like the activity in the answer to question 5, what's the next best activity to do to burn calories? _____

7. If you weigh about 120 pounds, how many hours/minutes per week would you

have to spend bowling in order to burn 1500 calories? _____

_____

8. Is bicycling a faster or slower way to burn calories than tennis? _____

Time: _____

Number correct: _____

Drill C-3: MAP, GRAPH, CHART

Directions: Using the map, graph, and chart on the opposite page, scan for the answers to the following questions. Circle the letter of the correct response. Answers are provided as a learning tool. Don't read them until after you have scanned.

1. The city having the lowest number of clear days during February is located in
    a. California
    b. Washington
    c. Arizona
    d. South Dakota
    The correct answer can be found by looking under "Average Temperature" on the weather report chart. The city is Seattle with five clear days. To find the state in which the city is located, look on the map provided. The correct answer is Washington.

2. The city having the same number of cloudy and clear days during February is
    a. Portland
    b. Denver
    c. Santa Fe
    d. Salt Lake City
    To find the correct answer you would compare the "Cloudy" and "Clear" columns on the weather report chart to find equal numbers of cloudy and clear days. The correct answer is Santa Fe with fourteen days of each.

3. The city having the lowest average temperature during February is
    a. Seattle
    b. Pierre
    c. Los Angeles
    d. Portland
    The correct answer can be found under "Average Temperature" on the weather report chart, or more quickly on the average temperature graph below it. The correct answer is Pierre with 46°, a high for that month!

4. The average temperature of the city shown in Colorado is
    a. 63°
    b. 58°
    c. 55°
    d. 65°
    The correct answer can be found by first finding the city in Colorado on the map, then looking down the weather report chart or the graph for the average temperature of Denver. The correct answer is 63°.

5. The city with the highest average temperature during February is nearest on the map to
    a. Salt Lake City
    b. Los Angeles
    c. Denver
    d. Portland
    The correct answer can be found by looking at the weather report chart or the graph for the highest average temperature, and then locating that city on the map. Look to the adjacent cities to see which one is nearest to it. The correct answer is Denver, which is nearest to Santa Fe.

6. The number of cloudy days in Los Angeles during February is equal to the number of cloudy days in
    a. Portland
    b. Santa Fe
    c. Seattle
    d. Phoenix
    The correct answer can be found by looking at the cloudy days for Los Angeles on the weather report chart and scanning the list to find

WEATHER REPORT—FEBRUARY		
City	Average Temperature	Number of days
		Cloudy	Clear
Seattle	60	23	5
Los Angeles	70	8	20
Santa Fe	75	14	14
Salt Lake City	65	18	10
Denver	63	10	18
Portland	55	10	8
Phoenix	72	8	20
Pierre	46	20	8

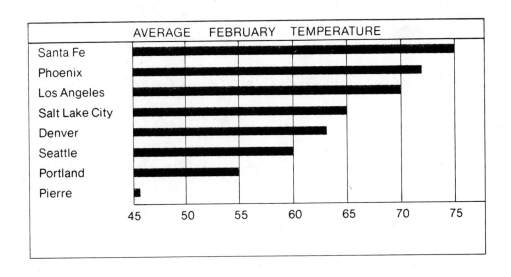

AVERAGE   FEBRUARY   TEMPERATURE

which other city has the same number of cloudy days. The correct answer is Phoenix with eight cloudy days.

7. The city located nearest the Pacific Ocean had how many clear days in February?
   a. 15
   b. 5
   c. 20
   d. 8
   The correct answer can be found by first looking at the map and locating the city nearest the Pacific. Then look at the clear days on the weather report chart to find the city. The city is Los Angeles and the correct answer is twenty clear days.

8. The city having the greatest number of cloudy days during February had what average temperature?
   a. 65°
   b. 60°
   c. 58°
   d. 63°
   The correct answer can be found by first looking under "Cloudy" on the weather report chart to locate the city with the greatest number of cloudy days. Then you should look

under "Average Temperature" for the correct answer. The correct answer is 60° for Seattle.

9. The city appearing nearest the middle of the map is located in which state?
   a. Arizona
   b. Utah
   c. Colorado
   d. California
   The correct answer can be found by simply locating the middle point of the map and looking to see what city is nearest that point. It is Salt Lake City, Utah.

10. The city farthest east on the map had how many cloudy days in February?
    a. 5
    b. 12
    c. 20
    d. 8
    The correct answer can be found by locating the city farthest east on the map. The city is Pierre, South Dakota. Then look under the "Cloudy" column of the weather report chart to find the number of cloudy days. The correct answer is twenty cloudy days.

Number correct: _____

Drill C-4: AN INDEX

Directions: Scan the index listing on page 204 for the answers to the following questions. Circle the letter of the correct answer. You should finish in less than three minutes.

Begin timing.

1. On what page would you find information about Mayan Indians?
   a. 6
   b. 44
   c. 243
2. On what pages would you find information about Meriwether Lewis?
   a. 136, 148–149
   b. 138–139
   c. 144–145
3. On what page would you find a definition of Manifest Destiny?
   a. 208
   b. 182
   c. 149

4. How many pages are listed for information on the Missouri Compromise?
   a. one
   b. two
   c. three
5. On what page would you find information on the "Log Cabin" Bill?
   a. 206
   b. 207
   c. 208
6. Are Mowhawk Indians listed in the index?
   a. no
   b. yes
   c. can't tell

7. On what pages will you find information about Lincoln's debates with Douglas?
   a. 237–246
   b. 233, 247
   c. 219, 231
8. How many pages are listed for Bishop Las Casas?
   a. one
   b. two
   c. three

9. Under what other listing besides "Massachusetts Bay Colony" could you find more information about the colony?
   a. founding of Maryland
   b. Puritan colonies
   c. Native Americans
10. How many pages are given to Moonshiners?
    a. one
    b. two
    c. three

Time: _____

Number correct: _____

Drill C-5: TEMPERATURE TABLE

Directions: Scan the temperature listings below for the answers to the following questions. Write your answers in the blanks that follow the questions. Try to finish in two minutes or less.

Begin timing.

Temperatures

Temperature and precipitation table for the 24-hour period ending at 4 a.m. Pacific Time, as prepared by the National Weather Service in San Francisco:

	High	Low	Pr.
Albany	69	45	...
Albuquerque	81	52	...
Atlanta	83	61	.16
Bakersfield	107	75	...
Bismarck	73	47	...
Boise	91	51	...
Boston	71	51	...
Brownsville	79	57	2.25
Buffalo	67	50	...
Charlotte	83	66	...
Chicago	64	54	.12
Cincinnati	86	62	...
Cleveland	76	64	...
Dallas	78	52	.01
Denver	74	43	...
Des Moines	64	53	.01
Detroit	70	59	...
Eureka	56	48	...
Fairbanks	55	37	.02
Fresno	103	66	...
Helena	83	52	.01
Honolulu	85	72	.01
Indianapolis	82	62	.37
Kansas City	67	47	...
Las Vegas	96	66	...
Los Angeles	88	59	...
Louisville	87	63	.24
Memphis	75	61	.16
Miami	82	78	...
Milwaukee	60	48	.03
Minneapolis	63	43	...
New Orleans	81	69	.54
New York	64	58	...
North Platte	63	34	.05
Oakland	86	54	...
Oklahoma City	70	46	...
Omaha	68	53	...
Palm Springs	104	71	...
Paso Robles	105	52	...
Philadelphia	71	61	...
Phoenix	100	70	...
Pittsburgh	75	56	...
Portland, Me.	62	42	...
Portland, Ore.	69	43	...
Rapid City	71	47	...
Red Bluff	100	66	...
Reno	91	59	...
Richmond, Va.	76	59	...
Sacramento	104	59	...
St. Louis	65	55	.30
Salt Lake City	78	53	...
San Diego	74	62	...
San Francisco	80	52	...
Seattle	62	47	...

1. What is the temperature high in Honolulu? _____

2. What is the temperature low in Fairbanks? _____

3. In what city is the highest temperature listed? _____

4. In what city is the lowest temperature listed? _____

5. What city received the most rain (Pr.)? _____

6. In how many cities was there rain? _____

7. Who prepared the weather listings? _____

Time: _____

Number correct: _____

Drill C-6: TELEPHONE DIRECTORY

Part 1

Directions: Using the telephone directory listings on the opposite page, answer the following questions by circling the letter of the correct response. You should be able to finish in less than 70 seconds.

Begin timing.

1. The phone number of John M. Bowman is
    a. 967–9460   b. 967–9410   c. 947–4960
2. The phone number of the Boys' Club in Goleta is
    a. 684–4018   b. 962–2382   c. 967–1612
3. M. L. Boyd's office is on
    a. Anacapa   b. Arbolado   c. Mission
4. The phone number of Bowman & Son Tree Surgery is
    a. 962–5387   b. 962–9967   c. 987–4876
5. Albert H. Bowker is
    a. an attorney   b. a captain in the navy   c. a retired naval captain

Time: _____ seconds

Total correct of 5: _____

Part 2

Directions: Using the same telephone listings, answer the following questions by circling the letter of the correct response. Try to finish in less than 70 seconds.

Begin timing.

1. The phone number for Boy Scout Troop 3 is
    a. 967–0105   b. 966–7027   c. 966–4810
2. William Brace is an attorney for
    a. himself   b. Hollister, Brace, Angle   c. does not say
3. Elmo Bowers lives on
    a. Castillo   b. Anapamu   c. San Jose Lane
4. The second listing under Boyer is
    a. Alton   b. Anthony   c. Barton
5. Jack Boydston is a building designer.
    a. yes   b. no   c. does not say

Time: _____ seconds

Total correct of 5: _____

Bowdon R S 2831 EVallyRdMont 969-4558
Bowdon's Welding Repairs 375PineAvGol 964-5050
Bowdry Sarah 233WValerio SBar 963-3148
Bowen Andrew 1111SnAndresSBar 963-4061
Bowen Asa 4799BaxtrSBar 967-8347
Bowen B A 1432SnPascualSBar 962-2764
Bowen Bertha 1130PuntaGorda SBar 965-4679
Bowen C J 1804MountnAvSBar 965-3431
Bowen Chas W 2526ModocRdSBar 963-2457
Bowen Darwin 1130PuntaGorda SBar 965-4679
Bowen Fredrick Talbot 3644SnGabrielLnSBar .687-3558
Bowen Geo 6621AbregoRdGol 968-2810
Bowen Jas T 5823BerkelyRdGol 964-3464
Bowen R W 2804MiraderoDrSBar 687-3501
Bowen Robt A 2945DeLaVinaSBar 687-6273
Bowen Robt Lee 5622BerkelyRdGol 967-0085
Bowen Robt M 468CamInoLagunaVstaGol 967-3776
Bowen W E 5557CameoRdCarp 684-2905
Bower C S 2ElVedadoLnSBar 687-7324
Bower Jas S 4490ViaAlegreHpeRnch 967-2833
Bower L E 1426GardenSBar 963-7103
Bower Lester B 3655RockCrkRdSBar 687-6053
Bower W M 6754AbregoRdGol 968-8885
Bower W M DMD
    Ofc 6134CalleRealGol 964-2211
Bowers Ada-Marie 1266SnAntonIoCrkRdSBar .964-2262
Bowers Allan T 3195SerenaAvCarp 684-3268
Bowers Ellen E 3529SnJoseLnSBar 687-1466
Bowers Elmo 1517CastilloSBar 962-8632
Bowers Guy A 409EAnapamuSBar 962-1637
Bowers John N 7465HollistrAvGol 968-2447
Bowers John N Jr 1103WPedregosaSBar 962-9243
Bowers Michael T 301StaRosaliaWySBar ...967-2659
Bowersox Lee 455ScandiaDrBuellton 688-5976
Bowes Donald F 1360LimuCarp 684-2552
Bowie Abbie 702PilgrmDrSBar 965-7423
Bowie Bill G 5396AngosaSBar 964-5567
Bowie Frank L 450ViaRoma SBar 967-6423
Bowie Harry 201 OlivrRdSBar 963-2816
Bowie Jack 1515½GillespieSBar 963-9121
Bowie Judie K 722PilgrmDrSBar 962-5792
Bowie Mary Mrs 730DeLaVina SBar 966-4425
Bowie Robt W 1620Payeras SBar 962-1522
Bowker Albert H Capt USN Ret
              5461BerkelyRdSBar..967-4629
Bowler Robt CateSchoolCarp 684-4048
Bowles Stephen 6717AbregoRdGol 968-7035
Bowley Michael 6725AbregoRdGol 968-2824
Bowling Howard 5016AnitaLnSBar 964-1963
Bowlus Jack E 4731Amarosa SBar 967-9284
Bowman Bernard C 5086SnBernardoDrSBar ..967-3579
Bowman David C 6592SabadoTardeRdGol 968-7641
Bowman Dorothy 602GroveLnSBar 687-7178
Bowman Douglas T 463A WhitmnGol 968-5486
Bowman Eugene H 2661PuestaDlSolRdSBar ..962-5666
Bowman Geo D 426RosarioDrSBar 967-1354
Bowman George Motors 118StateSBar 966-3936
Bowman Harry J Mrs 1763 OvrlookLnSBar ..962-7862
Bowman Hubert D 2310 State SBar 962-7501
Bowman Jeffrey 70SurreyPlGol 968-8692
Bowman John 1531VeronIcaPlSBar 963-4803
Bowman John K 616EdgewdDrGol 964-1177
Bowman John M 375MoretnBayLnSBar 967-9410
Bowman John T 5174SnLorenzoDrSBar 964-1664
Bowman Karen 1000CliffDrSBar 963-2348
Bowman Kenneth C 430ElCielito SBar 965-3204
Bowman Leora J 1605SnPascualSBar 966-1847
Bowman Melvin E Mrs 393LasAlturasRdSBar .962-3155
Bowman Olma June 618WPedregosaSBar 962-3237
Bowman Pan Mrs 823LagunaSBar 962-2626
Bowman Philip G 3330CalleRosalesSBar ...687-4876
Bowman Robt F 6285NewcastleAvGol 964-5382
Bowman & Son Tree Surgery SBar 962-9967
Bowman Walter E 1225MissionRdgeRdSBar ..965-8244
Bowman Wm H LosPrietos SBar 967-1152
Bowne V W 4715AndritaSBar 967-1023
Bowser Barry AlamoPintadoRdLosOlivos ...688-3548
Bowser Gordon W 1261DovrLneSBar 962-6625
Bowser H S 802KentiaAvSBar 966-4541
Bowser Irene Mrs SnMarcosAvLosOlivos ...688-4338
Bowser J I 4454LaPalomaAvSBar 967-1170
Bowser Vera 469PaseoDlDescansoSBar 687-6526
BOWSER'S JEWELRY & GEMS
   3317B StateSBar 687-1715
Box Richard 4175StateSBar 964-1020
Boxberger Mary Ellen 431EVictoriaSBar ..966-0952
Boxer Diana Gail 564RIcardoAvSBar 965-3350
Boxer Rubin 564RicardoAvSBar 966-7027
Boy Scout Troop No 3 1605GillespieSBar ..966-4810
BOY SCOUTS OF AMERICA MISSION COUNCIL
   4000ModocRdSBar 967-0105

Boyd Bruce Allen 765HollyAvCarp 684-5105
Boyd C H 2514DeLaVina SBar 962-4527
Boyd Carroll V 2374ShelbySummerlnd 969-1493
Boyd Celia B 36RomaineDrSBar 962-4504
Boyd Francis E 229WAlamrAvSBar 962-6462
Boyd Gary E 429PacIfcOksRdGol 968-4193
Boyd Gayle 1050ChannIDrMont 969-0526
Boyd Gladys A 3079CallePinonSBar 687-7978
Boyd Harry S 3079CallePinonSBar 687-7978
Boyd Janet MacMaster 717 SnYsidroLneMont .969-2387
Boyd John 6559SabadoTardeRdGol 968-4982
Boyd Lance 1250CliffDrSBar 963-3271
Boyd Lila M 431EVictoriaSBar 966-4958
Boyd M L Bud rl est
   Ofc 1500AnacapaSBar 963-1391
   Res 1054ArboladoRdSBar 962-5472
Boyd Myron L 314EValerioSBar 962-8838
Boyd Oran C Jr 19NVoluntario SBar 962-6752
Boyd Patricia 865EmbarcaderoDlMarGol ...968-2358
Boyd Rebecca 320 OceanoAvSBar 966-1015
Boyd Reva L 1255MesaRdMont 969-2806
Boyd Ronald E 497HalkrkSBar 964-7950
Boyd Stephen 4189FoothlRdCarp 684-4645
Boyd Wm V 1236CliffDrSBar 965-4481
Boydston Jack bldg desgnr 94HumphryRdMont .969-0112
Boydston Scott 109DearbrnPlGol 964-7952
Boydstun Linda 6594MadridRdGol 968-4822
Boyer Alton C 1921Castillo SBar 966-7376
Boyer Anthony 150VeronaAvGol 968-4775
Boyer Barton 4977ToreroRdSBar 967-2545
Boyer Gerald E 527½BathSBar 966-0074
Boyer Gordon 210 OldMillRdSBar 964-6193
Boyer Jas 514½WArrellagaSBar 966-7942
Boyer M A 246PebblHIDrSBar 964-3289
Boyes Terry W 975GarciaRdSBar 966-0070
Boyle Edw 700BuenaVstaRdMont 969-2768
Boyle John A 141CarloDrGol 964-4030
Boyle Michael R 6509SevleRdGol 968-2767
Boyle Robt J 2830StateSBar 687-4829
Boyle Stephen R 4447ViejaDrHopeRnch 967-6764
Boyles Robt W 1423HarbrVwDrSBar 963-6189
Boyne Wm W 333 OldMillRdSBar 964-7020
Boynton C W 204ElSuenoRdSBar 967-2972
Boynton Carlita 1018CaciqueSBar 965-9508
Boynton Clarence W Jr 3553LaEntrada SBar ..965-0720
Boynton Fredrick R 322LaderaSBar 963-7929
Boynton John B 305MoretnBayLnGol 967-3636
Boys' Club
   Carpinteria 4545CarpinteriaAv 684-4018
   Goleta 5701HollistrAv 967-1612
   Santa Barbara 632ECanonPerdido 962-2382
   Westside 602WAnapamuSBar 966-2811
Boysel H B 1024NOntareRdSBar 687-4872
Boysel L E 102NHopeAvSBar 687-8261
Boysen Hans A 7167AlamedaAvGol 968-7633
Boysen Philip T 3754SnRemoDrSBar 687-2294
Boysen Robt E 30WalnutLnSBar 967-2766
Boza David 1615BathSBar 966-7096
Bozarth Chas 429WValerioSBar 962-2359
Bozarth E A Col 275ButtrflyLnMont 969-4844
Bozeman Jas 7275YoloLnGol 968-6688
Bozsik Albert S 6565SabadoTardeRdGol ...968-1397
Braaten Willard C 16EPedregosaSBar 965-4653
Brabo Henry M 1703SnAndresSBar 962-0820
Brabo J Henry Mrs 1425Castillo SBar 962-5439
Brabo J R Mrs 112½ WMicheltorena SBar ..966-4272
Brace Chas E 629EValerio SBar 965-4287
Brace Joe W 3625TivolaSYnez 688-4755
Brace Virginia 206EPadreSBar 966-5282
Brace Wm A atty Hollister Brace & Angle
   Ofc 125EVictoriaSBar 963-6711
   Res 1021MissnRdgeRdSBar 962-2884
   Sandra's Phone 962-5844
Bracken Leilani 850FortunaLnGol 968-7352
Bracken Pearl 1716Chino SBar 966-9446
Brackenhamer Paul Jr 430HarvrdAvSBar ...967-7064
Bracker Lewis 3269PadaroLnCarp 684-3355
Brackett J Frank 410WPueblo SBar 962-9432
Brackley Art 1745GrandAvSBar 966-9773
Brackney R H 620EMicheltorena SBar 965-2166
Bradburn Flossie L Mrs 1327HarmnSBar ...965-3147
Bradburn Jas G 111DearbrnPlGol 964-3150
Bradbury C W 123EMicheltorenaSBar 965-1401
Bradbury E P 1525CliffDrSBar 965-4675
Bradbury Elaine R 1530BathSBar 966-6307
Bradbury Harold G RAdm USCG Ret
            30LangloTerSBar.687-2221
Bradbury Howard 4485MeadowlrkLnSBar 967-0922
Bradbury Jack 1628StateSBar 966-4861
Bradbury John V 141 OlivrRdSBar 966-9581

D. Reading Practices

The following two reading practices are provided to help you practice your skimming and scanning ability. Apply what this chapter has taught you about the difference between the two reading techniques. The first five comprehension questions following each reading selection check your skimming skills, while the second five questions check your scanning ability. There are also vocabulary checks so that you can continue to develop your word knowledge.

Drill D-1

Directions: Before you read the following article, read the title and skim over the reading selection applying those skimming skills taught in this chapter. Take no more than 30 seconds to read the opening paragraph, a few first sentences of selected paragraphs, and the final paragraph. Then in the spaces below, write in what you think are the correct answers.

Subject or topic of the article: _____

Probable thesis: _____

_____

Now read the article, looking for the author's thesis and supporting details. When finished, answer the questions that follow.

CAN BAD AIR MAKE BAD THINGS HAPPEN?

Randi Londer

1   On hot, smoggy days in the pit of the Los Angeles basin, Sgt. Charles Mealey of the central area police precinct braces himself for an onslaught of calls. On those sweltering days, he says, when your eyes burn from the pollution and "You can't see the top of a building two blocks away, more people stay outdoors, argue and carry on."

2   And some of these citizens, he notes, will clobber each other. "That's when the police have to step in," the veteran cop declares.

3   Most policemen would agree that the hotter it

gets, the more incidents there are of family violence, muggings and assault. And lest you think that this sounds too much like the once-popular "lunar theory" (Remember when people believed that the crime rate was higher when the moon was full? Even the police believed it, until scientists debunked the myth.), there is scientific proof that bad air makes bad things happen.

4   Evidence that chemicals in the air we breathe affect our brains is growing. Scientists suspect that the airborne toxins turn some people to violence. In Los Angeles, for example, and other cities, hot weather can worsen the effects of pollution. That's when some people, goaded by bad air, come out swinging.

Reprinted with permission from *Parade,* copyright © 1987.

5   Researchers like the psychologist James Rotton of Florida International University in North Miami have linked higher crime rates to air fouled with chemicals. The worst pollutant, according to Rotton, is ozone. He estimates that, every year, ozone provokes hundreds of cases of family violence in big cities with bad air.

6   Potentially, this could be a huge problem. Consider, for example, that, of the 300 largest cities in this country, one-third have broken the federal clean-air laws on ozone in the last three years.

7   "If we reduce the ozone by 50 percent, we can reduce the incidence of violence by a thousand cases," says Rotton.

8   Ozone has some beneficial properties, however. When it appears in the stratosphere, 12 miles above the earth, ozone protects us from the harmful rays of the sun. But when ozone forms closer to the earth's surface—the sunlight helps to make ozone when it hits chemicals from car exhaust and industrial sources—it threatens our health.

9   Rotton and his colleagues studied two years worth of police and pollution data in Dayton, Ohio. They found that on warm, dry days—high pollution days—there were more assaults and cases of family violence. Rotton concludes that, without wind, rain or humidity to wash away air poisons, bad air moves people to mischief. To corroborate his theory that warm, pollution-racked air causes aggressive behavior, Rotton ran additional tests, using mathematical techniques to rule out factors other than pollution. His findings did not waver. He said: "If you already have some trouble in your life, irritating pollutants can push you over the edge."

10   Rotton is now studying how people react to low, sub-toxic levels of ozone. That is the kind of pollution—usually more than what is allowed by federal clean-air laws—found in cities with a population of more than 100,000 people.

11   Even the scientists advancing these theories agree that blaming antisocial behavior solely on hot, dirty air is risky business. "Behavior is complex and can be altered by so many things," says Lawrence Reiter of the Environmental Protection Agency (EPA). "So you have to make sure that behavioral changes are due to a chemical [in the air] and not some other factor."

12   Reiter studies how chemicals and pollutants affect our brains, nervous systems and behavior. His is an emerging field called neurotoxicology.

13   "One of the problems of this research," he says, "is that we are trying to evaluate an abnormal state of the brain when we still don't know enough about how the brain works normally."

14   But the findings which link high levels of both pollution and crime do fit into the growing knowledge that, in the long run, many chemicals can cause nerve damage and behavioral changes.

15   For example, scientists have known for years that mercury causes brain damage: The 19th century "mad hatters" stammered, twitched and trembled from inhaling mercury vapors in London hat factories. Today, many factories use masks and protective hoods to shield workers from the worst effects of chemicals.

16   In recent years, scientists have demonstrated that lead lowers children's intelligence. As a result, the EPA has slashed the amount of lead allowed in gasoline. In time, the agency may ban leaded gas altogether.

17   "The problem," says Reiter, "is how do you interpret behavioral change—and prove it is based directly on a chemical?"

18   This is the question that researchers like Gary Evans of the University of California at Irvine and Steve Jacobs, formerly at Harvard, are trying to answer. They searched for the subtle "other factors" that Reiter refers to. They studied people living in the chemical soup of Los Angeles.

19   The psychologists talked to 6000 people from all walks of life by telephone. They asked about stress on the job and at home, and about physical and mental health symptoms. Then they matched the levels of dirty air to the neighborhoods of a random group.

20   According to Jacobs, people showed an uncanny knack for knowing when the air was bad. Even without knowing the official measurements, they could tell that the invisible ozone was high. Jacobs said that Los Angeles residents felt depressed when they thought the air was dirty "*and* they had a major stress such as divorce or losing a job."

21   Interestingly, lower income people felt more smog, says Jacobs. He thinks this may be because they tend to live in more polluted areas.

22   If pollution makes people limp with depression, how can it also make them angry and aggressive?

23   "One explanation," says Jacobs, "is that we are seeing one problem with two stages. First you get irritable and aggressive. And then, due to chronic pollution and stress, the next stage is depression. This is a problem that's not going away."

24   Environmental watchdogs have fought hard to reduce the levels of smog choking our cities. Since 1970, when Congress passed the Clean Air Act, there has been a reduction in the six worst air pollutants: carbon monoxide from vehicle exhaust; nitrogen dioxide from industry and automobiles; sulfur dioxide from power plants; ozone from chemicals mixing with sunlight; lead from gasoline; and particulates such as dirt, dust and soot from industry. Yet, considerable levels of these poisons still wash over our cities, threatening our physical, and apparently, our mental health.

25　　"The Clean Air Act sets very strict health standards," says Lee M. Thomas, head of the EPA. "In many cities, it is impossible to reach those standards. To do it, we will call on state and local governments and individuals to make some tough choices. Ultimately, people may need to make basic lifestyle changes, such as limiting how often and where they drive their cars."

26　　"All federal laws on pollution have focused on death and disease," adds Rotton. "But crimes and mental illness cost us too. When planning our cities, we need to take that into account."

27　　The bottom line, some researchers maintain, is that if we don't clean up our air even faster, we can expect more mental depression and more crime.

COMPREHENSION CHECK

Directions: Answer the first five questions without looking back. The last five questions require scanning. More directions will be given when you get to them.

1. What is the thesis or main idea of the essay? _____

_____

2. T/F　Evidence is growing that chemicals in the air we breathe affect our brains.

3. The worst pollutant, according to one research scientist, is
   a. rotton
   b. ultraviolet rays from the sun
   c. ozone
   d. mercury

4. In Dayton, Ohio, on warm, dry days—high pollution days—it was found that there were more cases of
   a. assault
   b. family violence
   c. both a and b
   d. none of the above

5. Explain how air pollution can make people limp with depression and angry

and aggressive at the same time. _____

_____

_____

_____

Scan back through the article for the answers to the next five questions. The number following the question refers to the paragraph in the reading selection where you can find the answer.

6. At what level in the stratosphere is ozone beneficial? (8) _____

_____

7. Why did the EPA require that lower amounts of lead be used in gasoline?

(16) _____

_____

8. How many people did Gary Evans and Steve Jacobs talk to by telephone to ask about stress on the job and at home? (19) _____

_____

9. When did Congress pass the Clean Air Act? (24) _____

10. What scientific field is mentioned in paragraph 12? _____

VOCABULARY CHECK

Directions: Define the following italicized words from the article.

1. an *onslaught* of calls

_____

2. scientists *debunked* the idea

_____

3. *goaded* by bad air

_____

4. findings did not *waver*

_____

5. an *emerging* field

_____

6. *chronic* pollution

_____

7. *particulates,* such as dirt

_____

8. an *uncanny* knack

_____

9. a *random* group

_____

10. environmental *watchdogs*

_____

Record the results of both your comprehension and vocabulary checks on the Student Record Chart on page 495. Make certain that you understand any problems that you may have had with the questions before going on to the next drill.

Drill **D-2**

Directions: Before you read the following passage, skim it by reading the title, the headings, and selective paragraphs. Take no more than 30 seconds. Then, in the spaces below, write in your answers.

Subject or topic: _____

Probable thesis: _____

_____

Now read the article, looking for the author's thesis and supporting details. When finished, answer the questions that follow.

ADVICE THAT CAN HELP YOU SUCCEED ON CAMPUS

1   The fat letter has finally arrived welcoming you as a member of the class of 1992. You're about to become a college freshman.

2   Most students enter college expecting to leave with a bachelor's degree; only half ever do. The others drop out.

3   "Half of a college education has to come from the student," advises Fred Hargadon, former dean of admissions at Stanford University. But how?

4   College counselors, faculty advisers and one very successful student offer the following tips on how to get the most out of your college education.

5   **INVOLVEMENT.** The most successful students are those actively involved in their education. By interacting with classmates and faculty and participating in activities, you become part of the college community, developing support groups that you can turn to for help. Get involved, but not overcommitted. In the first term, focus on adjusting to the new academic demands.

6   Consider study groups in which you meet regularly with a few classmates to discuss course material. Find an upperclassman, someone from your hometown or down the hall who can be a mentor. Older students can offer advice on courses plus activities to join.

7   **TIME MANAGEMENT.** "Man is first a social animal, then a rational one," says E. Glenn Griffin, a professor emeritus at Purdue University. So you may find it hard to say "No" each time your roommate wants to see "Beverly Hills Cop" when you need to read *Paradise Lost*.

8   College is known for its distractions. In those first months, you'll meet people whose values and priorities are different from yours. The newness of the situation and the range of decisions you'll face could leave you confused.

9   Think about what you want from college—and from friends. Study after breakfast, between classes, whatever works best for you. Don't cut off all social contacts. They're as vital to surviving in college as reading. Study Hegel first, then catch the late showing of "Rambo."

10   **STUDY METHODS.** Would you take a trip by stopping for directions at every filling station instead of reading a map? Of course not, but that's how most people study, says Griffin, who teaches a course on preparing for college. Studying in college demands more reading and thinking, less memorization than in high school. Survey the material first to get a sense of it; formulate some questions. Jot down key ideas, tell yourself the essence of what you've read and review it. Does it make sense? Were your questions answered?

11   Get copies of old exams from the library so you can see what types of questions each professor asks. Preparing for an exam on the Civil War will be easier if you know whether to study broad themes or specific battles.

12   **KEEPING CURRENT.** Professors may not notice whether you attend a large lecture, but you could notice later on, says Lawrence Graham, a 1983 graduate of Princeton University who as a senior wrote *Conquering College Life: How to Be a Winner at College*.

13   Some professors use lectures to discuss material not found in the reading on which they will base an exam. Others stress key points. Skip at your own risk. If you must miss a lecture, get the notes promptly. If too much time elapses, the notes will make less sense than secondhand notes normally do. Never fall more than a week behind in reading. If you don't do the reading, you won't understand the lecture.

14   **SEEKING HELP.**   You may attend every calculus class, do each assignment and still watch your grade plummet. Or maybe you missed more classes than you should have. Get help. Most professors are very willing to talk about their courses. Just don't wait until a week before the midterm exam.

15   **THE MAJOR CHOICE.**   For a minimum of $4,000 a year and four years of your life, you expect a degree—and a job when it's over. Why not major in computer science or business and be more assured of work after graduation?

16   "When choosing a major, look inside yourself as well as at the economic pattern," advises Ernest Boyer, president of the Carnegie Foundation for the Advancement of Teaching. If you're genuinely interested in computers, major in them. If you're happiest reading *Beowulf,* don't force yourself to study business. Think carefully before choosing a major. What excites and intrigues you? Knowing that may help you avoid changing disciplines several times.

17   It is quite appropriate to view college as a broadening experience, a preparation for life. Indeed, many college students do not select their ultimate career path until *after* they graduate. So take occupational courses if you like, but don't feel compelled to mold your major to the market.

18   **FINDING TOP TEACHERS.**   On every campus, there are professors noted for their inspirational teaching style, for their way of making a course an exciting voyage into the unknown. Don't spend four years on campus without taking their classes. So what if the professors teach modern art and Chinese history, subjects you know nothing about? When Hargadon was admissions dean at Stanford, he told parents to worry if their children were earning all A's by the end of the first quarter, which showed they were only taking subjects they would do well in. "College is a great feast from which to choose," he says. "Don't order the same meal every day."

COMPREHENSION CHECK

Directions: Answer the first five questions without looking back. The last five questions require scanning. More directions will be given when you get to them.

1.   What is the thesis or main idea of the essay? _____

_____

2.   T/F   The most unsuccessful students are those who are not actively involved in their education.

3.   Social contacts are
    a.   something you should temporarily give up while in college
    b.   distractions to good study habits
    c.   as important to surviving college as reading
    d.   none of the above

4.   Advice given for keeping current is
    a.   don't skip classes
    b.   get notes from someone if you do have to miss class
    c.   never fall more than a week behind in reading assignments
    d.   all of the above

5.   Explain what the following statement means: "College is a great feast from

which to choose. Don't order the same meal every day." _____

_____

_____

_____

Scan back through the article for the answers to the following five questions. The number after the question refers to the paragraph in the reading selection where you can find the answer.

6. What technique for studying is mentioned that you have already been taught to do? (10) _____

_____

7. Who is the author of *Conquering College Life: How to Be a Winner at College?* (12) _____

_____

8. How should you view college? (17) _____

_____

9. What is the best time to study? (9) _____

_____

10. What advice is given for choosing a major? (16) _____

_____

VOCABULARY CHECK

Directions: Define the following italicized words from the article.

1. find someone who can be a *mentor*

_____

2. *formulate* some questions

_____

3. the *essence* of what you read

_____

4. time *elapses*

_____

5. watch your grade *plummet*

_____

6. their *ultimate* career path

_____

7. a *rational* animal

_____

8. their *inspirational* teaching style

_____

9. their *priorities* are different

_____

10. feel *compelled* to

_____

Record the results of both your comprehension and vocabulary checks on the Student Record Chart on page 495. Make certain that you understand any problems that you may have had before going on to the next chapter.

CHAPTER 5

Developing Speed of Comprehension

How fast a person reads is irrelevant if good comprehension doesn't match the speed. Yet, with a little training, most people can easily increase their reading rate without a loss in comprehension. Most people read as slowly as they do because they've never been shown how to read faster.

There are several factors that need to be considered when discussing reading speed. First, not everything can be nor should be read quickly. How fast you read depends on your *purpose* for reading. In the last chapter you were shown how and when to skim and scan. Surveying to get an idea of what you will be reading, looking for specific items, and reviewing for tests are purposes that allow fast reading rates. You don't need to read everything on the page. But if you have been assigned to write an essay about a poem in your English textbook, you may need to read that poem several times before you can even begin to get an idea for your essay. You may need to look up many of the definitions of the words used, considering their connotative meanings. You may need to consider the rhyme schemes used and the form of the poem. You will probably even read it aloud. The reading and understanding of that poem may take longer than the reading of fifty pages in a psychology text. Reading rates vary with reading purposes.

A second factor in reading speed has to do with your *familiarity with the material* being read. For instance, if you read a great deal of material on computers and know the jargon of computer literacy, chances are you can read articles, textbooks, and computer manuals more quickly than you might read materials on subjects you know little about. Most professionals can read materials in their fields rather quickly because much of it is familiar already. Time isn't wasted reading slowly and carefully information already known. A good reader will race quickly over familiar information and only slow down on new or unfamiliar material.

A third reason most people read more slowly than they need to is from *poor habits*. Old reading habits are hard to lose. Since most people are never trained to read quickly, reading habits learned early in life are never broken. Researchers have found that training in four areas can help people speed up their reading with no loss in comprehension. These are (1) *development of visual perception*, (2) *reduction of vocalization*, (3) *vocabulary level*, and (4) *practice in reading faster*. Let's look at each one of these.

DEVELOPMENT OF VISUAL PERCEPTION

In order to read rapidly, we must see correctly the words being read. Our eyes only "see" what we are reading when they make brief pauses known as *eye fixations*. As you are reading right now, your eyes are making slight pauses, from three to five stops per second. In fact, we cannot read while our eyes are in motion. How many words you can accurately "see" during these fixation pauses also has to do with how fast you can read. Those readers who need to fixate on every word are naturally going to be slower than those who can take in three or four words per eye fixation.

These fixation pauses need to be quick and accurate; otherwise, reading will be slow and comprehension poor. For instance, inaccurate perception could cause a statement such as

He thought it might taste bitter.

to seem to read

He taught it night taste bitten.

Such inaccurate perception causes not only a lack of comprehension because it makes no sense, but forces the reader to reread the passage, resulting in a very slow reading rate. The fewer and faster the eye fixations, the faster the reading rate.

Related to this is another problem called *regression*. Regression is a tendency or need to back up on a line and reread part or all of it. Regression is not the same thing as rereading consciously. There are times when we need to reread something. However, regression is just a bad habit that has developed because of poor vocabulary, poor eye fixations, or just lack of training. It is a habit that can and must be overcome if speed of reading is to be gained.

In the last chapter, drills on rapid word and phrase perception were used to help you skim and scan faster. A few more of these are provided in this chapter to help you overcome regression tendencies and to develop visual clarity in perceiving words and phrases at a faster rate of speed.

REDUCTION OF VOCALIZATION

You may have seen people reading to themselves but their lips are moving. Some people, unknown to themselves, actually read aloud even though they think they are reading silently. This habit is known as *vocalization*. When we first learn to read, we are taught to read orally. We sound out the words to help us identify and understand their meaning. Some readers never get enough practice in overcoming vocalization and it gets carried into their adult reading habits.

While many people don't actually vocalize when they read, most *subvocalize*. Subvocalization is sounding out in the head the words the eyes see. While there is nothing wrong with this habit, it limits reading speeds because of the time it takes to sound out the words in your head. Our minds can work much faster than we can speak. Except for some forms of reading, we don't read for sound; we read for the meaning beyond the sounds. By reading for ideas, not sounds, our comprehension grows. Fast readers claim they don't need to hear the sound of the words to comprehend them. They respond to the visual shape and position of the words in sentences for meaning. However, some subvocalization will always occur at some point as we read.

The same drills that can help you develop accurate word and phrase recognition can also help overcome vocalization and some subvocalization. Force yourself to read so quickly on these drills that you don't have time to sound out all the words or phrases, but learn to respond to their meaning through shape.

VOCABULARY LEVEL

You have no doubt noticed that there are many drills dealing with vocabulary in this text. As mentioned earlier, a good vocabulary is the backbone to good reading. If you don't have a strong vocabulary, reading comprehension suffers. It follows that a strong vocabulary and an awareness of how words are positioned in sentences is also a step toward faster reading. Consequently, vocabulary will continue to be stressed throughout this book. It is hoped that you are continually expanding yours.

PRACTICE IN READING FASTER

Developing speed of comprehension means more than recognizing words and phrases quickly, overcoming vocalization, and enlarging your vocabulary. It requires an understanding of what words mean and how they are used in context; it requires all the skills this unit has been presenting, such as knowing where to find main ideas and supporting details, identifying an author's thesis, and knowing when and where to read carefully or to skim or scan.

If you *really* want to increase your reading rate, do the following in addition to what this book offers:

1. Set aside at least 20 minutes a day to practice reading faster than you normally do. Since most of your reading will be study-type reading, you need to practice on materials you won't be tested on. Use newspapers, easy reading magazines, and novels that aren't important for good grades.
2. Practice at a regular time every day. Don't practice when you are tired.
3. Don't worry if you feel you aren't getting much comprehension at first. You probably aren't. But you need to stretch yourself. Remember, you are trying to break years of reading habits that feel comfortable. Anything different or new will naturally seem awkward at first.

This chapter provides more training for developing the areas just mentioned. Use the drills to continue practicing what has been taught and to consciously attempt to raise your speed of comprehension when possible. Use the drills to experiment, to try new approaches, and to break out of habits that may be holding you back from better and faster reading.

A. Developing Visual Perception

Drill   A-1: DEVELOPING WORD RECOGNITION

Directions: The following five sets of word recognition drills are similar to the ones you did in the last chapter. The object is to move your eyes quickly from left to right along each line looking for the word by the number. Each time the word by the number appears on the line, make a quick mark with your pen or pencil to show that you saw it. The following tips are important:

1.   Don't look back on a line. Looking back could cause you to develop regression habits, the very thing you want to overcome.
2.   Don't sound out every word your eyes see. Try to respond to the visual shape of the word you are looking for.
3.   Emphasize speed, not accuracy, so that you can get used to moving faster than you do now.
4.   Don't worry about mistakes. Rapid visual perception takes place in the mind, even though you can't physically match that speed as you mark the words.
5.   Have some fun racing the clock. What have you got to lose?

Set 1

Begin timing.

1.   adopt   adopt   adapt   adapt   adapt   adopt
2.   deplore   deplace   deplace   deplore   deplore   deplore
3.   curtail   curtain   curtain   curtail   curtain   curtail
4.   implore   implore   implore   implant   implant   implore
5.   reduce   redeem   redeem   redeem   reduce   reduce
6.   relish   relish   release   release   relish   relish
7.   wrest   wrist   wrist   wrist   wrist   wrest
8.   obscene   obsess   obsess   obsess   observe   observe
9.   counsel   council   counsel   council   counsel   counsel
10. meditate   mediate   mediate   mediate   meditate   mediate
11. feint   feint   faint   feint   faint   faint
12. pensive   pension   pension   pensive   pensive   pension
13. calm   calm   calm   clam   clam   calm
14. severe   severe   serene   serene   serene   severe
15. reverie   reverence   reverence   reverence   reverie   reverie

Time: _____44_____ **seconds.**

Look over each line carefully. Did you mark the correct word? Did you mark it each time it appeared? Did you go back on line 8? The word "obscene" does not appear on the line. It was left out deliberately to see whether or not you would go back to look. Remember, don't regress; don't sound out words in your head, at least not every word on the line; and don't worry about missing any words. For now, speed of eye movement is being stressed.

Number of lines correct: ___13_____

Set 2

Begin timing.

1.	swine	swine swipe swipe swine swine
2.	pervade	prevent prevent prevent pervade pervade
3.	purge	purge plunge plunge plunge purge
4.	portent	pretend pretend portent portent portent
5.	chide	chimes chimes chide chimes chide
6.	permeate	permeate permeate permit permit permit
7.	defiance	defence defence defiance defence defiance
8.	restraint	restraint restrict restrict restraint restraint
9.	transfigure	transference transference transference transfigure
10.	defective	detective defective defective defective detective
11.	frugal	fragile frugal fragile frugal fragile
12.	hostile	hospital hospital hospital hostile hostile
13.	offensive	offense offense offensive offense offensive
14.	process	process procede procede process process
15.	inane	insane insane insane inane inane

Time: _____38_____ seconds. Check each line carefully for mistakes.

Number of lines correct: _____15_____

Set 3

Begin timing.

1.	stationery	stationary stationary stationary stationery
2.	sanction	suction suction suction sanction sanction
3.	valiant	variant valiant valiant variant valiant
4.	servile	servant servant servant servile servile
5.	impart	impart impart imprint imprint impart
6.	martial	marital marital martial marital martial
7.	harlot	harbor harlot harbor harbor harlot
8.	canon	canon cannon cannon cannon canon
9.	momentum	memento memento memento memento momentum
10.	initiative	initiate initiative initiate initiative initiate
11.	majority	majority minority minority minority majority
12.	indent	indulge indulge indulge indent indent
13.	involved	invented invented invented involved invented
14.	internal	internal intended intended internal intended
15.	digest	divest divest divest divest digest

Time: _____28_____ seconds. Check each line carefully for mistakes.

Number of lines correct: _____14_____

Set 4

Begin timing.

1.	discrete	discrete	discover	discover	discover	discrete
2.	exalt	exalt	exalt	exact	exact	exalt
3.	qualify	quality	quality	qualify	qualify	quality
4.	imperial	imperial	impervious	impervious	imperial	impervious
5.	commend	command	command	command	command	commend
6.	bibliography	bibliography	biography	bibliography	biography	biography
7.	revel	revel	reveal	reveal	revel	revel
8.	intent	intend	intent	intend	intent	intent
9.	narrative	narrative	narration	narration	narrative	narration
10.	watt	watt	wait	wait	watt	watt
11.	radial	radius	radial	radius	radial	radius
12.	antiseptic	antecedent	antecedent	antiseptic	antecedent	antecedent
13.	explosive	explosion	explosive	explosion	explosive	explosion
14.	disease	despair	disease	disease	despair	disease
15.	caucus	circus	circus	caucus	circus	caucus

Time: _____30_____ seconds. Check each line carefully for mistakes.

Number of lines correct: __14__

Set 5

Begin timing.

1.	consumer	consumes	consumes	consumer	consumes	consumer
2.	collision	collusion	collusion	collusion	collusion	collision
3.	studious	student	studious	student	studious	student
4.	pleasant	pleasure	pleasure	pleasure	pleasant	pleasure
5.	tolerant	tolerable	tolerable	tolerable	tolerant	tolerant
6.	courage	currency	courage	currency	currency	courage
7.	flatter	flatter	flatter	flatten	flatter	flatten
8.	revised	reviewed	reviewed	revised	reviewed	reviewed
9.	freak	frank	frank	frank	freak	freak
10.	placid	placid	placard	placard	placard	placard
11.	bungle	bugle	bungle	bugle	bungle	bugle
12.	astonish	astound	astound	astonish	astound	astound
13.	instigate	investigate	investigate	instigate	investigate	instigate
14.	construct	construct	contract	contract	contract	contract
15.	fini	finish	finish	fini	finish	fini

Time: _____25_____ seconds. Check each line carefully for mistakes.

Number of lines correct: __15__

Drill A-2: DEVELOPING PHRASE READING

Directions: Use the next five sets of phrase-reading drills to help you develop
your ability to read whole phrases rather than one word at a time. As you do these
drills, move your eyes from left to right, looking for the key phrase. Every time the
key phrase appears, mark it quickly. Don't move back or regress on any line. Work so
quickly that you can't sound aloud or in your head all the words you see. The only

sounds you should be hearing are the words in the key phrases. Work as fast as you can, experimenting with faster rates of speed than you are used to. Mistakes are not as important as doing the drills correctly for their intended purpose. Have some fun!

Set 1

Key phrase: **seating thousands**

Begin timing.

standing in shade	standing in shade	semblance of speed
something for success	seating thousands	seating thousands
semblance of speed	semblance of speed	seems to me
seating thousands	still stands there	still stands there
still stands there	seating hundreds	seating hundreds
seems to me	something for success	something for success
standing in shade	seating thousands	semblance of speed
seating thousands	something for success	seating thousands
semblance of speed	seating thousands	seems to me
something for success	semblance of speed	still stands there
seating thousands	seems to me	seating thousands
still stands there	still stands there	semblance of speed
seems to me	seating hundreds	something for success
		seating hundreds

Time: _____ 15 _____ seconds

The key phrase appears nine times. Check your responses.

Number of key phrases you marked: _____ 9 _____ out of 9

Set 2

Key phrase: **a cleaner operation**

Begin timing.

a century capitalist	a chief reason	a contemporary way
a cleaner operation	a cleaner oven	a century capitalist
a better way	a contemporary way	a chief reason
a contemporary way	a class conflict	a cleaner operation
a class conflict	a cleaner operation	a better way
a competitive society	a century capitalist	a class conflict
a cleaner operation	a competitive society	a competitive society
a contemporary way	a competitive society	a cleaner operation
a century capitalist	a century capitalist	a century capitalist
a chief reason	a chief reason	a contemporary way
a class conflict	a cleaner operation	a cleaner oven
a cleaner operation	a class conflict	a class conflict
a competitive society	a cleaner oven	a competitive society
		a chief reason

Time: _____ 9 _____ seconds

The key phrase appears seven times. Check your responses.

Number of key phrases you marked: _____ 6 _____ out of 7

Set 3

Key phrase: **he wanted it**

Begin timing.

to this day   he wanted it   like no other   in a troubled world   she wanted it   shake your hand   to this day   no more bad times   a popular classic   should not have   he wanted it   nor can I   much of the lure   we wanted it   to test your luck   almost too much   within the limit   enjoyed the idea   he wanted it   expect the unexpected   in all those areas   nice and easy   inherent in us   show to remember   he wanted it   over the hill   not on your life   to look upon   trouble and expense   not now or ever   we wanted it   when we were young   inherent in us   never on time   he wanted it   not now   heard it before   may be wrong   over the edge   he wanted it

Time: _____ seconds

The key phrase appears six times. Check your responses.

Number of key phrases you marked: _____ out of 6

Set 4

Key phrase: **much of the lure**

Begin timing.

struggle to win   much of the lure   nor can I   music should be   like no other   much of the time   a paper doll   within the limit   much of the lure   like all others   much of the time   a popular classic   much of the land   much of the lure   compared to what   over the hill   like no other   shake your hand   to this day   share the land   much of the lure   struggle to win   within the limit   much of the time   compared to what   much of the lure   share the land   a popular classic   like no other   much of the lure   enjoyed the idea   music should be   much of the time   much of the lure   boggles the mind   much of the lure   share the land   to look upon   over the edge   much of the lure

Time: _____ seconds

The key phrase appears ten times. Check your responses.

Number of key phrases you marked: _____ out of 10

Set 5

Key phrase: **good at its thing**

Begin timing.

once in a lifetime   what I wanted   good at it   over and over   good at its thing
may be vulgar   expect to win   nor can I   heard it before   good at its thing
in all those areas   much of the lure   over the ground   not displeased   good at
its thing   its own reward   not for me   never on time   its own reward   good
at its thing   the current passion   on the market   not now or ever   endless
flirtation   good at its thing   what I wanted   something just beyond   endless
remarks   good at its thing   heard it before   to look at   endless trouble   may
be wrong   within the limit   good at its thing

Time: _____ seconds

The key phrase appears seven times. Check your responses.

Number of key phrases you marked: _____ out of 7

B. Eliminating Vocalization

Drill   B-1: ELIMINATING VOCALIZATION

Directions: If you have been doing the previous drills correctly, chances are you are not vocalizing or moving your lips as you read. But here's a way to find out. Place a pencil or a pen lightly between your lips. Don't hold it in your teeth. As you read the following drill, the pencil or pen should stay in your mouth. If it wiggles or falls out, you may be moving your lips.

Read the following paragraph as fast as you can. Move your eyes quickly across the lines. Try to respond to the meaning of the paragraph through the shapes of the words, not the sounds. When you notice the phrase *don't vocalize* somewhere in the paragraph, stop reading, and mark down your time. Try to finish in less than ten seconds.

Begin timing.

If you're planning to buy or start a business, don't use the word *enterprise* after its name; it makes your firm sound like an amateur operation. That's the number one in a list of 101 business don'ts. Among the other nine lists included to help you with a business start-up are new business opportunities for both grown-ups and teenagers, things to do before buying a business, and a directory of useful business publications. The booklet is don't vocalize published by a business consulting group, Success Group, in Palm Beach Gardens, Florida.

Time: _____ **seconds**

Drill B-2: ELIMINATING VOCALIZATION: REDUCING SUBVOCALIZATION

Directions: If you noticed the pencil in your mouth wiggling or if it fell out, continue practicing reading with it in your mouth. In this drill there are two paragraphs. You will be asked to read them three times. Record your time for each of the three readings. Try to go faster each time by noticing that the more familiar you are with the paragraphs the easier it is to respond to the shapes of the words rather than their sounds.

Begin timing.

Breathes there an American who hasn't at one time said, "Gee, if I'd gotten in on McDonald's (or Domino's Pizza or Holiday Inns or Radio Shack) when their franchises were cheap, I'd be rich today." There's just enough truth to that remark to cause tens of thousands of would-be business owners to take the plunge each year, hoping they have a hold of the next Big Mac of franchising. They aren't crazy. Although Dun & Bradstreet says 55% of all new businesses fail within five years, Commerce Department figures suggest the failure rate of franchise units is about one-third of that.

Now comes the rub. Buying a franchise of a well-established brand-name company is apt to be financially out of the reach for all but the wealthy. Even if the cost is relatively low, key territories may be closed to new entrants. What you're left with are mostly newer companies with short track records and names that are not widely recognized.

Time: _____ **seconds**

Reading 2

Now read the passage again, this time faster. Begin timing.

Time: _____ **seconds**

Reading 3

Now read it again, going even faster. Begin timing.

Time: _____ **seconds**

C. Rapid Word Identification

Drill   C-1: RAPID WORD MEANING RECOGNITION

Directions: In the next five sets of exercises, a definition appears by the number. Somewhere along the same line is a word that fits that definition. As you move your eyes from left to right looking for the correct word, don't regress or look back on a line. If you get to the end of the line and have not found the word, go directly to the next line. Try not to sound out every word you see. Instead try to respond to the shape of the words; that is, try to recognize a word by its shape rather than its sound. Research shows that we can recognize words and phrases much faster visually than in the time it takes to sound out the words in our heads.

Again, mistakes are not as important as doing the drill correctly. These are just one of several types of exercises designed to help you increase your comprehension speed. Answers are provided after each set, but don't look at them until you have finished it. They are all good words to know.

Set 1

Begin timing.

1.	decisive, convincing	deficient conclusive adequate strewn oral
2.	distinguishing mark	comfort benefactor stigma ignore silhouette
3.	ask earnestly for, beg	subside petite invoke disuse enhance
4.	make believe, pretend	dissect feign enthrall seethe dilate
5.	unaffected, natural	dainty coy petite naive silly
6.	very important, critical	crucial peculiar regular loyal indifferent
7.	find value or amount of	guess check evaluate deduce transform
8.	obstinate, headstrong	genteel lazy mediocre dogged eccentric
9.	skillful, nimble	mature deft unskilled certain modest
10.	instruct, teach, inform	steadfast consider reject enlighten sincere
11.	lowliness, modesty	humiliate humility charity honesty sincere
12.	inhabit	provoke immigrant populate invade density
13.	little, of small size	narrow petite amazon huge titanic
14.	repeal, cancel, withdraw	display produce keep persist revoke
15.	lack of use	prepare disuse utilize stagnant exploit

Time: _____ **seconds**

Check your answers with these:

1. conclusive   2. stigma   3. invoke   4. feign   5. naive   6. crucial   7. evaluate
8. dogged   9. deft   10. enlighten   11. humility   12. populate   13. petite
14. revoke   15. disuse

Number correct: _____

Make vocabulary cards for words you need to learn.

Set 2

Begin timing.

1.	withdrawn, isolated	sequester secluded allocate distract distant
2.	vital force	inactive creativity reality vitality alien
3.	captivate, fascinate	origin archaic enthrall entangle entrance
4.	forgetfulness	oblivion ecstasy jubilant hard remember
5.	flesh-eating	scrimmage diligent carnivorous help hoard
6.	fill with energy	desirable invigorate episode profit mire
7.	skilled, expert	sober proficient serious neglect rejected
8.	rough fight or struggle	encounter congregation scrimmage entail fit
9.	hard-working	diaphragm exuberant discourage diligent keep
10.	discouraged, dejected	joyful elated spirited anxious despondent
11.	soft deep mud, bog	caress mire mangle stroke delve
12.	very abundant	hysteria sparse barren steep exuberant
13.	search carefully	meditate delve decay foliage glance
14.	senseless excitement	disaster somber hysteria happy critical
15.	being alone	together distant foreign solitude crowded

Time: _____ seconds

Check your answers with these:

1. secluded 2. vitality 3. enthrall 4. oblivion 5. carnivorous 6. invigorate

7. proficient 8. scrimmage 9. diligent 10. despondent 11. mire 12. exuberant

13. delve 14. hysteria 15. solitude

Number correct: _____

Make vocabulary cards for words you need to learn.

Set 3

Begin timing.

1.	not active, sluggish	deadly stagnant havoc induce relate
2.	tell a story	define conclusion drama narrate deduce
3.	mysterious	patient prevent cryptic opaque persuade
4.	very famous, great	illustrious customary infamous unknown mite
5.	lead on, persuade	trace immobile induce lecture transparent
6.	devastation, ruin	detect havoc demented transitory develop
7.	a feudal estate	mediocre radiate manor camp malady
8.	insane, crazy	eliminate control relieve demented reverie
9.	average, ordinary	naive harmonious mediocre superior equal
10.	get rid of	eradicate adorn refuse stupefy dilate
11.	dreamy thoughts	uproar joy mirth reverie fury
12.	sickness, illness	mutation bedlam malady recovery health
13.	uproar, confusion	dispel conflict ambush massacre bedlam
14.	restore to good condition	remove exaggerate rehabilitate donate aid
15.	disperse, scatter	defeat pervade decide dispel compel

Time: _____ seconds

Check your answers with these:

1. stagnant 2. narrate 3. cryptic 4. illustrious 5. induce 6. havoc

7. manor 8. demented 9. mediocre 10. eradicate 11. reverie 12. malady

13. bedlam 14. rehabilitate 15. dispel

Number correct: _____

Make vocabulary cards for words you need to learn.

Set 4

Begin timing.

1.	destruction, ruin	retain demolition revise nimble collect
2.	appearing true	plausible powerful pleasing athletic retreat
3.	active, forceful	approach untamed dynamic foreign discard
4.	gash, cut	uproot incision valve ascend reduce
5.	curious	lost pointed inquisitive related ideal
6.	funeral song	dirge dense wake plot vault
7.	center, core	atom nucleus seed order require
8.	incomplete, defective	revise sufficient perfect deficient super
9.	require, demand	persuade design restore prepare necessitate
10.	shorten, reduce	pleasant curtail deject clever rare
11.	bearable, endurable	remove mixture tolerable change transfer
12.	change, alteration	mutation create ripe balance mute
13.	god or goddess	conserve spirit chorus deity invalid
14.	arrange data	design form purpose harmony tabulate
15.	skillful, expert	adept strong lazy smooth pretense

Time: _____ seconds

Check your answers with these:

1. demolition 2. plausible 3. dynamic 4. incision 5. inquisitive 6. dirge
7. nucleus 8. deficient 9. necessitate 10. curtail 11. tolerable 12. mutation
13. deity 14. tabulate 15. adept

Number correct: _____

Make vocabulary cards for words you need to learn.

Set 5

Begin timing.

1.	indifferent, languid	heavy listless energetic serene cheerful
2.	make greater, add to	exhaust exhale empire interest enhance
3.	return to health	recuperate reiterate reenlist regain hope
4.	hidden room or vault	cave cramp crypt saturn embryo
5.	foreign	unusual different alienate exotic ornamental
6.	not ripe, not full-grown	immune immature innocent adolescent mature
7.	hard to get at	obtain procure produce inaccessible hold
8.	impulse, force	continue momentum action delivery adequate
9.	before proper time	accident promptly deliberate premature aid
10.	having to do with cities	metropolis town urban residential suburban
11.	annoy	enervate harass fluster yearly nuisance
12.	of or like a college	connect collector collegiate campus quarry
13.	grind to powder or dust	pulverize desolate distant contract halt
14.	lingo, slang	seclude jargon vital enthrall expand
15.	become larger or wider	oblivion scholar dilate capacity captured

Time: _____ seconds

Check your answers with these:

1. listless 2. enhance 3. recuperate 4. crypt 5. exotic 6. immature
7. inaccessible 8. momentum 9. premature 10. urban 11. harass 12. collegiate
13. pulverize 14. jargon 15. dilate

Number correct: _____

Make vocabulary cards for words you need to learn.

Drill   C-2: VOCABULARY QUICK QUIZ

Directions: Match the definitions in the column on the right with the words in the list on the left. Write the letter of the correct answer in the blanks provided. There are more definitions than you need.

Words

Definitions

_____ **1.** crucial

a. cancel, repeal

_____ **2.** populate

b. discouraged, dejected

_____ **3.** revoke

c. very important, critical

_____ **4.** secluded

d. insane, crazy

_____ **5.** despondent

e. funeral song

_____ **6.** delve

f. get rid of

_____ **7.** stagnant

g. isolated

_____ **8.** demented

h. persuade

_____ **9.** eradicate

i. mysterious

_____ **10.** mediocre

j. reduce, shorten

_____ **11.** induce

k. sluggish, not active

_____ **12.** incision

l. average, ordinary

_____ **13.** curtail

m. inhabit

_____ **14.** nucleus

n. gash, cut

_____ **15.** dirge

o. arrange data

_____ **16.** listless

p. center, core

_____ **17.** tabulate

q. return to health

_____ **18.** deity

r. languid, indifferent

_____ **19.** recuperate

s. look into

_____ **20.** cryptic

t. pertaining to God

u. disperse, scatter

v. devastation, ruin

D. Timed Reading Practices

The following articles are for timed reading practice. Remember that word—practice. They are provided to give you practice in reading faster, in developing your comprehension, and in learning vocabulary in context. In addition, some of the questions you will be asked to answer are designed to help you continue practicing your skimming and scanning.

The articles deal with a variety of subjects. Some will be more interesting to you than others. Interest can affect your speed and your comprehension. In some cases, you may get "hung up" on the article's subject and forget you are practicing reading skills. Other articles will be less interesting, and your comprehension will suffer because you are not concentrating. Try to remember that you are using these articles to develop your reading versatility. Use these drills to break old habits, not confirm them.

In all cases, read faster than you normally do, but not so fast that you don't get the main idea of the article. Speed is never more important than comprehension, but you are practicing for faster speeds. Sometimes your comprehension scores may drop because of a faster reading speed. That's all right here because you are practicing. This is the place to make mistakes. The point is that the more you push yourself to read faster during practice, the faster you will read when you return to what you think is your "normal" reading rate.

Learn from the errors you make in comprehension and vocabulary checks. Understanding why you miss a question is more important than missing it. Sometimes answer keys contain mistakes. Don't be afraid to challenge an answer. Often discussing the contents of an article or particular questions about the article helps develop comprehension skills.

Use the vocabulary checks to continue developing your word power. Learning words in context is the best way to strengthen your vocabulary. See how the words are used and make vocabulary cards for any new words you want to learn.

Your instructor may ask you to do one or two word or phrase perception exercises before doing a timed reading. It's a good way to warm up before the timed practice.

So remember, the following articles are for practice in rate, comprehension, and vocabulary development. As you record the results of your efforts on the Timed Reading Chart on page 495, don't be concerned if your scores go up and down; that is not unusual. What you learn about reading versatility is more important than the scores.

Drill   D-1: WARM-UP EXERCISE

Directions: Below are two rapid phrase perception exercises. Do each one separately under the pressure of time. Try to finish each exercise in 15 seconds or less.

Key phrase: **the casino contains**

Begin timing.

the house contains	the casino contains
the less cycles	the classical writers
the casino contains	the casino remains
the classical writers	the house contains
the catastrophic intervention	the less cycles
the casino remains	the catastrophic intervention
the house contains	compensation for frustrations
compensation for frustrations	the casino contains
the casino contains	the Christian church
the house contains	the classical writers
the casino remains	the house contains
the less cycles	the casino remains
the classical writers	the Christian church
the casino contains	the casino contains
the casino remains	the less cycles
the catastrophic intervention	the classical writers
the casino contains	the catastrophic intervention
the house contains	compensation for frustrations
the less cycles	the Christian church
the classical writers	the house contains

Time: _____ seconds
The key phrase appears seven times. Check your responses.

Number of key phrases you marked: _____ out of 7

Key phrase: **its own reward**

Begin timing.

in our society   a showgirl's smile   forever and ever   what I wanted   its own regard   inherent in us   over and over   its own reward   hit the right note over the hill   on the market   cost the management   its own reward   when we were young   endless flirtation   compared to what   its own reward   something just beyond   endless remarks   on the way   endless rewards   to look at   its own reward   enjoyed it some   to look at   not on your life   nor can I   music should   its own reward   to test your luck   struggle to see   in all those areas   within the limit   its own reward   may be wrong   expect to lose almost too much   may be good   its own reward   to this day   like no other in a troubled world   its own reward   over and over

Time: _____ seconds
The key phrase appears eight times. Check your responses.

Number of key phrases you marked: _____ out of 8

Drill   D-2

Directions: Quickly skim the following article by checking the title, first paragraph, headings, and last paragraph in as few seconds as possible. Then read the article rapidly, looking for the answer to the question raised in the title and the headings. Remember, you are practicing comprehension speed. Record your total reading time when you have finished.

Begin timing. Starting time:_____

CAN BILLIONS BUY SURVIVAL IN ATOMIC WAR?

Some Contend Americans Can Be Protected. Others Insist Civil Defense Is Useless. At Stake: Vast Sums of Money—and a Lot More Besides.

1   Government officials are nearing a difficult decision on whether to spend billions of dollars to protect American civilians in event of a nuclear attack.

2   The choice, which could mean life or death for millions, is being forced by international events and technical developments after years in which the U.S. largely ignored civil defense while the Soviet Union pressed efforts to protect its population.

3   The question now: Should the U.S. follow the lead of Russia and other countries—such as China, Finland, Sweden, Norway and Switzerland—to develop an intricate and costly program to reduce casualties in an all-out missile war? Or, despite the urge to take such action, would any such efforts be fruitless as well as a huge waste of national resources?

NO RESULTS

4   Officials reluctantly concede that the 100 million dollars a year the U.S. is spending on civil defense has bought little or no real protection. Bardyl R. Tirana, who headed the Defense Civil Preparedness Agency for the last 2½ years, told Congress that the amount being spent on civil defense was money down a rathole.

5   "At the present time, the United States has, for all practical purposes, no genuine defense against the threat of nuclear attack," Tirana declared.

6   Now, for the first time since the early 1960s, serious attention is focused on the adequacy of and need for civil defense. Pentagon experts have come up with two plans—both admittedly imperfect—to save up to two-thirds of the U.S. population in a nuclear war.

7   One proposal calls for a massive program of building underground urban blast shelters to which people could rush in the half hour between the time an attack against the U.S. was launched from Russia and the time the missiles landed. The shelters would cost about 90 billion dollars, nearly three times as much as the new MX-missile system.

8   The other plan calls for preparations to evacuate major cities if war seems imminent. The program would cost an estimated 2 billion dollars. A reduced version of the empty-the-cities plan is pending in Congress.

9   There are serious problems, however, with evacuating cities. Getting everyone out into the country may take a week or more—no help in the event of a true surprise attack, which could come with less than a half-hour warning that missiles had been launched. Also, Pentagon experts figure that even a false alarm would cost the nation 90 billion dollars in lost production and other expenses to clear the cities, wait a week and then let people return. Faced with that kind of bill, a President might hesitate too long before ordering an evacuation.

10   The Soviet Union has combined the two approaches. It has built about 15,000 blast shelters that could protect national and local leaders and 10 to 20 million others. The rest of the population would be moved out of the cities, many of them on foot.

11   The Soviet program involves the full-time efforts of about 100,000 persons, according to the Central Intelligence Agency study, and would cost more than 2 billion dollars a year if duplicated in the U.S. Some American experts think the system is so good that it would help the Russians "win" a nuclear war. Others insist it would save relatively few lives and have little effect on a conflict.

12   U.S. civil-defense planning is being taken over by a new agency, the Federal Emergency Management Agency, which pulls together five government units dealing with everything from home fires to nuclear attack. John W. Macy, chairman of the Civil Service Commission in the Kennedy and Johnson administrations, heads it.

13   Macy faces formidable problems in devising a program that is both realistic and economically feasible to cope with nuclear war. Some of the serious questions that must be faced:

WHAT IS TO BE DONE ABOUT PEOPLE WHO LIVE IN ESPECIALLY HIGH-RISK AREAS?

14   In the event of a surprise attack aimed at destroying weapons that could retaliate against the Soviet Union—the most likely contingency—the greatest casualties would not be inflicted on New York or Chicago or Los Angeles, but on central Missouri.

15   Government experts predict that at least 300 warheads would thunder down on the 150 Minuteman-missile silos in the Whiteman Air Force Base complex in west central Missouri. In that event, more than half the state's population of 4.8 million inhabitants is considered likely to die.

16   Blast shelters might cut that toll in half. What needs to be decided is whether residents of Missouri and other states where missiles, bomber bases and submarine docks are situated should be given this special protection.

WILL GOVERNMENT SURVIVE A NUCLEAR WAR?

17   The federal government already has established several underground command centers in a 300-mile arc around Washington, D.C. In one of them, huge piles of currency are stored, ready to replace the nation's money supply after a war. Theoretically, teams of officials in these shelters would keep the government operating.

18   Some civil-defense experts, however, say it is more likely the country would be divided into clusters of people depending on their own resources, rather than on federal or state authorities.

19   This raises the question of whether civil-defense planning should focus on insuring the survival of existing governments or on preparing communities to fend for themselves.

EVEN IF AN EMERGENCY PROGRAM SAVES MUCH OF THE POPULATION, WHAT HAPPENS TO PEOPLE AFTER THE DUST HAS SETTLED?

20   Critics say far too little attention has been paid to chances for long-term survival of those who escape the blast and initial radioactive fallout. Even a shift in the wind, carrying fallout in an unexpected direction, could make a big difference in the number of casualties.

WOULD THE U.S. ACTUALLY HAVE A BETTER CHANCE OF SURVIVING AS A NATION IF THERE WERE MORE RUSSIANS THAN AMERICANS LIVING AT THE END OF A WAR?

21   Strange as it may sound, that question is one that the experts are afraid to ask aloud.

22   It is based on the presumption that, after a nuclear exchange, the survivors would be in a race to get production going again before they used up the food and other products grown and manufactured prior to the war. If output matched or exceeded consumption by the time the leftovers ran out, society would be on the way to recovery. If not, it could decline into a long dark age. Conceivably, the nation with fewer mouths to feed might have a better chance to rebuild.

23   It is because of sticky questions such as these that some American experts doubt that an expanded U.S. civil-defense program, or even the huge Soviet effort, would really make much difference in wartime.

24   But of one thing there is no doubt: The best civil defense to date is the mutual knowledge in the U.S. and in the Soviet Union that, no matter how much is spent on protection, a full-scale exchange of nuclear weapons is certain to be a disaster of unprecedented proportions for both sides.

Finishing time: _____

Starting time: _____ **(subtract)**

Reading time: _____

Check the Reading Conversion Chart on page 499 to determine how many words per minute you read.

WPM: _____

LITERAL COMPREHENSION CHECK

1. The author's main idea or thesis is that
   a. The government should spend billions on civil defense against nuclear attack.
   b. The government should *not* spend billions on civil defense against nuclear attack.
   c. The government should build a civil defense system to match the Soviet Union's.
   d. The government has inadequate plans for civil defense and isn't certain what to do.

2. The government is giving attention to _____ major proposals related to civil defense in case of a nuclear attack.

3. T/F   The Soviet Union has spent more money on civil defense than the United States.

4. The greatest casualties in the event of a major nuclear attack against our defense systems would occur in
   a. New York
   b. Chicago
   c. Los Angeles
   d. central Missouri

5. Approximately how much time would there be before the landing of Soviet missiles launched against the U.S.? _____

6. Considering the time factor, which of the proposed plans do experts favor in

   the event of a surprise attack? _____

   _____ Why? _____

   _____

7. Which of the following factors must the U.S. government consider in devising
   a civil defense plan? Circle all that apply.
   a. cost differential between blast shelter and evacuation plans
   b. insuring the survival of the federal government
   c. special protection for people in high risk areas
   d. whether an expanded civil defense program is even worth the effort

8. What has the U.S. government done in the Washington, D.C., area to try to

   insure its survival in the event of nuclear war? _____

   _____

   _____

9. The Soviet Union has built about 15,000 blast shelters designed to protect

   _____

   in case of nuclear attack by the U.S.

10. Why would the U.S. have a better chance of survival as a nation if there were

    more Soviet citizens than U.S. citizens living at the end of a war? _____

    _____

    _____

Number correct: _____

VOCABULARY CHECK

A. Define the underlined words in the following phrases and sentences from the
   article you just read.
1. to develop an intricate and costly program

   _____

2. would such efforts be fruitless

   _____

3. Officials reluctantly concede that the 100 million dollars a year the U.S. spends
   on civil defense has bought little protection.

   _____

4. if war seems imminent

   _____

5. Macy faces formidable problems

   _____

B. Select from the list below the proper word for each blank in the following paragraph.

exchange   presumption   decline
production   exceeded

"It is based on the (6) _____ that, after a nuclear (7) _____,

the survivors would be in a race to get (8) _____ going again.... If output

matched or (9) _____ consumption by the time leftovers ran out, society

would be on the way to recovery. If not, it could (10) _____ into a long dark

age."

Number correct: _____ **Learn any words you don't know.**

Turn to the Timed Readings Chart on page 497. Record your rate (WPM), comprehension, and vocabulary scores. Each question counts 10 percent. Do this with all of the timed readings. Discuss with your instructor any questions or problems you may have. When you make mistakes, don't worry about them; learn from them. What you learn is always more important than what you record on your chart.

Drill   D-3: WARM-UP EXERCISE

Directions: Below are two rapid phrase perception drills. Do each one separately under the pressure of time. Try to finish each exercise in 15 seconds or less.

Key phrase: **seating thousands**

Begin timing.

standing in shade	standing in shade	semblance of speed
something for success	seating thousands	seating thousands
semblance of speed	semblance of speed	seems to me
seating thousands	still stands there	still stands there
still stands there	seating hundreds	seating hundreds
seems to me	something for success	something for success
standing in shade	seating thousands	semblance of speed
seating thousands	something for success	seating thousands
semblance of speed	seating thousands	seems to me
something for success	semblance of speed	still stands there
seating thousands	seems to me	seating thousands
still stands there	still stands there	semblance of speed
seems to me	seating hundreds	something for success
		seating hundreds

Time: _____ **seconds**

The key phrase appears nine times. Check your responses.

Number of key phrases you marked: _____ **out of 9**

Key phrase: **how they felt**

Begin timing

once in a lifetime   like no other   now or never   how they felt   inherent in us   in a troubled world   how we felt   he wanted it   its own reward   in our society   not now   how they felt   heard it before   may be vulgar   to come here   how we felt   may be right   how they felt   in all those areas   may be wrong   within the limit   a class conflict   how they felt   seems to me   almost too much   shake your hand   how they felt   much of the time   over the edge   to look upon   how they felt   share the land   how we felt   boggles the mind   how they feel   much of the lure   how they felt   to this day   he wanted it   not on your life   may be wrong   inherent in us

Time: _____ **seconds**

The key phrase appears seven times. Check your responses.

Number of key phrases you marked: _____ **out of 7**

Drill **D-4**

Directions: Quickly skim the following article by checking the title, first paragraph, headings, and last paragraph in as few seconds as possible. Then read the article rapidly, looking for main ideas. Practice speed and concentration. Record your total reading time when finished.

Begin timing. Starting time: _____

USING DRUGS? YOU MAY NOT GET HIRED

Tests That Employees Call an Invasion of Privacy Are Seen by Companies as Insurance Against Accidents and Waste.

Ted Gest

1   Scores of applicants today are facing more than job-competency exams. They need to pass urine tests as well.

2   The problem is illicit drugs. Companies are cracking down to prevent accidents, absenteeism and low productivity that they blame on wide use of marijuana, cocaine and other substances ranging from illegal "angel dust" to prescription medications.

3   A new survey shows that 1 in 5 of the nation's biggest companies now give tests, and an additional 19 percent may join the trend within two years. Employers are beginning to test workers already on the payroll, and a few school systems may test both teachers and students.

4   The practice is spreading rapidly even though critics say tests are often inaccurate and that the drugs they do detect may have no effect on job performance.

5   Testing got its foothold in the armed services, which long have insisted on strict prohibition against drug use by their personnel. In recent years, business owners and government officials have turned up more and more cases of civilian mishaps linked to drugs.

Although no one has compiled a national toll of drug-caused accidents, several cases have been documented in the transportation and utility industries.

6   Drugs were a factor in a Burlington Northern rail crash in Wyoming last year in which two crewmen were killed. The railroad dismissed an engineer who had been smoking marijuana. Tests of crewmen on a train parked nearby turned up several more drug users, who also were fired.

7   The crash of a small plane last year in northern New Jersey that killed the pilot and three passengers also was the result of drug use, reports the National Transportation Safety Board. The board suspects that drug use was involved in train collisions in Arkansas, Atlanta and Miami. The Federal Aviation Administration fired three Miami air-traffic controllers found with marijuana and cocaine at work.

8   To weed out drug abusers, many firms require job applicants to submit urine for analysis that can detect a half-dozen or more drugs. The exam can find cocaine traces for two days after use and marijuana for several weeks.

9   Critics complain that the test often is inaccurate. Some samples are handled improperly, causing "false positives"—persons tagged as drug users when they are not. A study of 13 laboratories by the federal Centers for Disease Control showed an error rate of up to 66 percent. "Some testing is done by untrained people," notes Richard Hawks of the National Institute on Drug Abuse.

10   Others say initial indications of drug use should be rechecked on more-sophisticated equipment. When that is done, "results are almost 100 percent accurate," contends Claude Buller of North Carolina-based CompuChem Laboratories. Preliminary tests cost only a few dollars, but many firms don't pursue follow-up tests that often cost $50 or more.

11   When companies use the tests as a screening device, there is little that applicants can do to protest. As long as exams are required of everyone, discrimination claims are likely to fall flat. It may be a different story for tests of those already on the job, and some of these employees are charging that their privacy is being violated.

12   What may be the first drug-testing dispute to enter the courts erupted last summer in San Francisco at Southern Pacific Transportation Company, which forced nearly 500 workers without warning to submit urine samples. Computer programer Barbara Luck was dismissed after she refused to participate on privacy grounds. Luck has a lawsuit pending against the company, as does an office manager whose test showed that he had used cocaine—a charge he denies. The man says he was sent to rehabilitation classes even though a follow-up test showed no evidence of drug abuse.

13   After reports of such cases, San Francisco last month became the first major U.S. city to bar employers from ordering tests unless there is clear evidence that a worker's drug use endangers others. The measure permits tests only for police, firefighters and rescue units.

14   Even so, more public and private employers whose work involves public safety are likely to continue drug checks. Burlington Northern intensified testing after last year's crash. Unions unsuccessfully challenged a plan by the Federal Railroad Administration to require all railroad job seekers to submit to tests.

15   Urinalysis may spread in sports. Big-league baseball was embarrassed last summer when the Pittsburgh trial of a drug dealer included extensive testimony on cocaine use by major-league players. Commissioner Peter Ueberroth has asked all 650 players to take tests. But the players' union has balked, arguing that all players shouldn't be made to comply if only a few have a drug problem.

16   Moves to test teachers and students have run into roadblocks. A New York judge barred urinalysis for teachers on Long Island, and a New Jersey judge ruled December 10 against a plan to test high-school students. The courts said the procedure violated constitutional protections against unreasonable searches.

17   No court has stopped testing in a private firm, although the question of whether privacy rights are violated by such procedures may eventually end up in the Supreme Court.

18   In the meantime, the question facing businesses is whether testing is worth the costs. Some companies insist that it is. After Pacific Gas & Electric Company began to screen applicants, injuries among newly hired construction workers fell 40 percent. But North Carolina toxicologist Arthur McBay says he has seen no scientific evidence that the "millions of dollars being spent on handy-dandy screening programs" have reduced drug problems on the job.

19   Still, growing public pressure to do something about substance abuse will make screening routine in many employment offices.

Finishing time: _____

Starting time: _____ **(subtract)**

Reading time: _____

Check the Conversion Chart on page 499 to determine how many words per minute you read.

WPM: _____

LITERAL COMPREHENSION CHECK

1. The author's thesis or main point is that
   a. If you use drugs, you may not get hired.
   b. Drugs have been a factor in many accidents.
   c. A survey showed that 1 in 5 of the nation's biggest companies now give drug tests.
   d. Growing public pressure to do something about drug abuse on the job is causing more companies to screen applicants as well as current employees for drug use.
2. Circle the items below that were mentioned in the article as reasons for the public's growing concern over drug-related accidents.
   a. a Burlington Northern rail crash in Wyoming
   b. train collisions in Arkansas, Atlanta, and Miami
   c. a small plane crash in New Jersey that killed four people
   d. six overdose deaths in the army
3. T/F Critics of drug-use testing claim that the tests are often inaccurate and that samples are often handled improperly.
4. T/F When companies use the tests as a screening device, there is little that applicants can do to protest.
5. The first major U.S. city to bar employers from ordering drug-use testing unless there is clear evidence that a worker's drug use endangers others was
   a. Los Angeles
   b. San Francisco
   c. Chicago
   d. Philadelphia
6. Why don't many companies do follow-up tests when an error rate of up to 66 percent has been shown? _____

   _____

7. T/F As of the writing of this article, no court has stopped testing by private firms.

8. According to the article, is testing for drug use worth the cost? _____

   Explain. _____

   _____

9. T/F Unions successfully challenged a plan by the Federal Railroad Administration to require all railroad job seekers to submit to tests.
10. T/F Urine analysis tests for drug use can only detect cocaine and marijuana use.

   For every question you missed, find the place in the article that contains the correct answer. Try to determine why you missed the questions you did. If you read faster than you normally do, a score of 60 percent correct is considered good. As you get used to faster speeds, you'll discover your comprehension will also start to improve.

Number correct: _____

VOCABULARY CHECK

A. Define the underlined words in the following phrases from the article.

1. <u>scores</u> of applicants today are facing tests

   _____

2. testing got its <u>foothold</u> in the armed services

   _____

3. she has a lawsuit <u>pending</u>

   _____

4. to prevent accidents, <u>absenteeism</u> and low productivity

   _____

5. the union has <u>balked</u>

   _____

   _____

B. Select from the list below the proper word for each blank in the following paragraph:

   submit   erupted   adamantly
   coerced   dispute   routine

   What may be the first drug-testing (6) _____ to enter the

courts (7) _____ last summer in San Francisco at Southern Trans-

portation Company, which (8) _____ nearly 500 workers without

warning to (9) _____ urine samples. One employee was dis-

missed because she (10) _____ refused to participate.

Number correct: _____ **Learn any words you don't know.**

   Turn to the Timed Readings Chart on page 497. Record your WPM (words per minute), comprehension, and vocabulary scores for this article on the chart. Each question counts 10 percent. An average score is around 250 WPM with 70 percent comprehension. Discuss any problems, concerns, or questions you have with your instructor.

Drill D-5: WARM-UP EXERCISE

Directions: Below are two rapid phrase perception drills. Do each one separately under the pressure of time. Try to finish each exercise in 15 seconds or less.

Key phrase: **still stands there**

Begin timing.

standing in shade	standing in shade	semblance of speed
something for success	seating thousands	seating thousands
semblance of speed	semblance of speed	seems to me
seating thousands	still stands there	still stands there
still stands there	seating hundreds	seating hundreds
seems to me	something for success	something for success
standing in shade	seating thousands	semblance of speed
seating thousands	something for success	seating thousands
semblance of speed	seating thousands	seems to me
something for success	semblance of speed	still stands there
seating thousands	seems to me	seating thousands
still stands there	still stands there	semblance of speed
seems to me	seating hundreds	something for success
		seating hundreds

Time: _____ seconds

The key phrase appears six times. Check your responses.

Number of key phrases you marked: _____ **out of 6**

Key phrase: **how we felt**

Begin timing.

once in a lifetime   like no other   now or never   how they felt   inherent in us
in a troubled world   how we felt   he wanted it   its own reward   in our society
not now   how they felt   heard it before   may be vulgar   to come here
how we felt   may be right   how they felt   in all those areas   may be wrong
within the limit   a class conflict   how they felt   seems to me   almost too
much   shake your hand   how they felt   much of the time   over the edge
to look upon   how they felt   share the land   how we felt   boggles the mind
how they feel   much of the lure   how they felt   to this day   he wanted it   not
on your life   may be wrong   inherent in us

Time: _____ seconds

The key phrase appears three times. Check your responses.

Number of key phrases you marked: _____ **out of 3**

Drill   D-6

Directions: Quickly skim the following article by checking the title, first paragraph, headings, and last paragraph in as few seconds as possible. Then read the article as rapidly as you can, looking for the main ideas and supporting details. Remember, this is a chance to practice reading faster than you normally do. Push yourself to read quickly. You are not expected to get high comprehension scores during these practices. This does not mean that speed is more important than comprehension; the purpose here, however, is to try out faster rates than usual.

Begin timing. Starting time: _____

THE LAW OF SOCIAL CYCLES

Ravi Batra

1   While man is free to decide his own course of action, he faces limits imposed by the society in which he lives. He can determine his own evolution but not social evolution, which, in the interest of order in the universe, must follow the dictates of nature.

THE FOUR SOCIAL CLASSES

2   It can be safely stated that most social phenomena are in one way or another related to human nature. Thus, P. R. Sarkar [*Human Society,* Part 2, Proutist Universal, 1967] begins with general characteristics of the human mind. He argues that even though most people have common goals and ambitions, their methods of achieving their objectives may differ from person to person, depending on inner qualities of the individual. But some of us try to attain them by developing intellectual skills, some by developing physical skills, and some by accumulating wealth. Finally, some people have little ambition in life, and they form a class by themselves. Thus, society is basically composed of four types of people, each endowed with a different frame of mind.

WARRIORS

3   People have common objectives, but their modus operandi to attain them differs because of sharp differences in their innate abilities and qualities. Some persons, born with superior bodily strength, excel in physical skills requiring stamina, courage, and vigor. Such people are usually employed in occupations involving physical risks. Sarkar calls them persons of warrior mentality. In his view, soldiers, policemen, fire fighters, professional athletes, skilled blue-collar workers, and the like belong to the class of warriors in the sense that all these occupations require physical skills. Thus, anyone who tries to solve his problems with the help of his might and muscle can be said to have a warrior turn of mind.

INTELLECTUALS

4   There is another type of person who lacks the physical energy of the warrior but is endowed with a relatively superior intellect. Being so endowed, he or she tries to

From *The Great Depression of 1990* by Ravi Batra. Copyright © 1985 by Ravi Batra. Copyright © 1987 by Venus Books. Reprinted by permission of Simon & Schuster, Inc.

develop mental skills to do well in society. To Sarkar, everyone attempting to solve his problems with the help of his brains rather than brawn is an intellectual. Sarkar's use of the term is much broader than is generally conceived. To him, not just philosophers, writers, and scholars, but lawyers, physicians, poets, engineers, scientists, white-collar workers, and priests are intellectuals because they all utilize their minds rather than muscle power to attain their goals.

ACQUISITORS

5   There is yet another type of person who, according to Sarkar, strives to accumulate wealth to achieve what is generally regarded as the good life. Such people are also bright, but their minds run mainly after money. They are smarter than the warrior type but not as intelligent as the intellectual. Yet they are usually more affluent than the other two. Such people are called acquisitors, because virtually all their propensities are engaged in amassing wealth. To them money is all that matters in life; it alone is their key to success and prosperity. Merchants, bankers, moneylenders, businessmen, and landlords generally belong to the class of acquisitors. While other classes seek wealth to enjoy material goods, the acquisitor generally covets money for its own sake.

LABORERS

6   Finally, there is a fourth type of person who is altogether different from the other three. He is the unskilled worker or the physical laborer. He lacks the vigor of the warrior, the brilliance of the intellectual, and the accumulating instinct of the acquisitor. He is also lacking in the high ambition of the other three. His level of education is relatively low, and he is usually deficient in marketable skills. Because of these handicaps the unskilled worker is, and has always been, exploited by the rest of society. He does the work deemed dirty by others, and is the poorest among all classes. Farm workers and unskilled factory workers generally belong to the class of physical laborers.

7   Exceptions, of course, may be found among those engaged in unskilled occupations. They may be persons of keen intelligence who perhaps perform hard labor not by choice but because of economic necessity or social coercion. Such persons do not belong to the laboring class. Similarly, in virtually all societies in the past slavery was common, and slaves were forced to do servile work. But in no way does that mean that slaves belonged to the class of unskilled workers. The laboring class is simply composed of people who perform physical labor by choice, or because they are unable to acquire technical skills. They lack the initiative, ambition, and drive to succeed in the world; seldom do they shine in society.

8   These, then, are the four classes which exist in every society and have existed since ancient times in what Sarkar calls the quadridivisional social system. He differs sharply from those who define classes on economic grounds—on the basis of income and wealth. Sarkar does not neglect the economic aspect, but to him it is only one component among many. Class divisions, in his view, persist because of inherent differences in human nature.

SOCIAL MOBILITY

9   Sarkar's division of society into four classes is by no means inflexible. Social mobility may occur if an individual's mentality changes over time. Through diligent effort, or through prolonged contact with others, a person may move into another class. For example, a laborer may hone his skills to become an accomplished warrior, or through diligence and vigorous education he or she may become an intellectual. Similarly, an intellectual may turn into an acquisitor, or an acquisitor into a laborer. Thus even though class distinctions in society derive from innate differences in human endowments and nature, they may or may not be hereditary.

10   Yet the possibility of social mobility should not be exaggerated. Although it is

possible for a person of one class to acquire the skills of another, it is not easy. A boxer would find it hard to become a scientist, and vice versa. An acquisitor would have the same difficulty in becoming a warrior or an intellectual. But the point is that it is not impossible.

11   Wherever civilization developed, a careful examination of its history reveals the existence of the four-pronged division of society sketched by Sarkar. His categories of mind are broad enough to cover the full range of a mature society. Thus every civilization, which is what a mature society is, consists of four classes, each comprising people reflecting the predominance of a certain type of mind. Although individual behavior might display two, or even all, of the four mental attitudes, for the most part, and especially under duress, only one of them predominates. There is a bit of acquisitive instinct in most of us, but only a few make money the consuming obsession of their lives. We are all after a comfortable living standard and social prestige, but some of us attain them by means of physical skills, some through intellectual pursuits, and some by ceaselessly chasing after money. In this order, we are warriors, intellectuals and acquisitors. Largely left behind are the laborers, imbued with little ambition or drive, wanting in basic education and essential skills.

12   In every society, generally warriors maintain law and order, intellectuals supply philosophy and religion, acquisitors are adept at managing the economy, and laborers do the unskilled jobs.

13   Although some people display two or more mentalities—for instance, an accomplished army general may also be a superb writer, or an intellectual may also have the great business sense of an acquisitor—such individuals are rare, constituting an exception to the rule.

Finishing time: _____

Starting time: _____

Reading time: ___2:30___ (subtract)

Check the **Conversion Chart** on page 499 to determine how many words per minute you read.

WPM: ___535___

LITERAL COMPREHENSION CHECK

1. Which of the following best expresses the article's thesis?
    a. There is a law of social cycles in all societies.
    b. People have common objectives but their methods to attain them differs because of their innate abilities and qualities.
    c. Society is basically composed of four types of people.
    d. Society is basically composed of four types of people, each with a different frame of mind.

2. T/F   Most of the information in this selection is based on the work of P. R. Sarkar, not the author of the article.

3. Which of the following are *not* classified as warriors?
    a. soldiers
    b. fire fighters
    c. professional athletes
    d. farm workers

4. T/F   To Sarkar, everyone attempting to solve problems with the help of brains rather than brawn is classed as an acquisitor.

5. Acquisitors are mostly interested in ___money___.

6. T/F   Acquisitors are not as smart as the warrior type, but as bright as the intellectuals.

7. Which of the following are classed as acquisitors?
   a. merchants
   b. bankers
   c. landlords
   d. businessmen

8. The educational level of the laborer group is usually _very low._

9. *T/F* Persons of keen intelligence who perform hard labor not by choice but because of economic necessity are still classified as laborers.

10. The division of society into four classes is by no means _inflexable_

Number correct: _____8_____

Find the place in the article that provides the correct answer to any questions you missed. Make certain you understand why you missed any question.

VOCABULARY CHECK

Directions: Define the following underlined words from the article.

1. he faces limits imposed by <u>society</u>

2. <u>exploited</u> by the rest of society

3. forced to do <u>servile</u> work

4. the <u>quadridivisional</u> social system

5. because of <u>inherent</u> differences

6. differences in human <u>endowments</u>

7. all their <u>propensities</u> are engaged in amassing wealth

8. <u>covets</u> money for its own sake

9. one of them <u>predominates</u>

10. <u>imbued</u> with little ambition

Number correct: _____ **Learn any words you don't know.**

Turn to the Timed Reading Chart on page 497. Record your rate (WPM), comprehension, and vocabulary scores for this article on the chart. Each correct answer counts 10 percent. Discuss any problems or questions you may have with your instructor. Feel free to share any improvements, too!

Don't forget to learn any vocabulary words you need to add to your repertoire.

Drill   D-7: WARM-UP EXERCISE

Directions: Below are two rapid perception drills. Do each one separately under the pressure of time. Try to finish each one in 15 seconds or less.

Key phrase: **the principal pleasures**

Begin timing.

the profound changes	the principal pleasures
the principal pleasures	the predestined part
the predestined part	the profound changes
the philosophy itself	the philosophy itself
the physical environment	the physical environment
perfection by being	perfection by being
the principal pleasures	the principal pleasures
the profound changes	the profound changes
the philosophy itself	the philosophy itself
the physical environment	the physical environment
the predestined part	perfection by being
the principal pleasures	the principal pleasures
perfection by being	the predestined part
pressure of social	the profound changes
the principal pleasures	the principal pleasures
the physical environment	the predestined part
the predestined part	the profound changes
the profound changes	the philosophy itself
the philosophy itself	the physical environment
perfection by being	the principal joys

Time: _____ **seconds**

The key phrase appears eight times. Check your responses.

Number of key phrases you marked: _____ **out of 8**

Key phrase: **rather than me**

Begin timing.

over the ground   the idea of   rather than me   much of the lure   rather
enjoyed it   compared to what   rather than me   within the limit   almost too
much   on one stage   rather than me   within the limit   almost too much   on
one stage   inherent in us   rather than me   boggles the mind   the struggle is
one   what I wanted   its own reward   not from me   rather than me   never on
time   never you mind   rather than me   to look upon   the current passion
not for me   rather than me   no more bad times   over the hill   all good times
rather than me   nice and easy   something just beyond   endless flirtation
rather than me   endless trouble   on the way   rather than me   nor can I

Time: _____ seconds

The key phrase appears ten times. Check your responses.

Number of key phrases you marked: _____ out of 10

Drill   D-8

Directions: Before you do this last speed drill, look again at your reading rate
and comprehension score for Drill D-2. Try to read twice as fast as you did on that
drill with 60–70 percent comprehension. Remember, your reading rate depends
on your purpose for reading. In this case, your purpose is to practice reading faster
than you normally do.

Quickly skim the following article, checking the title, first paragraph, headings, and last paragraph in as few seconds as possible. Then read the article
rapidly, looking for the main idea and any supporting details you can identify.

Begin timing. Starting time: _____

IN AMERICA, FAME IS AN OPEN DOOR

Leo Braudy with Alvin P. Sanoff

1   Fame is really our religion in America. And we
have a constantly changing calendar of saints whom
we encounter in our media churches, especially films
and television, which have the largest congregations.

2   There is a heightened reality to the larger-than-
life images of film that's different from the more domestic reality surrounding performers who appear in
smaller dimension on TV. On television, performers
often look directly at the audience; on film, they rarely
do so. Television breaks the psychic distance between
performer and audience. There's a more familiar relationship between us and the stars; they're like members of the family. So television is less conducive to a
grand kind of fame like that of the old movie stars. It
promotes instead a type of fame that seems much more
accessible to many more people.

RENOWN ISN'T ALWAYS THE ANSWER

3   Increasingly, ordinary people seem to feel that
without fame they are somehow incomplete. In part
that's because there are so many more avenues for
achieving fame. People see someone on the TV screen
and think: "Why can't I be up there, too?" If you are not
on television, you feel that you are lacking something.

If people do not pay attention to you, you feel as if you don't exist. Yet many performers have found that fame does not necessarily lead to completeness. They get to the top and discover that they are still themselves—with the same void in the center they were looking for fame to fill.

4   It has always intrigued me that in the old fan magazines you rarely saw a story about Fred Astaire or Gene Kelly. My explanation is that when dancers were on film they knew they were working because there was real exertion involved. But when other performers—especially the old Hollywood stars—were on film they often weren't sure whether they were working since their main role was to "be themselves." The fan-magazine stories were a way of reassuring them that they were indeed doing something. It was an effort to fill up the feeling that they were empty. Marilyn Monroe is an extreme example of that hunger. The more you are just a body—the more you are famous just because you happen to look a certain way—the greater the psychic pressure on you.

5   I would call Monroe a martyr to fame, as were Elvis Presley and Judy Garland. They were not prepared for the tremendous expansion of the media after World War II and cracked either because of the attention or because of the disparity between that attention and who they thought they really were. Stars who followed have learned from these experiences. Some, such as Barbra Streisand, ration themselves out.

ATHLETES, WARRIORS WERE FIRST

6   Preoccupation with fame has a long history that dates back to ancient Greece, where fame was connected to a warrior aristocracy whose members were regarded as heroes. Over the centuries the nature of fame has changed—as well as the means of bestowing it. At one point it was the artists, who bestowed fame on individuals. Today it is the increasingly complicated visual media that do so.

7   Athletes were probably the first famous people—right along with heroic warriors. The athletes at the Olympic Games were known all over Greece. In fact Alexander the Great modeled himself after athletes as a kind of physical hero. There was then—and remains now—the notion that athletic fame is somehow purer than other kinds because it is primarily physical. That's why we get more upset when athletes are accused of corrruption.

HEMINGWAY: THE WRITER AS PERFORMER

8   Writers occupy an interesting category of fame. All through history they have been on the edge between visibility and invisibility. They wrote books and usually put their names on the title pages. But the books were not really them; the books were intermediaries between the writers and their audiences. Then writers gradually started having their pictures in their books. With the rise of 19th-century show business, writers like Dickens and Twain began to develop a performing side. But it was confined to the stage until the publicity culture of the 20th century helped create a fame like that of Ernest Hemingway.

9   The desire to be famous now is also infecting business executives. It used to be that, with the exception of an Andrew Carnegie or a John D. Rockefeller, money tended to be quiet. But in the late 19th and early 20th centuries there was an effort to turn business into a spiritual calling. In 1925 Bruce Barton wrote *The Man Nobody Knows,* which essentially argued that Jesus was the world's greatest businessman. That was an early step toward the business executive presenting himself as a figure who ought to be admired for himself. To achieve that status, as Lee Iacocca has done, you cannot operate behind the scenes; you have to step on center stage and be a performer.

10 America has taught the world about both the dissemination and power of fame. In the U.S., fame has been democratized. As a result it is now the performer—not the monarch or the Roman general—who is the model for fame. Fame is no longer restricted to a dynastic, political elite; it is open to everyone. But immortality doesn't last as long as it used to.

Finishing time:

Starting time: _____

Reading time: _____ **(subtract)**
Check the Conversion Chart on page 499 to determine how many words per minute you read.

WPM: _____

LITERAL COMPREHENSION CHECK

1. The thesis or main idea of this article is that
   a. television creates a type of fame that seems more accessible to many more people.
   b. ordinary people seem to feel that without fame they are somehow incomplete.
   c. preoccupation with fame has a long history.
   d. fame has become our religion in America with a constantly changing category of famous people.

2. Which of the following are discussed as categories where fame can or has been achieved?
   a. film and television
   b. athletics
   c. art and writing
   d. business

3. T/F   Television is less likely to create the kind of fame that the old movie stars used to enjoy.

4. T/F   Many performers have found that fame does not lead to completeness.

5. Which of the following are not labeled as "martyrs to fame"?
   a. Gene Kelly
   b. Marilyn Monroe
   c. Elvis Presley
   d. Barbra Streisand

6. T/F   Preoccupation with fame has a long history that dates back to ancient Rome.

7. Explain what is meant by the statement that before the late 19th and early

   20th centuries "money tended to be quiet." _____

   _____

   _____

8. In the U.S., what type of person has become the model for fame? _____

   _____

9. T/F   The media has opened the door to fame for everyone.

10. Explain what is meant by the statement, "But immortality doesn't last as long

    as it used to." _____

   _____

   _____

Number correct: _____

Make certain you understand why you may have missed any questions. Look back in the article to the spot where the answer appears or is explained.

VOCABULARY CHECK

A. Define the following underlined words from the article.

1. television breaks the <u>psychic</u> distance between performer and viewer

_____

2. television is less <u>conducive</u> to a grand kind of fame

_____

3. <u>preoccupation</u> with fame

_____

4. because of the <u>disparity</u> between them

_____

5. connected to a warrior <u>aristocracy</u>

_____

B. Using the words in the list below, fill in the blanks with the correct answer.

essential   exertion   elite
reassuring   bestowed   disparity

My explanation is that when dancers were on film they knew they were

working because there was real _____ involved. But when other per-

formers—especially the old Hollywood _____—were on film they

often weren't sure they were working since their _____ role was to

"be themselves." The fan-magazine stories were a way of _____ them
that they were indeed doing something. It was an effort to fill up the

_____ between that attention and who they thought they really were.

Number correct: _____ **Learn any words you missed.**

Turn to the Timed Reading Chart on page 497. Record your rate (WPM), comprehension, and vocabulary scores for this article. Each correct answer counts 10 percent. Compare these scores with those for Drill D-2. Discuss any problems or successes with your instructor.

Drill D-9: QUIZ ON UNIT I

Directions: Answer the following questions on a separate sheet of paper.

1. Define, as thoroughly as possible, literal comprehension.
2. Explain the reason for making and practicing with vocabulary flash cards.
3. Define skimming and scanning, giving examples of when to use these skills.

4. Briefly explain each of the following writing patterns:
   a. illustration/example
   b. definition
   c. cause/effect
   d. comparison/contrast
   e. description
   f. sequence of events
   g. combination of patterns
5. How can being aware of writing patterns help you distinguish the main ideas from the details?

Drill D-10: SELF-EVALUATION

Directions: On a separate sheet of paper, write an evaluation that discusses what you learned in this unit, any problems you had, and an appraisal of your attitude toward the drills in this unit.

UNIT I
PROGRESS CHECK

At the beginning of this unit, you took an inventory of your rate, comprehension, vocabulary, and scanning abilities based on the reading of a passage from a sociology textbook. This progress check presents another passage from the same textbook chapter. The questions are similar to the ones you answered in the inventory. If you apply what you have learned in this unit, the results of this check should be as good as or better than the scores you received on the inventory.

Before you begin, turn to the Inventory Progress Chart on page 493. Notice your scores. Your purpose here is to try to beat your previous scores.

When you are ready, write your starting time in the blank below. Try to begin exactly on the minute.

Begin timing. Starting time: _____

CONCEPTS FOR CULTURAL ANALYSIS

Rodney Stark

1   Each human must learn the culture of his or her society. Among the most significant elements of culture each must learn are *values, norms,* and *roles.* We will begin by exploring these three concepts, and then we will examine concepts involving cultural conflicts within a society.

VALUES AND NORMS

2   The **values** of a culture identify its details—its ultimate aims and most general standards for assessing good and bad or desirable and undesirable. When we say people need self-respect, dignity, and freedom or that we must all stand up for our country, we are invoking values. Values are not only lofty but also quite general.

3   **Norms,** on the other hand, are quite specific. They are *rules governing behavior.* Norms define what behavior is required, acceptable, or prohibited in particular circumstances. Norms indicate that a person should, ought, or must act (or must not act) in certain ways. We have all been in situations where we were somewhat anxious about how we ought to act. Such anxiety reflects not only that we are sometimes not sure what the norms are but also that violation of the norms will often lead to disapproval or even punishment. Conversely, conforming to the norms often

From *Sociology,* 2nd ed., by Rodney Stark © 1987 by Wadsworth, Inc. Reprinted by permission of the publisher.

brings approval and other rewards. In the next chapter we shall begin discussing a theme that runs throughout the book. Why do people conform or fail to conform to the norms?

4   Values and norms are related. Values *justify* the norms. For example, values of human dignity and self-respect can be invoked to explain the norm against ridiculing people who are physically handicapped. That is, calling someone a "gimp" not only is violating a norm but is also morally *wrong*. As another example, many societies value the intellectual development of the individual. As we shall see in Chapter 15, this value is the basis for many norms, including the norm that children shall be enrolled in school.

ROLES

5   A **role** is a collection of norms associated with a particular position in a society. That is, these norms describe how we expect someone in a particular position to act or not to act.

6   Consider a church during Sunday services. To keep things simple, let's assume that there are three roles: minister, organist, and member of the congregation. Each person in each of these roles is expected to act in different ways. The minister is expected to lead the service in the proper sequence and to preach a sermon. The organist is expected to play appropriate selections accurately and at the right times. The members of the congregation are expected to join in hymns, prayers, and rituals at the proper moments and to sit attentively the rest of the time. A minister who gets prayers mixed up violates a norm attached to his or her role, as does the organist who plays wrong notes or the churchgoer who falls asleep.

7   Of course, it would be a much more serious violation of role behavior if a member of the congregation ran up and pounded on the organ or if the minister fell asleep during the services. When people blatantly disregard their roles, the integrity of the social situation is called into question. We may begin to ask ourselves, "Is that person really a minister?" "Is that person really a member of this church?" "Is this really a church service or a hoax?" (Goffman, 1959).

8   Social life is structured by roles. In virtually every social situation, we have a relatively clearly defined role to fulfill: student, friend, woman, husband, shopper, pedestrian, cop, nun, bartender, wife, and so on. Each of these roles involves a "script" that we are expected to follow.

9   Some roles are thought to be more demanding than others, and some are thought to be more important than others. Virtually everyone is thought to be competent enough to fulfill the role of friend or spouse, but few are considered able to fulfill roles such as mathematician or sports star. A role that is believed to be more demanding and more important earns greater rewards than roles that are considered less demanding and less important. However, societies differ in their evaluations of various roles. For example, the role of priest is considered much more important in Italy than in the Soviet Union, while the role of chess player is more highly valued in the Soviet Union than in Italy.

10   Differences in the rewards attached to various roles in a particular society largely influence what roles persons will seek and what aspects of roles people will try to adopt in their own behavior. For example, if people in the most exalted roles in a society are required to demonstrate intense religious faith, then many other people in that society will attempt to do likewise.

11   In later chapters (especially Chapter 6) much will be said about roles—about how people learn to perform roles, about conflicts among roles, and the like. For now, it is enough to understand that different cultures can evaluate a given role quite differently.

12   Since cultures can differ greatly, what happens when several cultures exist within a single society—as they must in any society undergoing substantial rates of immigration? The result has often been violent conflicts (see Chapter 11). But Canadian and American history also provide examples of more pleasant possibilities.

ASSIMILATION AND ACCOMMODATION

13   The term **assimilation** refers to the process of exchanging one culture for another. Usually the term is applied to people who adjust to new surroundings by adopting the prevailing culture as their own. Think of assimilation in terms of fitting into or *disappearing into* a new culture. For example, to be fully assimilated into Canadian society an immigrant from the United States would have to drop ways of speaking, acting, and thinking that distinguish the two cultures and would have to substitute Canadian patterns. Or a Mexican would be assimilated into Amerian culture by becoming just like people born and raised in the United States.

14   Only rarely do individuals manage to become fully assimilated, especially if the cultures differ greatly. Usually it is their children or grandchildren who become assimilated. Moreover, many groups are unwilling *ever* fully to assimilate. Thus, for example, when British immigrants began to arrive in Canada they did not begin to speak French or become Roman Catholics, nor did the French switch to English and Anglicanism. Indeed, most immigrant groups in the United States have maintained some central aspects of their original culture, and this tendency is thought to be even more pronounced in Canada. (Shaffir and Weinfeld, 1981; Isajiw, 1977).

15   The failure of newcomers to assimilate has often caused intense conflicts. But not always and not forever. A second outcome is called **accommodation**—which describes the situation where two groups find they are able to ignore some important cultural differences between them and emphasize common interests instead.

16   In the nineteenth century, Catholic-Protestant cultural conflicts agitated American society. A rapid influx of Irish Catholics, fleeing the terrible famine of 1845–46 in Ireland, caused many Protestants in the United States to fear that their religious culture was threatened. Over the decades the cultural antagonisms between Catholics and Protestants waned until it became possible for them to emphasize their common Christianity rather than historic theological feuds. At that point accommodation had occurred.

CULTURAL PLURALISM AND SUBCULTURES

17   Accommodation results in the continued existence of several distinctive cultures within a society—or **cultural pluralism.**

18   Considerable cultural pluralism exists in both the United States and Canada. In each nation immigration has created a cultural mosaic, for most groups have retained some distinctive elements of their native culture—especially religion and food. Moreover, there is constant addition to the overall culture as material from various groups comes to be shared by all. For example, *everybody* eats Italian food and many Italian and Yiddish words have crept into the vocabulary of English-speaking North Americans (Rosten, 1968). Yet, even as the larger culture has embraced elements of ethnic cultures, distinctively Jewish and Italian cultures still flourish (as do many other ethnic cultures). There still are Italian and Jewish neighborhoods, easily recognized as such. Thus, to some extent, Canada and the United States are societies that have not only a distinctive culture but also many cultures.

19   To deal conceptually with this situation, sociologists have developed the concept of subcultures. A **subculture** is a culture within a culture—in other words, a distinctive set of beliefs, morals, customs, and the like developed or maintained by a group within a larger society. Sometimes the differences between the general culture and a subculture are not very great, as is the case today between general American culture and the subculture of Italian-Americans. Sometimes the differences are very great, as between the general Canadian culture and that of the Mennonite communities of Saskatchewan (Driedger, 1982). Often, people are born and raised in a subculture. But often, too, they *join* subcultures such as those sustained by convents.

Finishing time: _____

Starting time: _____

Reading time: ___3:00_____ (subtract)

Check page 499 for your reading rate, or words per minute.

WPM: ___766_____

LITERAL COMPREHENSION PROGRESS CHECK

Part A

Directions: In the space below, write a summary of the reading selection you just read.

Part B

Directions: Answer the following questions without looking back at the reading selection.

1. State in your own words what you think the main idea of the reading selection is. *the effect of cultures on society* _____

_____

_____

_____

2. What are the three most significant elements of culture each of us must learn? *roles, values, norms* _____

_____

3. Give an example of what is meant by roles in society. *the preacher is expected to act like a preacher* _____

_____

4. Define *assimilation* as used in sociology. *someone from a different culture takes on the new one.*

5. When two groups find they are able to ignore some important cultural differences and emphasize common interests instead, sociologists call this *accomodation*.

6. Give an example of cultural pluralism that exists in the United States. ____
Italian - American sub - culture

7. How are values and norms related? *values justify the norms*

8. What can happen when newcomers to a country fail to assimilate? ____
there may be cultural unrest

9. How do sociologists define a subculture? *a culture within a culture.*

10. Social life is structured by *norms roles*

VOCABULARY PROGRESS CHECK

Part A

Directions: Define the following underlined words as they appear in context.

1. their <u>vociferous</u> chatter

2. the <u>elite</u> group on campus

3. usually <u>morose</u> when sick

4. the judge showed <u>clemency</u> toward her

5. she's <u>astute</u> in business matters

6. they <u>enhanced</u> the property

7. <u>rapport</u> between us was good

_____

8. she acts <u>pretentious</u> around us

_____

9. the <u>prevailing</u> notions

_____

10. his <u>indolence</u> caused his failure

_____

Part B

Directions: Define the following word parts.

1. psych _____

2. logy _____

3. bio _____

4. ist _____

5. vis _____

6. in _____

7. gen _____

8. aud _____

9. phil _____

10. mono _____

Go on to the next page.

SKIMMING/SCANNING PROGRESS CHECK

Directions: Take no more than two minutes to scan the reading sociology selection for the answers to the following questions.

1. What is the definition for *norms* in paragraph 3? _____

   _____

2. List three examples of *roles* given in paragraph 8. _____

   _____

3. In what years was there a rapid influx of Irish Catholics to the U.S.? _____

   _____

4. In paragraph 18, what two elements of their native culture do most people

   retain? _____

5. According to paragraph 11, what chapter from the textbook this passage is

   taken from will discuss more on roles? _____

   Once this progress check has been scored, enter the results on the Inventory Progress Chart on page 493. When you have finished, share the results with your instructor. Discuss your successes or any areas you need to review before going on to the next unit.

UNIT II

CRITICAL COMPREHENSION

CRITICAL COMPREHENSION INVENTORY

Before you begin to work in this unit, quickly skim the article below by checking the title, first paragraph, headings, and last paragraph in as few seconds as possible. Then read the article rapidly but with good comprehension. Time yourself or have someone time you so that you can get an inventory of your reading rate and critical understanding.

Begin timing. Starting time: _____

WHY I WANT TO HAVE A FAMILY

Lisa Brown

1   For years the theory of higher education operated something like this: men went to college to get rich, and women went to college to marry rich men. It was a wonderful little setup, almost mathematical in its precision. To disturb it would have been to rock an American institution.

2   During the '60s, though, this theory lost much of its luster. As the nation began to recognize the idiocy of relegating women to a secondary role, women soon joined men in what once were male-only pursuits. This rebellious decade pushed women toward independence, showed them their potential and compelled them to take charge of their lives. Many women took the opportunity and ran with it. Since then feminine autonomy has been the rule, not the exception, at least among college women.

3   That's the good news. The bad news is that the invisible push has turned into a shove. Some women are downright obsessive about success, to the point of becoming insular monuments to selfishness and fierce bravado, the condescending sort that hawks: "I don't need *anybody*. So there." These women dismiss children and marriage as unbearably outdated and potentially harmful to their up-and-coming careers. This notion of independence smacks of egocentrism. What do these women fear? Why can't they slow down long enough to remember that relationships and a family life are not inherently awful things?

Reprinted from *Newsweek*, Oct. 1984.

4   Granted that for centuries women were on the receiving end of some shabby treatment. Now, in an attempt to liberate college women from the constraints that forced them almost exclusively into teaching or nursing as a career outside the home—always subject to the primary career of motherhood—some women have gone too far. Any notion of motherhood seems to be regarded as an unpleasant reminder of the past, when homemakers were imprisoned by husbands, tots and household chores. In short, many women consider motherhood a time-consuming obstacle to the great joy of working outside the home.

5   The rise of feminism isn't the only answer. Growing up has something to do with it, too. Most people find themselves in a bind as they hit their late 20s: they consider the ideals they grew up with and find that these don't necessarily mix with the ones they've acquired. The easiest thing to do, it sometimes seems, is to throw out the precepts their parents taught. Growing up, my friends and I were enchanted by the idea of starting new traditions. We didn't want self-worth to be contingent upon whether there was a man or child around the house to make us feel wanted.

6   I began to reconsider my values after my sister and a friend had babies. I was entertained by their pregnancies and fascinated by the births; I was also thankful that I wasn't the one who had to change the diapers every day. I was a doting aunt only when I wanted to be. As my sister's and friend's lives changed, though, my attitude changed. Though these two women lost the freedom to run off to the beach or to a bar, they gained something else—an abstract happiness that reveals itself when they talk about Jessica's or Amanda's latest escapade or vocabulary addition. Still in their 20s, they shuffle work and motherhood with the skill of poker players. I admire them, and I marvel at their kids. Spending time with the Jessicas and Amandas of the world teaches us patience and sensitivity and gives us a clue into our own pasts. Children are also reminders that there is a future and that we must work to ensure its quality.

7   Now I feel challenged by the idea of becoming a parent. I want to decorate a nursery and design Halloween costumes; I want to answer my children's questions and help them learn to read. I want to be unselfish. But I've spent most of my life working in the opposite direction: toward independence, no emotional or financial strings attached. When I told a friend—one who likes kids but never, ever wants them—that I'd decided to accommodate motherhood, she accused me of undermining my career, my future, my life. "If that's all you want, then why are you even in college?" she asked.

8   The answer's simple: I want to be a smart mommy. I have solid career plans and look forward to working. I make a distinction between wanting kids and wanting nothing but kids. And I've accepted that I'll have to give up a few years of full-time work to allow time for being pregnant and buying Pampers. As for undermining my life, I'm proud of my decision because I think it's evidence that the women's movement is working. While liberating women from the traditional childbearing role, the movement has given respectability to motherhood by recognizing that it's not a brainless task like dishwashing. At the same time, women who choose not to have children are not treated as oddities. That certainly wasn't the case even 15 years ago. While the graying, middle-aged bachelor was respected, the female equivalent—tagged a spinster—was automatically suspect.

9   Today, women have choices: about careers, their bodies, children. I am grateful that women are no longer forced into motherhood as a function of their biology; it's senseless to assume that having a uterus qualifies anyone to be a good parent. By the same token, it is ridiculous for women to abandon all maternal desire because it might jeopardize personal success. Some women make the decision to go childless without ever analyzing their true needs or desires. They forget that motherhood can add to personal fulfillment.

10   I wish those fiercely independent women wouldn't look down upon those of us who, for whatever reason, choose to forgo much of the excitement that runs in tandem with being single, liberated and educated. Excitement also fills a family life; it just comes in different ways.

11 I'm not in college because I'll learn how to make tastier pot roast. I'm a student because I want to make sense of the world and of myself. By doing so, I think I'll be better prepared to be a mother to the new lives that I might bring into the world. I'll also be a better me. It's a package deal I don't want to turn down.

Finishing time: _____

Starting time: _____ **(subtract)**

Reading time: _____*2:00*_____

Check page 500 for your rate.

WPM: _____*545*_____

COMPREHENSION INVENTORY

Directions: The point of this inventory is to see what you already know about critical comprehension before you begin working in this unit. Don't worry if you don't understand some of the terminology or questions. Answer whatever questions that follow without guessing or looking back at the reading selection.

1. The best statement of the thesis or main idea from this essay is
   a. "I'm a student because I want to make sense of the world and of myself."
   b. "I wish those fiercely independent women wouldn't look down upon those of us who . . . choose to forgo much of the excitement that runs in tandem with being single, liberated and educated."
   c. "Today, women have choices: about careers, their bodies, and children."
   d. "While liberating women from the traditional childbearing role, the movement has given respectability to motherhood by recognizing that it's not a brainless task like dishwashing."

2. The author's *attitude* toward her thesis can be be described as
   a. lighthearted   c. serious
   b. pessimistic   d. sad

3. The *tone* of the essay can best be described as
   a. ironic   c. humorous
   b. angry   d. pleased

4. T/F The author, once for the feminist movement, is now opposed to it because of the harm it has brought upon women.

5. Is the essay expressed mostly in fact or opinion? _____*opinion*_____

6. T/F We can infer from some of the author's comments that she is envious of her married sister and friend she mentions.

7. Is the author's statement, "Children are also reminders that there is a future and that we must work to ensure its quality," mostly fact or opinion? _____*opinion*_____

8. T/F We can infer that the author is now no longer interested in a career, but motherhood.

9. T/F We can infer that the author has little patience with those women who say, "I don't need *anybody*. So there."

10. What personal reasons does the author give for attending college? _____*To be a smart*_____ _____*Mommy. Be better prepared*_____ _____*to be a mother*_____

 _____

Number correct: _____*6*_____

VOCABULARY CHECK

Part A

Directions: Define the following underlined words or terms used in the reading selection.

1. the idiocy of <u>relegating</u> women to a secondary role

     _____

2. feminine <u>autonomy</u>

     _____

3. <u>insular</u> <u>monuments</u> to selfishness

     _____

4. smacks of <u>egocentrism</u>

     _____

5. from the <u>constraints</u> that forced them

     _____

6. throwing out the <u>precepts</u> their parents taught

     _____

7. it might <u>jeopardize</u> personal success

     _____

8. runs in <u>tandem</u> with being single

     _____

9. choose to <u>forgo</u> much

     _____

10. <u>fierce</u> <u>bravado</u>

     _____

Part B

Directions: Define the following terms. They are words used in this unit. Don't guess. Define only the ones you believe you know.

1. author's attitude

   _____

2. tone of an essay

   _____

3. reader bias

   _____

4. draw an inference

   _____

5. author's intent

   _____

Number correct: _____

Record the results of this inventory on the Inventory Progress Chart on page 493.

INTRODUCTION TO CRITICAL COMPREHENSION

WHAT IS CRITICAL COMPREHENSION?

Critical comprehension is that level of understanding which entails the distinguishing of fact from opinion, the recognition of an author's intent, attitude, or bias, the drawing of inferences, and the making of critical judgments. It's the second branch on the comprehension triangle explained in Unit I. Critical comprehension is a more sophisticated level of understanding than literal comprehension. A well-known reading expert, Dr. Francis Triggs, says that "Critical reading requires a contribution by both the author and the reader and an interplay which usually results in a new understanding." For instance, Jonathan Swift's *Gulliver's Travels* appeals to young people because at the literal level it reads like a fairy-tale adventure story about a man who lives with giants and miniature people. However, when the story is read at a more critical level of understanding, it is a very bitter satire on mankind. In other words, an understanding beyond the literal level is necessary for thorough comprehension.

WHAT DOES THIS UNIT COVER?

There are three chapters in this unit, each one covering a different facet of critical comprehension. Chapter 6 deals with the development of the skill of separating fact from opinion. Exercises will call your attention to how we think we are dealing with fact when often we are accepting opinion.

Chapter 7 provides exercises for developing the ability to recognize an author's intent, that is, the real purpose of writing. Sometimes authors "disguise" their true purpose or thesis by the use of metaphor, satire, irony, or humor. Other times, authors use propaganda or present their evidence in a biased way. Chapter 7 should help you analyze an author's actual intention and evaluate bias.

Chapter 8 contains drills for discovering how both the author and the reader often draw inferences. Rather than coming right out and saying what they mean, authors sometimes imply or suggest what they want the reader to understand. Likewise, readers often draw inferences about what an author says. When you hear students talking about the "hidden meaning" of a work, or when you hear the statement "Read between the lines," drawing inferences is what is meant. This chapter also provides an opportunity to react to quoted statements, advertisements, and short articles, using what you learned in previous chapters to help you make critical judgments and draw conclusions.

A comment regarding reading rate is in order here. As you learned in Unit I, speed of reading is not as important as good comprehension. By now you should have realized that although you can increase your overall speed, your reading rate fluctuates with your interest in the topic, the length of the reading selection, your knowledge of the subject, the level of difficulty, and even how you feel on a certain day. That is natural. Some reading selections in this section of the book are timed, mostly for your own concern. Most students developing their reading versatility like to have some idea how fast they are reading. That's fine. Go ahead and practice reading faster. Just remember not to let speed be your goal. As you get to be a better reader, your reading speed also will increase.

At the end of this unit is another Progress Check so that you can compare your reading progress in rate and comprehension at both the literal and critical levels.

WHAT SHOULD YOU KNOW UPON COMPLETION OF THIS UNIT?

Here are six objectives to work toward in this unit. By the time you complete this unit, you should be able to

1. Distinguish fact from opinion.
2. Recognize an author's intent, attitude, and tone.
3. Recognize an author's bias and use of propaganda.
4. Recognize inferences being made by an author and make your own inferences from what you read.
5. Make critical judgments and draw conclusions by analyzing the author's diction, style, and use of figurative language.
6. Write a definition of critical comprehension.

For now, concentrate on objective 1, distinguishing fact from opinion, which is covered in the next chapter.

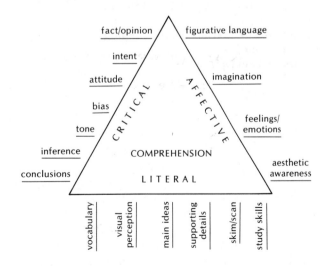

CHAPTER 6

Distinguishing Fact from Opinion

Distinguishing fact from opinion is not always easy. A fact is usually defined as a truth, something that can be tested by experimentation, observation, or research and shown to be real. But even that is an elusive definition. For example, in 1930 it was generally accepted as fact that the atom was the smallest particle of an element and could not be split. With the advent of atomic power in the 1940s, scientists split the atom, making what was once thought to be a fact a fallacy. Today, physicists are just beginning to understand subatomic particles and refer to much of their findings as theory rather than fact. The point is that facts are sometimes "slippery."

An opinion, on the other hand, is often easier to distinguish. Your belief, feeling, or judgment about something is an opinion. It is a subjective or value judgment, not something that can be objectively verified. Even though you base your opinion on fact, others may not agree; an opinion cannot be proven to everyone's satisfaction. For instance, you may be of the opinion that Martin Sheen is the greatest movie star of the 1980s, but there is no way to make your opinion fact. Others have their own favorite actors, while still others do not know who Martin Sheen is. The only fact that you can prove is that Martin Sheen is an actor.

Test your skill in recognizing fact from opinion by placing an F in the blank in front of any of the following statements you believe to be fact.

_____ 1. Harry S. Truman was the president of the United States.

_____ 2. Truman was one of the best presidents the U.S. has had.

_____ 3. Generally speaking, movies are more entertaining than books.

_____ 4. *Time* is a better magazine than *Reader's Digest*.

_____ 5. Columbus, in 1492, was the first person to discover America.

Now see how well you did. You should have marked the first one. It is a fact that can be verified objectively. The second statement, however, is not a fact. It is a subjective statement claiming Truman was "one of the best." This claim is a value judgment; although we can prove that Truman was a president, historians may never agree that he was one of the best, even though he might have been. Words that give something value, such as *great, wonderful, beautiful, ugly, intelligent,* or *stupid,* make statements subjective opinions, not verifiable facts.

The third statement is not fact; it is a value judgment. To say something is "more entertaining" or "better" or "worse" is to place a personal value on something. Value judgments may be based on facts, but they are opinions nonetheless.

Number four is not a fact. You may believe one magazine is better than another, but *Reader's Digest* has a much larger circulation than *Time,* so many readers disagree. However, the fact—and it *is* a fact—that *Reader's Digest* has a larger circulation than *Time* does not mean it is any better either. The use of the word "better" needs clarification. Better in what way? Paper? Size? Cost? Contents? Again, "better" implies a value judgment.

The fifth statement is one of those "slippery" facts. According to many sources, Columbus did discover America in 1492. Yet, factually, he never actually landed on the continent; Vikings are said to have explored America long before Columbus, and evidence indicates that native Americans inhabited America over 25,000 years or more before Columbus. Obviously, he wasn't the first person to discover America. It is a European viewpoint that many history books continue to express; yet many textbooks are now changing wording to clarify this historical point. As stated, number five is not an opinion; it is more an erroneous statement than anything else.

On the other hand, if someone were to claim that Columbus sailed to the New World in 1592 rather than 1492, it would be easy enough to consult historical records to show the correct date was 1492. Knowledge that we share and agree upon as a society is called *shared knowledge.* Agreed upon facts, then, are generally referred to as objective. If we argue that Columbus was a better sailor than Magellan, we get into the subjective realm of opinion. Unless we can find objective evidence that one was better than the other, we can't speak factually.

Which of the following statements are based on objective evidence?

1. Coca-Cola tastes better than Pepsi-Cola.
2. The capital of Illinois is Springfield.
3. The moon revolves around the earth.
4. Italians make great lovers.

Both statements 1 and 4 are based on subjective evidence. You might get fifty people to say Coke tastes better than Pepsi, but you can get another fifty to say the opposite. The same goes for Italians as great lovers. These statements are opinions, not facts. Items 2 and 3 can be verified by checking agreed upon information; thus they are facts based on objective evidence until such time as Springfield is no longer the capital and the moon quits revolving around the earth.

Just as our purpose for reading affects our speed and comprehension needs, so does it affect the degree to which we must be aware of the differences in objective and subjective statements. When we read the paper for the news of the day, we want facts based on objective reporting. If we want to read someone's interpretation of the facts and what implications that news may have on us, we read editorials and columnists' opinions to see how they subjectively interpret the news. When we read a recipe, we want factual measurements, not opinions on how the finished product will taste. When we read an encyclopedia, we want the facts. But when we read a critic's opinion or interpretation of the importance of those facts, we are looking for a subjective reaction, an opinion.

As a critical reader of all kinds of writing, you need to be able to discern between objective and subjective statements and then draw your own conclusions. The following drills will help you develop your ability to distinguish facts, opinions, and erroneous-sounding statements. If some of the answers seem "picky," just remember that the point is to sharpen your reading versatility.

A. Fact-Finding

Drill A-1: FACT-FINDING

Directions: Read each of the following statements and place an *F* in the blanks of those statements that you feel are *mostly* fact and an *O* in the blanks of those statements that are *mostly* opinion.

1. _____ A world auction record for a single piece of furniture—$415,800 for a Louis XVI table—was set today at a sale of the French furniture collection of the late Mrs. Anna Thomson Dodge of the Detroit auto fortune. (From a United Press release.)

2. _____ The junior college is a better place to attend school for the first two years than is a university or four-year school. This is so primarily because classes are smaller at a junior college and more individualized attention can be given to students.

3. _____ Medsker and Trent found that four-year colleges draw approximately three-fourths of their freshmen from the upper 40 percent of the high school graduating class, whereas about half the junior college transfer students were in the upper 40 percent of their high school graduating classes. (From K. Patricia Cross, *The Junior College Student: A Research Description.*)

4. _____ A black can expect to live, on the average, seven years less than a white person of the same sex, to enjoy a little more than half the income—even if he has more education than his white brothers—and to suffer about twice the unemployment rate. (From Robert K. Carr et al., *Essentials of American Democracy.*)

5. _____ Not since the frontier days have Native Americans faced greater threats to their existence than they do today. Malnutrition, disease, and despair are rampant. Their school dropout rate is 50 percent greater than the national average. Unemployment is 10 times the rate of other Americans. The Native American today has the shortest life expectancy of any group in the country.

6. _____ Eric Larnabee's *Commander in Chief* is a bold, fresh, and utterly convincing portrait of F.D.R. as a war leader.

7. _____ Adolf Hitler's mistress, Eva Braun, was a pudgy, middle-class blonde who gloomed more than she glittered. Yet her name will go down in history alongside such famous and glamorous kept women as Lola Montez, Madame de Pompadour, Nell Gwyn, and Du Barry.

8. _____ America's Favorite Cigarette Break—Benson & Hedges 100's. (From Benson & Hedges advertising slogan.)

9. _____ The President is the only official who represents every American—rich and poor, privileged and underprivileged. He represents ... also the great, quiet, forgotten majority—the non-shouters and the non-demonstrators, the millions who ask principally to go their own way in decency and dignity ... (From a 1968 campaign speech by Richard M. Nixon.)

10. _____ Businessmen, especially big businessmen, do whatever they want to you: They set outrageously high prices on their products, bombard you with advertising so that you'll buy something you don't want and don't even need, and then make sure that what you've bought falls apart just when you get it home. (From Angus Black, *A Radical's Guide to Economic Reality.*)

Drill   A-2: MORE FACT-FINDING

Directions: Read each of the following paragraphs. Circle the number of any statements that you think are primarily factual or can be objectively proven. Then underline any words in the statements that you feel are too subjective to be verified as factual.

1. In the first seven months of 1988, once private companies raised $17.4 billion through initial public offerings, or two thirds more than in the same period of 1987.

2. There are still young persons who read for pleasure and who do well in school, but their number dwindles. The middle range of children muddles through high school and some go through college, but the general level of their academic achievement is significantly below what it was thirty years ago.

3. Ravi Batra's eye-catching book *The Great Depression of 1990* has jumped to number four in its sixth week on the *New York Times'* nonfiction bestseller list. At $17.95 a copy, it has been snapped up by some 175,000 buyers who are either curious or concerned—or both—about how high the current boom can go before it turns to bust.

4. Take the plunge into the splashiest resort on the most spectacular beach in the most exquisite island in Hawaii—the new Willoughby Maui Hotel. Join in the dreamlike atmosphere of waterfalls, tropical lagoons, and lush tiered gardens—or simply soak up the sun.

5. While grammar usage offers the most immediate clues to a person's educational background, another important clue is vocabulary. The writer or speaker who uses words appropriately and accurately is probably well educated. One who often misuses words or phrases is not soundly educated, because a major purpose of education is to teach people to use their native tongue with accuracy.

6. Since 1957, writes Ben J. Wattenberg in his *The Birth Dearth*, the average American woman's fertility rate has dropped from 3.77 children to 1.8— below the 2.1 size needed to maintain the present population level. Meanwhile, he argues, Communist-bloc countries are producing at a rate of 2.3 children per mother, while the Third World rate is rising so fast that within fifty years its population may be ten times that of the West.

7. But specific challenges to Wattenberg's data have been raised. Some demographers question his projections, since he gathered his information from population trends with little or no regard for such unpredictable factors as wars, epidemics, famines, and baby booms.

8. As of 1988, just two women serve in the U.S. Senate and twenty-three in the House of Representatives. Does that mean voters are more at ease with the idea of a woman on the local school board than in the White House? The electoral gender gap, according to a report by the National Women's Political Caucus, is beginning to break down. Fifty-seven percent polled said they believed that a female president could be as good or better than a male.

Drill   A-3: FACT VS. OPINION

Directions: Each sentence is lettered in the following statements. On the line below each statement, write the letter of each sentence you think can be accepted as a statement of fact. The first one has been done for you.

1. (a) The last great Greek astronomer of antiquity was Claudius Ptolemy (or Ptolemeus), who flourished about A.D. 140. (b) He compiled a series of 13 volumes on astronomy known as the *Almagest*. (c) All of the *Almagest* does not deal with Ptolemy's own work, for it includes a compilation of the astronomical achievements of the past, principally of Hipparchus. (d) In fact, it is our main source of information about Greek astronomy. (e) The *Almagest* also contains accounts of the contributions of Ptolemy himself. (From George Abell, *Exploration of the Universe*.)

    <u>*a*, although the phrase "last great" may not be fact; *b, c, d, e*</u>

2. (a) The July 1987 Almanac states that there are four West Coast species of salmon. This is incorrect. (b) There are five species. (c) The West Coast species belong to the genus *Oncorhynchus*. (d) Their common names are chinook, also called the spring or king salmon; the chum or dog salmon; the coho or silver salmon; the pink salmon; and the sockeye or red salmon.

    _____

3. We hold these truths to be self-evident, (a) that all men are created equal; (b) that they are endowed by their Creator with certain unalienable rights; (c) that among these are life, liberty, and the pursuit of happiness; (d) that to secure these rights, governments are instituted among men. (From the Declaration of Independence.)

    _____

4. (a) If the American political system is to survive without repression, it will be because of positive political leadership that faces up to the problems and convinces both private citizens and public officials that these problems are serious and interrelated; (b) that they must be attacked, attacked immediately, and attacked together by coordinated and probably expensive programs. (c) As we have said so many times . . . , if there is to be positive leadership in American politics, it can only come from the President. (d) Even then the Madisonian system may stalemate. (e) But without presidential leadership there is no hope that the system can move with any speed or controlled direction.

    _____

5. (a) *The Glass Bead Game* by Hermann Hesse appeared in Switzerland in 1943. (b) It was his last major work of any importance. (c) It is also the best of all his novels, an "act of mental synthesis through which the spiritual values of all ages are perceived as simultaneously present and vitally alive." (d) It was with full artistic consciousness that Hesse created this classic work.

    _____

6. (a) Although over 500 ruins are recorded within the Grand Canyon National Park, we know only the outline of this area's prehistory. (b) Most ruins are small surface pueblos in and along the north and south rims of the canyon. (c) No large communal centers have been found. (d) Small cliff dwellings and numerous granaries occupy caves and niches in the canyon walls. (e) A few early pit houses, some ruins of late Havasupai houses, and occasional hogans and sweat lodges left by the Navajos complete the roster. (From Joe Ben Wheat, *Prehistoric People*.)

    _____

Drill A-4: INTERPRETING "FACTS"

Directions: Read the two passages below. They are accounts of the same historical event written by two different historians. Notice how they both use facts and
how they interpret these facts.

When anarchy visited Nicaragua, Coolidge had no choice but to act
unilaterally. First, in 1925, he withdrew a token force of marines from that
nation, which then seemed capable of servicing its foreign debt and preserv-
ing its internal stability. But the appearance was deceptive. Almost at once
revolution broke out, and Coolidge again landed the marines, in time some
five thousand. Regrettably, in its quest for order, the United States chose to
support the reactionary faction, whose identification with large landowners
and foreign investors had helped provoke the revolution in the first place.
(From John Blum et al., *The National Experience*, Harcourt Brace Jovanovich,
1963, p. 617.)

The United States, despite the current anti-war sentiment, was reluctantly forced to adopt warlike measures in Latin America. Disorders in
Nicaragua, perilously close to the Panama Canal jugular vein, had jeopar-
dized American lives and property, and in 1927 President Coolidge felt
compelled to dispatch over 5000 troops to this troubled banana land. His
political foes, decrying mailed-fist tactics, accused him of waging a "private
war," while critics south of the Rio Grande loudly assailed *Yanqui* imperi-
alism. (From Thomas A. Bailey, *The American Pageant*, 2nd ed., D. C. Heath,
1961, p. 503.)

1. What facts reported in the first passage are also reported in the second one?

   Are there any differences in the reporting of the facts? _____

   _____

   _____

2. Explain whether or not the two authors agree on the reason Coolidge sent

   troops to Nicaragua. _____

   _____

   _____

3. Do the two authors agree on the reactions to Coolidge's action? Explain.

   _____

   _____

   _____

Drill   A-5: COMPARING "FACTS"

Directions: Forty years after the United States dropped the atomic bomb on Hiroshima during World War II, two essays on the rightness or wrongness of this act were published in the *New York Times*. One of the authors believes that the U.S. was right to drop the bomb; the other believes it was wrong. Even today the argument continues.

Before you read the essays, check one of the following statements:

1. I believe the U.S. should have dropped the bomb.
2. I believe the U.S. should not have dropped the bomb.
3. I don't know.

Now read both of the following essays. As you read them, underline any statements you think are factual. Then answer the questions that follow each reading selection.

THE U.S. WAS RIGHT

John Connor

1   Forty years ago this week in Hiroshima: the dreadful flash, the wrist watches fused forever at 8:16 A.M. The question still persists: Should we have dropped the atomic bomb?

2   History seldom gives decisive answers, but recently declassified documents point to a clear judgment: Yes, it was necessary to drop the bomb. It was needed to end the war. It save countless American and Japanese lives.

3   In the early summer of 1945, Japan, under tight control of the militarists, was an implacable, relentless adversary. The Japanese defended territory with a philosophy we had seldom encountered: Soldiers were taught that surrender was worse than death. There was savage resistance to the end in battle after battle.

4   Of the 5,000-man Japanese force at Tarawa in November 1943, only 17 remained alive when the island was taken. When Kwajalein was invaded in February 1944, Japanese officers slashed at American tanks with samurai swords; their men held grenades against the sides of tanks in an effort to disable them.

5   On Saipan, less than 1,000 of the 32,000 defending Japanese troops survived. Casualties among the Japanese-ruled civilians on the island numbered 10,000. Parents bashed their babies' brains out on rocky cliff sides, then leaped to their deaths. Others cut each other's throats; children threw grenades at each other. America suffered 17,000 casualties.

6   Just 660 miles southeast of Tokyo, Iwo Jima's garrison was told to defend the island as if it were Tokyo itself. They did. In the first day of fighting, there were more American casualties than during "D-Day" in Normandy. At Okinawa—only 350 miles south of Kyushu—more than 110,000 Japanese soldiers and 100,000 civilians were killed. Kamikaze attacks cost the Navy alone some 10,000 casualties. The Army and Marines lost more than 50,000 men.

7   In the early summer of 1945, the invasion of Japan was imminent and everyone in

the Pacific was apprehensive. The apprehension was justified, because our intelligence was good: With a system code-named "Magic," it had penetrated Japanese codes even before Pearl Harbor. "Magic" would play a crucial role in the closing days of the war.

8   Many have maintained that the bomb was unnecessary because in the closing days of the war intercepted Japanese diplomatic messages disclosed a passionate desire for peace. While that is true, it is irrelevant. The Japanese government remained in the hands of the militarists: *Their* messages indicated a willingness to fight to the death.

9   Japanese planes, gasoline and ammunition had been hoarded for the coming invasion. More than 5,000 aircraft had been hidden everywhere to be used as suicide weapons, with only enough gas in their tanks for a one-way trip to the invasion beaches. More than two million men were moving into positions to defend the home islands.

10   The object was to inflict such appalling losses that the Americans would agree to a treaty more favorable than unconditional surrender. The Army Chief of Staff, Gen. George C. Marshall, estimated potential American casualties as high as a million.

11   The willingness of the Japanese to die was more than empty bravado. Several of my colleagues at Kyushu University told me that as boys of 14 or 15, they were being trained to meet the Americans on the beaches with little more than sharpened bamboo spears. They had no illusions about their chances for survival.

12   The Potsdam declaration calling for unconditional surrender was beamed to Japan on July 27. On July 30, the Americans were informed that Japan would officially ignore the ultimatum. A week later, the bomb was dropped.

13   Could we not have warned the Japanese in advance, critics asked, and dropped a demonstration bomb? That alternative was vetoed on the grounds the bomb might not work, or that the plane carrying it might be shot down. Moreover, it is questionable how effective a demonstration bomb might have been. The militarists could have imposed a news blackout as complete as the one imposed after the disastrous battle of Midway and continued on their suicidal course. That is exactly what happened at Hiroshima. Within hours, the Japanese Government sent in a team of scientists to investigate the damage. Their report was immediately suppressed and was not made public until many years after the war.

14   After midnight on Aug. 10, a protracted debate took place in an air-raid shelter deep inside the Imperial Palace. The military insisted that Japan should hold out for terms far better than unconditional surrender. The peace faction favored accepting the Potsdam declaration, providing that the Emperor would be retained. The two factions remained at an impasse. At 2 A.M., Prime Minister Kantaro Suzuki asked the Emperor to decide. In a soft, deliberate voice, the Emperor expressed his great longing for peace. The war had ended.

15   It was impossible, in August 1945, to predict the awesome shadow the bomb would cast on humanity. The decision to drop it seemed both simple and obvious. Without it, the militarists might have prevailed, an invasion ordered. And the loss of both American and Japanese lives would have been awesome.

16   The atomic bomb accomplished what it had been designed to do. It ended the war.

Now answer the following questions:

1. Is this essay mostly fact or opinion? _____

2. What is the author's main argument in favor of dropping the bomb? _____

_____

3. Is the main argument based on facts? _____ Explain.

_____

_____

4. Did the author convince you that the U.S. was right in using the bomb?

_____ Explain. _____

_____

_____

_____

The following essay offers the opposite opinion on dropping the bomb. As you read, underline any statements you feel are factual. Then answer the questions that follow the reading selection.

THE U.S. WAS WRONG

Gar Alperovitz

1   Though it has not yet received broad public attention, there exists overwhelming historical evidence that President Harry S. Truman knew he could almost certainly end World War II without using the atomic bomb: The United States had cracked the Japanese code, and a stream of documents released over the last 40 years show that Mr. Truman had two other options.

2   The first option was to clarify America's surrender terms to assure the Japanese we would not remove their Emperor. The second was simply to await the expected Soviet declaration of war—which, United States intelligence advised, appeared likely to end the conflict on its own.

3   Instead, Hiroshima was bombed Aug. 6, 1945, and Nagasaki on Aug. 9. The planned date for the Soviet Union's entry into the war against Japan was Aug. 8.

4   The big turning point was the Emperor's continuing June–July decision to open surrender negotiations through Moscow. Top American officials—and, most critically, the President—understood the move was extraordinary: Mr. Truman's secret diaries, lost until 1978, call the key intercepted message "the telegram from Jap Emperor asking for peace."

5   Other documents—among them newly discovered secret memorandums from William J. Donovan, director of the Office of Strategic Services—show that Mr. Truman was personally advised of Japanese peace initiatives through Swiss and Portuguese channels as early as three months before Hiroshima. Moreover, Mr. Truman told several officials he had no objection in principle to Japan's keeping the Emperor, which seemed the only sticking point.

6   American leaders were sure that if he so chose "the Mikado could stop the war with a royal word"—as one top Presidential aide put it. Having decided to use the bomb, however, Mr. Truman was urged by Secretary of State James F. Byrnes not to give assurances to the Emperor before the weapon had been demonstrated.

7   Additional official records, including minutes of top-level White House planning meetings, show the President was clearly advised of the importance of a Soviet

declaration of war: It would pull the rug out from under Japanese military leaders who were desperately hoping the powerful Red Army would stay neutral.

8   Gen. George C. Marshall in mid-June told Mr. Truman that "the impact of Russian entry on the already hopeless Japanese may well be the decisive action levering them into capitulation at that time or shortly thereafter if we land."

9   A month later, the American-British Combined Intelligence Staffs advised their chiefs of the critical importance of a Red Army attack. As the top British general, Sir Hastings Ismay, summarized the conclusions for Prime Minister Winston Churchill: "If and when Russia came into the war against Japan, the Japanese would probably wish to get out on almost any terms short of the dethronement of the Emperor."

10   Mr. Truman's private diaries also record his understanding of the significance of this option. On July 17, 1945, when Stalin confirmed that the Red Army would march, Mr. Truman privately noted: "Fini Japs when that comes about."

11   There was plenty of time: The American invasion of Japan was not scheduled until the spring of 1946. Even a preliminary landing on the island Kyushu was still three months in the future.

12   Gen. Dwight D. Eisenhower, appalled that the bomb would be used in these circumstances, urged Mr. Truman and Secretary of War Henry L. Stimson not to drop it. In his memoirs, he observed that weeks before Hiroshima, Japan had been seeking a way to surrender. "It wasn't necessary," he said in a later interview, "to hit them with that awful thing."

13   The man who presided over the Joint Chiefs of Staff, Adm. William D. Leahy, was equally shocked: "The use of this barbarous weapon at Hiroshima and Nagasaki was of no material assistance in our war against Japan. The Japanese were already defeated and ready to surrender."

14   Why, then, was the bomb used?

15   American leaders rejected the most obvious option—simply waiting for the Red Army attack—out of political, not military, concerns.

16   As the diary of one official put it, they wanted to end the war before Moscow got "in so much on the kill." Secretary of the Navy James V. Forrestal's diaries record that Mr. Byrnes "was most anxious to get the Japanese affair over with before the Russians got in."

17   United States leaders had also begun to think of the atomic bomb as what Secretary Stimson termed the "master card" of diplomacy. President Truman postponed his Potsdam meeting with Stalin until July 17, 1945—one day after the first successful nuclear test—to be sure the atomic bomb would strengthen his hand before confronting the Soviet leader on the shape of a postwar settlement.

18   To this day, we do not know with absolute certainty Mr. Truman's personal attitudes on several key issues. Yet we do know that his most important adviser, Secretary of State Byrnes, was convinced that dropping the bomb would serve crucial long-range diplomatic purposes.

19   As one atomic scientist, Leo Szilard, observed: "Mr. Byrnes did not argue that it was necessary to use the bomb against the cities of Japan in order to win the war. Mr. Byrnes' . . . view [was] that our possessing and demonstrating the bomb would make Russia more manageable."

Now answer the following questions:

1. Is this essay mostly fact or opinion? _____

2. What is the author's main argument against dropping the bomb? _____

_____

3. Is the main argument based on facts? _____ Explain.

_____

_____

4. Did the author convince you that the U.S. was wrong in using the bomb?

_____ Explain. _____

_____

_____

5. Have you changed your opinion after reading these two essays? _____

Explain. _____

_____

_____

B. Reading Opinions of Others

Drill **B-1**

Directions: Take a few seconds to survey the following selection. Referring to the title, the headings, and your brief survey, write in the space below what you think the article will cover.

Probable coverage: _____

Now read the article, underlining factual statements. Then answer the questions that follow.

HOW GOOD ARE YOUR OPINIONS?

Vincent Ryan Ruggiero

1   "Opinion" is a word that is often used carelessly today. It is used to refer to matters of taste, belief, and judgment. This casual use would probably cause little confusion if people didn't attach too much importance to opinion. Unfortunately, most do attach great importance to it. "I have as much right to my opinion as you to yours," and "Everyone's entitled to his opinion," are common expressions. In fact, anyone who would challenge another's opinion is likely to be branded intolerant.

2   Is that label accurate? Is it intolerant to challenge another's opinion? It depends on what definition of opinion you have in mind. For example, you may ask a friend "What do you think of the new Buicks?" And he may reply, "In my opinion, they're ugly." In this case, it would not only be intolerant to challenge his statement, but foolish. For it's obvious that by opinion he means his *personal preference,* a matter of taste. And as the old saying goes, "It's pointless to argue about matters of taste."

3   But consider this very different use of the term. A newspaper reports that the Supreme Court has delivered its opinion in a controversial case. Obviously the justices did not state their personal preferences, their mere likes and dislikes. They stated their *considered judgment,* painstakingly arrived at after thorough inquiry and deliberation.

4   Most of what is referred to as opinion falls somewhere between these two extremes. It is not an expression of taste. Nor is it careful judgment. Yet it may contain elements of both. It is a view or belief more or less casually arrived at, with or without examining the evidence.

5   Is everyone entitled to his opinion? Of course. In a free country this is not only permitted, but guaranteed. In Great Britain, for example, there is still a Flat Earth Society. As the name implies, the members of this organization believe that the earth is not spherical, but flat. In this country, too, each of us is free to take as creative a position as we please about any matter we choose. When the telephone operator announces "That'll be 95¢ for the first three minutes," you may respond, "No, it won't—it'll be 28¢." When the service station attendant notifies you "Your oil is down a quart," you may reply "Wrong—it's up three."

6   Being free to hold an opinion and express it does not, of course, guarantee you favorable consequences. The operator may hang up on you. The service station attendant may threaten you with violence.

From Beyond Feelings: A Guide to Critical Thinking by Vincent Ryan Ruggiero by permission of Mayfield Publishing Company. Copyright © 1984 by Mayfield Publishing Company.

7   *Acting* on our opinions carries even less assurance. Some time ago in California a couple took their eleven-year-old diabetic son to a faith healer. Secure in their opinion that the man had cured the boy, they threw away his insulin. Three days later the boy died. They remained unshaken in their belief, expressing the opinion that God would raise the boy from the dead. The police arrested them, charging them with manslaughter. The law in such matters is both clear and reasonable. We are free to act on our opinions only so long as, in doing so, we do not harm others.

OPINIONS CAN BE MISTAKEN

8   It is tempting to conclude that, if we are free to believe something, it must have some validity. But that is not so. Free societies are based on the wise observation that since knowledge often comes through mistakes and truth is elusive, every person must be allowed to make his own path to wisdom. So in a way, free societies are based on the realization that opinions can be *wrong*.

9   In 1972 a British farmer was hoeing his sugar beet field when he uncovered a tiny statue. It looked to him like the figure of a man listening to a transistor radio. In his opinion, it was a piece of junk. Yet it turned out to be a work of art made of gilt bronze in the twelfth century and worth more than $85,000. He was free to have his opinion. But his opinion was wrong.

10   For scores of years millions of people lit up billions of cigarettes, firm in their opinion that their habit was messy and expensive, but harmless. Yet now we know that smoking is a significant factor in numerous diseases and even does harm to non-smokers who breathe smoke-polluted air and to unborn babies in the wombs of cigarette addicts. Those millions of people were free to believe smoking harmless. But that didn't make them right. Nor did it protect their bodies from harm.

KINDS OF ERROR

11   There are four general kinds of error that can corrupt anyone's beliefs. Francis Bacon classified them as follows: (1) errors or tendencies to error common among all people by virtue of their being human; (2) errors that come from human communication and the limitations of language; (3) errors in the general fashion or attitude of an age; (4) errors posed to an individual by a particular situation.

12   Some people, of course, are more prone to errors than others. John Locke observed that these people fall into three groups. He described them as follows:

> a.   Those who seldom reason at all, but do and think according to the example of others, whether parents, neighbors, ministers, or whoever else they choose or have implicit faith in, to save themselves the pain and trouble of thinking and examining for themselves.
>
> b.   Those who are determined to let passion rather than reason govern their actions and arguments, and therefore rely on their own or other people's reasoning only so far as it suits them.
>
> c.   Those who sincerely follow reason, but lack sound, overall good sense, and so do not have a full view of everything that relates to the issue. They talk with only one type of person, read only one type of book, and so are exposed to only one viewpoint.

INFORMED VS. UNINFORMED OPINION

13   In forming our opinions it helps to seek out the views of those who know more than we do about the subject. By examining the views of informed people, we broaden our perspective, see details we could not see by ourselves, consider facts we were unaware of. No one can know everything about everything. It is not a mark of inferiority but of good sense to consult those who have given their special attention to the field of knowledge at issue.

14   Each of us knows something about food and food preparation. After all, most of us have eaten three meals a day all our lives. But that experience doesn't make us experts on running a restaurant or on the food packaging industry. Many of us have played varsity sports in high school. But it takes more than that experience to make us authorities on a particular sport.

15   Some years ago the inmates of Attica prison in New York State overpowered their guards and gained control of the prison. They took a number of hostages and threatened to kill them if their demands were not met. Negotiations proceeded for a time. Then they were at an impasse. The situation grew tense. Finally lawmen stormed the prison and, before order was restored, a number of the hostages were killed. In the wake of the tragedy were two difficult questions: Had the prisoners' demands been reasonable? And who was responsible for the breakdown in negotiations?

16   A number of people in public and private life offered their opinions. One newspaper editorial stated that the main fault lay with the prisoners, that they had refused to negotiate reasonably. A letter to the editor explained that the prisoners were unquestionably in the wrong simply because they were prisoners, and thus had forfeited all rights and privileges. A U.S. senator from another state declared that the blame lay with American life in general. "We must ask," he said, "why some men would rather die than live another day in America."

17   The governor of New York State issued this statement: "The tragedy was brought on by the highly-organized, revolutionary tactics of militants who rejected all efforts at a peaceful settlement, forcing a confrontation, and carried out cold-blooded killings they had threatened from the outset."

18   In a much less publicized statement, a professor at a small liberal arts college, an expert in penology (the study of prison systems), expressed sympathy with the prisoners, criticized the terrible conditions in the nation's prisons, agreed fully with many of the prisoners' demands, rejected a few as absurd, and explained some of the underlying causes of prison unrest.

19   Now all those opinions deserved some consideration. But which was *most* helpful in coming to an understanding of the issue in all its considerable complexity? Certainly the most informed opinion. The opinion of the expert in penology.

20   For all of us, whether experts or amateurs, it is natural to form opinions. We are constantly receiving sensory impressions and responding to them first on the level of simple likes and dislikes, then on the level of thought. Even if we wanted to escape having opinions, we couldn't. Nor should we want to. One of the things that makes human beings vastly more complex and interesting than trees or cows is their ability to form opinions.

21   This ability has two sides, though. If it can lift man to the heights of understanding, it can also topple him to the depths of ludicrousness. Both the wise man and the fool have opinions. The difference is, the wise man forms his with care, and as time increases his understanding, refines them to fit even more precisely the reality they interpret.

COMPREHENSION CHECK

Directions: Answer the following questions. Don't look back unless you are referred to a particular paragraph for an answer.

Part A

1. Circle the letter of the statement that best expresses the thesis of the article:
    a. We need to form our opinions with care.
    b. It is natural to form opinions.
    c. The word "opinion" is used carelessly today.
    d. Everyone has a right to his or her own opinion.
2. T/F   The statement "Being free to hold an opinion and express it does not, of course, guarantee you favorable consequences" is a fact.
3. T/F   Paragraph 9 is mostly factual in content.
4. Which of the following are mentioned as the kinds of error that can corrupt anyone's beliefs?
    a. errors posed to an individual by a particular situation
    b. errors or tendencies to error common among all people by virtue of being human
    c. errors in the general fashion or attitude of an age
    d. errors that come from limitations of language
5. T/F   In forming our opinions, it helps to seek out the views of those who do not know more than we do about the subject.
6. T/F   "No one can know everything about everything" is an opinion.
7. In paragraph 19, the author claims the expert in penology was the most helpful in coming to an understanding of the prison riot issue. Why would

    this opinion be better than the others mentioned? _____

    _____

8. What is the difference between personal preference and considered judg-

    ment? _____

    _____

    _____

9. "One of the things that make human beings vastly more complex and interesting than trees or cows is their ability to form opinions," says the author. Is

    this a statement of fact or opinion? _____ Explain. _____

    _____

    _____

10. Is the article mostly fact or opinion? _____ Explain.

    _____

    _____

Number correct: _____

Part B

Directions: The preceding questions can be answered objectively. The following questions require subjective responses.

1.   "We are free to act on our opinions only as long as, in doing so, we do not harm

   others," says the author. Is this a good rule to follow? _____ Explain. _____

   _____

   _____

   _____

2.   The author refers to a couple who took their diabetic son to a faith healer as an example of how acting on our opinions can be dangerous. Give an example of an opinion you hold or held at one time that could be dangerous in certain

   circumstances. _____

   _____

   _____

   _____

3.   Reread paragraph 12. In your opinion, do you fit any one of the three groups?

   _____ Explain. _____

   _____

   _____

4.   Give an example of an opinion you once held but no longer do. Explain why

   you changed your viewpoint. _____

   _____

   _____

   _____

   _____

VOCABULARY CHECK

A. Write a definition for each underlined word in the blanks following each statement.

1. their <u>considered</u> judgment

_____

2. it must have some <u>validity</u>

_____

3. errors <u>posed</u> to an individual

_____

4. some are more <u>prone</u> to errors

_____

5. they have <u>implicit</u> faith in themselves

_____

B. Using the words from the list below, write the correct word in the appropriate blank.

overpowered	inmates
impasse	proceeded
tense	

"Some years ago the (6) _____ of Attica prison in New York State

(7) _____ their guards and gained control of the prison. Negotiations

(8) _____ for a time. Then they were at an (9) _____. The

situation grew (10) _____."

Number correct: _____

Record the results of the comprehension and vocabulary checks on the Student Record Chart on page 495. Discuss any problems or questions with your instructor before you continue.

Drill B-2

Directions: Read the title of the following selection. Based on the title, what do you think the article will be about? At this point, do you think you will agree or disagree with the author? Why? Write your answers in the spaces provided.

Probable thesis: _____

_____

Do you agree or disagree: _____
Now read the selection and answer the questions that follow it.

LIFEBOAT ETHICS: THE CASE AGAINST HELPING THE POOR

Garrett Hardin

1   Environmentalists use the metaphor of the earth as a "spaceship" in trying to persuade countries, industries and people to stop wasting and polluting our natural resources. Since we all share life on this planet, they argue, no single person or institution has the right to destroy, waste, or use more than a fair share of its resources.

2   But does everyone on earth have an equal right to an equal share of its resources? The spaceship metaphor can be dangerous when used by misguided idealists to justify suicidal policies for sharing our resources through uncontrolled immigration and foreign aid. In their enthusiastic but unrealistic generosity, they confuse the ethics of a spaceship with those of a lifeboat.

3   A true spaceship would have to be under the control of a captain, since no ship could possibly survive if its course were determined by committee. Spaceship Earth certainly has no captain; the United Nations is merely a toothless tiger, with little power to enforce any policy upon its bickering members.

4   If we divide the world crudely into rich nations and poor nations, two-thirds of them are desperately poor, and only one-third comparatively rich, with the United States the wealthiest of all. Metaphorically each rich nation can be seen as a lifeboat full of comparatively rich people. In the ocean outside each lifeboat swim the poor of the world, who would like to get in, or at least to share some of the wealth. What should the lifeboat passengers do?

5   First, we must recognize the limited capacity of any lifeboat. For example, a nation's land has a limited capacity to support a population and as the current energy crisis has shown us, in some ways we have already exceeded the carrying capacity of our land.

6   So here we sit, say fifty people in our lifeboat. To be generous, let us assume it has room for ten more, making a total capacity of sixty. Suppose the fifty of us in the lifeboat see 100 others swimming in the water outside, begging for admission to our boat or for handouts. We have several options: We may be tempted to try to live by the Christian ideal of being "our brother's keeper," or by the Marxist ideal of "to each according to his needs." Since the needs of all in the water are the same, and since they

Reprinted with permission from *Psychology Today* Magazine. Copyright © 1974 American Psychological Association.

can all be seen as "our brothers," we should take them all into our boat, making a total of 150 in a boat designed for sixty. The boat swamps, everyone drowns. Complete justice, complete catastrophe.

7   Since the boat has an unused excess capacity of ten more passengers, we could admit just ten more to it. But which ten do we let in? How do we choose? Do we pick the best ten, the neediest ten, "first come, first served"? And what do we say to the ninety we exclude? If we do let an extra ten into our lifeboat, we will have lost our "safety factor," an engineering principle of critical importance. For example, if we don't leave room for excess capacity as a safety factor in our country's agriculture, a new plant disease or a bad change in the weather could have disastrous consequences.

8   Suppose we decide to preserve our small safety factor and admit no more to the lifeboat. Our survival is then possible, although we shall have to be constantly on guard against boarding parties.

9   While this last solution clearly offers the only means of our survival, it is morally abhorrent to many people. Some say they feel guilty about their good luck. My reply is simple: "Get out and yield your place to others." This may solve the problem of the guilt-ridden person's conscience, but it does not change the ethics of the lifeboat. The needy person to whom the guilt-ridden person yields his place will not himself feel guilty about his good luck. If he did, he would not climb aboard. The net result of conscience-stricken people giving up their unjustly held seats is the elimination of that sort of conscience from the lifeboat.

10   This is the basic metaphor within which we must work out our solutions.

COMPREHENSION CHECK
Part A

Directions: Answer the following questions. Look back only if you are referred to a particular paragraph.

1. T/F   The author's thesis is that wealthy countries, contrary to what some environmentalists say, are obligated to help poor countries just because they have more.

2. The author _____ accept the analogy of the environmentalists who liken the earth to a spaceship.
    a. does
    b. does not
    c. does with limitations
    d. does with no limitations

3. The author says that the United Nations is a "toothless tiger." Is this fact or

    opinion? _____

4. According to the author, if we live by the Christian ideal of "being our brother's keeper," or the Marxist ideal of "to each according to his needs,"

    what will eventually happen? _____

    _____

5. The author, using an analogy, likens our planet to
    a. a spaceship
    b. a farm
    c. a factory
    d. none of the above

6. The author states, "If we divide the world into rich nations and poor nations, two-thirds of them are desperately poor, and only one-third comparatively rich, with the United States the wealthiest of all." Is this fact or opinion?

_____

7. T/F   According to the author, feelings of guilt are what cause many people to want to help those less fortunate than themselves.
8. T/F   The author feels that since we all share life on this planet, no single person or institution has the right to destroy, waste, or use more than a fair share of its resources.
9. T/F   Those who believe that question 8 is true see themselves as a part of a world population rather than a national group.
10. T/F   This article expresses more opinions than facts.

Number correct: _____

Part B

Directions: The following questions are more subjective than objective. You may look back if you need to.

1. Paragraph 2 opens with a question. Does the author answer the question?

_____

2. What is your answer to the question? _____

_____

3. Is your answer based on fact or opinion? _____
4. The author says that his "... solution clearly offers the only means of our survival," even though it is morally distasteful to many. Do you agree or

disagree with his conclusion? _____

Why? _____

_____

5. Has his article changed your opinions about the responsibility of wealthy

nations toward poorer countries? _____ Why?

_____

_____

_____

VOCABULARY CHECK

Directions: Define the following underlined words or phrases from the reading selection.

1. use the <u>metaphor</u> of the earth as a "spaceship"

_____

2. they confuse the <u>ethics</u> of a spaceship with a lifeboat

_____

3. full of <u>comparatively</u> rich people

_____

4. "<u>to each according to his needs</u>"

_____

5. we have several <u>options</u>

_____

6. it is morally <u>abhorrent</u> to many

_____

7. <u>yield</u> your place to others

_____

8. "<u>our brother's keeper</u>"

_____

9. through <u>uncontrolled immigration</u>

_____

10. when used by <u>misguided idealists</u>

_____

Number correct: _____

Record the results of the comprehension and vocabulary checks on the Student Record Chart on page 495. Discuss any problems or questions with your instructor.

Drill B-3: QUICK QUIZ ON FACT/OPINION

Part A

Directions: In the space provided, explain the differences between fact and opinion.

Part B

Directions: Place an *O* in the blank in front of all statements of opinion, an *F* if a statement is fact or can be verified.

_____ **1.** There are 57 items in the L. L. Bean Women's Outdoor Catalogue offered in various shades of pink.

_____ **2.** We can no longer get along in our present society without telephones.

_____ **3.** It is important for college students to have good study skills if they are to succeed in the academic world.

_____ **4.** The Tobacco Institute donated $70,000 to help underwrite the anti-drug booklet *Helping Youth Say No.*

_____ **5.** The two most interesting things in the world, for our species, are ideas and the individual human body, two elements that poetry uniquely joins together.

_____ **6.** Last year, as a result of the worldwide collapse of oil prices, the Mexican economy shrank 5 percent, and underemployment reached 50 percent. Things are worse in El Salvador.

_____ **7.** The United States is a nation of immigrants, and of immigration policies—policies designed to facilitate the orderly entry of people into the country, but also to keep them out.

_____ **8.** War against the Plains Indians in the early nineteenth century was a hopeless proposition for Europeans armed with swords, single-shot pistols, and breech-loading rifles. The Indians were infinitely better horsemen and could loose a continuous fusillade of arrows from beneath the neck of a pony going at full tilt.

_____ **9.** Mark Hunter's comments on the lack of spirit and spontaneity found in contemporary rock music are accurate. But his attack on MTV is misguided and his assertion that rock music is no longer worth listening to is absurd.

_____ **10.** Your jeweler is the expert where diamonds are concerned. His knowledge can help make the acquisition of a quality diamond of a carat or more a beautiful, rewarding experience.

Part C

Directions: In the space provided, explain what kind of evidence you would have to gather to prove the following statements as facts.

1. The viewing of violence on television has created a more violent society.

2. City slums breed crime.

3. Solar energy is the most efficient way to heat homes in some parts of the U.S.

4. A college education provides better job opportunities.

5. If you are rich, you probably won't get convicted of a crime as easily as you will if you are poor.

Turn in the quiz to your instructor.

C. Detecting Propaganda

Propaganda is the deliberate attempt on the part of a group or an individual to sway our opinions in their favor. Contrary to what some think, propaganda is not merely a tool used by dictatorial governments. We are exposed to various propaganda techniques nearly every day of our lives. Politicians use propaganda, along with other devices, to get us to accept their opinions and vote for them. Newspapers and magazines use propaganda techniques to influence our opinions on political and social issues. Religious leaders use propaganda to influence our opinions on morality. Advertisers, through television, radio, newspapers, and magazines, use propaganda techniques to get us to buy things we often don't need or to change the brand of soap we use.

Propaganda techniques usually appeal to our emotions or our desires rather than to our reason. They cause us to believe or do things we might not believe or do if we thought and reasoned more carefully. When we are too lazy to think for ourselves, we often become victims of propaganda. Propagandists are usually not concerned with good or bad, right or wrong. They are more concerned with getting us to believe what they want us to believe. The techniques they use can range from outright lies to subtle truths.

The power of propaganda cannot be overrated. While some propaganda may be socially beneficial, it can also be harmful. Through propaganda techniques, our opinions can be changed to be "for" or "against" certain nations, political rulers, races, moral values, and religions. What we must guard against is having our opinions formed for us by others. We must not let ourselves be used or fooled, even for good causes.

Those who investigate the way propagandists work have identified seven basic techniques that are used frequently:

1. *name calling* (using names that appeal to our hatred or fears; if the propagandists know a group fears communism, they might call an opponent a "commie" or a "red" to get the group to distrust the opponent)
2. *glittering generalities* (using words that appeal to our emotions such as justice, founding fathers, freedom fighters, love, loyalty, or the American way are vague but have positive connotations that appeal to us; they are often used because propagandists know we are touched by such words)
3. *transfer* (linking something we like or respect to some person, cause, or product; if we respect the flag or the Christian cross, our respect for the symbol is transferred to whatever use it is being associated with)
4. *testimonial* (using well-known people to testify that a certain person, idea, or product is "the best"; if we admire Robert Redford and we see him in advertising for a particular product or politician we then buy the product or vote for the person because of our respect for Redford, even though he may not be an authority on the subject)
5. *plain folks* (a device used by politicians, labor leaders, businessmen, ministers, educators, and advertisers to win our confidence by appearing to be just plain folks like ourselves; the good-old-boy image)
6. *card stacking* (stacking the evidence against the truth by lying, omitting, or evading facts, underplaying or overemphasizing issues, telling half-truths, stating things out of context; advertisers might say their product "helps stop bad breath," leading us to think it *does* stop it)
7. *the bandwagon* (appealing to our desire to be on the winning side, to be like or better than everyone else and follow the crowd or be one of the gang "in on the latest fad")

Most of these devices work because they appeal to our emotions, our fears, our ignorance, or our desire to do the "right thing." But by sorting facts from opinions, and by recognizing these propaganda techniques when used, we won't become victims, but rather thoughtful readers and thinkers.

Drill   C-1: DETECTING PROPAGANDA TECHNIQUES

Directions: Read each of the following items and in the space provided write in which propaganda technique is being used and why you think so.

1. "My opponent, Senator Glick, has a record of being soft on communism at a time when we need to be strong."

   _____

   _____

2. "Senator Cluck cares what happens to the farmers; he cares for the future of the American tradition of prosperity. He'll put this country back on track!"

   _____

   _____

3. "Wilt Chamberlain. Cardmember since 1976" (American Express advertisement).

   _____

   _____

4. "M Lotion helps skin keep its moisture . . . discourages tired-looking lines under eyes."

   _____

   _____

5. "Over 8,000,000 sold! Why would anyone want to buy anything else?"

   _____

   _____

6. "Buy Banhead. It contains twice as much pain reliever."

   _____

   _____

7. "Mayor Naste has shown time and again he's for the little guy. You don't see him driving a big limo, or wearing fancy suits. No, sir. You'll find him out talking to us folks to see how he can serve us better."

   _____

   _____

8. "Buy the Sportsman's Shaving System, appointed the exclusive skin care system for the Winter Olympics."

_____

_____

9. "Yes, I lied. But I did it for my country. As God is my witness, I felt in my heart—and still do—that what I did was right, and the people of this country who want to preserve its freedom will thank me some day."

_____

_____

10. "Drive to class reunions with this new Fone-E antenna on your car, and even Mr. Most-Likely-to-Succeed will be envious. Everyone will assume you have a cellular phone—_the_ mark of success!"

_____

_____

Drill C-2

Directions: Read the following selection that deals with some of the propaganda techniques already mentioned. Look for definitions and examples of the techniques discussed.

DETECTING PROPAGANDA

Richard D. Altick and Andrea A. Lunsford

1   All of us, whether we admit it or not, are prejudiced. We dislike certain people, certain activities, certain ideas—in many cases, not because we have reasoned things out and found a logical basis for our dislike, but rather because those people or activities or ideas affect our less generous instincts. Of course we also have positive prejudices, by which we approve of people or things—perhaps because they give us pleasure or perhaps because we have always been taught that they are "good" and never stopped to reason why. In either case, these biases, irrational and unfair though they may be, are aroused by words, principally by name-calling and the use of the glittering generality. Both of these techniques depend on the process of association, by which an idea (the specific person, group, proposal, or situation being discussed) takes on emotional coloration from the language employed.

2   _Name-calling_ is the device of arousing an unfavorable response by such an association. A speaker or writer who wishes to sway an audience against a person, group, or principle will often use this device.

The bleeding-heart liberals are responsible for the current economic crisis.

From _Preface to Critical Reading,_ 6th ed., by Richard D. Altick and Andrea A. Lunsford. Copyright © 1984 by Holt, Rinehart and Winston, Inc. Reprinted by permission of Holt, Rinehart and Winston, Inc.

> The labor union radicals keep honest people from honest work.
> Environmental extremists can bankrupt hard-pressed companies with their fanatical demands for unnecessary and expensive pollution controls such as chimney-scrubbers.

Name-calling is found in many arguments in which emotion plays a major role. It rarely is part of the logic of an argument but instead is directed at personalities. Note how the speakers here depend on verbal rock throwing in their attempt to win the day:

> He's no coach, but a foul-mouthed, cigar-chomping bully who bribes high-school stars to play for him.
> The Bible-thumping bigots who want to censor our books and our television shows represent the worst of the anti-intellectual lunatic fringe.
> Mayor Leech has sold the city out to vested interests and syndicates of racketeers. City Hall stinks of graft and payola.

The negative emotional associations of the "loaded" words in these sentences have the planned effect of spilling over onto, and hiding, the real points at issue, which demand—but fail to receive—fair, analytical, objective judgment. Generating a thick emotional haze is, therefore, an effective way for glib writers and speakers to convince many of the unthinking or the credulous among their audience.

3   The *glittering generality* involves the equally illogical use of connotative words. In contrast to name-calling, the glittering generality draws on traditionally positive associations. Here, as in name-calling, the trouble is that the words used have been applied too freely and thus are easily misapplied. Many writers and speakers take advantage of the glitter of these words to blind readers to real issues at hand. *Patriot, freedom, democracy, national honor, Constitution, God-given rights, peace, liberty, property rights, international cooperation, brotherhood, equal opportunity, prosperity, decent standard of living:* words or phrases like these sound pleasant to the listener's ear, but they can also divert attention from the ideas the speaker is discussing, ideas which are usually too complex to be fairly labeled by a single word.

> The progressive, forward-looking liberal party will make certain that we enjoy a stable and healthy economy.
> The practical idealists of the labor movement are united in supporting the right of every person to earn an honest living.
> Dedicated environmentalists perform an indispensable patriotic service for us all by keeping air-polluting industries' feet to the fire.

> He's a coach who is a shining light to our youth. He believes that football helps to build the character, stamina, and discipline needed for the leaders of tomorrow.
> The decent, God-fearing people who want to protect us from the violence and depravity depicted in books and on television represent the best of a moral society.
> Mayor Leech has stood for progress, leadership, and vision at a time when most cities have fallen into the hands of the corrupt political hacks.

4   The effectiveness of name-calling and the glittering generality depends on stock responses. Just as the scientist Pavlov, in a classic experiment, conditioned dogs to increase their production of saliva every time he rang a bell, so the calculating persuader expects readers to react automatically to language that appeals to their prejudices.

5   The abuse of authority is one of the *transfer devices* which exploit readers' willingness to link one idea or person with another, even though the two may not be logically connected. The familiar *testimonials* of present-day advertising provide an

instance of this device. In some cases, the "authority" who testifies has some connection with the product advertised. The problem to settle here is, when we try to decide which brand of sunburn cream is best, how much weight may we reasonably attach to the enthusiastic statements of certain nurses? When we are thinking of buying a tennis racket, should we accept the say-so of a champion who, after all, is well paid for telling us that a certain make is the best? In other cases, the testifying authorities may have no formal, professional connection with the products they recommend. An actor, who may very well be a master of his particular art, praises a whiskey, a coffee, or an airline. He likes it, he says. But, we may ask, does the fact that he is a successful actor make him better qualified than any person who is not an actor to judge a whiskey, a coffee, or an airline? Competence in one field does not necessarily "transfer" to competence in another.

6   Furthermore, advertisers often borrow the prestige of science and medicine to enhance the reputation of their products. Many people have come to feel for the laboratory scientist and the physician an awe once reserved for bishops or statesmen. The alleged approval of such people thus carries great weight in selling something or inducing someone to believe something. Phrases such as "leading medical authorities say . . ." or "independent laboratory tests show . . ." are designed simply to transfer the prestige of science to a toothpaste or deodorant. Seldom are the precise "medical authorities" or "independent laboratories" named. But the mere phrases carry weight with uncritical listeners or readers. Similarly, the title "Dr." or "Professor" implies that the person quoted speaks with all the authority of which learned people are capable— when as a matter of fact doctoral degrees can be bought from mail-order colleges. Therefore, whenever a writer or speaker appeals to the prestige that surrounds the learned, the reader should demand credentials. Just *what* "medical authorities" say this? Can they be trusted? What independent laboratories made the tests—and what did the tests actually reveal? Who are the people who speak as expert educators, psychologists, or economists? Regardless of the fact that they are "doctors," do they know what they are talking about?

7   Another closely related form of transfer is the borrowing of prestige from a highly respected institution (country, religion, education) or individual (world leader, philosopher, scientist) for the sake of enhancing something else. Political speakers sometimes work into their speeches quotations from the Bible or from secular "sacred writings" (such as a national constitution). Such quotations usually arouse favorable emotions in listeners, emotions which are then transferred to the speaker's policy or subject. When analyzing an appeal that uses quotations from men and women who have achieved renown in one field or another, the chief question is whether the quotation is appropriate in context. Does it have real relevance to the point at issue? It is all very well to quote George Washington or Abraham Lincoln in support of one's political stand. But circumstances have changed immensely since those statements were first uttered, and their applicability to a new situation may be dubious indeed. The implication is, "This person, who we agree was great and wise, said certain things which 'prove' the justice of my own stand. Therefore, you should believe I am right." But to have a valid argument, the writer must prove that the word of the authorities is really applicable to the present issue. If that is true, then the speaker is borrowing not so much their prestige as their wisdom—which is perfectly justifiable.

8   Another version of the transfer device is one which gains prestige not through quotations or testimonials of authorities but from linking one idea to another. Here is an advertisement that illustrates how this device works.

THE TELEPHONE POLE THAT BECAME A MEMORIAL

9   The cottage on Lincoln Street in Portland, Oregon, is shaded by graceful trees and covered with ivy.

10   Many years ago, A. H. Feldman and his wife remodeled the house to fit their dreams . . . and set out slips of ivy around it. And when their son, Danny, came along,

he, too, liked to watch things grow. One day, when he was only nine, he took a handful of ivy slips and planted them at the base of the telephone pole in front of the house.

11   Time passed . . . and the ivy grew, climbing to the top of the pole. Like the ivy, Danny grew too. He finished high school, went to college. The war came along before he finished—and Danny went overseas. And there he gave his life for his country.

12   Not very long ago the overhead telephone lines were being removed from the poles on Lincoln Street. The ivy-covered telephone pole in front of the Feldman home was about to be taken down. Its work was done.

13   But, when the telephone crew arrived, Mrs. Feldman came out to meet them. "Couldn't it be left standing?" she asked. And then she told them about her son.

14   So the pole, although no longer needed, wasn't touched at all. At the request of the telephone company, the Portland City Council passed a special ordinance permitting the company to leave it standing. And there it is today, mantled in ivy, a living memorial to Sergeant Danny Feldman.

15   What did the telephone company wish to accomplish by this ad? Readers are not urged to install a telephone, equip their homes with extra telephones, or use any of the various new services the company has developed. Nor are they told how inexpensive and efficient the telephone company thinks those services are. Instead, this is what is known as an "institutional" advertisement. Its purpose is to inspire public esteem, even affection, for the company.

16   How do such advertisements inspire esteem and respect? Simply by telling an anecdote, without a single word to point up the moral. In this ad, every detail is carefully chosen for its emotional appeal: the cottage ("home, sweet home" theme), the ivy (symbol of endurance through the years; often combined, as here, with the idea of the family home), the little boy (evoking all the feelings associated with childhood), the young man dying in the war (evoking patriotic sentiment). Thus at least four symbols are combined—all of them with great power to touch the emotions. Then the climax: Will the company cut down the ivy-covered pole? To many people, *company* has a connotation of hardheartedness, impersonality, coldness, which is the very impression this particular company, one of the biggest in the world, wants to erase. So the company modestly reports that it went to the trouble of getting special permission to leave this one pole standing, "mantled in ivy, a living memorial."

17   The writer of this advertisement has, in effect, urged readers to transfer to the telephone company the sympathies aroused by the story. The ivy-covered pole aptly symbolizes what the writer wanted to do—"mantle" the pole (symbolizing the company) with the ivy that is associated with home, childhood, and heroic death. If it is possible to make one feel sentimental about a giant corporation, an advertisement like this one—arousing certain feelings by means of one set of objects and then transferring those feelings to another object—will do it. But the story, although true enough, is after all only one incident, and a sound generalization about the character of a vast company cannot be formed from a single anecdote. The company may well be as "human" as the advertisement implies, but readers are led to that belief through an appeal to their sympathies, not their reason.

18   A third kind of fallacy involves *mudslinging,* attacking a person rather than a principle. Mudslingers make personal attacks on an opponent (formally known as *ad hominem* arguments, those "against the man"), not merely by calling names, but often by presenting what they offer as damaging evidence against the opponent's motives, character, and private life. Thus the audience's attention is diverted from the argument itself to a subject which is more likely to stir up prejudices. If, for example, in denouncing an opponent's position on reducing the national debt, a candidate refers to X's connection with certain well-known gamblers, then the candidate ceases to argue the case on its merits and casts doubt on the opponent's personal character. The object is not to hurt X's feelings but to arouse bias against that person in the hearer's mind. Critical readers or listeners must train themselves to detect and reject these irrelevant aspersions. It may be, indeed, that X has shady connections with underworld gamblers. But that may have nothing to do with the abstract right or wrong of his stand

on the national debt. Issues should be discussed apart from character and motives. Both character and motives are important, of course, since they bear on any candidate's fitness for public office and on whether we can give him or her our support. But they call for a separate discussion.

19 A somewhat more subtle kind of personal attack is the *innuendo,* which differs from direct accusation roughly as a hint differs from a plain statement. Innuendo is chiefly useful where no facts exist to give even a semblance of support to a direct charge. The writer or speaker therefore slyly plants seeds of doubt or suspicion in the reader's or listener's mind, as the villainous Iago does in the mind of Shakespeare's Othello. Innuendo is a trick that is safe, effective—and unfair. "They were in the office with the door locked for four hours after closing time." The statement, in itself, may be entirely true. But what counts is the implication it is meant to convey. The unfairness increases when the doubts that the innuendo raises concern matters that have nothing to do with the issue anyway. An example of the irrelevant innuendo is found in the writings of the historian Charles A. Beard. In assailing the ideas of another historian, Admiral Alfred T. Mahan, Beard called him "the son of a professor and swivel-chair tactician at West Point," who "served respectably, but without distinction, for a time in the navy" and "found an easy berth at the Naval War College." Actually, the occupation of Mahan's father has nothing to do with the validity of the son's arguments. But observe the sneer—which is meant to be transferred from father to son—in "professor" and "swivel-chair tactician." Beard's reference to Mahan's naval record is a good elementary instance of damning with faint praise. And whether or not Mahan's was "an easy berth" at the Naval War College (a matter of opinion), it too has no place in a discussion of the man's ideas or intellectual capacities.

20 Newspapers often use this device to imply more than they can state without risking a libel suit. In reporting the latest bit of gossip about celebrated members of the "jet set" or the "beautiful people" (what do the terms suggest about the habits and tastes of the people referred to?), a paper may mention the fact that "gorgeous movie actress A is a frequent companion of thrice-divorced playboy B" or that they "are seen constantly together at the Vegas night spots" or that they are "flitting from the Riviera to Sun Valley together." The inference suggested, however unfounded it may be, is that their relationship is not just that of good friends who happen to be in the same place at the same time. Similarly, newspapers which value sensationalism more than responsibility may describe an accused "child slayer" or "woman molester" as "dirty and bearded" (implication: he is a suspicious-looking bum). His face may, in addition, be "scarred" (implication: he is physically violent). Such literal details may be true enough. But how much have they to do with the guilt or innocence of the person in this particular case? The effect on the reader is what courts of law term "prejudicial" and therefore inadmissible. Unfortunately the law does not extend to slanted writing, however powerfully it may sway public opinion.

21 Another instance of the way in which emotionally loaded language can be combined with unproved evidence to stir up prejudice may be taken from the field of art. A modern critic condemned certain paintings as "a conventional rehash of cubist patterns born among the wastrels of Paris forty years ago." In so doing, the critic attacked the art through the artist. The artistic merit of paintings has nothing to do with the private lives of the people who paint them. The painters referred to may well have been wastrels. But that fact—if it is a fact—has no bearing on the point at issue. The assumed connection between the personal virtues or shortcomings of artists and the artistic value of their productions has resulted in a great deal of confused thinking about literature, music, and the other arts.

22 Another diversionary tactic which introduces an irrelevant issue into a debate is the *red herring.* It too may involve shifting attention from principles to personalities, but without necessarily slinging mud or calling names. Since neither relaxing at a disco nor having a taste for serious books is yet sinful or criminal, a political party slings no mud when it portrays the other party's candidate as a playboy or an intellectual. Still, such matters are largely irrelevant to the main argument, which is

whether one or the other candidate will better serve the interests of the people. The red-herring device need not involve personalities at all; it may take the form simply of substituting one issue for another. If a large corporation is under fire for alleged monopolistic practices, its public relations people may start an elaborate advertising campaign to show how well the company's workers are treated. Thus, if the campaign succeeds, the bad publicity suffered because of the assertions that the company has been trying to corner the market may be counteracted by the public's approval of its allegedly fine labor policy.

23   Unfortunately, most of us are eager to view questions in their simplest terms and to make our decisions on the basis of only a few of the many elements the problem may involve. The problem of minority groups in North America, for instance, is not simply one of abstract justice, as many would like to think. Rather, it involves complex and by no means easily resolvable issues of economics, sociology, politics, and psychology. Nor can one say with easy assurance, "The federal government should guarantee every farmer a decent income, even if the money comes from the pocketbooks of the citizens who are the farmer's own customers" or "It is the obligation of every educational institution to purge its faculty of all who hold radical sympathies." Perhaps each of these propositions is sound; perhaps neither is. But before either is adopted as a conviction, intelligent readers must canvass their full implications.... After the implications have been explored, more evidence may be found *against* the proposition than in support of it.

24   Countless reductive generalizations concerning parties, races, religions, and nations, to say nothing of individuals, are the result of the deep-seated human desire to reduce complicated ideas to their simplest terms. We saw the process working when we touched on stereotypes in Chapter 1 and in our discussion of rhetorical induction in this chapter. Unfortunately, condemning with a few quick, perhaps indefensible assumptions is easier than recognizing the actual diversity in any social group. But every man and woman has an urgent obligation to analyze the basis of each judgment he or she makes: "Am I examining every aspect of the issue that needs to be examined? Do I understand the problem sufficiently to be able to make a fair decision? Or am I taking the easiest and simplest way out?"

Now answer the following questions:

1. According to the authors, what two propaganda devices are used to stir up our

    prejudices? _____

    _____

2. What part do our emotions play in the effectiveness of some propaganda techniques?

    _____

    _____

3. What do the authors mean when they say that "advertisers often borrow the

    prestige of science and medicine to enhance the reputation of their

    products"? _____

    _____

    _____

4. What is meant by the term "transfer device"? Give some examples.

_____

_____

_____

5. Name the three devices or methods frequently used to attack a person rather than a principle. _____

_____

6. Define the following terms:

    a. transfer devices: _____

    _____

    b. testimonials: _____

    _____

    c. mudslinging: _____

    _____

    d. innuendo: _____

    _____

    e. red herring: _____

    _____

    f. oversimplification: _____

    _____

7. Why is it important to recognize and understand how propaganda is used?

_____

_____

_____

Drill C-3: RECOGNIZING PROPAGANDA AT WORK

Directions: Find an example of one of the seven propaganda techniques used in a current magazine or newspaper advertisement. Write a brief explanation of how the technique is being used, attach it to the ad, and share it in class.

CHAPTER 7

Recognizing Intent, Attitude, and Tone

A. Recognizing Intent, Attitude, and Tone

In addition to distinguishing fact from opinion, critical reading requires an awareness of an author's *intent, attitude*, and *tone*.

An author's *intent* is not always easy to recognize. Let's say, for instance, that you are reading Jonathan Swift's essay "A Modest Proposal," an essay that appears frequently in English literature anthologies. At the time he wrote this essay in the eighteenth century, many Irish people were dying from famine. To read his essay at the literal level, Swift would seem to be in favor of taking the profusion of children in Ireland and treating them as cattle, fattening up some for slaughter, exporting some to boost the economy, and raising some strictly for breeding. However, to accept his essay on the literal level would be to miss his intent. His essay is a satire, and his intent was to make his readers more aware of a social problem that existed in his day. His real purpose was to ridicule the people in power at the time. He intentionally wrote in a rather cold, uncompassionate way to shock his readers into action. Yet, if you were not perceptive enough to understand Swift's intent, you could completely miss his point.

An author's intent may be to satirize a problem or condition, to amuse readers, to make them cry by arousing sympathy, pity, or fear, to argue a point that another writer has made, or to accuse someone of something. But whatever an author's intent may be, you, as a critical reader, need to be absolutely certain that you understand what it is.

An author's treatment of a subject reflects an *attitude* toward it. Swift, for instance, in the essay mentioned here, uses satire, but his attitude is serious. He is not serious about using children as an economic commodity, even though he provides a detailed plan for doing so. He was angry at the people of his day for allowing such deplorable conditions to exist. He was serious about wanting to change these conditions. An author's attitude, then, is the author's personal feeling about a subject. Attitudes can range from sad to happy, angry to delighted, sympathetic to unsympathetic, tolerant to furious.

The language an author uses is frequently a clue to that writer's attitude both to his subject and to the reader. In his book, *Preface to Critical Reading*, Richard Altick provides a good example of how paying attention to the language a writer uses can reflect intent and attitude:

> Compare the two ways in which a person could express the desire [intent] to borrow some money: (1) "Hey, good buddy, how about loaning me a ten for a few days? I'm in a bind. You'll get it back on Friday." (2) "I'm very sorry to impose on you, but I'm in a bit of a predicament, and I need ten dollars just until payday. I'd be extremely grateful." The language of the first appeal suggests that slang is the normal means of expression for this speaker. The meaning of the second appeal is identical, and the general approach is the same. But whereas the first speaker is forthright and unembarrassed, the other seems hesitant and apologetic. The personalities of the two seem as different as the connotations of *bind* and *predicament*.

In other words, the intent of both the appeals in the example is the same; they want to borrow money. But the attitudes are different. Critical reading requires an ability to distinguish such differences.

How an author uses language creates what is called a *tone*. Tone in writing is similar to what we call a tone of voice. For instance, the phrase "Thanks a lot!" can have different meanings based on the tone of voice used to express it. If we are truly grateful we will say it one way; if we want to be sarcastic, we'll say it another way;

and if we are angry or disgusted, we'll say it still another way. When reading, however, we can't hear an author's tone of voice. But as critical readers, we must be able to recognize the true tone intended by the author.

Frequently writers use *figurative language* to express their tone. Figurative language is used in an imaginative way rather than in a literal sense. For instance, when a writer says "her eyes flashed fire," the intent is not for us to imagine real fire coming from someone's eyes, but to realize that the character is angry. Or, when we read that a lawyer "dropped his client like a hot potato," we are given to understand that the lawyer's actions were quick, just as we'd be quick to drop a hot potato.

Figurative language is familiar to everyone. A great deal of our slang and ordinary speech is based on figurative language, as well as a great many works in literature. Without figures of speech our language would be dull and mechanical. It becomes, therefore, important in developing reading comprehension to know the difference between literal and figurative language. It also becomes important to know the difference between literal and figurative language in developing your aesthetic understanding of what you read.

One form of figurative language is the *metaphor.* A metaphor is a comparison of two things without the use of the words "like" or "as." For instance, when you say someone "clammed up and wouldn't talk," you are comparing the person's closed mouth with the tightness of a closed clam. When you say someone has a "stone face," you are comparing the unchanging expression with the immobility of stone.

Dead metaphors are metaphors that have been used so frequently that we accept them almost literally. Terms such as "a tenderfoot," "hands" on a watch, the "head" of a cane, a "run" in a stocking, or an engine "knocking" are all dead metaphors, yet they help us convey meaning that is seldom misunderstood. S. I. Hayakawa says that metaphors are probably the most important of all the means by which language develops, changes, grows, and adapts itself to our changing needs.

A *simile* is another form of figurative language. It, like a metaphor, compares one thing with another but uses the words "like" or "as." Examples of similes are: "out like a light," "sparkles like a lake," "sounds like a machine gun," "cool as spring water," and "phony as a three-dollar bill."

When metaphors and similes are overused, they turn into *clichés.* Clichés are worn-out figures of speech such as "a blanket of snow covered the hill," or "the silence was broken," or "my old lady." Such terms have been used so often in speech and writing that they lose their real effectiveness and seem stale.

Still another type of figurative language is *hyperbole.* Hyperbole is a deliberate exaggeration or overstatement used to emphasize a point being made. For instance, if a friend tells you she can't go to the movies because she has "mountains of homework" to do, she is using hyperbole. If someone tells you that the story was "so funny he almost died laughing," he's using hyperbole. If you "love someone to pieces," know someone who "talked your arm off," or couldn't get your work done because "the phone rang ten thousand times," then you have been dealing with hyperbole. Like overused similes and metaphors that have become clichés, it can happen with hyperbole, too.

Recognizing how authors use figurative language helps us clarify whether or not an author's attitude is serious, playful, sympathetic, outraged, sarcastic, bitter, humorous, and so on. Thus, attitude and tone are closely allied through the use of figures of speech.

A writer's attitude toward a subject may not be ours. However, as critical readers it is important not to let either the author's *bias* or our own interfere with critical comprehension. Being biased means being prejudiced about or having a special leaning toward something. For instance, you may be biased about the type of music you listen to. Maybe you have no patience with classical music and prefer hard rock. That is a bias. Perhaps you are biased when it comes to food and would rather eat vegetables than meat. Everyone is biased about something, whether it's music, food, religion, politics, or people. Many of our biases are unconsciously learned from parents, friends, people we admire, or teachers. Reading critically can help us examine our own biases for their value.

While we are free to make up our own minds about a subject, we must still examine carefully the arguments and reasons of an author with opinions different from ours. We must recognize those biases of the author and not allow our own biases to interfere or shut out those of the author. Once we critically examine what we read, we should reflect on its worth before accepting or rejecting it.

Most of us tend to accept readily the ideas of writers who have the same biases we do, and we tend to reject the views of those we have biases against. To do so is to be closed minded. As critical readers, we must be willing to make critical judgments based on reason rather than emotions.

As you learn to read critically, you need to recognize bias in writing. If you don't, you may become the victim of an author's propaganda. You may miss seeing how an author takes facts and misrepresents them. You may not see that an author is being more subjective (using personal opinions) than objective (using undistorted facts). Or you may be unaware of how one-sided some writing is.

Sometimes recognizing an author's bias is easy; at other times it isn't. Bias is apt to be present in advertisements, newspaper and magazine editorials, and religious and political pamphlets. You generally pay little attention to an author's bias when it matches your own. When you don't agree with an author, the reverse is true. To read critically requires real involvement in the text and in thinking through what is being read. In effect, critical reading *is* thinking.

The following passage appeared in *Consumer Reports*, a publication of Consumers Union, a nonprofit organization. Read it and then answer the questions that follow.

> The letter, marked, "confidential," was from the R.I. Research Special Human Being Laboratory in New York City and was signed by one Dr. Roger Grimstone. It informed the recipient that, based on the date and hour of her birth, she was an extraordinary individual, "apart from the rest of humanity," a "Beyonder."
>
> "Owing to some cosmic quirk," the letter went on, "your destiny operates independently of any stars.... Why have you suffered so much? *Why has true happiness, true love, wealth, a happy home always been out of your reach?* Why have the things you've yearned for most been snatched away?"
>
> Simple. According to the good Dr. Grimstone, it's because the recipient has yet to send him 20 bucks for something entitled "The Guide."
>
> The reader who sent us Dr. Grimstone's solicitation has a different theory, however. He believes that his daughter, the recipient of the letter, has yet to find happiness, companionship, and financial security because she is only four months old. (Copyright © 1987 by Consumers Union of United States, Inc., Mount Vernon, NY 10553. Reprinted by permission from *Consumer Reports*, September, 1987.)

1. What is the intent of the "confidential" letter sent by the R.I. Research Special Human Being Laboratory?

_____

_____

2. What is the intent of the article from *Consumer Reports?*

_____

_____

3. What attitude toward the recipient is implied by the originators of the letter?

_____

_____

4. What is *Consumer Reports*'s attitude toward the laboratory?

_____

_____

5. What is the tone of the letter sent by Dr. Grimstone?

_____

_____

6. What is the tone of the passage from *Consumer Reports?*

_____

_____

Your answers to the questions may be worded differently from the following, but see if they don't match up. The answer to the first question is to sell "The Guide" for twenty dollars by appealing to the recipient's "uniqueness" and desire for more wealth, happiness, and health, things most all of us want more of. The intent of *Consumer Reports*, the second question, is to expose the "Laboratory" as a fraud.

The third question can be answered by looking at such phrases as "apart from the rest of humanity," "owing to some cosmic quirk," and "Beyonder." The laboratory believes there are enough people (suckers?) who believe in astrology and who are dissatisfied enough with their lives (or curious enough) that they are willing to spend twenty dollars to find "the answer." *Consumer Reports*'s attitude is that the whole thing is phony.

The tone of the letter is tied in with attitude. The letter's tone, based on what quotes are given, seems serious about wanting to help. Even the "doctor's" name is serious sounding—Grimstone (or is it a subtle touch of humor on the sender's part?). *Consumer Reports*'s tone is humorous. Waiting until the end of the passage to let us know that the "confidential" letter was sent to a four month old makes us chuckle. We realize that phrases such as "the good Dr. Grimstone" and "20 bucks" provide a light, playful tone to it.

The following drills will help you practice finding intent, attitude, and tone in various types of writing.

Drill A-1

Directions: Read the following newspaper article, looking for fact, opinion, intent, attitude, and tone. Then answer the questions that follow it.

TV "ANGEL" DRAWS DEVOTED, DISBELIEVERS

1 MOUNT SHASTA—Thousands of people have trekked to a house in this Northern California resort town to see what they claim is an image of an angel that appeared on a woman's television set.

2 But the police chief and a TV repairman claim the image is caused by the TV set's bad capacitator and its low voltage power supply.

3 "I was sitting around watching TV Friday night," said Diane Boettcher, 40, on Wednesday. "I switched on the news to see about the harmonic convergence when a bright light came out . . . this image appeared. She has in the last few days become brighter and more defined. She is definitely an angel."

4 Mount Shasta, about 50 miles south of the Oregon border, was one of several sites around the world that last weekend attracted crowds of people who believed in a galactic "harmonic convergence" that would signal either a new age of peace, or doom, for mankind. About 6,000 people turned out to meditate and watch the sun rise over Mount Shasta Sunday.

5 Boettcher, a drug counselor-turned-writer, said about 5,000 people have come to the house she shares with her two teen-age daughters to see the image.

6 "She's really beautiful," she said. "People have been really touched by this."

7 Bob Wilson, owner of Shiloh Electronics in Mount Shasta, said he saw the television Tuesday and immediately identified the problem. In fact, he has duplicated it in his shop for anyone who wants to see it.

8 "The only reason I didn't say anything in the house was because there were people praying in front of the TV and I didn't know how to break it to them," Wilson said.

9 But Boettcher is convinced otherwise. She said the TV set is three years old, and that a psychic named Solara meditated in front of it on Tuesday and talked to the angel.

10 "I think (the angel's appearance) has everything to do with harmonic convergence. Although we all know God is in our hearts, most people need something to visualize.

11 "(The angel) has been wonderful. She loves children . . . She's real beautiful—all rainbow colored."

Now answer these questions.

1. T/F   The article is mostly opinion.
2. Which of the following is the best statement regarding the news item's intent?
    a. to report an unusual fact
    b. to report an unusual occurrence
    c. to make fun of the woman who claims an angel has appeared on her television set
    d. to objectively present two sides of an unusual occurrence
3. Which of the following best describes that author's attitude toward the occurrence?
    a. serious   d. disbelief
    b. humorous   e. none of the above
    c. sarcastic
4. The tone of the article is
    a. subjective   d. humorous
    b. objective   e. none of the above
    c. sarcastic
5. Based on what is presented in this article, do you believe the woman and the others who claim to have seen an angel on the television set? _____ Why?

_____

_____

Reprinted by permission of The Associated Press.

Drill   A-2

Directions: Read the following article and answer the questions as they appear. As you read, look for fact, opinion, intent, and attitude. Part of being a good critical reader is to be alert and to react to an author's ideas.

WE MUST BEGIN A CELESTIAL SEARCH FOR CIVILIZATION

Isaac Asimov

1   It is quite possible that somewhere far out in space on a planet circling a star perhaps 50 light-years away—perhaps 500, perhaps more—is a technological civilization more advanced than ours. Here and there in our galaxy, there may even be millions of them.

2   It may be that one or more of these civilizations is sending a beacon of some sort of radiation out into space, either as a deliberate signal or for other purposes. Or it may be that in the course of its ordinary use of energy (at a much higher level than our own) there is some disregarded leakage.

3   If we were to build a large array of radio telescopes (such an array, called Project Cyclops, has actually been proposed by a group of NASA scientists) we might detect this radiation.

4   Building such an array and making an adequate study of all stars closer than 1,000 light-years might take, perhaps, 20 years and might cost $100 billion. And in the end, we might detect no signals anywhere—or if we did, we might not be sure whether they represent a civilization, and even if we were sure that they did, we couldn't figure out what it all meant?

5   Is there any point, then, in spending all that time and money?

6   I and many others would answer that question with an emphatic "yes." To begin with, the expenditure would not be too great. It might come to $5 billion a year. The nations of the earth already spend $400 billion a year on armaments alone.

1.   Is the author for or against spending billions of dollars on radio telescopes to

detect other civilizations in outer space? _____

_____

2.   Are paragraphs 1 and 2 mostly fact or opinion? _____

_____

3.   Can you guess what the intent of this article is? _____

_____

Reprinted by permission of Isaac Asimov.

7   And whereas money spent on armaments only stimulates hatred and fear, and steadily increases the chance that the nations of the earth may wipe out themselves and humanity, the search for extraterrestrial civilizations would have a unifying effect on all of us. The mere thought of civilizations advanced beyond our own could not but emphasize the pettiness of our own quarrels and shame us into more serious attempts at international cooperation.

8   But what if we don't find anything? Then we wouldn't have the inspirational thought that other civilizations exist, and we would be out all that time and money for nothing, wouldn't we?

9   Not so. Even if we find nothing—not a single sign of civilization—we will have achieved something.

10   In the first place, the very attempt to construct the equipment for Project Cyclops would teach us a great deal about radiotelescopy and would undoubtedly advance the state of the art greatly even before a single observation of the sky is made.

11   Besides, it is impossible to use new expertise, new delicacy, new persistence and new power to search the heavens, and fail to discover a great many things about the universe that have nothing to do with advanced civilizations. Even if we failed to detect signals, we would not return from the task empty-handed.

   4.   Is paragraph 7 mostly fact or opinion? _____

   5.   T/F   The intent of this passage is to argue that spending money on arms is not as beneficial as spending money on Project Cyclops.

12   No one can say what discoveries we will make or in what direction they will enlighten us, or just how they may prove useful to us, but history shows that all knowledge *wisely applied* has the capacity to prove useful. This will undoubtedly hold true in the future as well.

13   Nor does it mean, if we find nothing, that other civilizations do not exist. It may mean only that we have been looking in the wrong place, or in the wrong way. The search would then have eliminated some blind alleys.

14   And suppose we *do* find a signal of some sort and decide that it must be of intelligent origin, but that we can't decide anything else about it. Does it do us any good at all just knowing civilizations are out there somewhere?

15   Certainly—think of the psychological significance!

16   We have had an industrial civilization for only 200 years and already we're stockpiling nuclear weapons; overpopulating the planet; poisoning the air, the water and the soil; destroying fertile land; developing an energy crisis, and running low on resources.

17   Many think glumly that there is no solution to all this—that we are headed on a collision course with damnation and that we are the last generation of civilization. It can even be argued that this is the inevitable consequence of intelligence: that intelligent beings anywhere gradually develop a greater and greater understanding of the laws of nature until their power exceeds their wisdom and they destroy themselves. If that is so, we may find no evidence of civilizations elsewhere, not because none have developed, but because none have endured.

   6.   T/F   The author's attitude about the future of civilization on earth is more optimistic than pessimistic.

   7.   What is the intent of paragraph 16? _____

   _____

18   But if we *do* find evidence of a civilization, one that is further advanced than our own (or its signals would not be so powerful as to reach us, since we can't dispose of

enough power to reach it), it would mean that at least one civilization had reached the crisis of power, surmounted it and survived. Perhaps it was differently constituted from our own and its beings were wiser—but perhaps it is just that the crisis that now seems so deadly to us is surmountable, given good will and strenuous effort.

19   The receipt of such signals could give us hope, then, and remove the currently gathering despair just a little. Perhaps, if we are tottering on the brink, that hope can provide the added bit of strength that can pull us through and supply the crucial feather's weight to swing the balance toward survival and away from destruction.

20   It is impossible to get *no* information at all from the signal. At the very least, its characteristics should tell us the rate at which the signal-sending planet revolves about its star and rotates about its axis, together with other physical characteristics of interest. Even if a message seems unintelligible, astronomers can still try to interpret it, and that in itself is an interesting challenge, a fascinating scientific game. Even if we cannot reach any conclusion as to specific items of information, we might reach certain generalizations about alien psychology—and that, too, is valuable knowledge.

   8. T/F   Most of paragraphs 18–20 is fact.
   9. T/F   The author's intent is to convince readers that sending signals to planets would not be a waste of time.

21   Besides, even the tiniest breaks in the code could be of interest. Suppose that from the message we get one single hint of some relationship unsuspected by ourselves that, if true, might give us new insight into some aspect of physics. Scientific advances do not exist in a vacuum. That one insight could then stimulate other thoughts and, in the end, greatly accelerate the natural process by which our scientific knowledge advances.

22   If we do come to some detailed understanding of the message, we might learn enough to be able to deduce whether the civilization sending it is benign or not. If it is malevolent and warlike (a very slight chance, in my opinion) then we will be encouraged to keep quiet, make no reply and to do our best to shield any inadvertent leakage into outer space of any radiation that would hint of our presence.

23   If the civilization seems benign, however, we might decide to answer, using the code we have learned. The civilization may be so far away that it could take a century for our answer to reach it, but then we would just go about our business as usual and wait.

24   The advanced civilization at the other end, receiving our answer and learning that someone is listening, may perhaps at once begin to transmit in earnest. Though we may have to wait generations for the reply, we would find ourselves, in the end, getting a crash course in all kinds of knowledge. There is no way that we can predict how useful such information will prove to be, but surely it cannot be altogether useless.

25   The search for extraterrestrial civilizations cannot possibly hurt us, or even be useless. It can only help us earthlings—just possibly to an immeasurable extent.

   10. T/F   The author's tone and attitude toward his thesis that we will benefit from a search for extraterrestrial civilizations is serious.

Expressing your attitude and bias, write your reaction to the ideas in this essay in the space provided.

B. Recognizing Figurative Language

Drill B-1: IDENTIFYING LITERAL VS. FIGURATIVE LANGUAGE

Directions: The following statements are either literal or figurative. Place an F in the blanks below for each statement that uses figurative speech.

_____ **1.** Mr. Timpkin went through the ceiling when his son told him that he had wrecked the car.

_____ **2.** Alyce waited eagerly for the show to start.

_____ **3.** Doreen's checks are bouncing all over town.

_____ **4.** The crowd was getting increasingly angry waiting for the musicians to show up.

_____ **5.** The battery is dead as a doornail.

_____ **6.** Prices are being slashed to rock bottom.

_____ **7.** Mom really stuck her neck out for you this time.

_____ **8.** I find myself out on a limb.

_____ **9.** When Jimmy screamed, her hair stood on end.

_____ **10.** The Giants were defeated 18–4 in the last game.

Drill B-2: RECOGNIZING TONE THROUGH FIGURATIVE LANGUAGE

Directions: Read the following paragraphs and answer the questions that follow them.

1.   There is an appalling cloud of illiteracy shadowing America's pride. We would do well to attack some basic causes for the lack of literacy facing us. Instead, we seem to throw more money down the drain for more grants and studies.

    a. The expression "cloud of illiteracy shadowing America's pride" means

_____

_____

    b. T/F   The literary term for the phrase in *a*. is simile.

    c. T/F   Using the phrase "money down the drain" lets us know the author is happy with what efforts are taking place.

    d. The tone of this passage is best described as

_____ serious concern   _____ concerned displeasure

_____ humorous concern   _____ sarcastic

2.   My job was really starting to get to me. It seemed a dead end, a treadmill taking me nowhere. If I was to keep from blowing a fuse, I had to somehow shatter my negativity toward my work or go for broke and resign. After what seemed centuries of indecisiveness, one day I plunked myself down at the typewriter, quickly tossed off my resignation, and boldly signed it with great flair. So I wouldn't chicken out at the last minute, I sailed into the boss's office and slapped it down on her desk.

a. The tone of this passage is best described as

_____ one of relief   _____ frustration

_____ fear of losing a job   _____ indecision

b. The phrase "go for broke" here means _____

_____

c. T/F   "My treadmill job was a dead end" is an example of a metaphor.

d. T/F   It is possible to literally shatter a negative attitude.

3.   Out deeper, in cooler water, where trout live, floating on one's back is a kind of free ride, like being fifteen again, like being afloat upon another sky. Perhaps there is a bit of Tom Sawyer's pleasure at watching his own bogus funeral in this, but before we get overly morbid, a fish begins nibbling our toes. Floating on one's back is like riding between two skies.... (From Edward Hoagland, "Summer Pond," *New York Times*.)

a. T/F   The author mostly uses similes in the above passage.

b. The tone of the paragraph is best described as

_____ lazy   _____ morbid

_____ pleasant   _____ sad

c. T/F   The intent of the passage is to relive the joys of swimming in a pond or lake.

4.   "C'mon, we're supposed to be having fun," snaps her companion, a clone. In razor-crease jeans and stiletto heels they stamp into the ladies room, flounce around the corner past the polished washbasins and disappear into the two long rows of toilet stalls. They are the kind of girls who obey their mothers' warnings never to sit on strange toilet seats. Attendants have to nip in after that type, making sure the next woman will have no unpleasant surprises. (From Jane O'Reilly, "In Las Vegas: Working Hard for the Money," *Time*, January 9, 1984.)

a. T/F   The phrase "razor-crease jeans and stiletto heels" reflects a negative attitude toward the girls.

b. T/F   The intent of the passage is to gain sympathy for the two girls.

c. T/F   The tone of the passage can best be described as

_____ humorous   _____ sweet

_____ sarcastic   _____ apathetic

Drill B-3

Directions: Read the following essay looking for intent, attitude, and tone.

ESCAPING THE DAILY GRIND FOR LIFE AS A HOUSE FATHER

Rick Greenberg

1   "You on vacation?" my neighbor asked.

2   My 15-month-old son and I were passing her yard on our daily hike through the neighborhood. It was a weekday afternoon and I was the only working-age male in sight.

3   "I'm, uh . . . working out of my house now," I told her.

4   Thus was born my favorite euphemism for house fatherhood, one of those new life-style occupations that is never merely mentioned. Explained, yes. Defended. Even rhapsodized about. Or in my case, fibbed about. I was tongue-tied then, but no longer. People are curious and I've learned to oblige.

5   I joined up earlier this year when I quit my job—a dead-end, ulcer-producing affair that had dragged on interminably. I left to be with my son until something better came along. And if nothing did, I'd be with him indefinitely.

6   This was no simple transition. I had never known a house father, never met one. I'd only read about them. They were another news magazine trend. Being a traditionalist, I never dreamed I'd take the plunge.

7   But as the job got worse, I gave it serious thought. And more thought. And in the end, I still felt ambivalent. This was a radical change that seemed to carry as many drawbacks as benefits. My dislike for work finally pushed me over the edge. That, and the fact that we had enough money to get by.

8   Escaping the treadmill was a bold stroke. I had shattered my lethargy and stopped whining, and for that I was proud.

9   Some friends said they were envious. Of course they weren't quitting one job without one waiting—the ultimate in middle-class taboos. That ran through my mind as I triumphantly, and without notice, tossed the letter of resignation on my boss' desk. Then I walked away wobbly-kneed.

10   The initial trauma of quitting, however, was mitigated by my eagerness to raise our son. Mine was the classic father's lament. I felt excluded. I had become "the man who got home after dark," that other person besides Mama. It hurt when I couldn't quiet his crying.

11   I sensed that staying home would be therapeutic. The chronic competitiveness and aggressiveness that had served me well as a daily journalist would subside. Something better would emerge, something less obnoxious. My ulcer would heal. Instead of beating deadlines, I'd be doing something important for a change. This was heresy coming from a newspaper gypsy, but it rang true.

12   There was unease, too. I'd be adrift, stripped of the home-office-home routine that had defined my existence for more than a decade. No more earning a living. No benchmarks. Time would be seamless. Would Friday afternoon feel the same?

13   The newness of it was scary.

14   Until my resignation, my wife and I typified today's baby-boomer couples, the want-it-all generation. We had two salaries, a full-time nanny and guilt pangs over practicing parenthood by proxy.

15   Now, my wife brings home the paychecks, the office problems and thanks for good work on the domestic front. With me at home, her work hours are more flexible. Nanny-less, I change diapers, prepare meals and do all the rest. And I wonder what comes next.

16   What if I don't find another job? My field is tight. At 34, I'm not getting any more marketable and being out of work doesn't help.

17   As my father asked incredulously: "Is this going to be what you do?"

18   Perhaps. I don't know. I wonder myself. It's even more baffling to my father, the veteran of a long and traditional 9-to-5 career. For most of it, my mother stayed home. My father doesn't believe in trends. All he knows is that his only son—with whom he shares so many traits—has violated the natural order of men providing and women raising children. In his view, I've

Reprinted by permission of Rick Greenberg, Washington-based writer.

shown weakness and immaturity by succumbing to a bad job.

19 But he's trying to understand, and I think he will.

20 I'm trying to understand it myself. House fatherhood has been humbling, rewarding and unnerving.

21 "It's different," I tell friends. "Different."

22 Imagine never having to leave home for the office in the morning. That's how different. No dress-up, no commute. Just tumble out of bed and you're there. House fathering is not for claustrophobics.

23 I find myself enjoying early morning shopping. My son and I arrive right after the supermarket opens. The place is almost empty. For the next hour we glide dreamily, cruising the aisles to a Muzak accompaniment. This is my idyll. My son likes it, too; he's fascinated by the spectacle.

24 Housekeeping still doesn't seem like work, and that's by design. I've mastered the art of doing just enough chores to get by. This leaves me enough free time. Time to read and write and daydream. Time with my son. Time to think about the structure.

25 So much time, and so little traditional structure, that the days sometimes blur together. I remember on Sunday nights literally dreading the approaching work week, the grind. Today, the close of the weekend still triggers a shiver of apprehension; I now face the prospect of a week without tangible accomplishments, a void.

26 On our hikes to the playground, I can feel my old identity fading. All around are people with a mission, a sense of purpose. Workers. And then there's the rest of us—the stroller and backpack contingent. The moms, the nannies, and me. I wonder if I've crossed over a line never to return.

27 Still, the ulcer seems to be healing. I take pride in laying out a good dinner for the family and in pampering my wife after a tough day at the office. I love reading to my son. Running errands isn't even so bad. A lot of what had been drudgery or trivia is taking on new meaning; maybe I'm mellowing.

28 Which is ironic. To be a truly committed and effective at-home parent, there must be this change—a softening, a contentment with small pleasures, the outwardly mundane. This is a time of reduced demands and lowered expectations. Progress is gradual, often agonizingly so. Patience is essential. Ambition and competitiveness are anathema. Yet eliminating these two qualities—losing the edge—could ruin my chances of resurrecting my career. I can't have it both ways.

29 The conflict has yet to be resolved. And it won't be unless I make a firm commitment and choose one life style over the other. I'm not yet ready for that decision.

30 In the meantime, a wonderful change is taking place in our home. Amid all the uncertainties, my son and I have gotten to know each other. He can't put a phrase together, but he confides in me. It can be nothing more than a grin or a devilish look. He tries new words on me, new shtick. We roll around a lot; we crack each other up. I'm no longer the third wheel, the man who gets home after dark. Now, I'm as much a part of his life as his mother is. I, too, can stop his crying. So far, that has made the experiment worthwhile.

Now answer the following questions:

1. What is the intent of this article?
    a. to describe the author's experiences as a house father
    b. to explain why the author became a house father
    c. to convince more men that they should give up their jobs and become house fathers
    d. to share the pros and cons of the author's experience in giving up his job and becoming a house father
2. Which of the following best describes the author's attitude toward being a house father?
    a. regretful
    b. ecstatic
    c. worthwhile
    d. worried
3. Which of the following best describes the author's attitude toward giving up his career?
    a. satisfied
    b. satisfied for the present
    c. apprehensive that he may be sorry later
    d. sorry that he acted rashly

4. What is the attitude of the author's father?
   a. happy for his son
   b. wishes he'd done the same thing when younger
   c. feels his son made a weak and immature decision
   d. feels his son is a trendsetter
5. T/F The intent of paragraph 9 is to show how easy it was for the author to give up his career.
6. T/F The intent of paragraph 14 is to contrast the author's values with others of his generation.
7. T/F The intent of paragraph 28 is to show that the author is still not certain he wants to remain a house father.
8. The overall tone of this article is best described as
   a. humorous
   b. honest
   c. sarcastic
   d. ironic
9. The tone of paragraph 16 mostly reflects
   a. happiness
   b. worry
   c. pride
   d. strength

10. What biases did you detect in the article? _____

_____

_____

_____

Drill B-4

Directions: Read the following essay looking for intent, attitude, and tone.

A LITTLE BANNING IS A DANGEROUS THING

Loudon Wainwright

1   My own introduction to sex in reading took place about 1935, I think, just when the fertile soil of my young mind was ripe for planting. The exact place it happened (so I've discovered from checking the source in my local library) was the middle of page 249, in a chapter titled "Apples and Ashes," soon after the beginning of Book III of a mildly picaresque novel called *Anthony Adverse*. The boy Anthony, 16, and a well-constructed character named Faith Paleologus ("Her shoulders if one looked carefully were too wide. But so superb was the bosom that rose up to support them. . . .") made it

Loudon Wainwright, *Life* Magazine © 1982 Time Inc. Reprinted with permission.

right there in her apartment where he'd gone to take a quick bath, thinking (ho-ho) that she was out.

2   Faith was Anthony's sitter, sort of, and if author Hervey Allen was just a touch obscure about the details of their moon-drenched meeting, I filled in the gaps. "He was just in time," Allen wrote, "to see the folds of her dress rustle down from her knees into coils at her feet. . . . He stood still, rooted. The faint aroma of her body floated to him. A sudden tide of passion dragged at his legs. . . . He was half blind, and speechless now. All his senses had merged into one feeling. . . . To be supported and yet possessed by an ocean of unknown blue depths below you and to cease to think! Yes, it was something like swimming on a transcendent summer night."

3   Wow! Praying that my parents wouldn't come home and catch me reading this terrific stuff, I splashed ahead, line after vaguely lubricious line, exhilarated out of my mind at Anthony's good fortune. "After a while he was just drifting in a continuous current of ecstasy that penetrated him as if he were part of the current in which he lay." I still don't understand *that* line, but I sure feel the old surge of depravity. And reading it again, I thank God there was no righteous book banner around at the time to snatch it from me. *Anthony Adverse* doesn't rank as literature, or even required reading, but I'm convinced it served a useful, even educational, purpose for me at the time.

4   Alert vigilantes of the printed word worked hard to suppress the novel then. The wretched little war to keep the minds of children clean is always going on. In fact, it has heated up considerably since President Reagan came to power, with libraries around the country reporting a threefold increase in demands that various volumes even less ruinous than *Anthony Adverse* be withdrawn. School boards, too, are feeling the cleansing fire of assorted crusaders against dirty words and irreverent expressions of one sort or another. Protestors range from outraged individual parents to teachers to local ministers to such well-organized watchdog outfits as the Gabler family of Texas, Washington's Heritage Foundation and, of course, the Moral Majority.

5   The victims are fighting back. Writers are leading public "read-ins" of their banned words. One school board case, which actually dates to 1976, has gone all the way to the U.S. Supreme Court. Before the end of the current term, the court is expected to rule on whether or not the First Amendment rights (to free expression) of five students in Island Trees, N.Y., were denied when the board took nine books out of circulation. A far more personal thrust against censorship was made recently by authors Studs Terkel. At the news that his book *Working* was in danger of being banned in Girard, Pa., Terkel went there and standing before the whole school in assembly made his own eloquent case for the book, for the so-called bad language in it and for reading in general. Six weeks later the school board voted unanimously to keep *Working* in the reading program where it had initially been challenged. Presumably they were persuaded, in part at least, that Terkel was *not,* as Kurt Vonnegut wrote in a furious and funny defense of his own *Slaughterhouse-Five,* one of those "sort of ratlike people who enjoy making money from poisoning the minds of young people."

6   What gets me is the weird presumption that the book banners actually know something about the minds of young people. Vonnegut, among others, suspects that a lot of censors never even get around to reading the books they suppress. And just the briefest scanning of the list of titles currently banned or under threat in various communities calls the banners' credentials to rude question. *The Scarlet Letter, The Great Gatsby, A Farewell to Arms, Huckleberry Finn, The Grapes of Wrath* are a few of the variously seminal works challenged as somehow being dangerous to the stability of impressionable young minds. *Mary Poppins* and *The American Heritage Dictionary* have been under attack, too, the former after protests that its black characters were stereotypes, the latter presumably as a storehouse of words that shouldn't be viewed by innocent eyes, much less defined.

7   More critically, the censors forget, if they ever knew, many of the needs of childhood. One, obviously, is the need for privacy, for a place to get away from the real world, a place where one is safe from—among other things—difficult or boring adult

demands. The world that a reader makes is a perfect secret world. But if its topography is shaped by adults pushing their own hardened views of life, the secret world is spoiled.

8   Yet the world of the young human mind is by no means a comfy habitat, as much as a lot of interfering adults would like to shape it that way. In *The Uses of Enchantment,* Bruno Bettelheim's book about the great importance of folk and fairy tales to child development, the author writes: "There is a widespread refusal to let children know that the source of much that goes wrong in life is due to our very own natures—the propensity of all men for acting aggressively, asocially, selfishly, out of anger and anxiety. Instead, we want our children to believe that, inherently, all men are good. But children know that *they* are not always good; and often, even when they are, they would prefer not to be." In the fantasies commonly churned out in the mind of a normal child, whatever that is, bloody acts of revenge and conquest, daredevil assaults and outlandish wooings are common currency. To achieve the bleak, cramped, sanitized, fear-ridden state of many adults takes years of pruning and repression.

9   Books, as everyone but the censors knows, stimulate growth better than anything—better than sit-coms, better than *Raiders of the Lost Ark,* better than video games. Many books, to be sure, are dreadful heaps of trash. But most of these die quickly in the marketplace or become best-sellers incapable of harming the adults who buy them.

10   It's often the best books that draw the beadiest attention of the censors. These are the books that really have the most to offer, the news that life is rich and complicated and difficult. Where else, for example, could a young male reader see the isolation of his painful adolescence reflected the way it is in *The Catcher in the Rye,* one of the *most* banned books in American letters. In the guise of fiction, books offer opportunities, choices and plausible models. They light up the whole range of human character and emotion. Each, in its own way, tells the truth and prepares its eager readers for the unknown and unpredictable events of their own lives.

11   *Anthony Adverse,* my first banned book, was just a huge potboiler of the period. Still, it tickled my fantasy. And it sharpened my appetite for better stuff, like *Lady Chatterley's Lover.* Actually I didn't read that tender and wonderful book until I was almost 50. I wish I'd read it much sooner while we were both still hot.

Now answer the following questions:

1. The best statement of thesis is
    a. There will always be people or groups who want to ban books.
    b. Books, better than anything else, stimulate the growth of young minds and should not be banned.
    c. Those who want to censor certain books from children forget the many needs of childhood.
    d. Everyone should read the author's favorite novel, *Anthony Adverse.*
2. According to the author, what type of people or groups are book banners?

    _____

    _____

3. Which of the following are benefits children get from reading books, even so-called bannable ones?
    a. a secret world of their own
    b. fantasies of revenge, conquests, and daredevil actions
    c. the knowledge that all men are not always good
    d. all of the above

4. The author's attitude toward J. D. Salinger's novel *The Catcher in the Rye* is
   a. negative
   b. positive
   c. that it is not as good as *Anthony Adverse*
   d. none of the above

5. The author's intent is to
   a. put down those who want to ban books
   b. show that even books such as *Anthony Adverse* have their place
   c. discourage book banning
   d. all of the above

6. The author uses some language that carries negative connotations. For instance, in paragraph 4 he calls those who would ban books "vigilantes of the printed word." What are some other negatively charged words he uses?

   _____

   _____

7. In the first paragraph the author says, "...the fertile soil of my young mind was ripe for planting." This is an example of a metaphor.

   a. True because _____

   b. False because _____

8. Explain what the figurative language in question 7 means. _____

   _____

   _____

9. Explain what the author means when he says in paragraph 8, "To achieve the bleak, cramped, sanitized, fear-ridden state of many adults takes years of

   pruning and repression." _____

   _____

   _____

   _____

10. What is the author's tone in the final paragraph? (It may help to know that the book he mentions, *Lady Chatterley's Lover*, was banned from this country until early 1960.)
    a. humorous   c. nasty
    b. bitter   d. hopeful

C. Comparing Biased Points of View

Critical reading requires identifying an author's point of view and motives. Nearly all controversial subjects are written from a particular point of view or bias. By their very nature, such controversial subjects cannot be written about with complete objectivity. For instance, if a Catholic priest were to write about abortion, chances are his point of view would reflect opposition by the very nature of his training and religious beliefs. On the other hand, a social worker who has seen many teenage lives destroyed because of unwanted pregnancies might very well speak in favor of abortion. Even though the priest and the social worker have different points of view, their motives are the same—to convince us their particular viewpoint is the correct one. As critical readers—and thinkers—we need to be alert to as many points of view as possible before making up our own minds on controversial issues. Then we need to examine the reasoning used to support those viewpoints.

Here are a few guides to follow so that you don't fall victim to poor reasoning. Watch out for

1. statements that oversimplify or distort the issue being discussed.
2. irrelevant or unsupported evidence.
3. left out or suppressed information or evidence.
4. appeals to the emotions rather than reasonable evidence.
5. mudslinging, or attacks on people or groups rather than the issue itself.
6. references to or quotations from the Bible or historical figures even though there is no connection to the issue.

These are the most frequent, although not all, of the devices used to sway people to accept a particular point of view. They appear in advertisements, political campaigns, newspaper and magazine columns, editorials, and television commentaries.

The following is a syndicated column from the *Boston Globe* newspaper that appeared in hundreds of newspapers around the country. The subject has to do with the censorship of movies, videocassettes, television programs, and rock music. Before you read it, answer the following questions about your own biases regarding censorship.

1. Do you believe in censorship of any kind? _____

    Explain. _____

    _____

    _____

2. Do you believe that the electronic media (TV, videocassettes, records, radio) are generally responsible for the rise in drug addiction, adolescent suicides, and a

    decline in Scholastic Aptitude Test (SAT) scores? _____ Explain. _____

    _____

    _____

Now read the following essay using the six previously listed guidelines that outlined what you should watch for when reading about controversial issues. Then answer the questions that follow the essay.

SHIELD OUR YOUTH WITH CENSORSHIP

William Shannon

1 The United States today has a popular culture at war against the nation's children and youth. Movies, video cassettes, television programs and rock music have produced what the late Harvard sociologist Pitirim Sorokin called a "sensate culture." The message of this popular culture is, "Feel good." What one thinks hardly matters.

2 These media bombard young people with sounds and images for several hours each day. The two dominant themes are sexual pleasure and sadistic violence. The indescribable "highs" and mysterious charms of using drugs also lurk as subsidiary themes.

3 The effect of this non-stop sensual assault is anti-intellectual and anti-academic. It is difficult for any classroom teacher to compete with the exciting images projected by television and films. Serious use of the mind requires patience, self-discipline and the ability to defer present gratification in favor of future achievement. Very little in our culture supports these serious values. On the contrary, the fast pace and pounding rhythms of rock music and violent films tells impressionable youngsters "Go, go, go . . . now, now, now."

4 Parents are engaged in an uneven battle against this popular culture. There are still young persons who read for pleasure and who do well in school, but their number dwindles. The middle range of children muddles through high school and some go through college, but the general level of their academic achievement is significantly below what it was 30 years ago. The number of vulnerable youngsters cruelly damaged or destroyed by this culture grows. Victims are at every level of intelligence and family income. Their vulnerability is a matter of temperament, family history and perhaps genetic endowment.

5 The casualty figures in this uneven battle between conscientious parents and the popular culture appear in the form of a rising number of adolescent suicides and drug addicts and in the Scholastic Aptitude Test scores, which have fallen significantly from their levels of 20 years ago. Parents try various expedients. Wealthy families send their children to private boarding schools in the hope that tight scheduling of time and close supervision by teachers will reduce the risks.

6 Other families—some of them non-Catholic—turn to the Catholic schools, in the hope that the schools' traditionally stricter discipline and the greater respect for authority that they inculcate will save their children.

7 No place in this society is a sanctuary, however, from the brutal and corrupting pressures of our popular culture. Schools of every kind, public and private, secular and religious, struggle valiantly to instill good work habits and encourage intellectual values, but the opposing cultural pressures are too pervasive.

8 The film industry makes much of ratings such as "R" for restricted to adults, and "PG" for parental guidance suggested, but these ratings are close to useless.

9 The only solution is to restore prior censorship over the electronic media. Everyone older than 50 grew up in a time when Hollywood films were strictly censored by the industry itself to exclude explicit sexual scenes, gruesome violence and vulgar language. The Supreme Court in the 1950s struck down movie censorship. It extended to film makers the First Amendment protection traditionally enjoyed by newspapers and book publishers. The court also redefined the anti-pornography and anti-obscenity statutes into meaninglessness.

10 Those decisions were praised as liberal advances, but their consequences were unforeseen and disastrous. It would require a constitutional amendment to reverse those decisions. Unless they are reversed, the coarsening and corrupting of the nation's youth will continue.

Reprinted courtesy of The Boston Globe.

Now answer the following questions:

1. What is the author's point of view toward censorship? _____

_____

2. What is his attitude toward movies, videocassettes, and rock music? _____

_____

3. What is his intent in writing this essay? _____

_____

4. The statements made in paragraph 3 are factual.

    a. True because _____

    b. False because _____

5. The statements made in paragraph 3 are supported with evidence.

    a. True because _____

    b. False because _____

6. Statements such as, "The only solution is to restore prior censorship over the electronic media," oversimplify the issue being discussed.

    a. True because _____

    b. False because _____

7. By blaming today's problems on the Supreme Court of the 1950s, the author is mudslinging rather than dealing rationally with the issue.

    a. True because _____

    b. False because _____

8. Circle any of the following that you feel the author does:
    a. makes irrelevant or unsupported statements
    b. oversimplifies the problem and solution
    c. refers to the Bible for support
    d. appeals to the emotions rather than providing reasonable evidence

9. For each of the items you circled in question 8, find a passage in the essay that

serves as an example. _____

_____

_____

_____

_____

    It's not too difficult to answer the first question. The title of the essay provides us with our first clue: "Shield Our Youth with Censorship." As we read through the essay, the author makes it clear he blames the electronic media as the corrupting pressure on today's youth. Thus, his attitude is negative. His intent seems to be to push for censorship of some kind, to bring about a constitutional amendment that would reverse the Supreme Court's earlier decision. Otherwise, he says in the last paragraph, "the coarsening and corrupting of the nation's youth will continue."

    Both questions 4 and 5 are false. The author makes three statements in paragraph 3, each one an opinion as stated. Though he may be correct, he needs facts to support his opinions. But instead of providing facts, he moves on to "the effects of this non-stop sensual assault."

Questions 6 and 7 are both true. The issue is too complex for such a simple solution. When he blames the Supreme Court of the 1950s for today's problems, he not only simplifies the issue again but also enters into what is called "mud-slinging," attacking the court rather than the problem he claims the electronic media are causing.

As to questions 8 and 9, he uses all but *c*. We've already seen that paragraph 2 is full of unsupported statements. Other examples are the last sentence in paragraph 3. The last three sentences in paragraph 4 are unsupported. In paragraph 5 he links adolescent suicides, drug addiction, and a decline in SAT scores together as though all of these are related to the electronic media. Admittedly, he could be correct, but his argument is not very convincing. His tone is frequently emotional. Wording and phrases such as, "vulnerable youngsters cruelly damaged," "no place is a sanctuary," "a popular culture at war against the nation's children" all appeal to our emotions. Censorship of any type is a serious matter. To accept the author's premise and solution as written is to do so without solid facts or rational reasoning.

It's important to remember that Shannon may be right. What we as critical readers must do is recognize his point of view or bias, then see what facts he provides to support his thesis. If his facts or supporting arguments are valid, then we should consider his point of view before making up our minds, especially if we disagree with him. If we already agree with him, but have no more facts or reasons to support our point of view than he has, then we need to critically evaluate our own reasons for having the views we do. One of the primary reasons for reading a wide range of viewpoints is to acquire, broaden, and strengthen intelligent views of our own.

Too often we tend to accept the views of others we trust or admire without examining the logic or reasoning behind them. Many people practice the religion they do, not because they have truly examined the creeds, but because parents or friends are members of that religion. Many politicians have been elected to office not because they are the best qualified, but because they make a good impression in public. Many countries have gone to war not because it was the right thing to do, but because people were led to believe it was the only solution to a problem.

The next set of drills will help you develop your critical reading skills in these areas.

Drill   C-1: COMPARING TWO AUTHORS

Directions: Skim back over "A Little Banning Is a Dangerous Thing" on page 318 and "Shield Our Youth with Censorship" on page 323. You may want to look over the answers to the questions that follow the two essays. Then answer the following questions:

1. Do you think the two authors would agree on the subject of book banning?

_____   Explain. _____

_____

_____

_____

2. Which essay has more facts to support its thesis? Explain. _____

_____

_____

_____

3. With which author do you agree? _____

Why? _____

_____

_____

4. Which essay is the most convincing? Explain. _____

_____

_____

_____

5. Upon what is your bias based? _____

_____

_____

Drill   C-2

Directions: Before reading the next selection, answer the following questions:

1. I feel that there should be
    a.   stronger gun control laws
    b.   fewer gun control laws
    c.   I don't know

2. I feel as I do because _____

_____

_____

_____

Now read the following editorial from *The American Rifleman,* a publication of the National Rifle Association. Look for the author's thesis, supporting points, intent, attitude, and bias. Considering the source of this editorial, can you anticipate what the author's bias is toward gun control?

UNITED WE STAND

1   Members of the National Rifle Association of America and other reputable gun owners are being maligned by sensational reporting on the part of some writers. By means of cleverly written articles, these authors are presenting vehement diatribes against firearms of all description, against NRA, and against gun owners in general. Some reek of bigotry and parochial thinking, while others appear to be a deliberate attempt to divide and conquer.

2   The time has come to make a positive effort to overcome the ignorance and misunderstanding about firearms and the people who use them. Those who appreciate and enjoy guns and shooting must share their knowledge and their beliefs with others in their home communities. They must emphasize to public officials and people in general the importance of firearms in America; the positive values of shooting and hunting; the necessity for firearms safety programs and marksmanship training activities of the National Rifle Association, and the contribution of these programs to the American way of life. Those who have most to gain, and most to lose, must convince their friends and associates that guns and shooting are an essential part of our priceless heritage which must be cherished and encouraged. They must make known the true facts about the NRA, its affiliated shooting organizations, and its members in every state of the Union.

3   The NRA, more than any other organization, promotes the best interests of gun owners and shooters. As a public service, it is dedicated to firearms safety education, marksmanship training, and shooting for recreation. It stands squarely behind the premise that the lawful ownership of firearms must not be denied American citizens of good repute so long as they continue to use them for lawful purposes. The NRA is recognized as the leading authority in the field of firearms safety education and marksmanship training because of its nationwide programs for the youth of America. It has demonstrated the soundness of the theory that the educational approach is the most effective method of avoiding gun accidents in the home and in the field. It has developed shooting activities for young people which bring out the qualities of sportsmanship, fair play, self-control, and cooperation so essential to responsible citizenship and to success in life. Its instruction guides and training courses have been prepared as aids for teaching proper gun handling in local communities. The program is conducted on a volunteer basis by thousands of NRA certified instructors in schools, summer camps, shooting clubs and other youth groups, in cooperation with state agencies and local organizations. The NRA is the governing body of competitive rifle and pistol shooting in the United States and, in this capacity, establishes rules and regulations, sanctions tournaments, recognizes national champions, and maintains official records. It represents the shooters of America in the United States Olympic Committee and the International Shooting Union.

4   The strength of the NRA, and therefore the ability to accomplish its objects and purposes, depends entirely upon the support of loyal Americans who believe in the right to "keep and bear arms." Every reputable citizen who owns a gun or who shoots a gun should be a member. The small investment for dues will return to each individual member valuable dividends in tangible benefits and in the personal satisfaction derived from being a part of a great patriotic organization.

5   Notwithstanding libelous statements and false information appearing in a few publications, the National Rifle Association of America is composed of loyal, law-abiding American citizens. Anyone who has an affection for guns and shooting, and anyone who believes in the right to keep and bear arms, belongs in the NRA, because *united we stand.*

Permission has been granted to reprint this editorial by *The American Rifleman,* Washington, D.C.

Answer the following questions by writing your own comment or circling the correct response. More than one response may be necessary in some cases.

1. Circle the best statement of thesis for this essay:
   a. We must convince friends and associates that guns and shooting are an essential part of our priceless heritage which must be cherished and encouraged.
   b. The NRA more than any other organization promotes the best interests of gun owners and shooters.
   c. The NRA is composed of loyal, law-abiding American citizens.
   d. It's time for gun owners to join with the NRA in fighting back against the ignorance and misinformation being spread by some against people who appreciate and enjoy guns and shooting.

2. The author's intent is
   a. to persuade the reader that the NRA should not be maligned by sensational reporting
   b. to rally support against gun control laws
   c. to praise the NRA
   d. to encourage people to join the NRA

3. The author's attitude is
   a. humorous   c. sarcastic
   b. serious   d. neutral

4. The author is strongly biased in favor of
   a. gun control laws
   b. the NRA and its services
   c. keeping and bearing arms
   d. all of the above

5. T/F Paragraph 2 is mostly based on fact.

6. The tone of paragraph 1 is
   a. angry   c. sad
   b. sarcastic   d. sympathetic

7. Is the editorial mostly objective or subjective? Explain.

_____

_____

8. Does the editorial convince you of its intent? Explain.

_____

_____

_____

9. Do you think that your own bias or lack of interest has anything to do with your reaction to this editorial? Explain.

_____

_____

_____

Drill **C-3**

Directions: The following article is also about gun control laws, but the bias is different from the bias found in Drill C-2. Look for the author's thesis, intent, attitude, and bias toward the subject.

GUNS AND BATTER

Richard Lipez

1   The hue and cry over the so-called American gun problem is being raised again, but what the "liberal" advocates of gun control continue to overlook are the *legitimate* uses to which guns are put by millions of law-abiding Americans. Guns don't kill people, *people* do. The gun critics conveniently choose to forget that the vast majority of gun owners in this country use their weapons only for peaceful purposes.

2   Despite the popular misconceptions, most Americans' rifles, for example, are used as tomato stakes. Or as curtain rods, or softball bats. Sometimes as rudders (or extra oars) on small rafts. Many rifle owners also stuff bundles of straw up the barrels of their rifles and—*presto!*—they've got a child's toy broom. (Gun owners know that the sooner children start "pretending" to help keep the house clean, the sooner they'll get into the habit of helping to do the real thing.)

3   Hardly anybody ever loads and shoots a rifle at somebody or something. The last thing a rifle owner would do with his weapon would be to use it for its intended purpose.

4   Likewise with handguns. Many well-meaning but misguided "liberals" are trying to restrict the ownership and use of handguns. Again, the critics are ignoring the peaceful uses to which most handguns are put.

5   A popular use of the handgun, for example, is to take two large pistols and have them serve as shelf brackets. A gun lobbyist friend of mine was recently explaining to some members of Congress how the average handgun owner does this, and the lobbyist let me listen in.

6   You get a power drill with a tough, well-tempered one-eighth inch bit. Drill two holes through the barrel (top to bottom) and the butt (front to back) of each pistol. Place the guns against the wall where you want the shelf. The barrels should be pointing down, with the butts protruding away from the wall.

7   Next, screw the barrels into the wall with plaster screws. Lay the shelf across the protruding gun butts, and mark with a pencil where the holes should be drilled in the shelf. Remove the shelf and drill holes in it. Replace the shelf on the gun butts, and secure it with nuts and bolts.

8   Place books or *objets d'art* on the shelf, and there you are. Dangerous? Harmful? Not on your life! This admittedly widespread use of the handgun is practical and ecologically sound. It may even be *necessary*. Man's primal urge to put up shelves cannot be denied, and doing it with handguns provides a "double-barreled" outlet that is wholesome and *so far* (cross your fingers!) socially acceptable.

9   Another gun lobbyist friend of mine described, over dinner at the Washington Jockey Club, how millions of American handgun owners who prefer to take a shower under a hard shooting stream of water instead of a soft spray use *their* handguns as shower nozzles.

10   First, you remove the hammer from a well-made pistol and have a pipe fitter thread the (upper) end of the firing chamber. Remove your shower nozzle and screw on the pistol. This will give you a good, stimulating shower, and it will keep you plenty clean if you remember to shower at least once a day. As they say down at the National Rifle Association, "Shower nozzles don't let people get smelly, people do." And, "Register stinky people, not shower nozzles."

11   Yet another gun lobbyist acquaintance explained how handguns are used quite often for whipping up a mouth-watering batch of blueberry-and-sour-cream muffins:

Pre-heat oven to 400 degrees

Sift before measuring: 2 cups cake flour or 1¾ cups all-purpose flour

Resift with: 1 teaspoon double-acting baking powder; ½ teaspoon salt; 2 tablespoons sugar; ½ teaspoon soda

Measure: 1 cup cultured sour cream; 1 cup blueberries

Combine with: 1 beaten egg

12   Pick up (unloaded) handgun by barrel and beat batter for ten to twenty seconds. Pour batter into well-greased muffin tin and bake for twenty to twenty-five minutes. Then pop 'em into your mouth, lean back, and say, "Mmm! Mmm! *Mmmm!*"

Answer the following questions by writing your own comment or circling the correct response. More than one response may be correct.

1. Circle the best statement of thesis for this essay.
   a. Guns don't kill people, people do.
   b. The gun critics conveniently choose to forget that the vast majority of gun owners in this country use their weapons for peaceful purposes.
   c. Gun owners' reasons for liberal gun laws are as ridiculous as the examples of gun uses mentioned in the essay.
   d. The NRA has a powerful lobby in Washington that has been successful in maintaining liberal gun control laws.

2. The author's intent is to
   a. support gun control laws
   b. show that gun owners use their guns for peaceful purposes
   c. make fun of NRA's gun control position
   d. show that guns are *not* used for peaceful purposes
   e. argue against the NRA position

3. The author's attitude toward guns as expressed in the article is
   a. neutral
   b. negative
   c. positive
   d. not apparent

4. The author is strongly biased *against*
   a. strong gun control laws
   b. NRA arguments for lax gun laws
   c. guns
   d. keeping and bearing arms

5. Is the article mostly subjective or objective?

_____

_____

6. The tone of this essay is
   a. sarcastic
   b. humorless
   c. silly
   d. sympathetic

7. Which of the following statements show bias on the author's part?
   a. "A popular use of the handgun, for example, is to take two large pistols and have them serve as shelf brackets."
   b. "As they say down at the National Rifle Association, 'Shower nozzles don't let people get smelly, people do.' "
   c. "Despite the popular misconceptions, most Americans' rifles, for example, are used as tomato stakes."
   c. "The last thing a rifle owner would do with his weapon would be to use it for its intended purpose."

8. Write a statement that expresses the major bias of each article:

   a. "United We Stand" _____

   _____

   _____

   b. "Guns and Batter" _____

   _____

   _____

9. Which of the two essays is most convincing?

   Explain. _____

   _____

   _____

D. Critical Reading Practices

The next two reading selections provide practice in what you have learned in this chapter and previous ones.

Drill   D-1

Directions: Read the following essay by a frustrated English teacher. Look for her thesis, supporting points, intent, attitude, and tone.

"I WANTS TO GO TO THE PROSE"

Suzanne Britt Jordan

1   I'm tired—and have been for quite a while. In fact, I think I can pinpoint the exact minute at which I first felt the weariness begin. I had been teaching for three years at a community college. I had, for quite a while, overlooked ignorance, dismissed arrogance, championed fairness, emphasized motivation, boosted egos and tolerated laziness. I was, in short, the classic modern educator.

2   One day a student, Marylou Simmons, dropped by my office. She had not completed a single assignment and had missed perhaps 50 percent of her classes. Her writing, what little I saw of it, was illogical, grammatically incorrect and sloppy. "Can I help you, Marylou?" I said cheerily, ever the understanding and forgiving teacher. Her lip began to tremble; her eyes grew teary. It seemed she had been having trouble with her boyfriend. "I'm sorry, but what can *I* do?" I asked. Suddenly all business, Marylou said "Since I've been so unhappy, I thought you might want to just give me a D or an Incomplete on the course." She smiled encouragingly, even confidently. That's when the weariness set in, the moment at which I turned into a flaming conservative in matters educational. Whatever Marylou's troubles, I suddenly saw that I was not the cause, nor was I about to be the solution.

NAMBY-PAMBY COURSES

3   When I read about declining SAT scores, the "functional illiteracy" of our students, the namby-pamby courses, the army of child psychologists, reading aides, educational liaisons, starry-eyed administrators and bungling fools who people our school systems, my heart sinks. Public schools abide mediocre students; put 18-year-olds, who can't decide what to wear in the morning, into independent study programs; excuse every absence under the sun, and counsel, counsel, counsel. A youngster in my own school system got into a knife fight and was expelled—for one week. I noticed in the paper that bus drivers regularly see riders smoking marijuana and drinking wine on the bus at, for God's sake, 8 in the morning. I could go on, but the public knows well enough the effects of a system of education gone awry.

4   Consider for a moment what caused the mess. A few years ago people began demanding their rights. Fair enough. They wanted equal education under the law. I'm for it. Social consciousness was born. Right on. Now, enter the big wrong turn, the one that sent our schools into never-never land. We suddenly, naïvely, believed that by offering equal opportunities we could (1) make everybody happy, (2) make everybody

Reprinted by permission of Suzanne Britt.

well-adjusted, (3) forgive everybody who failed, and (4) expect gratitude to boot. When students were surly, uncooperative, whiny and apathetic, educators decided they themselves didn't know how to teach. So they made it easier on the poor, disadvantaged victims of broken homes, the misfits, the unloved. Well and good. But the catch to such lofty theories is evident. Poverty, ignorance and just plain orneriness will always abound. We look for every reason in the world for the declining test scores of our children, except for stupidity and laziness.

A CURMUDGEON SPEAKS

5   I'm perfectly aware that I sound like an old curmudgeon and it frightens me more than it offends you. But I have accepted what educators can't seem to face. The function of schools, their first and primary obligation, is not to probe tender psyches, to feed and clothe the homeless, nor to be the papa and mama a kid never had. The job is to teach.

6   The teacher's job is to know his subject, inside out, backward, forward and every which way. Nothing unnerves a student more than to have a teacher who doesn't know his or her stuff. Incompetence they cannot abide. Neither can I.

7   Before educators lost their way and tried to diversify by getting into the business of molding human beings, a teacher was, ideally, someone who knew a certain body of information and conveyed it. Period. Remember crotchety old Miss Dinwiddie, who could recite 40 lines of the "Aeneid" at a clip? Picture Mr. Wassleheimer, who could give a zero to a cheating student without pausing in his lecture on frog dissection. Every student knew that it wasn't wise to mess around with a teacher who had the subject down cold. They were the teachers we once despised and later admired.

8   I want them back, those fearsome, awe-inspiring experts. I want them back because they knew what a school was for and didn't waste any time getting on with the task at hand. They were hard, even at times unjust, but when they were through, we knew those multiplication tables blindfolded with both trembling hands tied behind our backs.

9   Before the schoolmasters and the administrators change they will have to shake off the guilt, the simpering, apologetic smiles and the Freudian theories. Which is crueler? Flunking a kid who has flunked or passing a kid who has flunked? Which teaches more about the realities of life? Which, in fact, shows more respect for the child as a human being?

10   Just today I talked to a big blond bruiser of a football player who wants to learn the basics of grammar. I didn't tell him it was too late. You see, he was a very, very good football player, so good that he never failed a course in high school. He had written on a weekly theme, "I wants to go to the prose and come fames." He may become a pro, may even become famous, but he will probably never read a good book, write a coherent letter or read a story to his children. I will, however, flunk him if he does not learn the material in the course. My job means too much to me to sacrifice my standards and turn soft. Suppose that every time my student played football badly, the coach said it was "just a game." Suppose the coach allowed him to drink booze, stay up all night, eat poorly and play sloppily. My student would be summarily dismissed from the team or the team would lose a game. So it goes with academic courses.

LIFE IS REAL

11   The young people are interested, I think, in taking their knocks, just as adults must take theirs. Students deserve a fair chance, and, failing to take advantage of that chance, a straightforward dismissal. It has been said that government must guarantee equal opportunity, not equal results. I like that. Through the theoretical fog that has clouded our perceptions and blanketed our minds, we know what is equitable and right. Mother put it another way. She always said, "Life is real; life is earnest." Incidentally, she taught me Latin and never gave me air in a jug. I had to breathe on my own. So do we all.

COMPREHENSION CHECK

1. The best statement of the main idea or thesis of the essay is
   a. The author is tired of teaching lazy students.
   b. Teachers must know their subject well.
   c. Everyone is being blamed for poor scholastic performance of students when most of the blame belongs to the students.
   d. The function of schools is not only to teach, but to make students happy and well adjusted.
2. The author's *attitude* toward her thesis can best be described as
   a. lighthearted
   b. pessimistic
   c. bored
   d. serious
3. The tone of the essay can best be described as
   a. ironic
   b. sarcastic
   c. angry
   d. ridiculous
4. T/F   The author is biased against equal opportunity in education.
5. Is the essay mostly fact or opinion?

_____

6. T/F   We can infer from paragraph 2 that the author hates Marylou.
7. T/F   We can infer from paragraph 5 that the author thinks she is more aware of the real educational issues than most educators.
8. Is paragraph 6 mostly fact or opinion?
9. T/F   According to paragraph 9, the author thinks it is better to fail students who have failed than it is to pass them.
10. Explain how the last two sentences fit the thesis of the essay.

_____

_____

_____

_____

_____

_____

Number correct: _____

VOCABULARY CHECK

Directions: Define the following words and phrases

1. championed fairness

_____

2. functional illiteracy

_____

3. mediocre students

_____

4. curmudgeon

_____

5. abide

_____

6. turned into a flaming conservative

_____

7. educational liaisons

_____

8. lofty theories

_____

9. crotchety

_____

10. prose

_____

Record the results of both checks on the Student Record Chart on page 495. Make certain you understand any problems you may have had before going on.

Number correct: _____

Drill D-2

Directions: Read the following essay on the battle between humans and inanimate objects. Look for the author's thesis, any use of facts and opinions, and determine the author's intent, attitude, and bias.

THE PLOT AGAINST PEOPLE

Russell Baker

1   Inanimate objects are classified into three major categories—those that don't work, those that break down and those that get lost.

2   The goal of all inanimate objects is to resist man and ultimately to defeat him, and the three major classifications are based on the method each object uses to achieve its purpose. As a general rule, any object capable of breaking down at the moment when it is most needed will do so. The automobile is typical of the category.

3   With the cunning typical of its breed, the automobile never breaks down while entering a filling station with a large staff of idle mechanics. It waits until it reaches a downtown intersection in the middle of the rush hour, or until it is fully loaded with family and luggage on the Ohio Turnpike.

4   Thus it creates maximum misery, inconvenience, frustration and irritability among its human cargo, thereby reducing its owner's lifespan.

5   Washing machines, garbage disposals, lawn mowers, light bulbs, automatic laundry dryers, water pipes, furnaces, electrical fuses, television tubes, hose nozzles, tape recorders, slide projectors—all are in league with the automobile to take their turn at breaking down whenever life threatens to flow smoothly for their human enemies.

6   Many inanimate objects, of course, find it extremely difficult to break down. Pliers, for example, and gloves and keys are almost totally incapable of breaking down. Therefore, they have had to evolve a different technique for resisting man.

7   They get lost. Science has still not solved the mystery of how they do it, and no man has ever caught one of them in the act of getting lost. The most plausible theory is

that they have developed a secret method of locomotion which they are able to conceal the instant a human eye falls upon them.

8   It is not uncommon for a pair of pliers to climb all the way from the cellar to the attic in its single-minded determination to raise its owner's blood pressure. Keys have been known to burrow three feet under mattresses. Women's purses, despite their great weight, frequently travel through six or seven rooms to find a hiding space under a couch.

9   Scientists have been struck by the fact that things that break down virtually never get lost, while things that get lost hardly ever break down.

10   A furnace, for example, will invariably break down at the depth of the first winter cold wave, but it will never get lost. A woman's purse, which after all does have some inherent capacity for breaking down, hardly ever does; it almost invariably chooses to get lost.

11   Some persons believe this constitutes evidence that inanimate objects are not entirely hostile to man, and that a negotiated peace is possible. After all, they point out, a furnace could infuriate a man even more thoroughly by getting lost than by breaking down, just as a glove could upset him far more by breaking down than by getting lost.

12   Not everyone agrees, however, that this indicates a conciliatory attitude among inanimate objects. Many say it merely proves that furnaces, gloves, and pliers are incredibly stupid.

13   The third class of objects—those that don't work—is the most curious of all. These include such objects as barometers, car clocks, cigarette lighters, flashlights and toy-train locomotives. It is inaccurate, of course, to say that they never work. They work once, usually for the first few hours after being brought home, and then quit. Thereafter, they never work again.

14   In fact, it is widely assumed that they are built for the purpose of not working. Some people have reached advanced ages without ever seeing some of these objects—barometers, for example—in working order.

15   Science is utterly baffled by the entire category. There are many theories about it. The most interesting holds that the things that don't work have attained the highest state possible for an inanimate object, the state to which things that break down and things that get lost can still only aspire.

16   They have truly defeated man by conditioning him never to expect anything of them, and in return they have given man the only peace he receives from inanimate society. He does not expect his barometer to work, his electric locomotive to run, his cigarette lighter to light or his flashlight to illuminate, and when they don't, it does not raise his blood pressure.

17   He cannot attain that peace with furnaces and keys and cars and women's purses as long as he demands that they work for their keep.

COMPREHENSION CHECK

1. The author's main point or thesis is that _____

_____

2. The author's *attitude* toward his subject is _____

_____

3. The author's *intent* is _____

_____

4. The author is biased against _____

_____

5. Is the essay mostly fact or opinion? _____

6. The author claims there are three major classifications of inanimate objects.

What are they? _____

_____

_____

7. Which of the three classifications does he feel is the most curious of all?

_____

8. The author uses anthropomorphism, the technique of attributing human qualities to inanimate or nonhuman objects. With what objects does he do

this? _____

_____

9. Explain how paragraphs 9 and 15 help reveal the author's attitude toward his

subject. _____

_____

_____

10. The author claims that we cannot achieve peace with furnaces, keys, and cars

as long as we demand _____

_____

Number correct: _____

For further discussion: The author uses the pronoun "he" to refer to both sexes. What is your reaction to this?

VOCABULARY CHECK

Directions: Define the following underlined words from the essay.

1.   the goal of all <u>inanimate</u> objects is to resist man

_____

2.   with the <u>cunning</u> typical of its breed

_____

3.   are in <u>league</u> with the automobile

_____

4. the most <u>plausible</u> theory

_____

5. a furnace will <u>invariably</u> break down at ... the first cold wave

_____

6. has some <u>inherent</u> capacity for breaking down

_____

7. a furnace could <u>infuriate</u> a man even more by getting lost

_____

8. a <u>conciliatory</u> attitude among inanimate objects

_____

9. the state to which things can still only <u>aspire</u>

_____

10. they have defeated man by <u>conditioning</u> him never to expect

_____

Number correct: _____

Record the results of both checks on the Student Record Chart on page 338. Make certain you understand any problems or questions you have before going on.

CHAPTER 8

Recognizing Inferences and Drawing Conclusions

A. Recognizing Inferences

All the skills you have been practicing in this unit are a basis for making critical judgments. You have been learning to recognize an author's attitude, intent, tone, and bias. Here's another important aspect of reading critically; recognizing *inferences*. An inference is a conclusion or an opinion drawn from reasoning based on known facts or events. For instance, when people smile we infer that they are happy. We base our inference on the fact that most smiles are from happiness or pleasure. A frown, we know from experience, generally means displeasure or pain. Thus, when someone frowns we infer that person is displeased. Our inferences are based on experience and/or knowledge. In his famous book, *Language in Thought and Action*, S. I. Hayakawa defines an inference as "a statement about the unknown made on the basis of the known."

Drawing inferences is something we do everyday. For instance, if you met a woman wearing a large diamond necklace and three platinum rings with rubies and pearls, you would no doubt infer that she is wealthy. You may not be right; the jewelry could belong to someone else or it could be fake. But because we know from experience that the type of jewelry she is wearing is expensive, it is natural to assume she is wealthy. It's a good educated guess based on experience and knowledge. Without experience or knowledge, however, any inferences we make are based on shaky ground.

Complete the following statements by drawing inferences from what is known in each case:

1. We may infer from the boy's crying and a melting ice cream cone on the

   ground that the boy _____.
2. We may infer from a woman's grease-stained hands and fingernails that she

   probably has been _____.
3. We may infer from the many whitecaps on the ocean that sailing would be

   _____
4. We may infer from the way the man threw his food on the floor and refused to

   pay the restaurant bill that he was _____.

5. We may infer from an F grade on a test that we _____.

Let's look now at some of the possible inferences. As to the first item, we can assume the boy dropped his ice cream cone; however, we don't know for a fact that is what happened. Someone may have knocked it out of his hands, or even thrown it at him. But based on the circumstances described, a good inference to draw is that he dropped it and is unhappy.

In the second item, we can infer that the woman has been working on something mechanical, such as an oily engine. Since we know that our hands and fingernails get greasy from such work, it's a good inference to make.

The circumstances in item 3 lead us to believe that sailing conditions might be rough, since whitecaps are caused by strong winds. However, a good sailor might like the conditions and think of it as a challenge. Of course, if you have never been around the sea, whitecaps might provide no information for drawing any kind of inference.

The man in item 4 might be angry, drunk, or "spaced out" on something. We might further infer that he didn't like the food, didn't get what he ordered, or hated the service. Most of us don't make a habit of throwing our food on the floor and making a scene, so we can infer that something is greatly upsetting him to act this way.

In the last item we probably infer that we failed. But is that technically an inference? The F grade is a symbol for failure. No inference need be drawn. But *why* did we fail? Maybe we didn't study hard enough, misunderstood the directions, studied the wrong material, the test was a poor one, or the instructor made a mistake.

Drawing inferences while we read critically is no different from the kind of thinking done in the preceding examples. For example, read the following passage and then answer the questions that follow.

If we compare college textbooks of just two decades ago with those of today, we see a dramatic decrease in the number of words, vocabulary level, and specificity of detail, but a sharp increase of graphics and, particularly, illustrations. Such textbook pictures can scarcely convey as well as words the subtle distinctions that emerge from scholarly or scientific work.

1. What is being compared in this paragraph? _____

_____

2. What inference can be drawn about the author's attitude toward college

textbooks today? _____

_____

3. What inference can be drawn about today's college students? _____

_____

Notice that the first question has nothing to do with inference, but it serves to remind you that in order to read critically you also have to put to use literal comprehension skills. The paragraph contrasts college textbooks of today with those published twenty years ago. In order to draw inferences, you have to understand that first. The answer to question 2 is that the author's attitude is negative. We can infer that because of the last sentence of the paragraph. The answer to question 3 is that today's college students' reading levels are probably lower than they were twenty years ago. Because of the decrease in words, lower vocabulary level, and more pictures, we can infer that today's students don't read as well. However, we could also infer that publishers are merely changing their way of publishing, but chances are that's not the author's intent here.

Here's a passage taken from a short story. Read it and answer the questions that follow.

In walks these three girls in nothing but bathing suits. I'm in the third checkout slot, with my back to the door, so I don't see them until they're over by the bread. The one that caught my eye first was the one in the plaid green two-piece. She was a chunky kid, with a good tan and a sweet broad soft-looking can with those two crescents of white just under it, where the sun never seems to hit, at the top of the back of her legs. I stood there with my hand on a box of HiHo crackers trying to remember if I rang it up or not. I ring it up again and the customer starts giving me hell. She's one of those cash-register-watchers, a witch about fifty with rouge on her cheekbones and no eyebrows, and I know it made her day to trip me up. She'd been watching cash registers for fifty years and probably never seen a mistake before. (From John Updike's "A & P," which appears in its entirety in Chapter 10.)

Based on the information provided, answer the following questions by drawing inferences:

1. How old and what sex is the narrator or person telling the story? _____

What makes you think so? _____

_____

_____

2. Where is the story taking place? _____

3. People in bathing suits coming into the place where the narrator is working is not an everyday occurrence.

    a. True because _____

    b. False because _____

4. The narrator is not distracted by the girls.

    a. True because _____

    b. False because _____

5. The narrator is very observant.

    a. True because _____

    b. False because _____

As we find out later in the story, the answer to the first question is a nineteen-year-old male. But we can guess from the passage that the narrator is male because of his reaction to the girls, because of the language he uses, and because of his comments about the "witch about fifty" who catches his mistake. The tone has a youthful, informal quality about it.

It's not too difficult to infer that the story is taking place in a supermarket of some type, probably a grocery store. He is working at a checkout slot ringing up HiHo crackers, and he comments that the girls were "over by the bread" before he saw them. These are clues to us.

Question 3 is probably true, making question 4 false. He is distracted by the girls. No doubt girls come into the store all the time, but in this case they are wearing "nothing but bathing suits," making this an unusual event. It causes him to forget whether or not he has already rung up the crackers.

Question 5 is true; he is very observant. His description of the one girl and the "cash-register-watcher" are full of details, reflecting an observant person.

The word "critical" often connotes finding fault with something. But making valid critical judgments, in its strictest sense, implies an attempt at objective judging so as to determine both merits and faults. Critical reading is thoughtful reading because it requires that the reader not only recognize what is being said at the literal level but also distinguish facts from opinions, recognize an author's intent, attitude, and biases, and draw inferences. A reader who is not actively involved is not reading critically.

Drill A-1: DRAWING INFERENCES

Part A

Directions: An inference, remember, is "a statement about the unknown made on the basis of the known." Complete the following statements drawing inferences from what is known. The first one has been done for you.

1. We may infer from the smile on the girl's face that she is probably _____

    _____ *happy, pleased* _____ .

2. We may infer from the scratchy noise that we hear every time we play a

    particular phonograph that there is _____

    _____ .

3. We may infer from the fact that when the light does not go on when we turn on

    a lamp that is plugged in that the bulb may be _____ .

4. We may infer from circling vultures that something near their circle of flight

    is _____ .

5. We may infer from a police car's flashing lights and siren close behind us that

    we _____ .

Part B

Directions: Read the following passages and answer the questions that follow them.

1. The word *concerto* originally meant a group of performers playing or singing together, as "in concert," or making a "concerted effort" of entertaining. The Gabrielis of sixteenth-century Venice called their motets, scored for choir and organ, *concerti ecclesiastici*. Heinrich Schutz, a seventeenth-century German composer, titled his similar works *Kleine geistliche Konzerte*.

    a. What is the intent of this paragraph? _____

    _____

    b. T/F   The German word *Konzerte* probably means concerto.
    c. T/F   We can infer that the author probably knows quite a bit about music.

2. Man, I screwed up royally. Like, I blew my allowance in Palm Springs during spring break, ya' know? When I called my ol' man to ask him to send me some more bread, he literally blew his stack. No way, man, am I gonna' be able to make it through the month. I don't know why he's so uptight, ya' know? He can afford it.

    a. What words best describe the person in the preceding passage? _____

    _____

    b. T/F   The person is a male college student.
    c. T/F   The person is angry at his father.
    d. T/F   The person is working his way through college.

3. Infer as much as you can from each of the following statements:
   a. The evening has proved to be most entertaining. I extend my deepest

      appreciation. _____

      _____   _____

   b. Tonight's been a real blast! Thanks a bunch.

      _____

   c. Like, I mean, funwise, this night has blown me away, babe.

      _____

4. There are all kinds of rumors about Ed Cantrell. Some say he can ride a horse
   for days without eating and still bring down a man at a thousand yards with a
   rifle. Some say he is almost deaf from practicing every day with a .38. Others say
   he can quote long passages from Hemingway's novels. And still others claim he
   has the eyes of a rattlesnake and faster hands. Most all who know him claim he
   is the last of the hired guns.

   a. What is Ed Cantrell's occupation? _____

      _____

   b. T/F   Based on the rumors, most people seem to admire him.
   c. T/F   Cantrell probably lives somewhere in the western states.
   d. What can we infer about Cantrell if it is true that he can quote long

      passages from Hemingway's works? _____

      _____

   e. Why would a man such as Cantrell be interested in Hemingway's works?

      _____

      _____

5. During the Middle Ages many scholars regarded printed books with apprehension. They felt that books would destroy the monopoly on knowledge.
   Books would permit the masses to learn to improve their lives, and to realize
   that no man is better than another. And not too long ago, slaves were strictly
   forbidden to learn to read and had to pretend that they were illiterate if they
   had learned how. Societies based on ignorance or repression cannot tolerate
   general education.
   a. T/F   The first sentence is fact.

   b. What is the author's attitude toward education? _____

      _____

   c. What is the intent of the statement? _____

      _____

Drill A-2: RECOGNIZING INFERENCES

Directions: Read the following passages and answer the questions that follow them.

1.   "Social science" in cold print gives rise to images of some robot in a statistics laboratory reducing human activity to bloodless digits and simplified formulas. Research reports filled with mechanical sounding words like "empirical," "quantitative," "operational," "inverse," and "correlative" aren't very poetic. Yet the stereotypes of social science created by these images are, I will try to show, wrong.

     Like any other mode of knowing, social science can be used for perverse ends; however, it can also be used for humane personal understanding. By testing thoughts against reality, science helps liberate inquiry from bias, prejudice, and just plain muddleheadedness. So it is unwise to be put off by simple stereotypes—too many people accept these stereotypes and deny themselves the power of social scientific understanding. (From Rodney Stark, *Sociology*, 2nd ed., Wadsworth Publishing Co., 1987, p. 28.)

    a. The author's intent in this passage is to _____

_____

    b. T/F   We can infer that the author feels some of his readers have a negative attitude toward social science.

    c. T/F   The author believes strongly in the scientific method of inquiry.

    d. T/F   The author is probably a science teacher.

2.   On July 10, 1985, the following events worth reporting occurred around the world:

—An Israeli court convicted fifteen Jewish terrorists of murder and violence against the Arabs.

—Bishop Desmond Tutu, Nobel laureate, pushed himself through an angry mob to save an alleged police informer from being burned alive.

—An Iraqi missile struck and heavily damaged a Turkish supertanker.

—A ship photographer was killed when a Greenpeace protest ship was blown up in New Zealand.

—The Nuclear Regulatory Commission (NRC) was accused of not properly considering earthquake hazards at the Diablo Canyon, California, atomic energy plant.

—Numerous major fires in Northern California burned over 300,000 acres of forests and destroyed many homes.

Yet the lead story of the day on two of the three major American television news broadcasts that evening had to do with the Coca-Cola Company's decision to return to its original formula after experimenting with a new taste that few seemed to like. Even the country's major newspapers featured the Coke story on their front pages at the expense of more newsworthy events. The headline of the *Denver Post*, for example, stated "'The Real Thing' Is Back." In addition, a six-square-inch picture of a can of Coke in two colors appeared next to the column.

    a. The intent of the passage is to _____

_____

b. T/F The passage is mostly opinion.

c. T/F The author feels that the type of news reporting described reflects an erosion of values in our society.

d. T/F The author of the passage would probably agree with this statement: Coca-Cola has become a national institution of sorts and what it does is of interest to almost all Americans.

e. State the author's attitude toward the reporting he describes. _____

_____

_____

3.   The United States Atomic Energy Commission, created by Congress in 1946, grew into a uniquely powerful, mission-oriented bureaucracy. One of its main goals, which it pursued with exceptional zeal, was the creation of a flourishing commercial nuclear power program.

By the late 1950s, the AEC began to acquire frightening data about the potential hazards of nuclear technology. It decided, nevertheless, to push ahead with ambitious plans to make nuclear energy the dominant source of the nation's electric power by the end of the century. The AEC proceeded to authorize the construction of larger and larger nuclear reactors all around the country, the dangers notwithstanding.

The AEC gambled that its scientists would, in time, find deft solutions to all the complex safety difficulties. The answers were slow in coming, however. According to the AEC secret files [obtained through the Freedom of Information Act], government experts continued to find additional problems rather than the safety assurances the agency wanted. There were potential flaws in the plants being built, AEC experts said, that could lead to "catastrophic" nuclear-radiation accidents—peace-time disasters that could dwarf any the nation had ever experienced.

Senior officials at the AEC responded to the warnings from their own scientists by suppressing the alarming reports and pressuring the authors to keep quiet. Meanwhile, the agency continued to license mammoth nuclear power stations and to offer the public soothing reassurances about safety. (From Daniel Ford, *The Cult of the Atom*, pp. 11–12. Copyright © 1982, 1984 by Daniel Ford. Reprinted by permission of Simon & Schuster, Inc.

a. The intent of the passage is to _____

_____

b. Describe the author's attitude toward the AEC. _____

_____

c. T/F The passage is mostly opinion rather than factual.

d. T/F We can infer from the passage that the author is probably not worried about the number of atomic energy plants built and being built.

e. T/F The author implies that the AEC placed its own commercial desires over the safety of the American people.

f.   What is your reaction to this passage and why? _____

_____

_____

_____

_____

4.   Futurists generally assume that twenty-first-century medicine will include new and more powerful drugs and technologies to fight diseases. They tend to forget, however, the serious problems presently arising from conventional medication prescribed by the average doctor. According to 1987 statistics, the average American receives 7.5 prescriptions per year. This is even more frightening when we realize that many people have not been prescribed any medication at all. This means that someone else is getting *their* 7.5 medications.

Most drugs have serious side effects, some quite serious. Since the sick person is often prescribed several drugs at the same time, there is often unfavorable reaction or illness from the drugs themselves. Studies also show that 25 to 90 percent of the time, patients make errors when taking their prescribed drug dosage. Despite the respect that people generally have for present-day doctors, there doesn't seem to be equal confidence in the treatments they prescribe because 50 percent of the time people do not even get their prescriptions filled.

Homeopathic medicine (using natural means to help the body build immune systems) offers an alternative. Instead of giving a person one medicine for headache, one for constipation, one for irritability, and so on, the homeopathic physician prescribes one medicine at a time to stimulate the person's immune system and defense capacity to bring about overall improvement in health. The procedure by which the homeopath finds the precise substance is the very science and art of homeopathy. (From Dana Ullman, "Royal Medicine," *New Age Journal,* Sept./Oct. 1987, p. 46.)

a.   The intent of the passage is to _____

_____

b.   T/F   The author's attitude toward conventional doctors and homeopathic doctors is equal.

c.   T/F   The passage is mostly opinion.

d.   T/F   We can infer from the passage that the author is biased against homeopathic medicine.

e.   T/F   The author implies that many patients do not trust or want to take the medications prescribed by their doctors.

f.   Would you be willing to go to a homeopathic doctor rather than a

conventionally trained physician? _____ Explain. _____

_____

_____

_____

_____

B. Recognizing Inferences and Facts

When inferences are based on facts, much useful information can be obtained. Scientists and historians, to name a few, have been able to infer from facts and observation most of the knowledge we have today. Below is a passage based on fact with many inferences that are probably true. As you read, note the inferences and the facts.

1   Nine hundred years ago, in what is now north-central Arizona, a volcano erupted and spewed fine cinders and ash over an area of about 800 square miles. The porous cinder layer formed a moisture-retaining agent that transformed the marginal farmland into a country of rich farmland.

2   Word of this new oasis spread among the Indians of the Southwest, setting off a prehistoric land rush that brought together the Pueblo dry farmers from the east and north, the Hohokam irrigation farmers from the south, and probably Mogollon groups from the south and east and Cohonino groups from the west. Focal points of the immigrants were the stretches of land lying some 15 miles northeast and southeast of the volcano, bordering territory already occupied by the Sinagua Indians.

3   Nudged out of their now-crowded corner by the newcomers, some of the Sinagua moved to the south of the volcano to a canyon that offered building sites and a means of livelihood. Here they made their homes.

4   Remains of the Sinagua's new homes, built in the early 1100s, are now preserved in Walnut Canyon National Monument; the cone of the benevolent volcano, in Sunset Crater National Monument; and part of the focal points of the immigrants, in Wupatki National Monument.

Now answer these questions.

1. T/F   The first paragraph is mainly fact rather than inference
2. T/F   The first sentence of paragraph 2 is inference.
3. T/F   The information in the last sentence of paragraph 2 is based on inference.
4. T/F   Paragraph 3 is mostly inference.
5. T/F   The last paragraph is mostly inference.
6. T/F   Chances are that someday this information will prove to be in error.

The answer to question 1 is false; it's mainly inference based on facts or evidence that when put together leads scientists to believe the events described happened 800 years ago. We have no way to prove the eruption occurred as stated, yet scientists basically agree that this is what did happen.

Questions 2 and 3 are true. Again, no one was around to verify these statements, but the inference that it happened can be made from present-day evidence.

While question 4 is basically true, at least the first part, the last part is fact because the remains are still there to see. Question 5 is false since all statements can be verified by visiting those places mentioned.

Question 6 is false; it's probable, but highly unlikely because of present-day facts and remains. However, in the future, this might be a "slippery fact," like the atom being thought of as the smallest particle at one time. But based on all the known facts we have at present, the best answer is false.

You can see that much of what we call "fact" today is based on inferences.

From the brochure *Walnut Canyon*, 1968–306–122/97, revised 1982, Superintendent of Documents, Washington, D.C.

When scientists agree on inferences that are drawn from what is known, we tend to accept as fact their conclusions until such time that more evidence can show the inferences drawn were wrong.

The following drills will help you recognize the difference between facts and inferences.

Drill B-1: DRAWING INFERENCES FROM FACTS

Directions: Read the following passages and answer the questions that follow them.

1.   The unit that is used to measure the absorption of energy from radiation in biological materials is the rem, usually abbreviated R. It stands for "Radiation Equivalent in Man." There is a unit called the rad, which corresponds to an amount of radiation that deposits 100 ergs of energy in one gram of material. The rem is defined as the radiation dose to biological tissue that will cause the same amount of energy to be deposited as would one rad of X rays.

A millirem (abbreviated mR) is one thousandth of a rem. To give some idea of the size of the things we are discussing, you get about 20 mR of radiation from a dental X ray, and about 150 mR of radiation from a chest X ray. Since the average dose of radiation to the average American is about 130 mR, it is not hard to see that it would be very easy to absorb in medical and dental X rays more radiation than one absorbs from natural causes.

The "average" dose of radiation, of course, varies as much as 150 or so mRs per year depending on where one lives. For example, in Colorado and Wyoming the average mR dose is about 250 per year, while in Texas the average dose is 100 mR. It is higher in the mountains because there is less air to shield us from cosmic rays and because there are more radioactive elements in the soil.

According to federal requirements in effect, the radiation dose at the fence of a nuclear plant can be no more than 5 mR per year. We can see that based on the average dose most of us receive, living near a nuclear plant offers relatively little dosage risk.

a. The intent of this passage is to _____

_____

a. T/F   The first paragraph is mostly factual.
c. T/F   Living in higher altitudes is safer from radiation doses than living at sea level, based on the information in the passage.
d. T/F   We can infer that the author is opposed to nuclear power plants.
e. T/F   The last sentence in the passage is factual.

2.   With that thought in mind, I raised my head, squared my shoulders, and set off in the direction of my dorm, glancing twice (and then ever so discreetly) at the campus map clutched in my hand. It took everything I had not to stare when I caught my first glimpse of a real live football player. What confidence, what reserve, what muscles! I only hoped his attention was drawn to my air of assurance rather than to my shaking knees. I spent the afternoon seeking out each of my classrooms

so that I could make a perfectly timed entrance before each lecture without having to ask dumb questions about its whereabouts.

The next morning I found my first class and marched in. Once I was in the room, however, another problem awaited me. Where to sit? ... After much deliberation I chose a seat in the first row and to the side. I was in the foreground (as advised), but out of the professor's direct line of vision.

I cracked my anthology of American literature and scribbled the date at the top of the crisp ruled page. "Welcome to Biology 101," the professor began. A cold sweat broke out at the back of my neck. (From Evelyn Herald, "Fresh Start," *Nutshell* magazine.)

a.   Where can we infer that the event described in the passage is taking

place? _____

How can you tell? _____

_____

b.   T/F   The narrator telling the story is female. Explain. _____

_____

c.   T/F   We can infer from the author's tone that the author has a sense

of humor. Explain. _____

_____

d.   Why did the author break out in a cold sweat when the professor

greeted the class? _____

e.   T/F   We can infer that the author is trying not to conceal his or her

true feelings. Explain. _____

_____

_____

3.   From the seller's viewpoint advertising is persuasion; from the buyer's viewpoint it is education. No single group of people spends as much time or money per lesson to educate the masses as do the creators of ads.

Ads participate in a feedback loop. They reflect a society they have helped to educate, and part of the advertising reflection is the effect of the advertising itself. Every ad that exploits a personality hole educates the audience toward using a particular product to fill that hole. Just as drug ads teach a crude and sometimes dangerous form of self-medication, psychosell ads teach a form of self-analysis and cure for psychological problems.

An ad that stirs a hidden doubt, that causes a person to ask, "Why does no one love me?"; "Why don't I have more friends?"; "Why am I lonely?" invariably goes on to suggest a partial cure—use our product. If an announcer for Pepsi would appear on screen and say:

> Are you lonely? Do you feel left out? Do you sometimes feel that everybody else has all the fun in life? Are you bored and isolated? Well, if you are, drink Pepsi and find yourself instantly a part of all those energetic, joyful, young-at-heart people who also drink Pepsi.

Such an ad would be greeted as either laughable or insulting by the viewing audience. Yet the old "Pepsi generation" campaign used pictures and a jingle to make exactly such a point.

The danger in psychosell techniques is not that people might switch from Coke to Pepsi in soft-drink loyalties or abandon Scope for Listerine. The danger is that millions learn (especially if the message is repeated often enough, as ads are) that problems in self-acceptance and boredom can be alleviated by corporate products. Which brand to buy is secondary to ads as education; the primary lesson is that the product itself satisfies psychological needs. (From Jeffrey Schrank, *Snap, Crackle and Popular Taste: The Illusion of Free Choice in America.* Delacorte Press, 1977.)

a. What is the intent of the author? _____

_____

_____

b. Is the passage primarily fact or opinion? _____ Explain.

_____

_____

c. T/F   The author thinks ads may be silly and repetitive, but basically

harmless. Explain. _____

_____

d. T/F   The author believes that some advertising is a dangerous form of education because it brainwashes us into thinking we can solve many of our personal problems by buying corporate products.

Explain. _____

_____

_____

e. T/F   The author's bias is easy to identify. Explain. _____

_____

_____

4.   Evolution has been made to appear a religious issue by two opposing groups of religious fundamentalists, each proposing a single-lens
view of reality. The biblical fundamentalists, interpreting the creation
narratives of Genesis as historical and scientific records dictated by God,
are compelled to reject any scientific theory which, like evolution,
appears to contradict what God said. Never mind that their biblicism
flies in the face of a century of biblical scholarship and is rejected by the
majority of religious denominations whose traditions stem from the
same biblical witness. This only reinforces their conviction that they are
the righteous few who will be saved. Never mind that, like the church-
men who refused to look through Galileo's telescope, they must deny an
enormous body of scientific evidence for evolution. This only proves that
scientists are the tools of Satan, using the theory of evolution to spread
vice and corruption everywhere. Never mind that many scientists see an
evolving universe as an even more magnificent tribute to a Creator than a
static one. They are lying, for only atheists "believe in" evolution. Salvation for us all lies in conversion to, or legal enforcement of, the biblical
fundamentalists' tribal myth, with its unquestionable morals and mores.

     The opposite extreme of religious fundamentalism is represented
by the "secular humanists." Their creed is the Humanist Manifesto, I and
II. Since they are neither secular nor humanistic, in the traditional sense,
and their basic premise seems to be that science has displaced religion
as the only valid way of acquiring knowledge of the real world, a better
name for them might be "scientistic fundamentalists." This group does
not seem bent on proselytizing, perhaps because it assumes that those
who can leave behind the religious myths (read "fantasies") of mankind's
childhood will be limited to the enlightened few. Their biases appear as
gratuitous snipes at religion, such as sometimes mar the otherwise lucid
writings of Isaac Asimov. (From Anne Marie Brennan, "Biblical Fundamentalists vs. Scientistic Ones: The Creationist Controversy," *Commonweal*, Oct. 22, 1982. Reprinted by permission of the Commonweal Foundation.)

a.   The intent of the paragraph is to _____

     _____

b.   T/F   The author is more biased against the "biblical fundamen-

     talists" than the "secular humanists." Explain. _____

     _____

c.   T/F   The author believes that only atheists "believe in" evolution.

     Explain. _____

     _____

d.   T/F   The author seems biased against Isaac Asimov's writings.

     Explain. _____

     _____

e. T/F   The author shares the views expressed in the Humanist Manifesto, I and II. Explain. _____

_____

_____

f. Do you agree or disagree with those views revealed in the passage? Explain. _____

_____

_____

Drill   B-2: INFERENCES IN ADVERTISEMENTS

Part A

Directions: Read the advertisement for "The Dry Look." Then answer the questions that follow.

1. T/F   The advertisement is aimed at both men and women.
2. What is the implication behind the statement "Get The Dry Look . . . and don't

   be a stiff"? _____

   _____

   _____

3. Obviously the intent of the ad is to persuade us to buy the product. Besides the
   promise of hair feeling soft and natural, the ad implies that use of the product
   will
   a. give you healthy hair
   b. make you attractive to the opposite sex
   c. keep your hair stiff
   d. make you feel happy
4. What purpose does the woman serve in the ad, especially the look on her

   face? _____

   _____

   _____

5. What social values are being taught through this ad? _____

   _____

   _____

Part B

Directions: Read the Antaeus cologne ad. Then answer the following questions:

1. The advertisement is aimed more toward women than men.

   a. True because _____

   b. False because _____
2. Based on the picture in the ad, what's the reason for using the product?
   a. You'll smell like a Greek god.
   b. You'll appear strong and sensitive.
   c. You'll get your back scratched.
   d. You'll be irresistible to women.
3. Antaeus, in Greek mythology, was a giant who was unbeatable as long as he
   was touching the ground. Hercules lifted him in the air and crushed him to
   death. Does this make Antaeus a good name for a cologne?

   a. Yes, because _____

   b. No, because _____

INSPIRED BY THE ANCIENT GREEK GOD

ANTAEUS

STRENGTH WITH SENSITIVITY IS NO LONGER A MYTH.

© 1987 CHANEL, INC. CHANEL® ANTAEUS®, ANTAEUS POUR HOMME™.

4. Antaeus Pour Homme (French meaning *for men*) Sport Cologne is designed especially for men who like sports.

    a. True because &rule;

    b. False because &rule;

5. Read the caption carefully, noting the use of the words "Greek god ...ANTAEUS... strength...no longer a myth." What does the ad imply about

   the use of the product? _____

   _____

6. What social values are implied through this ad? _____

   _____

   _____

C. Drawing Conclusions Using Induction and Deduction

A big part of critical reading is being able to draw conclusions based on what information authors provide. Once you understand the thesis or main idea of a reading selection, recognize fact from opinion, and understand intent, attitude, and inference, you almost automatically draw conclusions of your own. In fact, some of the questions you have been answering in the last drills require drawing conclusions based on the evidence provided.

Drawing conclusions is based on making *reasoned judgments*. Reasoned judgments usually come from two basic methods of reasoning: *deductive reasoning* and *inductive reasoning*. Deductive reasoning occurs when you begin with a general statement of truth and infer a conclusion about a particular specific. For instance, the old standby definition of deductive reasoning is shown through a *syllogism*, a three-step statement that begins with a general statement recognized as a truth and moves to a specific statement:

> All men are mortal.
> Bruce Springsteen is a man.
> Therefore, Bruce Springsteen is mortal.

Inductive reasoning, on the other hand, works in the opposite way. You begin with observing specifics and draw a general conclusion. You might move to a new town and notice that every time you see police officers they are wearing bright green uniforms. After seeing no police officer wearing anything other than this color, you might inductively reason that in this particular town the official police uniform is bright green.

Perhaps the best way to explain these two types of reasoning is to quote Robert M. Pirsig in a passage from his book *Zen and the Art of Motorcycle Maintenance:*

> If the cycle goes over a bump and the engine misfires, and then goes over another bump and the engine misfires, and then goes over another bump and the engine misfires, and then goes over a long smooth stretch of road and there is no misfiring, and then goes over a fourth bump and the engine misfires again, one can logically conclude that the misfiring is caused by the bumps. That is induction: reasoning from particular experiences to general truths.
>
> Deductive inferences do the reverse. They start with general knowledge and predict a specific observation. For example if, from reading the hierarchy of facts about the machine, the mechanic knows the horn on the cycle is powered exclusively by electricity from the battery, then he can logically infer that if the battery is dead the horn will not work. That is deduction.

We use these two types of reasoning every day, often without even knowing it.

Of course, we can make mistakes in our reasoning. Sometimes we make statements that draw the wrong conclusions. These are called *logical fallacies*. Here are some of the more common fallacies that you should avoid making and that you should look for when you are reading:

1. *Either-or thinking* or *oversimplification* occurs when a simplistic answer is given to a large problem: "You want to get rid of abortion clinics? Let's blow them up." *Either-or thinking* is also oversimplifying issues: "Let's

either get rid of all the nuclear weapons in the world, or learn to live with the bomb." Such thinking ignores or covers up other possible answers to a problem.

2. *Stereotyping* ignores individuality. There are stereotypes about political parties (Republicans are pro rich people; Democrats are pro poor people), stereotypes about Jews (they always look for bargains), stereotypes about blacks (they are better athletes), and so on. Stereotyping disallows looking at people, groups, or ideas on individual merit.

3. *Attacking a person's character* (the Latin term is *ad hominem*) to discredit someone's views is also a faulty way to reason: "Sure, Senator Nicely favors a bill to stop acid rain from being carried to Canada. Why shouldn't he? He owns a big farm in Canada and probably plans to retire there."

4. *Non sequiturs* (just a fancy Latin name for "it does not follow") occur when a logical reason is not provided for the argument being made. It's a contradiction when a person says, "Clint Eastwood would make a good president; his 'Dirty Harry' movies show you how tough he'd be on crime." The two assertions don't logically follow, since one has nothing to do with the other.

5. *Arguments because of doubtful sources* occur when an unknown source or a source lacking authority is cited: "The government doesn't want us to know about UFOs, but the *National Enquirer* has been providing a lot of evidence that proves contrary." While it might be true that the government is hiding something, the *National Enquirer's* reputation for sensationalism does not make it a good source to use as a convincing argument. Also, be careful when you read that a story comes from an unnamed "high level official."

6. *Begging the question* occurs when something that has already been proven as a truth is used to argue a point. Arguing that drunken drivers are a menace is begging the question since it's already been proven that they are.

7. *Irrational appeal* occurs when appeals to our emotions, to our religious faith, or to authority are made rather than appeals or reasons based on logic: "Of course you'll vote Republican; our family always has." "I'll get even. The Bible says 'an eye for an eye.' " "My country, right or wrong."

8. *Mistaking the reason for an occurrence* occurs when we fail to see there may be other causes or we are misled. "John is a naturally brilliant student." (Is John brilliant, or does he do well in school because his parents make him study more than others? Maybe he's trying to impress a girl in his class.) "Karla is absent from class again. She must not be a serious student." (Maybe Karla has a health problem, or a small child to attend, or lacks transportation to campus on certain days.)

If you read Chapter 3, you might want to review Drill C-4, which begins on page 138. If you haven't read that part of the book yet, you may want to read it now and compare these examples with the ones in the drill. That drill is based on a chapter from a textbook that deals with logical fallacies.

There are all kinds of faulty reasoning, but the ones described in this chapter are some of the more common ones you should begin to look for and avoid using when you draw conclusions or make inferences.

To look more closely at how we draw conclusions, read the following passage and then answer the questions that follow.

    In 1832, a twenty-four-year-old Englishman named Charles Darwin, aboard the HMS *Beagle* on a surveying expedition around the world, was collecting beetles in a rain forest near Rio de Janeiro. In one day, in one small area, he found over sixty-eight different species of small beetles. That there could be such a variety of species of one kind of creature astounded him. In his journal he wrote that such a find "...is sufficient to disturb the composure of an entomologist's mind...." The conventional view of his day was that all species were unchangeable and that each had been individually and separately created by God. Far from being an atheist, Darwin had taken a degree in divinity in Cambridge. But he was deeply puzzled by his find. (Adapted from James Burke, *The Day the Universe Changed*, Little, Brown & Co., 1985, p. 267.)

1. T/F   We can draw the conclusion that Darwin was not actually out searching for what he found.
2. T/F   The evidence provided for our conclusion is based partly on Darwin's journal.
3. T/F   What Darwin discovered was contrary to the beliefs of his day.
4. T/F   Darwin's later "theory of evolution," that species were not fixed forever, probably began with his discovery about the beetle.

All of the answers to these questions are true. Based on his journal statement that the find was "sufficient to disturb" his composure, the statement that he was "deeply puzzled," and the fact that what he found was contrary to what he had been taught to believe all provide evidence to support our conclusions that he was not looking for what he found.

Even though no one living today was with Darwin in 1832, his journal notes leave evidence to help answer question 2 as true. As to question 3, if Darwin had a degree in divinity from Cambridge, he would have been taught to believe what was accepted as "fact" in his day: that God individually and separately created all species. The fact that he found sixty-eight different species is contrary to such a belief.

Question 4 is true, but unless you have knowledge of what Charles Darwin's "theory of evolution" is, you might have difficulty drawing such a conclusion. If you know that he continued to pursue the suspicion in his mind that all species were not fixed forever, and that he eventually wrote *On the Origin of Species by Means of Natural Selection*, then there's no problem in answering this question as true.

The following drills are designed to help you develop your ability to draw conclusions from what you read.

Drill C-1: DRAWING CONCLUSIONS FROM AN AD

Directions: Read the advertisement about drug use. Then answer the following questions.

1. What is the intent of the ad? _____

    _____

    _____

2. T/F   One conclusion to be drawn is that drug use will "fry" your brains.
3. T/F   The creators of the ad probably believe that the pictures say more than the use of many words would against drug use.
4. T/F   The sponsors, "Partnership for a Drug-Free America," believe that their ad will effectively reduce drug use among teenagers.
5. To understand this advertisement, do you use inductive or deductive reason-

    ing? _____ Explain. _____

    _____

    _____

Drill C-2: DRAWING CONCLUSIONS FROM PARAGRAPHS

Directions: Read the following paragraphs and answer the questions that follow them.

1.   Look for a moment at the situation in those nations that most of us prefer to label with the euphemism "underdeveloped," but which might just as accurately be described as "hungry." In general, underdeveloped countries (UDCs) differ from developed countries (DCs) in a number of ways. UDCs are not industrialized. They tend to have inefficient, usually subsistence agricultural systems, extremely low gross national products and per capita incomes, high illiteracy rates, and incredibly high rates of population growth.... Most of these countries will never, under conceivable circumstance, be "developed" in the sense in which the United States is today. They could accurately be called "never-to-be-developed" countries. (From Paul and Anne Ehrlich, *Population, Resources and Environment.*)

    a.   The intent of the passage is to _____

         _____

    b.   T/F   The authors of the passage have drawn the conclusion that UDCs exist because they are not industrialized, have poor agricultural systems, high illiteracy rates, low incomes, and too much population growth.
    c.   T/F   If a UDC has a population growth that is too high for its agricultural system, we can draw the conclusion that it will never become a DC.

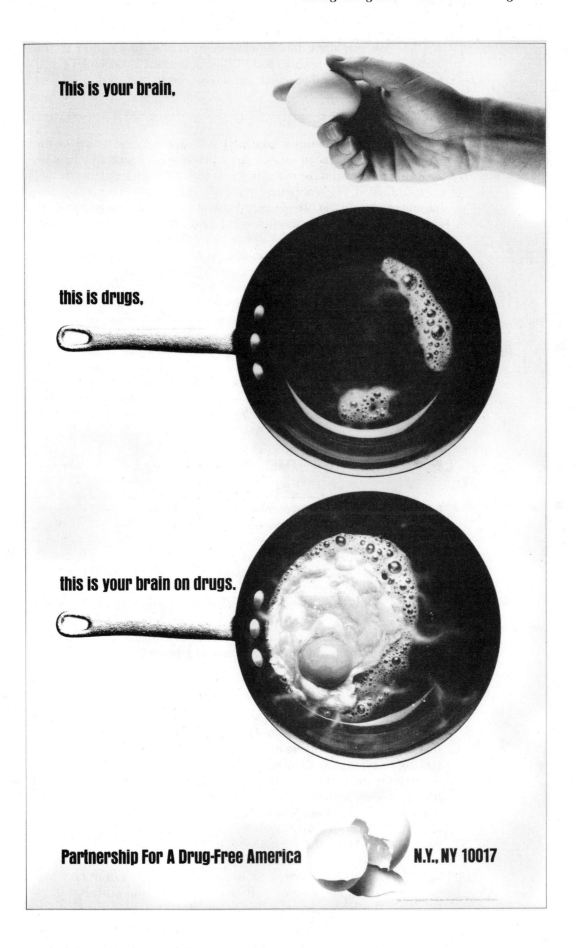

  d. T/F We can draw the conclusion from the information in the passage that the authors feel UDCs can eventually become DCs.

  e. Identify what kind of reasoning is required to answer *d.*

  _____

  2. Science is sometimes confused with technology, which is the application of science to various tasks. Grade-school texts that caption pictures of rockets on the moon with the title, "Science Marches On!" aid such confusion. The technology that makes landing on the moon possible emerged from the use of scientific strategies in the study of propulsion, electronics, and numerous other fields. It is the mode of inquiry that is scientific; the rocket is a piece of technology.

  Just as science is not technology, neither is it some specific body of knowledge. The popular phrase "Science tells us that smoking is bad for your health" really misleads. "Science" doesn't tell us anything; people tell us things, in this case people who have used scientific strategies to investigate the relationship of smoking to health. Science, as a way of thought and investigation, is best conceived of as existing not in books, or in machinery, or in reports containing numbers, but rather in that invisible world of the mind. Science has to do with the way questions are formulated and answered; it is a set of rules and forms for inquiry created by people who want reliable answers. (From Kenneth R. Hoover, *The Elements of Social Scientific Thinking*, 3rd ed., St. Martin's Press, 1984, pp. 4–5.)

  a. The intent of the passage is to _____

  _____

  b. T/F According to the author, some grade-school textbooks contribute to the confusion between science and technology.

  c. T/F The author does not think there is much difference between the terms *science* and *technology.*

  d. T/F The author does not believe that science is something that cannot be written down.

  e. T/F The author would agree with the statement, "Science has proven that too much sun causes skin cancer."

  f. T/F The author has respect for scientific thinking.

  g. What kind of reasoning did you use to answer *f?*

  _____

  3. Some years ago, I ran into an economist friend at the University of Michigan in Ann Arbor who told me, with concern bordering on shock, that assembly-line workers at the nearby Ford plant in Dearborn were making more money than an assistant professor at the University. It occurred to me that quite a few at Ford might prefer the more leisured life of a young professor. Certainly there seemed no need to fear any major movement of academic talent from Ann Arbor to the noisome shops in Dearborn. (From John Kenneth Galbraith, "When Work Isn't Work," *Parade* Magazine, February 10, 1985.)

  a. T/F The author's economist friend believes that a university professor should be paid more than an assembly-line worker.

  b. T/F The author agrees with his friend.

    c.   T/F   The author feels that a university professor's work is easier than factory work.

    d.   T/F   Because the pay is better for factory work, many professors will probably leave the university to seek factory jobs.

    e.   T/F   The author probably believes the usual definition for "work" can be misleading when comparing various types of jobs.

4.   Almost everyone in the middle class has a college degree, and most have an advanced degree of some kind. Those of us who can look back to the humble stations of our parents or grandparents, who never saw the inside of an institution of higher learning, can have cause for self-congratulation. But—inevitably but—the impression that our general populace is better educated depends on an ambiguity in the meaning of the word education, or fudging of the distinction between liberal and technical education. A highly trained computer specialist need not have any more learning about morals, politics or religion than the most ignorant of persons. . . . It is not evident to me that someone whose regular reading consists of *Time, Playboy* and *Scientific American* has any profounder wisdom about the world than the rural schoolboy of yore with his McGuffey's reader. (From Allan Bloom, *The Closing of the American Mind,* Simon & Schuster, 1987, p. 59.)

    a.   T/F   The author believes that the general public today is better educated than before.

    b.   T/F   The "McGuffey reader" must have been a widely used textbook in schools at one time.

    c.   T/F   The author believes that learning about morals, politics, and religion is not the function of institutions of higher learning.

    d.   T/F   The author favors a technical education over a liberal one.

    e.   T/F   The passage suggests that the author is pleased with the direction education is taking and thinks it is much better than it was in his grandparents' day.

    f.   Identify the type of reasoning the author uses to come to his con-

clusion. _____

Drill C-3: INDUCTION VS. DEDUCTION

Directions: Read the following passage to further develop your understanding of the difference between deductive and inductive reasoning. Also notice intent, attitude, and tone at work here.

DUELING DUALITIES

Two Pairs of Concepts Dear to the Hearts of Philosophers, Logicians, Literary Poseurs, and Intellectual Bullies Everywhere

Judy Jones and William Wilson

1   DEDUCTION VS. INDUCTION: Begin by forgetting what Sherlock Holmes used to do; to a philosopher, deduction is much more serious and far-reaching than being able to guess Watson was at his club all day because it's been raining and his clothes aren't wet. So what is it? It's a formal argument that assumes one or more principles as self-evident, then, following rigid rules and forms and proceeding from the general to the specific, infers one or more conclusions from those principles. The example you've heard before: "All men are mortal. Socrates is a man. Therefore, Socrates is mortal." Pay attention to that form. It's called a syllogism, and it's deduction at its most classic—though you can substitute Michael J. Fox for Socrates if you want.

2   Induction, by contrast, is empirical, factual, ordinary-feeling; it makes use of experiment and/or experience—the scientific method, if you will—to arrive at an inference and proceeds from the specific to the general. When you make an induction, you begin by recording instance, monitoring behavior, counting noses. If you go out to dinner at a Mexican restaurant a dozen times and each time you wake up at 3 A.M. with horrible indigestion, you may well induce that your digestive tract can't take Mexican food, at least not late at night. Of course, you could be wrong; maybe you'd have gotten sick those nights anyway, or maybe it's the particular Mexican restaurant, not Mexican food in general. Or maybe your roommate is poisoning you and trying to make it look like Mexican food. Don't worry, though: Unlike deduction, which, assuming its premises are sound, is certain, absolute, and airtight, induction is about mere probabilities; its success depends on how accurately you observe and over how many cases.

3   Historical note: For at least 200 years philosophers have been looking for a logical proof for why induction works as well as it does or, failing that, even just an orderly way to think about it. No soap. About the closest anybody's come to actually legitimatizing it as a philosophical entity, as opposed to a useful day-to-day skill, is John Stuart Mill, who cited "the uniformity of nature" as one reason why induction has such a good track record. Of course, that nature is uniform is itself an induction, but Mill was willing to give himself that much of a break.

4   Sometimes the line between deduction and induction is clear-cut: For instance, noting (with many a famous philosopher) that the sun always rises, you may have deduced it from the laws of planetary motion, or you may have induced it from the last 3,000-odd dawns. Sometimes you think you spot incest: After all, whoever first said that all men are mortal must surely have felt the need to do a little field work first, thereby inducing deduction's single most famous premise. But the flavors of the two will always be distinctive: Deduction is, in the end, all about the axiom ("A triangle has 180°"), while induction has the ring of the maxim ("Faint heart ne'er won fair lady").

Now answer the following questions:

1. T/F   Deductive reasoning begins with acknowledging an accepted principle or generality and proceeding from there to inferring or concluding something specific.
2. T/F   Syllogisms are the result of inductive thinking.
3. T/F   The following is an example of a valid syllogism:

    The sale to children of all things likely to hurt them should be prohibited.
    Sharp knives are likely to injure children.
    The sale of knives to children should be prohibited.

4. T/F   Inductive reasoning requires dealing with probabilities based on observation and numerous occurrences.
5. T/F   If you buy the same brand of ballpoint pen ten times and each time it runs out of ink after writing one page of notes, you can deduce that that brand of pens is probably no good.
6. T/F   Based on the last sentence, we could draw the conclusion that an axiom is to deduction what a maxim is to induction.
7. T/F   The tone of this passage contains a touch of humor.
8. T/F   The intent of the passage is to poke fun at the "dueling dualities," induction and deduction.
9. T/F   The authors are biased toward the inductive reasoning process.
10. List some phrases or sentences from the passage that create tone or attitude.

_____

_____

_____

_____

Drill   C-4: LOGICAL FALLACIES

Directions: Read the following dialogues and determine which of the following logical fallacies or errors in reasoning appear in the argument. There may be more than one type in a dialogue.

a. either-or thinking
   (oversimplification)
b. stereotyping
c. attacking character

d. non sequitur (contradiction)
e. doubtful sources
f. begging the question
g. irrational appeal

1. SAM: There's only one real aim of education—to learn all you can while going to school.

   GEORGE: Nonsense. Today, the only real reason to go to college is to get the skills necessary for a good job.

   Error in reasoning: _____

   Explain: _____

   _____

2. PAULA: Let's go hear the Nicaraguan ambassador at Fraley Hall tonight. It should be interesting to hear his views.

SUE: There's nothing that little commie's got to say that I want to hear.

Error in reasoning: _____

Explain: _____

3. HARRY: George is forming an organization to protest the dumping of toxic waste near the bird wildlife sanctuary. He really seems concerned about this. Quite a few people I know are joining with him. I think I will, too.

SALLY: Don't be a sucker. George's just doing it to bring attention to himself. He plans to run for president of the student body next term and wants to look good. Anyway, I dated him once and he came on too strong for me.

Error in reasoning: _____

Explain: _____

4. KIP: You going to vote for Sally? She'd make a good school representative on the board of education. She gets A's in all her classes.

PIP: You kidding? What does she know about politics? Anyway, a female's place is in the home, not running for office.

Error in reasoning: _____

Explain: _____

5. DALE: Did you hear that Sue is moving to the Midwest? She's convinced a major earthquake is going to hit us any day now.

FRED: She may be right. Have you been reading that series on natural disasters in the local newspaper? They predict an 8.8 earthquake will occur here in the next two years. The Midwest is a lot safer, that's for sure.

Error in reasoning: _____

Explain: _____

6. **RAUL:** Did you read about the junior-high kid who stabbed and killed his friend after they watched the movie "Friday the 13th" on TV?

PAM: Isn't that terrible? Maybe now they'll stop showing that worthless junk on television. Everybody knows what a big influence TV viewing has on kids.

RAUL: But how will this incident change anything?

PAM: Now there's proof of the harm.

Error in reasoning: _____

Explain: _____

Drill   C-5: QUIZ ON INTENT, ATTITUDE, BIAS, AND INFERENCE

Directions: As you read the following selection, look for the author's intent, attitude, bias, and inferences.

BIG WHITE

Skip Rozin

1   A strange calm settled over me as I stood before the large white vending machine and dropped a quarter into the appropriate slot. I listened as the coin clunked into register. Then I pressed the button marked "Hot Chocolate." From deep inside a paper cup slid down a chute, crackling into place on a small metal rack. Through an unseen tube poured coffee, black as night and smoking hot.

2   I even smiled as I moved to my customary place at the last table, sat down, and gazed across to the white machine, large and clean and defiant. Not since it had been moved in between the candy machine and the sandwich machine had I known peace. Every morning for two weeks I had selected a beverage, and each time the machine dispensed something different. When I pushed the button for hot chocolate, black coffee came out. When I pushed the button for tea with sugar, coffee with half and half came out. So the cup of coffee before me was no surprise. It was but one final test; my plan had already been laid.

3   Later in the day, after everyone else had left the building, I returned to the snack bar, a yellow legal pad in my hand and a fistful of change in my pocket. I approached the machine and, taking each button in order, began feeding in quarters. After the first quarter I pressed the button labeled "Black Coffee." Tea with sugar came out, and I recorded that on the first line of my pad. I dropped in a second quarter and pressed the button for coffee with sugar. Plain tea came out, and I wrote that down.

4   I pressed all nine of the buttons, noting what came out. Then I placed each cup on the table behind me. When I had gone through them all, I repeated the process, and was delighted to find the machine dispensing the same drinks as before.

5   None was what I had ordered, but each error was consistent with my list.

Reprinted by permission of Skip Rozin and Curtis Brown Assoc., Ltd. Copyright © 1975 by Skip Rozin.

6   I was thrilled. To celebrate, I decided to purchase a fresh cup of chocolate.

7   Dropping in two dimes and a nickel and consulting my pad, I pressed the "Coffee with Sugar and Half and Half" button. The machine clicked in response, and a little cup slid down the chute, bouncing as it hit bottom. But that was all. Nothing else happened. No hot chocolate poured into my cup. No black coffee came down. Nothing.

8   I was livid. I forced five nickels into the slot and punched the button for black coffee. A cup dropped into place, but nothing more. I put five more nickels in and pushed another button, and another cup dropped down—empty. I dug into my pocket for more change, but found only three dimes. I forced them in, and got back a stream of hot water and a nickel change. I went beserk.

9   "White devil!" I screamed as I slammed my fists against the machine's clean enamel finish. "You white devil!"

10   I beat on the buttons and rammed the coin-return rod down. I wanted the machine to know what pain was. I slapped at its metal sides and kicked its base with such force that I could almost hear the bone in my foot crack, then wheeled in agony on my good foot, and with one frantic swing, sent the entire table of coffee-, tea-, and chocolate-filled cups sailing.

11   That was last night. They have cleaned up the snack bar since then, and I have had my foot X-rayed and wrapped in that brown elastic they use for sprains. I am now sitting with my back to the row of vending machines. I know by the steadiness of my hand as I pour homemade hot chocolate from my thermos that no one can sense what I have been through—except, of course, the great white machine over against the wall.

12   Even now, behind me, in the space just below the coin slot, a tiny sign blinks off and on:

13   "Make Another Selection," it taunts. "Make Another Selection."

Now answer the following questions:

1. What is the author's general intent?
   a. to make us hate vending machines
   b. to share an experience with us
   c. to satirize the machine age
   d. to satirize the power of machines and human reactions

2. What is the author's attitude toward "Big White"?
   a. frustration
   b. hate
   c. defeat
   d. all of the above

3. T/F   The author seems to be biased toward the vending machine.

4. T/F   We can infer from paragraph 2 that the author has had trouble with "Big White" before.

5. T/F   We can infer from paragraph 4 that the author thinks he has outfoxed the machine.

6. What type of reasoning does the author use to outfox the machine?
   a. inductive
   b. deductive

7. T/F   From paragraph 11, we can infer no one knows the author was responsible for the mess he created the night before.

8. T/F   We can infer from the last three paragraphs that the author hates "Big White."

9. T/F   We can conclude that the author has given up trying to outwit "Big White."

Turn in the quiz to your instructor.

D. Practice Readings

The word "critical" often connotes finding fault with something. But as you have seen in this unit, reading critically implies an attempt at objective judging so as to determine both merits and faults. Critical reading is thoughtful reading because it requires that the reader recognize not only what is being said at the literal level but also facts, opinions, attitudes, inferences, and bias. A reader who is not actively involved is not reading critically.

Knowingly or unknowingly, you make critical judgments all the time, from deciding on the type of toothpaste to buy to choosing a topic for an English theme. The trick is always to be aware of your critical judgments and to know the reasoning behind your decisions.

Making critical judgments is a two-way street. As a reader you must be aware of the judgments the author is making and you must also be aware of the judgments you make, based on evidence rather than bias. For instance, you may dislike the subject of history so much that you have a bias against anything you read before you even get started. Your mind is already partly closed to the author. On the other hand, you could be biased in favor of what you read and accept what is being said simply because you already agree with the author. True critical reading should leave you a little wiser, a little better informed, and less biased than before—both about the subject and yourself.

Use the following practices to help you develop the critical reading skills taught in this unit.

Drill   D-1

Directions: Read the title and the first paragraph of the following essay. Then in the space provided, write what you think the essay will discuss.

_____

_____

Now, as you read the essay, apply all the reading techniques you have been learning. Then answer the questions that follow.

UNDERSTANDING NEED FOR KNOWLEDGE IS KEY TO "CULTURAL LITERACY"

William Raspberry

1   You cannot begin to understand E. D. Hirsch ("Cultural Literacy: What Every American Needs to Know") unless you first understand that there are two kinds of illiteracy.

2   Some illiterates, including many who have been to school, simply cannot read. That is, they cannot translate symbols on paper into words. They cannot decipher bus-route signs, simple instructions, application forms or letters from friends.

3   Others—"functional illiterates," as they are

called—do reasonably well at calling words but understand too little of what they have read. They may be able to recognize every word in, say, a newspaper article and still have little notion of what the article conveys.

4 They fail, in Hirsch's phrase, in "cultural literacy." That is, they know so little of what ordinary readers are presumed to know that they are unable to glean much meaning from what they read. Take this lead from a recent Associated Press story:

5 "The stock market retreated for the second straight session today in selling ascribed to concern over a weak dollar and rising interest rates."

6 The words, with the possible exception of "ascribed," are well within the grasp of an ordinary fourth-grade student. But what fourth-grader would understand what the reporter was talking about? He might know vaguely what a stock market is, but what is a market "session"? Just what does it mean to say that the market "retreated"? What was being sold? What is a "weak dollar"?

7 Those who would attack "illiteracy," perhaps calling for greater use of phonics, often have in mind the first variety—although the second may be far more common. Virginia Gov. Gerald L. Baliles, for instance, recently announced a major effort to help the "450,000 adult Virginians who cannot read, write or compute beyond the eighth-grade level."

8 But surely a reasonably bright eighth-grader is sufficiently adept at word-calling to handle the vocabulary of most newspaper articles or employment forms. The problem, Hirsch would insist, is they lack the background information necessary to give meaning to the words and phrases.

9 In short: "Literacy is more than a skill.... We know instinctively that to understand what somebody is saying, we must understand more than the surface meanings of words; we have to understand the context as well. To grasp the words on a page, we have to know a lot of information that isn't set down on the page."

10 That insight, in my view, explains why inner-city youngsters, who often read at or near the national norms while in the first three school grades, tend to fall further and further behind their national peers as they progress through the elementary grades. It is not that their word-attack skills decline, or that their teachers fail to teach them the "comprehension skills." The problem is that they lack the knowledge that the authors assume they possess.

11 That brings us to the most controversial part of Hirsch's book. Acting on his notion that the difference between cultural literacy and cultural illiteracy is "a limited body of knowledge" that can be catalogued, the University of Virginia professor ends his book with a long list of words, names and phrases: from Abraham and Isaac, agribusiness and albatross around one's neck through devaluation, détente and Don Quixote to Yellow Peril, xenophobia, zero-sum game and Zionism.

12 There will be—already have been—great arguments over what the list includes or omits. But his point is sound: There are things that literate Americans know, or at any rate know about. Only a tiny fraction of educated Americans have read *Mein Kampf*, but most of them at least have a pretty good idea of what it is.

13 Is the list, and authors' assumptions regarding what literate Americans ought to know, too "white"? Orlando Patterson, the black Harvard historian-sociologist, takes the question straight on.

14 "The people who run society at the macro-level must be literate in this culture. For this reason, it is dangerous to overemphasize the problems of basic literacy or the relevancy of literacy to specific tasks, and more constructive to emphasize that blacks will be condemned in perpetuity to oversimplified, low-level tasks and will never gain their rightful place in controlling the levers of power unless they also acquire literacy in this wider cultural sense."

15 A friend of mine puts it more simply: "If you don't know anything, it's hard to learn anything else."

COMPREHENSION CHECK

1. What is the thesis of the essay? _____

_____

_____

2. T/F The essay was written after the author read E. D. Hirsch's *Cultural Literacy: What Every American Needs to Know.*

3. T/F There are two kinds of illiteracy, according to the author: functional illiteracy and cultural illiteracy.

4. T/F The author of this essay disagrees with the findings of E. D. Hirsch.

5. T/F Someone who could read the words in this sentence, "Never has the world seen a nation so preoccupied with the buying and selling of the emblems of elitism," but not comprehend it is an example of a cultural illiterate.

6. T/F   The author of this essay feels that the items that every literate American should know listed at the end of Hirsch's book are geared more for whites than blacks.

7. T/F   Paragraph 14 implies that illiterate blacks need to first become functionally literate before worrying about the items on Hirsch's book list.

8. The author believes that literacy is
   a. a skill
   b. more than a skill
   c. understanding word meanings
   d. none of the above

9. Why does the author believe that inner-city school children who are reading at or near national norms while in the first three years of school fall behind as

   they progress through school? _____

   _____

   _____

   _____

10. Is the essay based mostly on fact or opinion? Explain. _____

   _____

   _____

   _____

Number correct: _____

VOCABULARY CHECK

Directions: Define the following underlined words from the essay.

1. They cannot <u>decipher</u> bus-route signs.

   _____

2. They still have little notion of what the article <u>conveys</u>.

   _____

3. The stock market retreated in selling <u>ascribed</u> to concern over the weak dollar.

   _____

4. An eighth-grader is sufficiently <u>adept</u> at word calling.

   _____

5. The people who run society at the <u>macro-level</u> must be literate.

   _____

6. Blacks will be condemned in <u>perpetuity</u> to oversimplified, low-level tasks.

_____

The following words are from examples of the list of items every American should know according to Hirsch's book. Define them.

7. devaluation

_____

8. détente

_____

9. xenophobia

_____

10. Zionism

_____

Number correct: _____

Record the results of both checks on the Student Record Chart on page 495. Make certain you understand any problems you may have had with any of the questions before going on.

Drill D-2

Directions: Read the title and the opening paragraph of the following selection. On the line provided, write what you think you will be reading about.

_____

Now read the selection, using all the literal and critical comprehension skills you have learned.

THE BAFFLING QUESTION

Bill Cosby

1   So you've decided to have a child. You've decided to give up quiet evenings with good books and lazy weekends with good music, intimate meals during which you finish whole sentences, sweet private times when you've savored the thought that just the two of you and your love are all you will ever need. You've decided to turn your sofas into trampolines, and to abandon the joys of leisurely contemplating reproductions of great art for the joys of frantically coping with reproductions of yourself.

2   Why?

3   Poets have said the reason to have children is to give yourself immortality; and I

"The Baffling Question" from *Fatherhood* by Bill Cosby, copyright © 1986 by Bill Cosby. Reprinted by permission of Doubleday, a division of Bantam, Doubleday, Dell Publishing Group, Inc.

must admit I did ask God to give me a son because I wanted someone to carry on the family name. Well, God did just that and I now confess that there have been times when I've told my son not to reveal who he is.

4   "You make up a name," I've said. "Just don't tell anybody who you really are."

5   Immortality? Now that I have had five children, my only hope is that they all are out of the house before I die.

6   No, immortality was not the reason why my wife and I produced these beloved sources of dirty laundry and ceaseless noise. And we also did not have them because we thought it would be fun to see one of them sit in a chair and stick out his leg so that another one of them running by was launched like Explorer I. After which I said to the child who was the launching pad, "Why did you do that?"

7   "Do what?" he replied

8   "Stick out your leg."

9   "Dad, I didn't know my leg was going out. My leg, it does that a lot."

10   If you cannot function in a world where things like this are said, then you better forget about raising children and go for daffodils.

11   My wife and I also did not have children so they could yell at each other all over the house, moving one to say, "What's the problem?"

12   "She's waving her foot in my room," my daughter replied.

13   "And something like that *bothers* you?"

14   "Yes, I don't *want* her foot in my room."

15   "Well," I said, dipping into my storehouse of paternal wisdom, "why don't you just close the door?"

16   "Then I can't see what she's doing!"

17   Furthermore, we did not have the children because we thought it would be rewarding to watch them do things that should be studied by the Menninger Clinic.

18   "Okay," I said to all five one day, "go get into the car."

19   All five of them ran to the same car door, grabbed the same handle, and spent the next few minutes beating each other up. Not one of them had the intelligence to say, "Hey, *look*. There are three more doors." The dog, however, was already inside.

20   And we did not have the children to help my wife develop new lines for her face, or because she had always had a desire to talk out loud to herself: "Don't tell *me* you're *not* going to do something when I tell you to move!" And we didn't have children so I could always be saying to someone, "Where's my change?"

21   Like so many young couples, my wife and I simply were unable to project. In restaurants, we did not see the small children who were casting their bread on the water in the glasses the waiter had brought; and we did not see the mother who was fasting because she was both cutting the food for one child while pulling another from the floor to a chair that he would use for slipping to the floor again. And we did not project beyond those lovely Saturdays of buying precious little things after leisurely brunches together. We did not see that *other* precious little things would be coming along to destroy the first batch.

COMPREHENSION CHECK

1. The title of this selection is "The Baffling Question." What is the question to which the title refers?
   a. Why do children act as they do?
   b. Why do people decide to have children?
   c. Why did the author have so many children?
   d. Why is raising children so difficult?

2. T/F   The question is never really answered.

3. The overall tone of this selection is
   a. gruesome
   b. bewilderment
   c. disgust
   d. humorous

4. T/F   The intent of the passage is to convince people not to have children.

5. T/F   The author's attitude toward his children is one of embarrassment. We can infer

this from his statement to one of his children, "Just don't tell anybody who you are."

6. T/F   The author wishes now that he had never had any children.

7. T/F   The author was happier before he had children than he is now so we can conclude he wants no more.

8. T/F   The author infers that their family dog is smarter than his children.

9. T/F   This reading selection cannot be read correctly only using literal comprehension skills.

10. We can infer that the author
   a. wishes he and his wife had spent more time deciding whether or not to have children
   b. wants his readers to think seriously before deciding to have children
   c. wishes his family were smaller
   d. loves his children even though he writes sarcastically about them

Number correct: _____

VOCABULARY CHECK

Part A

Directions: Define the underlined words in the following sentences or phrases from the selection.

1. You've decided to turn your sofas into <u>trampolines</u>.

   _____

2. Poets have said the reason to have children is to give yourself <u>immortality</u>.

   _____

3. You've <u>savored</u> the thought that just the two of you and your love are all you'll ever need.

   _____

4. ...these beloved sources of dirty laundry and <u>ceaseless</u> noises.

   _____

5. My wife and I were simply unable to <u>project</u>.

   _____

Part B

Directions: In the spaces provided, explain the following passages.

1. "You've decided...to abandon the joys of leisurely contemplating reproductions of great art for the joys of frantically coping with reproductions of yourself."

   _____

   _____

2. "If you cannot function in a world where things like this are said, then you better forget about raising children and go for daffodils."

   _____

   _____

3. "And we did not have children to help my wife develop new lines for her face...."

_____

_____

4. "We did not see the mother who was fasting because she was both cutting the food for one child while pulling another from the floor to a chair that he would use for slipping to the floor again."

_____

_____

5. "We did not see that *other* precious little things would be coming along to destroy the first batch."

_____

_____

Number correct: _____

Record the results of both checks on the Student Record Chart on page 495. Before going on, make certain that you understand any problem you may have had with any of the questions.

E. Timed Reading Practices

The following four reading selections can be used to practice increasing your reading speed of comprehension. You may want to look at your Timed Readings Record Chart on page 497 to review your rate and comprehension scores from the last timed readings you did. You may want to just use these as reading comprehension practices and not time yourself. It's up to you and your instructor.

Each of the reading drills contain comprehension and vocabulary checks that require using all the skills taught in this and the first unit of the book. Remember that you are competing against yourself. Try to learn from any mistakes you may make so that you can do better on each consecutive drill.

Drill E-1

Directions: Quickly read the title and skim over the headings in the following reading selection. Then answer these questions.

1. What do you think the article will be about? (Don't just write "birth.") _____

_____

2. What do you think you might learn about the subject? _____

_____

Now read the selection.

Begin timing. Starting time: _____

BIRTH

Stanley N. Wellborn

1   "Where do babies come from?"

2   That age-old question is provoking some startling new answers as doctors begin manipulating life.

3   Today, some children are created in test tubes. Others are carried in the wombs of surrogate mothers. And with sound-wave scans, prospective parents can know if their baby will be a boy or a girl months before birth. Soon, they will even be able to choose the sex.

4   In Australia and the Netherlands, five children have been born from frozen embryos. It is not beyond the imagination of doctors that parents one day may freeze their fertilized embryos for 100 years or more, leaving instructions for their children's births in another era.

"MIRACLE" CONCEPTIONS

5   Some 175 clinics in the U.S. offer in vitro fertilization (IVF). The technique benefits those who, because of functional sterility or infertility, cannot have children naturally.

6   In IVF, doctors surgically extract an egg from the mother and have it fertilized by the father's sperm in a laboratory dish. Once conception "takes," the fertilized egg is implanted in the mother.

7   Sometimes it takes repeated attempts to achieve fertilization. Dr. Michael Soules of the reproductive clinic at the University of Washington at Seattle estimates that a couple has about a 1-in-10 chance of having a baby on the first try with IVF.

8   Since the first test-tube baby was born in England in 1978, there have been roughly 1,000 births worldwide. The Eastern Virginia Medical School in Norfolk has produced 150 babies, including 20 sets of twins and two sets of triplets.

SURROGATES

9   At Cleveland's Mount Sinai Medical Center, doctors have performed the first implantation of an in vitro embryo in a surrogate mother.

10   Last August, doctors took an egg from a woman who was unable to have children because her uterus had been removed four years earlier. Once the egg was fertilized in a dish by the husband's sperm, it was transplanted into a good friend of the couple, who is now pregnant.

11   "I don't know of any previous case like this," says Dr. Wulf Utian, director of the medical center's obstetrics and gynecology department.

12   A growing number of surrogates are being artificially inseminated by a husband's sperm to produce a baby for him and his wife. In such instances, the baby has genetic characteristics of the father and surrogate mother.

13   In the Cleveland case, however, the child will carry the genes of its mother and father, not the surrogate.

EMBRYO TRANSFER

14   This technique is employed for women who cannot produce eggs but can carry a fetus.

15   Doctors first match up the infertile wife with an egg donor who ovulates at about the same time—a key step since hormone levels must be the same in both women for a successful transfer.

16   The donor then is artificially inseminated with the husband's sperm. Five days after fertilization, the egg is inserted into the wife's uterus.

17   A Chicago firm called Fertility & Genetics Research, Inc., has devised a procedure using a special catheter for embryo transfers. It forecasts a market of up to 50,000 candidates.

MULTIPLE BIRTHS

18   The most common therapy for the more than 2 million U.S. women who have difficulty getting pregnant involves fertility agents. These trigger increased ovulation and can lead to multiple births. The Frustaci septuplets, for example, were born to an Orange, Calif., couple on May 21. Only three of the seven survived—all three healthy.

FROZEN EMBRYOS

19   Through cryopreservation, eggs are fertilized and cooled to minus-321 degrees Fahrenheit in liquid nitrogen. In that condition, embryos could remain safe for centuries—and a couple could have their own genetic offspring even if one or both become sterile.

20   Yet frozen embryos present major ethical problems. "To whom do such embryos belong?" asks Michael Flower, a professor at the University of California. "To living parents, to the estate of deceased parents, to the storage facility that maintains them, or to the state?"

INFERTILITY

21   In the U.S., 1 in 6 couples has difficulty conceiving or bearing a child. About 27 percent of women between ages 15 and 44 can't have children because of physical problems. The sperm count of U.S. males has fallen more than 30 percent in 50 years. Some 25 percent of men are considered functionally sterile. Experts suspect that environmental pollution is a cause.

22   All this is spurring the race for ways to have a baby that are safe and ethically acceptable. In the process, "miracle" births are becoming part of the norm.

23   At the Eastern Virginia clinic, a poster reads, "They say that babies are made in heaven—but we know better."

Finishing time: _____

Starting time: _____ **(Subtract)**

Reading time: _1:30_____

Check your rate on the Conversion Chart on page 500.

WPM: _467_____

COMPREHENSION CHECK

1. The best statement of thesis for this article is
   a. New techniques are permitting otherwise childless couples to have babies of their own.
   b. Babies are no longer "made in heaven."
   c. In the U.S., 1 in 6 couples has difficulty conceiving or bearing a child.
   d. The new techniques allowing childless couples to conceive or bear children of their own are raising ethical problems.

2. The intent of the article is to ___*inform*___

3. The author's attitude toward his subject is
   a. biased in favor of the new technology
   b. fairly objective
   c. fairly subjective
   d. none of the above

4. T/**F** In vitro fertilization (IVF) is a process whereby doctors surgically extract an egg from the mother and have it fertilized by the father's sperm in a laboratory dish.

5. When doctors take an egg from a woman, fertilize it with the husband's sperm, and implant the fertile egg in another woman, it is called
   a. embryo transfer
   b. cryopreservation
   c. surrogate transfer
   d. infertility

6. T/**F** Soon it will be possible to choose the sex of the baby you want.

7. **T**/F The problem with using fertility agents to increase the chance of getting pregnant is that it can lead to dangerous multiple births.

8. **T**/F It is not beyond the imagination of doctors that parents may one day freeze their fertilized embryos for 100 years or more, leaving instructions for their children's births in another era.

9. Which of the following "miracle birth methods" are *not* mentioned in the article?
   a. "test tube" babies
   b. surrogate parenting
   c. embryo transfer
   d. cryopreservation
   e. none of the above

10. **T**/F There are probably people who are opposed to the techniques mentioned in the article.

Number correct: __8__

VOCABULARY CHECK

Directions: Define the underlined words in the following sentences or phrases.

1. Others are carried in the wombs of <u>surrogate</u> <u>mothers</u>.

   _____

2. because of <u>sterility</u>

   _____

3. It was <u>transplanted</u> into a good friend.

   _____

4. the medical center's <u>gynecology</u> department

   _____

5. using a special <u>catheter</u> for embyro transfers

   _____

6. their own <u>genetic</u> offspring

   _____

7. They create major <u>ethical</u> problems.

   _____

8. All this is <u>spurring</u> the race for ways to have babies.

   _____

9. They match up the infertile wife with an egg donor who <u>ovulates</u> at about the same time.

   _____

10. <u>prospective</u> parents can know

    _____

Number correct: _____

Record your rate, comprehension, and vocabulary scores on the Timed Readings Chart on page 497. Each correct answer is worth 10 percent. Discuss your results with your instructor.

Drill   E-2

Directions: Quickly read the title and skim over the first and last paragraphs of
the following reading selection. Then answer these questions:

1.   What do you think the article will deal with?   *genetic engineering*

_____

2.   What do you think you might learn from reading this article?

how it works _____

Now read the selection.

Begin timing. Starting time: _____

THE SPLICE OF LIFE

Judy Jones and William Wilson

1   Genetic engineering is a process that inserts genes from one living organism into
the cells of another, thereby custom-tailoring them to do work they weren't designed
for. (But they still won't do windows.) For example, thanks to genetic engineering, or
recombinant DNA technique, millions of bacteria are kept busy churning out precious
human insulin. Scientists build the microfactories by slipping the human gene responsible for the creation of insulin into *E. coli,* a mild-mannered bacterium found in our
digestive tract. So far, genetic engineering has been most successful with micro-
organisms and plants; science is still working on the problem of getting genetically
altered DNA back into a human cell. Someday, however, we may be able to replace,
remove, or repair bad genes, like the ones responsible for such diseases as cystic
fibrosis, sickle cell anemia, and perhaps even cancer.

2   To understand how genetic engineering works, you've got to know about deox-
yribonucleic acid, or DNA, three letters even more important than MSG or HBO. First,
go back to the days when you were a swinging single cell—a fertilized egg whose
nucleus contained forty-six particles called chromosomes, twenty-three from each
parent, carrying the coded information for all your inherited characteristics, from hair
color to disease susceptibility. As your cell divided, each new cell was issued forty-six
identical chromosomes (except your reproductive cells, which, in anticipation of
future mating, have only twenty-three apiece). The strandlike chromosomes are made
up of several thousand genes, each responsible for a particular trait. And the genes are
composed of DNA, the chemical that runs the show, controlling all life processes. All
living things have DNA in every cell. (The exception: Some viruses contain only a
chemical cousin of DNA called RNA.) Indeed, it has been said that if the instructions
coded in one person's DNA were written out, they would fill 1,000 encyclopedia-sized
volumes. You might want to wait for the movie.

3   In 1953, Francis Crick and James Watson earned a Nobel Prize for discovering
that DNA is shaped like a spiral staircase, the famous double helix. Phosphates and
sugars form the railing of the staircase, and pairs of four nitrogen bases in various

combinations form the steps—up to about 3 billion of them in human DNA. The order of the base pairs determines the particular characteristics of any shrub, egret, or standup comic.

4   Twenty years after this discovery, two California researchers, Stanley Cohen and Herbert Boyer, found a way to perform DNA transplants. For example, to turn bacteria into human insulin factories, DNA is first removed from a human cell and cut with special enzymes at the spot where the needed gene is found. Then, using more enzymes, the human gene is snapped into a plasmid, a strand of extra DNA found in bacterium. When the bacterium reproduces, it creates millions of copies of itself, each with the new gene. In this way, scientists are producing human insulin, growth hormone, and interferon. They may someday be able to insert the cattle gene responsible for producing muscle protein into bacteria, a glob of which would taste like steak.

5   There's already controversy and intrigue in the world of genetically altered organisms. In 1985, such an organism was tested for the first time outside the lab—semiofficially. A vaccine made by genetically altering a herpes virus was injected into 250 piglets. The test may have launched a golden age of agriculture—or a regulatory nightmare. What if the gene-altered vaccine goes wild, mutates, affects humans?

6   Gene splicing is not to be confused with cloning, replacing the nucleus of a fertilized egg with the nucleus from any cell in the body of a donor which upon division results in a perfect genetic copy of that donor. And don't get genetic engineering mixed up with in-vitro fertilization, the creation of test-tube babies. In that case, the ovum (or several ova) are removed from the mother, fertilized in a petri dish by a sperm from the father, and returned to the mother's womb. The world's first test-tube baby, born in England in 1978, now has a test-tube sister. (The term is unfair; the kid spends only a couple of days in a dish, as an egg $\frac{1}{25}$ of an inch in diameter.) There are now thousands of in-vitro children in the world.

7   In a newer procedure, so-called prenatal adoption, a woman needn't produce her own eggs. The fertilized ova of another woman, who has been artificially inseminated with sperm from the first woman's mate, can be implanted in the womb of the infertile woman and carried to term.

8   Yet another technique allows the freezing of fertilized and unfertilized eggs for future use. A woman may someday have her ova easy—she could deposit a fertilized egg, to be reimplanted later, once she's launched her career or sown her wild oats. Or she could rent a womb, paying someone else to carry her child. But mightn't that lead to the creation of a class of drone-moms employed by women who want to buy their way out of morning sickness?

9   Ah, that's just one of the ethical problems of biotechnology, the blanket term for all this fiddling around with Life Itself. Other sticklers: What if the wrong people start tampering with characteristics, like physique, building a brave new world of super-jocks and ultrawimps? What if a genetically engineered microbe escapes from the lab or the test area? There are still some bugs to be worked out.

Finishing time: _____

Starting time: _____ **(subtract)**

Reading time: _/:45_____

Check your rate on the Conversion Chart on page 500.

WPM: _____560_____

COMPREHENSION CHECK

1. The article is basically about genetic engineering.

   a. True because _that's the central focal point_

   b. False because _____

2. The intent of the article is to
   a. explain what DNA is
   b. give a history of the discovery of DNA
   c. show some outcomes of genetic engineering
   d. all of the above

3. The authors' attitude toward their subject is
   a. serious
   b. serious with a touch of humor
   c. playful
   d. sarcastic

4. The statement, "...thereby custom-tailoring them [cells] to do work they weren't designed for. (But they still won't do windows.)" is an example of how writers create tone.

   a. True because _it shows a touch of humor_

   b. False because _____

5. When the authors say that if one person's DNA were written out, they would fill 1,000 encyclopedia-sized volumes, but "you might want to wait for the movie," they are implying _humor. You wouldn't want to actually read that information_

6. T/F Gene splicing and cloning are the same thing.

7. Explain the statement "...DNA, three letters even more important than MSG or HBO." _humor again_

   _____

8. We can draw the conclusion that the authors have a sense of humor.

   a. True because _of all the puns_

   b. False because _____

9. The authors are not worried about future experimentation with genetic engineering.

   a. True because _Not really worried because of the humorous touch_

   b. False because _____

10. Explain one of the dangers that could occur, as the authors say, from "fiddling around with Life Itself." *what if the genetically altered virus got out of the lab?*

Number correct: _____

VOCABULARY CHECK

Directions:　Define the underlined words in the following sentences or phrases.

1. to understand how <u>genetic engineering</u> works

2. from hair color to disease <u>susceptibility</u>

3. <u>Strandlike</u> chromosomes are made up of several thousand genes

4. characteristics of any shrub, <u>egret</u>, or standup comic

5. What if it goes wild, <u>mutates</u>, affects humans?

6. fertilized in a <u>petri dish</u>

7. so-called <u>prenatal</u> adoption

8. once she's <u>sown her wild oats</u>

9. a brave new world . . . <u>ultrawimps</u>

10. the creation of a class of <u>drone-moms</u>

Number correct: _____

Record your rate, comprehension, and vocabulary scores on the Timed Readings Chart on page 497. Each correct answer is worth 10 percent. Discuss your results with your instructor.

Drill **E-3**

Directions: Survey the following essay before you begin timing. Then read rapidly, but not so quickly that you miss the main ideas and supporting details, or the author's attitude, tone, and bias.

Begin timing. Starting time: _____

AD PROVES BABY BOOMERS ARE MAINSTREAM AMERICA

Bob Greene

1   If you ever needed final proof that the Baby Boom generation has, indeed, taken over America, you will find that proof in a full-page advertisement that is currently running in many slick, upscale national magazines.

2   The ad is for Christian Brothers brandy. Most of the page is taken up by a picture of Chuck Berry, dressed all in orange. Berry is wearing orange shoes, orange socks, orange pants, a frilly orange shirt, an orange vest—and he is holding an orange guitar.

3   The caption at the bottom of the page reads: "C.B. in orange." And beneath that, in smaller letters: "With a little CB brandy and orange juice, Johnny B. very good indeed."

4   Now . . . the ad makes several assumptions. The first assumption is that mainstream America will instantly recognize Chuck Berry—his name never appears in the advertisement. The second assumption is that the caption "C.B. in orange" will be understandable to the reader—the double meaning, of course, being that C.B. (Chuck Berry) is dressed in orange, and that C.B. (Christian Brothers brandy) mixes well with orange juice. The third assumption is that the phrase "Johnny B. very good indeed" will make sense to the reader—the reference being to the old Chuck Berry song "Johnny B. Goode."

5   All these assumptions are right on the mark. The ad is quite effective, and it is based on the knowledge that the Baby Boom generation is now mainstream America—that the country's adult purchasing power is now in the hands of that generation.

6   Can you imagine, 20 years ago—even 10 years ago—a major consumer-products company trying to reach the masses by using Chuck Berry as a corporate symbol? It never would have happened. Chuck Berry

was the dividing line between generations. Let's start with the fact that the previous generation probably would not even have recognized Chuck Berry. And even if some members of that generation had recognized him, he would have been an extremely unlikely product spokesman. For one thing, of course, he was black, and most blacks—even the biggest black celebrities—traditionally have had a hard time being hired to promote products aimed at customers in a white marketplace.

7   In addition to this, Berry wasn't black in the way that, say, Fats Domino was black. Fats Domino was jolly and cheery and non-threatening. Chuck Berry—at least in his public persona—bordered on being downright nasty. Legend has it that, in the early '60s, when Berry was serving time in prison on a Mann Act conviction, he sat in his cell listening to the radio and heard a new hit. It was the Beach Boys' "Surfin' U.S.A."—and Berry was totally enraged and frustrated that the song was a blatant white-boys' ripoff of his "Sweet Little Sixteen."

8   Obviously, though, the manufacturers of Christian Brothers brandy realize that, to the Baby Boom generation, Chuck Berry now seems almost like a friendly, familiar, slightly eccentric uncle. My guess is that their decision to use him as a corporate symbol is a brilliant one. I can only go by my own experiences. In 1972, for the first time in my life, I bought a first-class airplane ticket—just so I could ride in the same cabin with Chuck Berry.

9   I was checking in at the gate for a flight from Chicago to St. Louis, and I noticed that the man in front of me in line was Chuck Berry. This was a little like seeing Santa Claus. As soon as I realized that Berry's ticket was first class, I made an impulsive decision and

Reprinted by permission: Tribune Media Services.

upgraded my coach ticket to first class. I was hoping that I would be seated next to him. Alas, Berry sat first-row aisle, and I sat second-row aisle. I never worked up the guts to say a word to him. But I have always considered that upgrade just about the best money I ever spent.

10   So from my point of view, Christian Brothers brandy has the right spokesman for the right times. If the Baby Boom generation is finally mainstream Amer-ica, then Chuck Berry is finally mainstream America, too. He turns 61 next month, by the way; he has an autobiography coming out, and also a movie—"Hail, Hail, Rock & Roll."

11   I don't know what I would have said to Chuck Berry in that airplane cabin even if I'd had the nerve. Probably just that "Brown-Eyed Handsome Man" is one of the best songs ever written.

Finishing time: _____

Starting time: _____ **(subtract)**

Reading time: ___*1:00*___

Check your rate on the Conversion Chart on page 500.

WPM: _____

COMPREHENSION CHECK

1. What is the thesis of the essay? *the baby-boomer generation has become the "adult's purchasing power".*

2. T/*F* The author deals primarily with fact.

3. The author's attitude about the ad for Christian Brothers brandy is that it
   a. stinks
   b. is effective
   c. won't be understood by most people
   d. uses too much orange color

4. The author's intent is to show that
   a. the major consumers today are from the Baby Boom generation
   b. Chuck Berry is well known
   c. Chuck Berry was the author's idol when he was younger
   d. the ad is effective

5. Which of the following are assumptions the Christian Brothers ad makes?
   a. that C.B. refers to both Christian Brothers and Chuck Berry
   b. that "C.B. in orange" refers both to Chuck Berry's attire and that C.B. brandy mixes well with orange juice
   c. that the phrase "Johnny B. very good indeed" is a reference to Chuck Berry's song "Johnny B. Goode"
   d. all of the above

6. For what reason is a comparison made between Chuck Berry and Fats Domino? *Because 10 or 20 years ago Chuck Berry was a bad guy & Domino was a good guy*

7. T/*F* We can infer that the author likes Christian Brothers brandy.

8. *T*/F We can infer that the author is a member of the Baby Boom generation.

9. T/*F* In order to write this essay the author had to apply critical reading skills to the ad he describes.

10. What conclusions can be drawn about advertising methods used to reach a

particular audience? *they're "on the mark"*

_____

_____

_____

Number correct: _____ *10* _____

VOCABULARY CHECK

Directions: Define the underlined words in the following phrases.

1. in many <u>slick</u>, <u>upscale</u> magazines

_____

2. a <u>frilly</u> orange shirt

_____

3. <u>mainstream</u> America

_____

4. Chuck Berry as a <u>corporate</u> <u>symbol</u>

_____

5. at least in his <u>public</u> <u>persona</u>

_____

6. on a <u>Mann</u> <u>Act</u> conviction

_____

7. a <u>blatant</u> white-boys' ripoff

_____

8. a familiar, slightly <u>eccentric</u> uncle

_____

9. I made an <u>impulsive</u> <u>decision</u>

_____

10. the <u>Baby</u> <u>Boom</u> <u>generation</u>

_____

Number correct: _____

Record your rate, comprehension, and vocabulary scores on the Timed
Readings Chart on page 497. Each correct answer is worth 10 percent. Discuss
your results with your instructor.

UNIT II PROGRESS CHECK

This check is the last timed reading selection in this unit. After you have finished it, compare the results with your scores for the Critical Comprehension Inventory you took at the beginning of this unit. Try to increase your scores over your first scores. Rate increase, however, is not as important as increase in comprehension.

Directions: Apply everything you have learned as you read the following article rapidly but with good comprehension.

Begin timing. Starting time: _____

THE TROUBLE WITH TELEVISION

Robert MacNeil

1   It is difficult to escape the influence of television. If you fit the statistical averages, by the age of 20 you will have been exposed to at least 20,000 hours of television. You can add 10,000 hours for each decade you have lived after the age of 20. The only things Americans do more than watch television are work and sleep.

2   Calculate for a moment what could be done with even a part of those hours. Five thousand hours, I am told, are what a typical college undergraduate spends working on a bachelor's degree. In 10,000 hours you could have learned enough to become an astronomer or engineer. You could have learned several languages fluently. If it appealed to you, you could be reading Homer in the original Greek or Dostoyevsky in Russian. If it didn't, you could have walked around the world and written a book about it.

3   The trouble with television is that it discourages concentration. Almost anything interesting and rewarding in life requires some constructive, consistently applied effort. The dullest, the least gifted of us can achieve things that seem miraculous to those who never concentrate on anything. But television encourages us to apply no effort. It sells us instant gratification. It diverts us only to divert, to make the time pass without pain.

Reprinted with permission from the March 1985 *Reader's Digest.*

4   Television's variety becomes a narcotic, not a stimulus. Its serial, kaleidoscopic exposures force us to follow its lead. The viewer is on a perpetual guided tour: 30 minutes at the museum, 30 at the cathedral, 30 for a drink, then back on the bus to the next attraction—except on television, typically, the spans allotted are on the order of minutes or seconds, and the chosen delights are more often car crashes and people killing one another. In short, a lot of television usurps one of the most precious of all human gifts, the ability to focus your attention yourself, rather than just passively surrender it.

5   Capturing your attention—and holding it—is the prime motive of most television programming and enhances its role as a profitable advertising vehicle. Programmers live in constant fear of losing anyone's attention—anyone's. The surest way to avoid doing so is to keep everything brief, not to strain the attention of anyone but instead to provide constant stimulation through variety, novelty, action and movement. Quite simply, television operates on the appeal to the short attention span.

6   It is simply the easiest way out. But it has come to be regarded as a given, as inherent in the medium itself; as an imperative, as though General Sarnoff, or one of the other august pioneers of video, had bequeathed to us tablets of stone commanding that nothing in television shall ever require more than a few moments' concentration.

7   In its place that is fine. Who can quarrel with a medium that so brilliantly packages escapist entertainment as a mass-marketing tool? But I see its values now pervading this nation and its life. It has become fashionable to think that, like fast food, fast ideas are the way to get to a fast-moving, impatient public.

8   In the case of news, this practice, in my view, results in inefficient communication. I question how much of television's nightly news effort is really absorbable and understandable. Much of it is what has been aptly described as "machine-gunning with scraps." I think the technique fights coherence. I think it tends to make things ultimately boring and dismissable (unless they are accompanied by horrifying pictures) because almost anything is boring and dismissable if you know almost nothing about it.

9   I believe that TV's appeal to the short attention span is not only inefficient communication but decivilizing as well. Consider the casual assumptions that television tends to cultivate: that complexity must be avoided, that visual stimulation is a substitute for thought, that verbal precision is an anachronism. It may be old-fashioned, but I was taught that thought is words, arranged in grammatically precise ways.

10   There is a crisis of literacy in this country. One study estimates that some 30 million adult Americans are "functionally illiterate" and cannot read or write well enough to answer a want ad or understand the instructions on a medicine bottle.

11   Literacy may not be an inalienable human right, but it is one that the highly literate Founding Fathers might not have found unreasonable or even unattainable. We are not only not attaining it as a nation, statistically speaking, but we are falling further and further short of attaining it. And, while I would not be so simplistic as to suggest that television is the cause, I believe it contributes and is an influence.

12   Everything about this nation—the structure of the society, its forms of family organization, its economy, its place in the world—has become more complex, not less. Yet its dominating communications instrument, its principal form of national linkage, is one that sells neat resolutions to human problems that usually have no neat resolutions. It is all symbolized in my mind by the hugely successful art form that television has made central to the culture, the 30-second commercial: the tiny drama of the earnest housewife who finds happiness in choosing the right toothpaste.

13   When before in human history has so much humanity collectively surrendered so much of its leisure to one toy, one mass diversion? When before has virtually an entire nation surrendered itself wholesale to a medium for selling?

14   Some years ago Yale University law professor Charles L. Black, Jr., wrote: "...forced feeding on trivial fare is not itself a trivial matter." I think this society is being

force-fed with trivial fare, and I fear that the effects on our habits of mind, our language, our tolerance for effort, and our appetite for complexity are only dimly perceived. If I am wrong, we will have done no harm to look at the issue skeptically and critically, to consider how we should be resisting it. I hope you will join with me in doing so.

Finishing time: _____

Starting time: _____ **(subtract)**

Reading time: _____
Check page 500 for your rate.

WPM: _____

CRITICAL COMPREHENSION PROGRESS CHECK

Part A

Directions: In the space below, write a summary of the reading selection you just read.

Part B

Directions: Answer the following questions without looking back at the reading selection.

1. The best statement of the main idea or thesis of the essay is
    a. The only things Americans do more than watch TV are work and sleep.
    b. Capturing and holding our attention is the prime motive of most TV programming and it is doing that very well.
    c. TV, while not the sole cause, contributes to and influences illiteracy because it deals more with visual stimulation than language stimulation.
    d. Society is being force-fed with trivial fare which is negatively affecting our minds, language, and tolerance for effort.

2. The author's attitude toward his subject can best be described as
   a. lighthearted   **c.** serious
   b. frightened   **d.** concerned

3. The tone of the essay is mostly
   a. ironic   **c.** serious
   b. silly   **d.** nasty

4. T/F   The author believes that literacy is an inalienable right that our Founding Fathers found reasonable and attainable.

5. Is the essay mostly based on fact or opinion? Explain. _____

_____

_____

6. We can infer from the essay that the author is not against TV as a medium itself, but with our seeming inability to resist its trivial fare.

   a. True, because _____

   b. False, because _____

7. The tone of the statement, "It is all symbolized in my mind by the hugely successful art form...the 30-second commercial: the tiny drama of the earnest housewife who finds happiness in choosing the right toothpaste," is
   a. sarcastic   **c.** angry
   b. serious   **d.** humorous

8. Which of the following does the author claim is the trouble with television?
   a. discourages concentration
   b. destroys the ability to focus your attention yourself
   c. is inefficient communication
   d. all of the above
   e. none of the above

9. T/F   According to the author, television programming creates the impression that the world is not as complex as it is and that there are quick solutions to problems.

10. Based on the author's statistical averages, when you are thirty years old, you

   will have watched about _____ hours of TV.
   a. 20,000   **c.** 40,000
   b. 30,000   **d.** 50,000

Number correct: _____

VOCABULARY PROGRESS CHECK

Part A

Directions: Define the following words or terms used in the reading selection. The number in parentheses refers to the paragraph where the term was used.

1. instant gratification (3)

_____

2. kaleidoscopic exposures (4)

_____

3. perpetual guided tour (4)

_____

4. television usurps (4)

_____

5. enhances its roles (5)

_____

6. inherent in the medium (6)

_____

7. august pioneers of video (6)

_____

8. aptly described (8)

_____

9. an anachronism (9)

_____

10. "machine-gunning with scraps" (8)

_____

Go to the next page.

Part B

Directions: Define the following terms. They were taught in this unit.

1. author's attitude

_____

2. the tone of an essay

_____

3. author's bias

_____

4. to infer

_____

5. author's intent

_____

Number correct: _____

Record the results of this progress check on the Inventory Progress Chart on page 493. Compare these scores with the Inventory Check scores and discuss them with your instructor.

UNIT III

AFFECTIVE COMPREHENSION

AFFECTIVE COMPREHENSION INVENTORY

Before beginning this unit, read the short story below and then answer the questions that follow it. Do not worry about any questions you can't answer or any terms you do not know. The purpose of this inventory is to see what you already know about affective comprehension.

Begin timing. Starting time: _____

LOVE

Jesse Stuart

1   Yesterday when the bright sun blazed down on the wilted corn my father and I walked around the edge of the new ground to plan a fence. The cows kept coming through the chestnut oaks on the cliff and running over the young corn. They bit off the tips of the corn and trampled down the stubble.

2   My father walked in the cornbalk. Bob, our Collie, walked in front of my father. We heard a ground squirrel whistle down over the bluff among the dead treetops at the clearing's edge. "Whoop, take him, Bob," said my father. He lifted up a young stalk of corn, with wilted dried roots, where the ground squirrel had dug it up for the sweet grain of corn left on its tender roots. This has been a dry spring and the corn has kept well in the earth where the grain has sprouted. The ground squirrels love this corn. They dig up rows of it and eat the sweet grains. The young corn stalks are killed and we have to replant the corn.

3   I can see my father keep sicking Bob after the ground squirrel. He jumped over the corn rows. He started to run toward the ground squirrel. I, too, started running toward the clearing's edge where Bob was jumping and barking. The dust flew in tiny swirls behind our feet. There was a cloud of dust behind us.

4   "It's a big bull blacksnake," said my father. "Kill him, Bob! Kill him, Bob!"

5   Bob was jumping and snapping at the snake so as to make it strike and throw itself off guard. Bob had killed twenty-eight copperheads this spring. He knows how to kill a snake. He doesn't rush to do it. He takes his time and does the job well.

6   "Let's don't kill the snake," I said. "A blacksnake is a harmless snake. It kills poison snakes. It kills the copperhead. It catches more mice from the fields than a cat."

7   I could see the snake didn't want to fight the dog. The snake wanted to get away. Bob wouldn't let it. I wondered why it was crawling toward a heap of black loamy earth at the bench of the hill. I wondered why it had come from the chestnut oak sprouts and the matted greenbriars on the cliff. I looked as the snake lifted its pretty head in response to one of Bob's jumps. "It's not a bull blacksnake," I said. "It's a she-snake. Look at the white on her throat."

8   "A snake is an enemy to me," my father snapped. "I hate a snake. Kill it, Bob. Go in there and get that snake and quite playing with it!"

9   Bob obeyed my father. I hated to see him take this snake by the throat. She was so beautifully poised in the sunlight. Bob grabbed the white patch on her throat. He cracked her long body like an ox whip in the wind. He cracked it against the wind only. The blood spurted from her fine-curved throat. Something hit against my legs like pellets. Bob threw the snake down. I looked to see what had struck my legs. It was snake eggs. Bob had slung them from her body. She was going to the sand heap to lay her eggs, where the sun is the setting-hen that warms them and hatches them.

10   Bob grabbed her body there on the earth where the red blood was running down on the gray-piled loam. Her body was still writhing in pain. She acted like a greenweed held over a new-ground fire. Bob slung her viciously many times. He cracked her limp body against the wind. She was now limber as a shoestring in the wind. Bob threw her riddled body back on the sand. She quivered like a leaf in the lazy wind, then her riddled body lay perfectly still. The blood colored the loamy earth around the snake.

11   "Look at the eggs, won't you?" said my father. We counted thirty-seven eggs. I picked an egg up and held it in my hand. Only a minute ago there was life in it. It was an immature seed. It would not hatch. Mother sun could not incubate it on the warm earth. The egg I held in my hand was almost the size of a quail's egg. The shell on it was thin and tough and the egg appeared under the surface to be a watery egg.

12   "Well, Bob, I guess you see now why this snake couldn't fight," I said. "It is life. Weaker devour the stronger even among human beings. Dog kills snake. Snake kills birds. Birds kill the butterflies. Man conquers all. Man, too, kills for sport."

13   Bob was panting. He walked ahead of us back to the house. His tongue was out of his mouth. He was tired. He was hot under his shaggy coat of hair. His tongue nearly touched the dry dirt and white flecks of foam dripped from it. We walked toward the house. Neither my father nor I spoke. I still thought about the dead snake. The sun was going down over the chestnut ridge. A lark was singing. It was late for a lark to sing. The red evening clouds floated above the pine trees on our pasture hill. My father stood beside the path. His black hair was moved by the wind. His face was red in the blue wind of day. His eyes looked toward the sinking sun.

14   "And my father hates a snake," I thought.

15   I thought about the agony women know of giving birth. I thought about how they will fight to save their children. Then, I thought of the snake. I thought it was silly for me to think such thoughts.

16   This morning my father and I got up with the chickens. He says one has to get up with the chickens to do a day's work. We got the posthole digger, ax, spud, measuring pole and the mattock. We started for the clearing's edge. Bob didn't go along.

17   The dew was on the corn. My father walked behind with the posthole digger across his shoulder. I walked in front. The wind was blowing. It was a good morning wind to breathe and a wind that makes one feel like he can get under the edge of a hill and heave the whole hill upside down.

18   I walked out the corn row where we had come yesterday afternoon. I looked in front of me. I saw something. I saw it move. It was moving like a huge black rope winds around a windlass. "Steady," I says to my father. "Here is the bull blacksnake." He took one step up beside me and stood. His eyes grew wide apart.

19   "What do you know about this," he said.

20   "You have seen the bull blacksnake now," I said. "Take a good look at him! He is

lying beside his dead mate. He has come to her. He, perhaps, was on her trail yesterday."

21   The male snake had trailed her to her doom. He had come in the night, under the roof of stars, as the moon shed rays of light on the quivering clouds of green. He had found his lover dead. He was coiled beside her, and she was dead.

22   The bull blacksnake lifted his head and followed us as we walked around the dead snake. He would have fought us to his death. He would have fought Bob to his death. "Take a stick," said my father, "and throw him over the hill so Bob won't find him. Did you ever see anything to beat that? I've heard they'd do that. But this is my first time to see it." I took a stick and threw him over the bank into the dewy sprouts on the cliff.

Finishing time: _____

Starting time: _____

Reading time: _____*2:30*_____

Check page 501 for your reading rate. WPM: _____*560*_____

COMPREHENSION CHECK

Now answer the following questions. Do not worry about any questions you can't answer or terms you may not know. Just answer them the best you can.

1. Based on the events and descriptions given, where does the story take place?
    a. on a farm *(circled)*
    b. in a city
    c. in a foreign country
    d. not enough information to tell

2. About how old is the main character in the story and how do you know? *late teens*

3. What is the major conflict between the father and the son?
    a. The son wants the dog to kill snakes; the father doesn't.
    b. Father and son have different ideas about snakes.
    c. The father hates snakes; the son doesn't.
    d. The son has more respect for life than the father, at least where snakes are concerned. *(circled)*

4. **T**/F   The following statement is a metaphor: "She was now limber as a shoestring in the wind." *(T circled)*

5. **T**/F   The following statement is a simile: "She quivered like a leaf in a lazy wind." *(T circled)*

6. The passage, "A lark was singing. It was late for a lark to sing. The red evening clouds floated above the pine trees on our pasture hill. My father stood beside the path. His black hair was moved by the wind. His face was red in the blue wind of the day," requires the reader to use which of the following senses?
    a. sight   **c.** touch
    b. sound   **d.** all three *(circled)*

7. **T**/F   We can infer that the person telling the story appreciates nature. *(T circled)*

8. T/**F**   We can infer that the father and son probably never agree on many things, and that the son can't wait to be out on his own. *(F circled)*

9. What conclusion can we draw at the end of the story regarding the father's attitude about snakes and life? *Snakes aren't deserved of life*

10. Why is the story called "Love"? *It's about all love between all species*

Number correct: _____*9*_____

VOCABULARY CHECK

Directions: Define or explain the following underlined words and phrases from the story.

1. My father walked in the cornbalk.

_____

2. toward a heap of black loamy earth

_____

3. my father snapped at me

_____

4. beautifully poised in the sunlight

_____

5. where the sun is the setting-hen that warms them

_____

6. Mother sun could not incubate it on the warm earth.

_____

7. I got up with the chickens.

_____

8. moving like a huge black rope winds around a windlass

_____

9. digger, ax, spud, measuring pole

_____

10. She acted like a greenweed held over a new-ground fire.

_____

Number correct: _____

Record your scores on the Inventory Progress Chart on page 493. Count 10 percent for each correct answer. If you are in doubt as to why any of your answers are wrong, check with your instructor.

NAME _____ SECTION _____ DATE _____

INTRODUCTION TO AFFECTIVE COMPREHENSION

WHAT IS AFFECTIVE COMPREHENSION?

Knut Hamsun wrote that "One must know and recognize not merely the direct but the secret power of the word." This unit is about the "secret power of the word," or affective comprehension.

Affective comprehension, most simply put, is your reaction to what you read at the literal and critical levels of understanding. It is your intellectual and emotional response to what you read. Why, for instance, do some people prefer to read factual materials rather than fiction? Why do some people react favorably and others negatively to a novel such as *Moby Dick?* Why do some people read fiction merely for recreation, whereas others find it personally enlightening? These differences are based on people's affective reaction to the type of material that they read.

The purpose of this book is not just to present you with various reading skills. While the development of skills is important, it is more important that you understand the distinction between the different kinds and levels of reading. As Frank Jennings says in his book, *This Is Reading:*

> We read to learn. We read to live another way. We read to quench some blind and shocking fire. We read to weigh the worth of what we have done or dare to do. We read to share our awful secrets with someone we know will not refuse us. We read our way into the presence of great wisdom, vast and safe suffering, or into the untidy corners of another kind of life we fear to lead. With the book we can sin at a safe distance. With Maugham's artist in *The Moon and Sixpence,* we can discommit ourselves of family responsibility and burn our substance and our talent in bright colors on a tropical isle.

Unless we react at an affective level, a personal, meaningful level, reading becomes dull and uninteresting. It becomes nothing more than a series of isolated drills where you read and answer questions to plot on a chart.

Once you have mastered the basic reading skills, it is important to move into the world of facts and opinions, ideas, and feelings. As a good reader, you will become your own teacher, using the learned skills to rebuild and reorganize your thoughts and beliefs. That can only happen when affective reactions to what is read take place.

WHAT DOES THIS UNIT COVER?

There are two chapters in this unit. The first one will help you understand your affective reaction to a variety of materials: pictures, cartoons, advertisements, and literature. Affective comprehension has to do with your personal reaction to what you read. Much of it has to do with our feelings. Someone once said that our *feelings* are our sixth sense, the sense that interprets, analyzes, orders, and summarizes the other five senses. Whether or not we feel and appreciate the fear, joy, shock, or passion an author wants us to feel through words depends on our ability to feel them in real life. The inability to react to what we read with appropriate feelings is to miss a large part of what total comprehension is all about. The drills in Chapter 9 are designed to get you to react to your feelings and to make sure they are the feelings the author intended you to feel.

Chapter 10 deals with recognizing figurative language used in imaginative literature. You have already done some drills with figurative language in the last unit, but this chapter will explore your affective reactions to words at the literal, critical, and affective levels of comprehension. Some readers lose the full "power of the word" because they read too literally or never have been shown the variety of figurative language that exists. Just as painters deal with different colors and designs to give us an image of how they see things, so writers paint pictures with words. They stimulate our senses—taste, touch, smell, sight, and sound—with words. How well a writer can create impressions and emotional reactions for us depends on the use of figurative language and imagery through the use of metaphors and similes.

Affective comprehension also has to do with our tastes and appreciation of the skills involved in writing. For instance, many people prefer to read *Reader's Digest* because it takes a collection of readings from a variety of sources and condenses them for easier and faster reading. What they end up reading is seldom the original work; in fact, the language is frequently changed or written at a lower level. This may be a convenient way to read from many sources, but some readers prefer reading the original works. It's a matter of preference and taste.

Our tastes in reading often change as we ourselves change. For example, as a college student you may be required to read a book that is considered a classic. At the time in your life that you are reading it, you may be bored by the work and wonder what all the praise is about. Years later, a rereading of that book may provide you with the answers to your own questions that you weren't ready for during college. Does your present lack of appreciation for, say, Herman Melville's *Moby Dick* mean you lack taste? Do you have poor affective comprehension? Will you "appreciate" it when you're eighty years old? Why do critics think it's such a great work? Answers to these questions are all part of developing affective comprehension.

Some people try to rely solely on their intellect as a way to see and respond to the world. While reason is important, it is also just as important to stay in touch with our feelings; it's what makes us human. When we lose touch with our feelings, we lose a part of our humanity, the part of us that lets us know we're alive. Reacting affectively is to react openly, to share our feelings with others, and to know that others can, have, and will feel as we do.

In this unit it is important to discuss some of the questions in class. Only through interacting with others, sharing your feelings and listening to those of others, will you begin to develop your affective levels of comprehension. Good discussions are frequently frustrating because there often doesn't seem to be a "correct" answer. (It's especially frustrating to instructors who want all questions to have right or wrong answers in order to make grading your responses easier!) But sometimes there are no "right" answers; it's important to listen to others as their sixth sense (feelings) interprets their literal and critical thought processes.

WHAT SHOULD YOU KNOW UPON COMPLETING THIS UNIT?

As in previous units, there are some objectives you should strive to accomplish by the time you finish this unit. You should be able to

1. Recognize how writers use figurative language to stimulate our senses.
2. Recognize images in both fictional and nonfictional writings.
3. Write a definition of affective comprehension.
4. See how closely tied together literal, critical, and affective levels of comprehension are.
5. Approach the various types of literature with an awareness of what is expected of you as a reader in each case.

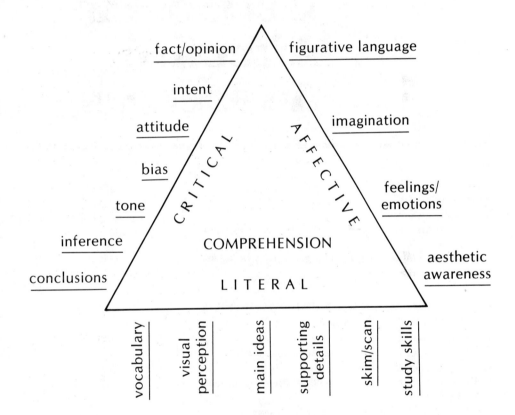

CHAPTER 9

Developing Affective Awareness

A. Responding Affectively

One important element involved in developing reading comprehension is your affective or emotional involvement with what you read. Without an affective reaction to what you read, comprehension would be just matter-of-fact and rather dull. Some things, such as scientific and historical facts, can be presented and received with little or no affective reaction. But the whole range of human emotions is also communicated through the written word. The concern of this chapter is your affective reaction to what you read.

There are both negative and positive affective reactions. You may begin reading a poem, story, or essay with a positive attitude, only to discover that what you are reading isn't really interesting or moving or agreeable to you. This legitimate type of negative response comes about because of the literature itself, not because of a prereading judgment on your part. It is also possible to approach something you read with a preconceived bias, or to let your emotional reaction to what you read warp your critical judgment. Only when your affective reaction is based on critical evaluation and judgment is it a valid reaction.

Everyone reacts affectively. The idea is to develop your awareness of why your affective reaction is what it is, to investigate the reasons behind your emotional and intellectual responses. For instance, many readers lack interest in fiction and its literary effects and values. They just want the facts, the quick bottom line. They think that reading fictional literature is useless and unproductive, perhaps even slightly immoral. Many people think that reading literature is too pleasure-oriented, too elite, or only for a select few oddballs. Some even feel that because literature is "made-up" it is not related to real life; it's untrue, humorless, and boring. These are all affective reactions, but they all are based on an unaware, undeveloped sense of aesthetics and reflect poor affective understanding. If nothing else, literature *is* a reflection of life, and because of the affective involvement necessary for reading fiction, it often can teach us more about ourselves and others than factual writings.

The point of this chapter is to help you open up to affective communication. Drills include reacting to pictures as well as to words in order to help you understand what affective comprehension is, give you more ways to develop your affective reactions, and expose you to a variety of affective experiences. As you do the exercises in this chapter, ask yourself why you are reacting as you do. When you have finished, you should be closer to reaching objectives 3, 4, and 5 for this unit: to be able to write a definition of affective comprehension and to approach various types of imaginative literature with the awareness of what is expected of you as a reader.

Drill A-1: AN AD

Directions: Answer the following questions about the advertisement on the opposite page.

1. Jot down a few words that express your first reaction to the ad. _____

   _____

2. What images of womanhood are being portrayed in the picture (mother, sister,

   wife, working woman, and so on)? _____

   _____

3. Is the ad directed primarily to men or women? _____

   Why do you think so? _____

   _____

4. Why is so much of the woman's face hidden behind her hair? _____

   _____

5. Notice the parallel between this ad and an animal peering out from behind a
   hiding place in the brush or jungle. We see only part of a face through the hair.

   Why is such an image used to sell perfume? _____

   _____

6. How do the caption under the picture and the name of the perfume fit the

   picture? _____

   _____

7. What, besides perfume, is the ad "selling"? _____

   _____

   _____

8. After examining the ad more carefully, now what is your affective reaction to

   the ad? _____

   _____

   _____

Jules Feiffer

Television Violence

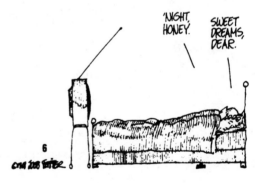

Drill A-2: A CARTOON

Directions: Read the cartoon on the opposite page and answer the following
questions

1. Jot down a few words or phrases that express your first reaction to the
cartoon.

   _____

2. Is the cartoon humorous? _____ Why? _____

   _____

   _____

3. The cartoon is composed of six panels. In the spaces provided, briefly state
what type violence each of the first five panels in the cartoon represents.

   Panel 1: _____

   Panel 2: _____

   Panel 3: _____

   Panel 4: _____

   Panel 5: _____

4. What is implied in panel 6? _____

   _____

5. Do you react more effectively to any one panel than to the others? _____

   If so, which one? _____

   Why? _____

   _____

6. What affective reaction do you think Jules Feiffer, the cartoonist, wants his

   readers to have? _____

   _____

   _____

Drill   **A-3: AN ESSAY**

Directions: Read the article below and answer the questions that follow.

CHUTING THE BREEZE

James Buden

1   There is something suicidal, something sexual about jumping out of an airplane. For me there was no turning back. My mind jerked and leaped. The simplest task seemed monumental. It took all my mental and physical powers to clip my static line to the static cable.

2   We had climbed to three thousand feet and taken two passes to check the winds before the spotter had waved me to the door.

3   Hooked up, I inched over and wrapped my gloved hands around the fuselage door frame, poked my toe over the precipice and stuck my head out of the plane. The wind cracked my neck. The height was unbearable.

4   I recoiled into the metallic cocoon—my heart jammed in my dry throat, my stomach heaving in protest. The engine fumes were nauseating, and my hands ached from gripping the door frame. My body buzzed with adrenaline, and every cell waited for the slap on my calf that would end the torment of anticipation.

5   Out of the corner of my eye I saw the jump master's hand go for the slap. That morning in the training session I had jumped off a one-foot platform again and again. The slap, the jump. The slap, the jump. Slap, jump. Slap, jump—until desire and thought were drummed out. I had become a Pavlovian parachutist.

6   *Whack!* I felt the slap on my calf.

7   I jumped and fell, and the fall was terror. Sheer terror—pencil-spinning, somersaulting, clutching-at-nothing terror.

8   BOOM! My chute opened. My eyes focused and turned upward. There it was! A bright-orange roulette wheel spinning above a tangle of shroud lines. I spun beneath it like a top until the lines fanned open into a symmetrical, sunlit cobweb. I could literally count the patches on the ripstop nylon. "Beautiful!" I screamed into the silence of an empty sky.

9   I hung like a marionette from the threads, my arms dangling, floating at the mercy of the breeze. Then I grabbed the toggles in each hand and tacked about the sky, soaring high over a green meadow. For a moment the sky was mine; I was in control. I directed my flight in perfect solitude and relaxation.

10   This bliss lasted two long minutes. Then the earth began to loom below, and what had looked from the plane like the green felt of a pool table now became pocked with rocks, fence posts and a few stray trees. The closer I got, the more dangerous landing looked. It dawned on me that jumping out of a plane couldn't hurt you, but hitting the ground might.

11   About a hundred feet above ground the earth began to magnify explosively. It raced at me faster and faster. I let go of the toggles to cushion the impact.

12   I smacked the ground and crumpled into a roll, then lay there breathless. Looking through the mask of my helmet I saw my chute fall and expire. The smell of the grass was good; the dirt between my fingers was real. I got to my feet, still connected to my silken rag. I looked up and saw another parachutist silently descending toward me. I laughed, laughed at my joy and relief. I knew the person above me wasn't listening.

Now answer these questions, rereading any paragraphs mentioned in the questions.

1. T/F   The article is basically an affective reaction, in words, to the author's first parachute jump.
2. T/F   The first paragraph reveals the nervousness and fear of the author.
3. Put yourself in paragraph 3. Describe how you would feel at that moment.

_____

_____

4. T/F   The author sounds happy in paragraph 4.
5. In paragraph 8 there is a metaphor and a simile. What are they?

   a. metaphor: _____

   _____

   b. simile: _____

   _____

6. Compare how the author felt in paragraph 1 with how he felt in paragraph 12.

_____

_____

_____

7. T/F   This description of a parachute jump helps those who have never done it to have some sense of what the experience is like.

8. How does this experience make you feel about parachute jumping? _____

_____

_____

_____

Drill **A-4: A MODERN FABLE**

Directions: Read the fable below and answer the questions that follow.

THE PRINCESS AND THE TIN BOX

James Thurber

1   Once upon a time, in a far country, there lived a king whose daughter was the prettiest princess in the world. Her eyes were like the cornflower, her hair was sweeter than the hyacinth, and her throat made the swan look dusty.

2   From the time she was a year old, the princess had been showered with presents. Her nursery looked like Cartier's window. Her toys were all made of gold or platinum or diamonds or emeralds. She was not permitted to have wooden blocks or china dolls or rubber dogs or linen books, because such materials were considered cheap for the daughter of a king.

3   When she was seven, she was allowed to attend the wedding of her brother and throw real pearls at the bride instead of rice. Only the nightingale, with his lyre of gold, was permitted to sing for the princess. The common blackbird, with his boxwood flute, was kept out of the palace grounds. She walked in silver-and-samite slippers to a sapphire-and-topaz bathroom and slept in an ivory bed inlaid with rubies.

4   On the day the princess was eighteen, the king sent a royal ambassador to the courts of five neighboring kingdoms to announce that he would give his daughter's hand in marriage to the prince who brought her the gift she liked the most.

5   The first prince to arrive at the palace rode a swift white stallion and laid at the feet of the princess an enormous apple made of solid gold which he had taken from a dragon who had guarded it for a thousand years. It was placed on a long ebony table set up to hold the gifts of the princess's suitors. The second prince, who came on a gray charger, brought her a nightingale made of a thousand diamonds, and it was placed beside the golden apple. The third prince, riding on a black horse, carried a great jewel box made of platinum and sapphires, and it was placed next to the diamond nightingale. The fourth prince, astride a fiery yellow horse, gave the princess a gigantic heart made of rubies and pierced by an emerald arrow. It was placed next to the platinum-and-sapphire jewel box.

6   Now the fifth prince was the strongest and handsomest of all the five suitors, but he was the son of a poor king whose realm had been overrun by mice and locusts and wizards and mining engineers so that there was nothing much of value left in it. He came plodding up to the palace of the princess on a plow horse and he brought her a small tin box filled with mica and feldspar and hornblende which he had picked up on the way.

7   The other princes roared with disdainful laughter when they saw the tawdry gift the fifth prince had brought to the princess. But she examined it with great interest and squealed with delight, for all her life she had been glutted with precious stones and priceless metals, but she had never seen tin before or mica or feldspar or hornblende. The tin box was placed next to the ruby heart pierced with an emerald arrow.

8   "Now," the king said to his daughter, "you must select the gift you like best and marry the prince that brought it."

9   The princess smiled and walked up to the table and picked up the present she liked the most. It was the platinum-and-sapphire jewel box, the gift of the third prince.

10   "The way I figure it," she said, "is this. It is a very large and expensive box, and when I am married, I will meet many admirers who will give me precious gems with which to fill it to the top. Therefore, it is the most valuable of all the gifts my suitors have brought me and I like it the best."

11   The princess married the third prince that very day in the midst of great merriment and high revelry. More than a hundred thousand pearls were thrown at her and she loved it.

12   *Moral: All those who thought the princess was going to select the tin box filled with worthless stones instead of one of the other gifts will kindly stay after class and write one hundred times on the blackboard "I would rather have a hunk of aluminum silicate than a diamond necklace."*

Now answer the following questions:

1. Which prince did you think the princess would choose? Why? _____

_____

_____

_____

2. Why is it important to the story that the poorest prince be described last?

_____

_____

_____

3. Much of the humor in this piece comes from the author's use of incongruity, things that don't fit or are illogical, such as the language the princess uses compared with the fairy-tale setting. What are some other incongruous

aspects of the story, language or otherwise? _____

_____

_____

4. Satire is used to poke fun at things. Here the author pokes fun at our human

frailties. Is he satirizing the princess, the reader, or both? Explain. _____

_____

_____

_____

5. If you were the princess, which prince would you have selected and why?

_____

_____

_____

6. What does the moral at the end of the tale imply? _____

_____

_____

_____

B. Recognizing Images and Analogies in Affective Language

In literature, *imagery* is a term used to refer to the use of words to compare ideas, things, or feelings with something else. A writer might say, "She looks very unhappy," or "Her face looks like she learned she only has twenty-four hours to live." The first statement is a literal one; the second an *analogy.* The second statement allows us to *imagine* (from which the term imagery comes) how the person feels rather than just telling us. Because we can imagine what it might feel like to learn we don't have long to live, our feelings are tapped by the author through the analogy.

Imagery is important in fiction and nonfiction. Almost all good writing uses imaginative or figurative language, but it is especially important in writing poetry, short stories, or novels. It often requires that a writer carefully select words that provide strong connotative feelings in us. In the example above "only twenty-four hours to live" connotes death within a day's time. In turn, that connotes a negative image, one we are supposed to feel.

Let's look more closely at how this works. Read the following short poem:

The Death of the Ball Turret Gunner

Randall Jarrell

From my mother's sleep I fell into the State
And I hunched in its belly till my wet fur froze.
Six miles from earth, loosed from its dream of life,
I woke to black flak and the nightmare fighters.
When I died they washed me out of the turret with a hose.

Now answer the following questions as best you can:

1. Write the denotative and connotative meanings in the words from the poem in the spaces provided.

		Denotation	Connotation
a.	mother	_____	_____
b.	sleep	_____	_____
c.	State	_____	_____
d.	fur	_____	_____

"The Death of the Ball Turret Gunner" from *The Complete Poems* by Randall Jarrell. Copyright © 1945, 1972 by Mrs. Randall Jarrell. Reprinted by permission of Farrar, Straus and Giroux, Inc.

2. What is the analogy being drawn between "my mother's sleep" and waking to the "black flak and the nightmare fighters"? _____

_____

_____

_____

3. What images are created in the following lines from the poem?
   a. "From my mother's sleep I fell into the State" (Why is "State" capitalized?)

   _____

   b. "I hunched in its belly"

   _____

   c. "my wet fur froze"

   _____

   d. "Six miles from earth"

   _____

   e. "washed me out . . . with a hose"

   _____

4. What is the tone of the poem?

   _____

5. What is the author's attitude toward his subject?

   _____

6. Write a one-sentence literal statement that says what the poem implies.

   _____

   _____

   _____

   Let's look at question 6 first. While wording will be different for everyone, the basic idea behind this poem is that "War is hell," or "In war, death is common and indiscriminate," or "Some lives are expendable in war." But rather than say such things at a literal level, the author chooses to make us *feel* the hell of war or the death of innocent people forced into a situation that is not their choosing. How do we know this?

   The author knows that the word "mother," literally the female parent, generally connotes feelings of love, security, warmth, and home life. *Sleep* connotes quiet, peacefulness, especially when the author says "my mother's sleep." It's a pleasant image; but it's quickly lost when he falls "into the State." The capital on the word causes us to think about government, an institution that has sent him to war. But the word also can refer to his state of mind, the change from a pleasant, safe home environment to now being at war in the belly of an airplane. It's a rude awakening from "my mother's sleep." It's also a strong analogy the author draws between the safety of home and the "black flak in the nightmare fighters." He's gone from pleasant dreams to nightmares.

Likewise, fur is soft. We use it for warmth and decoration on our clothes. But the use of the word *fur* could also remind us of the animal from which we get fur. Is the author implying through this image that man becomes animal-like by going to war? There's irony in this image. The image of "my wet fur froze" implies or suggests he may be sweating from fear. At the literal level, his perspiration freezes at six miles up in a bomber plane.

From the image, "From my mother's sleep I fell into the State," we then feel for this young man who recently was safe at home suddenly finding himself at war in a bomber (State could also refer to the actual plane itself). The image "hunched in its belly" offers a cramped feeling, like an animal hiding; in this case, he is both a hunter, looking for the enemy, and the hunted, being chased by an enemy. The word "belly" literally refers to the ball turret under the bomber where men manned machine guns to shoot down fighter planes. But "belly" (perhaps his mother's womb) is made analogous to the airplane's "womb." One is safe and one isn't; thus more contrast is made between the safety of home and the dangers of war six miles high.

The image of the last line is ugly. We are left with him dead and the almost callousness of washing out his remains from the turret in order to make room for the next person. When we put all these things together, we can say that the tone of the poem is ghastly, grim, deadly. The attitude of the author toward war is obviously negative, but more than that he wants us to see and feel for the innocent victims of the folly of war. By using figurative language, the author creates images that are hard to forget and affect us at a level a plain, literal statement never could.

The following drills will help you see how authors use affective language in a variety of ways.

Drill B-1: IMAGES IN FICTION

Directions: Read each of the following fictional selections. In the blanks that follow each selection write in the word *figurative* if you think the selection is mostly figurative or *literal* if you think it is mostly literal. Then write in the numbers of all of the sentences in the selection that you feel contain figurative language.

1.   (1) Dr. Rankin was a large and rawboned man on whom the newest suit at once appeared outdated, like a suit in a photograph of twenty years ago. (2) This was due to the squareness and flatness of his torso, which might have been put together by a manufacturer of packing cases. (3) His face also had a wooden and a roughly constructed look; his hair was wiglike and resentful of the comb. (4) He had those huge and clumsy hands which can be an asset to a doctor in a small upstate town where people still retain a rural relish for paradox, thinking that the more apelike the paw, the more precise it can be in the delicate business of a tonsillectomy. (From John Collier, "De Mortuis.")

_____

_____

2.   (1) The morning of June 27th was clear and sunny, with the fresh warmth of a full-summer day; the flowers were blossoming profusely and the grass was richly green. (2) The people of the village began to gather in the square, between the post office and the bank, around ten o'clock; in some towns there were so many people that the lottery took two days and had to be started on June 26th, but in this village, where there were only about three hundred people, the whole lottery took less than two hours, so it could begin at ten o'clock in the morning and still be through in time to allow the villagers to get home for noon dinner. (From Shirley Jackson, "The Lottery.")

_____

_____

3. (1) She was going the inland route because she had been twice on the coast route. (2) She asked three times at the automobile club how far it was through the Tehachapi Mountains, and she had the route marked on the map in red pencil. (3) The car was running like a T, the garage man told her. (4) All her dresses were back from the cleaners, and there remained only the lace collar to sew on her black crepe so that they would be all ready when she got to San Francisco. (5) She had read up on the history of the mountains and listed all the Indian tribes and marked the route of the Friars from the Sacramento Valley. (6) She was glad now that Clara Robbins, the "Math" teacher, was not going with her. (7) She liked to be alone, to have everything just the way she wanted it, exactly. (From Meridel Le Sueur, "The Girl.")

_____

_____

4. (1) Braggioni catches her glance solidly as if he had been waiting for it, leans forward, balancing his paunch between his spread knees, and sings with tremendous emphasis, weighing his words. (2) He has, the song relates, no father and no mother, nor even a friend to console him; lonely as a wave of the sea he comes and goes, lonely as a wave. (3) His mouth opens round and yearns sideways, his balloon cheeks grow oily with the labor of song. (4) He bulges marvelously in his expensive garments. (5) Over his lavender collar, crushed upon a purple necktie, held by a diamond hoop: over his ammunition belt of tooled leather worked in silver, buckled cruelly around his gasping middle: over the tops of his glossy yellow shoes Braggioni swells with ominous ripeness, his mauve silk hose stretched taut, his ankles bound with the stout leather thongs of his shoes. (From Katherine Anne Porter, "Flowering Judas.")

_____

_____

5. (1) The midafternoon winter sun burned through the high California haze. (2) Charles Dudley, working with a mattock in a thicket of overgrowth, felt as steamy and as moldy as the black adobe earth in which his feet kept slipping. (3) Rain had fallen for five days with no glimmer of sunshine, and now it seemed as if the earth, with fetid animation, like heavy breath, were giving all that moisture back to the air. (4) The soil, or the broom which he was struggling to uproot, had a disgusting, acrid odor, as if he were tussling with some obscene animal instead of with a lot of neglected vegetation, and suddenly an overload of irritations— the smell, the stinging sweat in his eyes, his itching skin, his blistering palms—made him throw the mattock down and come diving out of the thicket into the clearing he had already achieved. (From Mark Schorer, "What We Don't Know Hurts Us.")

_____

_____

Drill B-2: REACTING TO FICTIONAL PASSAGES

Directions: Following are some short fictional passages containing figurative language. Read each one and answer the questions that follow.

1. "...inside we ate in the steady coolness of air by Westinghouse." (From Philip Roth, _Goodbye, Columbus._)

a. The above quote is an example of figurative language. Restate the quote in

literal terms. _____

_____

b. What can you infer from the quote about the weather outside? _____

_____

2.   "...women, with their Cuban heels and boned-up breasts, their knuckle-sized rings, their straw hats, which resembled immense wicker pizza plates." (From Philip Roth, *Goodbye, Columbus.*)

a.   Would you call this a flattering description? _____

b.   What figurative phrases support your answer to *a?* _____

_____

3.   "When my parents have somebody over they get lemonade and if it's a real racy affair Schlitz in tall glasses with 'They'll Do It Every Time' cartoons stencilled on." (From John Updike, "A & P.")

a.   Literally state what the narrator is telling us about his parents. _____

_____

b.   What is the narrator's tone? Sarcastic? Friendly? Embarrassed? _____

_____

4.   "...The flames, as though they were a kind of wild life, crept as a jaguar creeps on its belly toward a line of birch-like saplings that fledged an outcrop of the pink rock. They flapped at the first of the trees, and the branches grew a brief foliage of fire. The heart of flame leapt nimbly across the gap between the trees and then went swinging and flaring along the whole row of them." (From William Golding, *Lord of the Flies.*)

a.   Why is the fire like a wild animal? _____

_____

b.   List four descriptive words or phrases the author uses to give the fire life.

_____

_____

5.   "She slides through the door with a gust of cold and locks the door behind her and I see her fingers trail across the polished steel—tip of each finger the same color as her lips. Funny orange. Like the tip of a soldering iron. Color so hot or so cold if she touches you with it you can't tell which." (From Ken Kesey, *One Flew Over the Cuckoo's Nest.*)

a.   From this description can you infer whether the narrator likes or dislikes

the woman? _____

b.   What feelings do you get from the description of the woman? _____

_____

c.   List at least three phrases that cause you to feel the way you do. _____

_____

_____

6.   "Lying in this third-story cupola bedroom, he felt the tall power it gave him, riding high in the June wind, the grandest tower in town. At night, when the trees washed together, he flashed his gaze like a beacon from this lighthouse in all directions over swarming seas of elm and oak and maple." (From Ray Bradbury, *Dandelion Wine.*)

a.   Is the overall mood of this passage pleasing or frightening? _____

_____

b.   Why? _____

_____

c.   What is meant by "the trees washed together"? _____

_____

d.   The bedroom is being compared to what? _____

e.   How can you tell? _____

_____

7.   "The fresh-plowed earth heaved, the wild plum buds puffed and broke. Springs and streams leapt up singing. He could hear the distant roar of the river swelling in the gorge. The clear blue skies stretched out above him like the skin of a puffed fiesta balloon. The whole earth strained and stretched with new life." (From Frank Waters, *The Man Who Killed the Deer.*)

a.   Is the overall mood of this passage pleasing or frightening? _____

_____

b.   Why? _____

_____

c.   What time of year would you infer is being described? _____

d.   Why? _____

8.   "It unrolled slowly, forced to show its colors, curling and snapping back whenever one of us turned loose. The whole land was very tense until we put our four steins on its corners and laid the river out to run for us through the mountains 150 miles north. Lewis' hand took a pencil and marked out a small strong X in a place where some of the green bled away and the paper changed with high ground, and began to work downstream, northeast to southwest through the printed woods." (From James Dickey, *Deliverance.*)

a.   What is the "it" that "unrolled slowly"? _____

b.   How do you know? _____

_____

c. What clue does the author give as to how many people the "us" and "we"

refer? _____

d. What can you infer from the passage is going on? _____

_____

_____

_____

9.   "The red sunset, with narrow black cloud strips like threats across it, lay on the curved horizon of the prairie. The air was still and cold, and in it settled the mute darkness and greater cold of night. High in the air there was wind, for through the veil of the dusk the clouds could be seen gliding rapidly south and changing shapes. A queer sensation of torment, of two-sided, unpredictable nature, arose from the stillness of the earth air beneath the violence of the upper air. Out of the sunset, through the dead, matted grass and isolated weed stalks of the prairie, crept the narrow and deeply rutted remains of a road. In the road, in places, there were crusts of shallow, brittle ice. There were little islands of an old oiled pavement in the road too, but most of it was mud, now frozen rigid. The frozen mud still bore the toothed impress of great tanks, and a wanderer on the neighboring undulations might have stumbled, in this light, into large, partially filled-in and weed-grown cavities, their banks channeled and beginning to spread into badlands. These pits were such as might have been made by falling meteors, but they were not. They were the scars of gigantic bombs, their rawness already made a little natural by rain, seed, and time. Along the road there were rakish remnants of fence. There was also, just visible, one portion of tangled and multiple barbed wire still erect, behind which was a shelving ditch with small caves, now very quiet and empty, at intervals in its back wall. Otherwise there was no structure or remnant of a structure visible over the dome of the darkling earth, but only, in sheltered hollows, the darker shadows of young trees trying again." (Reprinted by permission of International Creative Management, Inc. Copyright © 1941, 1969, by Walter Van Tilburg Clark.)

a. The opening paragraph does what a camera does on film; it provides a setting and a sense of time for a story about to unfold. What has obviously

taken place? _____

_____

b. How recently? _____

c. What time of year is it? _____

d. What is the tone of the story so far? _____

_____

e. Would you want to read the rest of the story? _____

Why? _____

_____

_____

Drill   B-3: LINES FROM POETRY

Directions: Following are some short passages from poetry and some quotations. Read each one and in the blanks provided write what you think is the *literal* meaning of the passage.

1.   "The pen is mightier than the sword." (Edward Bulwer-Lytton)

_____

_____

_____

2.   "The Lord is my shepherd; I shall not want." (Psalms 23:1)

_____

_____

_____

3.   "Was this the face that launched a thousand ships,
      And burnt the topless towers of Ilium?" (Christopher Marlowe)

_____

_____

_____

4.   "There is no frigate like a book
      To take us lands away." (Emily Dickinson)

_____

_____

_____

5.   "God's in his heaven—
      All's right with the world!" (Robert Browning)

_____

_____

_____

6.   "A little learning is a dangerous thing." (Alexander Pope)

_____

_____

_____

7. "But love is blind." (Shakespeare)

_____

_____

_____

Drill   B-4: IMAGES IN A POEM

Directions: Read the following poem and answer the questions.

A WHITE ROSE

John Boyle O'Reilly

The red rose whispers of passion
And the white rose breathes of love;
Oh, the red rose is a falcon,
And the white rose is a dove.

1. Which rose is equated to physical desire?

_____

2. Are the last two lines examples of simile or metaphor?

_____

3. Which rose does the author seem to like best?

_____

4. How can you tell? _____

_____

Drill   B-5: TWO VERSIONS OF THE LORD'S PRAYER

Directions: Below are two published versions of Matthew 6:9–13, more commonly known as The Lord's Prayer. Read both of them and then answer the questions that follow.

Version A

Our Father who art in heaven,
Hallowed be thy name.
Thy Kingdom come.
Thy will be done,
   On earth as it is in heaven.
Give us this day our daily bread;
And forgive us our debts,
   As we also have forgiven our debtors;
And lead us not into temptation,
   But deliver us from evil.

Version B

Our Father in heaven:
May your name be kept holy,
May your Kingdom come,
May your will be done on earth
   As it is in heaven.
Give us today the food we need;
Forgive us the wrongs that we have done,
As we forgive the wrongs that others have
    done us;
Do not bring us to hard testing, but
    Keep us safe from the Evil One.

1.   Which version do you think is a more recent translation of the Bible? _____

_____

2.   Why? _____

_____

3.   Which version do you prefer? _____

4.   Why? _____

_____

5.   Which version uses more figurative language than the other? _____

_____

6.   Is there any difference in the meaning of the two versions? _____

7.   Explain your answer to question 6. _____

_____

_____

_____

Drill B-6: QUICK QUIZ

Directions: Answer the following questions as thoroughly as you can. There are two parts to the quiz.

Part A

Below are some quotations and short passages from poetry. In the blanks provided, write what you think is the literal meaning of the passage.

1. "...ignorance is bliss." (Thomas Gray)

_____

_____

2. "Where liberty dwells, there is my country." (John Milton)

_____

_____

3. "Husbands are awkward things to deal with; even keeping them in hot water will not make them tender." (Mary Buckley)

_____

_____

4. "Early to bed, early to rise, Makes a man healthy, wealthy, and wise." (Benjamin Franklin)

_____

_____

5. "All the world's a stage." (Shakespeare)

_____

_____

_____

Part B

Define the following terms.

1. figurative language

_____   _____

_____

_____

_____

2. simile

_____

_____

3. imagery

_____

_____

4. affective comprehension

_____

_____

5. "the secret power of the word"

_____

_____

Turn in the quiz to your instructor.

C. Reading Practices

The following practices will help you put to use the information from this chapter and all the previous ones. As you do them, apply all the reading skills you have learned so far.

Drill   C-1

Directions: Quickly read the title and first paragraph of the following essay, then answer the questions here.

1.   What do you think the essay will discuss? _____

_____

_____

2.   Do you think you will enjoy reading the essay? _____ Why? _____

_____

Now read the essay, applying all the skills you have learned.

FRESH START

Evelyn Herald

1   I first began to wonder what I was doing on a college campus anyway when my parents drove off, leaving me standing pitifully in a parking lot, wanting nothing more than to find my way safely to my dorm room. The fact was that no matter how mature I liked to consider myself, I was feeling just a bit first-gradish. Adding to my distress was the distinct impression that everyone on campus was watching me. My plan was to keep my ears open and my mouth shut and hope no one would notice I was a freshman.

2   With that thought in mind, I raised my head, squared my shoulders, and set off in the direction of my dorm, glancing twice (and then ever so discreetly) at the campus map clutched in my hand. It took everything I had not to stare when I caught my first glimpse of a real live college football player. What confidence, what reserve, what muscles! I only hoped his attention was drawn to my air of assurance rather than to my shaking knees. I spent the afternoon seeking out each of my classrooms so that I could make a perfectly timed entrance before each lecture without having to ask dumb questions about its whereabouts.

3   The next morning I found my first class and marched in. Once I was in the room, however, another problem awaited me. Where to sit? Freshman manuals advised sitting near the front, showing the professor an intelligent and energetic demeanor.

Reprinted by permission. Copyright *Nutshell* magazine, Whittle Communications, 505 Market Street, Knoxville, TN 37902.

After much deliberation I chose a seat in the first row and to the side. I was in the foreground (as advised), but out of the professor's direct line of vision.

4   I cracked my anthology of American literature and scribbled the date at the top of a crisp ruled page. "Welcome to Biology 101," the professor began. A cold sweat broke out on the back of my neck. I groped for my schedule and checked the room number. I *was* in the right room. Just the wrong building.

5   So now what? Get up and leave in the middle of the lecture? Wouldn't the professor be angry? I knew everyone would stare. Forget it. I settled into my chair and tried to assume the scientific pose of a biology major, bending slightly forward, tensing my arms in preparation for furious notetaking, and cursing under my breath. The bottled snakes along the wall should have tipped me off.

6   After class I decided my stomach (as well as my ego) needed a little nourishment, and I hurried to the cafeteria. I piled my tray with sandwich goodies and was heading for the salad bar when I accidentally stepped in a large puddle of ketchup. Keeping myself upright and getting out of the mess was not going to be easy, and this flailing of feet was doing no good. Just as I decided to try another maneuver, my food tray tipped and I lost my balance. As my rear end met the floor, I saw my entire life pass before my eyes; it ended with my first day of college classes.

7   In the seconds after my fall I thought how nice it would be if no one had noticed. But as all the students in the cafeteria came to their feet, table by table, cheering and clapping, I knew they had not only noticed, they were determined that I would never forget it. Slowly I kicked off my ketchup-soaked sandals and jumped clear of the toppled tray and spilled food. A cleanup brigade came charging out of the kitchen, mops in hands. I sneaked out of the cafeteria as the cheers died down behind me.

8   For three days I dined alone on nothing more than humiliation, shame, and an assortment of junk food from a machine strategically placed outside my room. On the fourth day I couldn't take another crunchy-chewy-salty-sweet bite. I needed some real food. Perhaps three days was long enough for the campus population to have forgotten me. So off to the cafeteria I went.

9   I made my way through the food line and tiptoed to a table, where I collapsed in relief. Suddenly I heard a crash that sounded vaguely familiar. I looked up to see that another poor soul had met the fate I'd thought was reserved for only me. I was even more surprised when I saw who the poor soul was: the very composed, very upperclass football player I'd seen just days before (though he didn't look quite so composed wearing spaghetti on the front of his shirt). My heart went out to him as people began to cheer and clap as they had for me. He got up, hands held high above his head in a victory clasp, grinning from ear to ear. I expected him to slink out of the cafeteria as I had, but instead he turned around and began preparing another tray. And that's when I realized I had been taking myself far too seriously.

10   What I had interpreted as a malicious attempt to embarrass a naive freshman had been merely a moment of college fun. Probably everyone in the cafeteria had done something equally dumb when he or she was a freshman—and had lived to tell about it.

11   Who cared whether I dropped a tray, where I sat in class, or even whether I showed up in the wrong lecture? Nobody. This wasn't like high school. Popularity was not so important; running with the crowd was no longer a law of survival. In college, it didn't matter. This was my big chance to do my own thing, be my own woman—if I could get past my preoccupation with doing everything perfectly.

12   Once I recognized that I had no one's expectations to live up to but my own, I relaxed. The shackles of self-consciousness fell away, and I began to view college as a wonderful experiment. I tried on new experiences like articles of clothing, checking their fit and judging their worth. I broke a few rules to test my conscience. I dressed a little differently until I found the Real Me. I discovered a taste for jazz, and I decided I liked going barefoot.

13   I gave up trying to act my way through college (this wasn't drama school) and

began not acting at all. College, I decided, was probably the only time I would be completely forgiven for massive mistakes (including stepping in puddles of ketchup and dropping food trays). So I used the opportunity to make all the ones I thought I'd never make.

14 Three years after graduation, I'm still making mistakes. And I'm even being forgiven for a few.

COMPREHENSION CHECK

1. Which of the following best states the thesis of this essay?
  a. College is not the place to make mistakes.
  b. College is not like high school.
  c. College students can be cruel sometimes.
  d. College is a good place to discover who you are.

2. The tone of the essay is mostly
  a. humorous   **c.** sarcastic
  b. serious   **d.** nasty

3. The author's intent is to _____

_____

4. T/F   We can infer from the essay that the author had prepared for her first days of college by reading materials on how to be a successful student.

5. What does the author mean when she says, "I realized I had been taking

myself far too seriously"? _____

_____

6. T/F   We can infer that the author was away from home for the first time.

7. T/F   By sharing her embarrassing moments, the author gains our sympathy and reminds us of ourselves in similar situations.

8. The author mentions the "upperclass football player" twice. How does she

use him to make a point? _____

_____

9. T/F   It is difficult to relate to the author's feelings because most of us have not felt the way she does.

10. Based on what the author tells us in this essay, what advice do you think she

would give to a college freshman? _____

_____

_____

_____

Number correct: _____

VOCABULARY CHECK

Directions: Define the following underlined words or phrases.

1. I had the <u>distinct</u> <u>impression</u> that everyone was watching me.

    _____

2. glancing twice, ever so <u>discreetly</u>

    _____

3. showing the professor an intelligent and energetic <u>demeanor</u>

    _____

4. I <u>cracked</u> <u>my</u> <u>anthology</u> of American literature

    _____

5. a cleanup <u>brigade</u> came charging out

    _____

6. the very <u>composed</u>, very upperclass football player

    _____

7. a <u>malicious</u> attempt to embarrass

    _____

8. a <u>naive</u> freshman

    _____

9. The <u>shackles</u> <u>of</u> <u>self-consciousness</u> fell away.

    _____

10. If I could get past my <u>preoccupation</u> with being perfect

    _____

Number correct: _____

Record your scores on the record chart on page 495. Count 10 percent for each correct answer. Make certain you understand any errors before going on to the next drill.

Drill **C-2**

Directions: Read the following poem, more than once if you wish. Then take a moment to think about the poem and your reactions before answering the questions that follow it.

FORGIVE MY GUILT

Robert P. Tristram Coffin

Not always sure what things called sins may be,
I am sure of one sin I have done.
It was years ago, and I was a boy,
I lay in the frostflowers with a gun,
The air ran blue as the flowers, I held my breath,
Two birds on golden legs slim as dream things
Ran like quicksilver on the golden sand,
My gun went off, they ran with broken wings
Into the sea, I ran to fetch them in,
But they swam with their heads high out to sea,
They cried like two sorrowful high flutes,
With jagged ivory bones where wings should be.

For days I heard them when I walked that headland
Crying out to their kind in the blue,
The other plovers were going over south
On silver wings leaving these broken two.
The cries went out one day; but I still hear them.
Over all the sounds of sorrow in war and peace
I ever have heard, time cannot drown them,
Those slender flutes of sorrow never cease.
Two airy things forever denied the air!
I never knew how their lives at last were spilt,
But I have hoped for years all that is wild,
Airy, and beautiful will forgive my guilt.

From *Atlantic Monthly,* 1949.

COMPREHENSION CHECK

1. What feelings and emotions did you feel as you read the poem?

_____

_____

_____

2. Paraphrase briefly what happens in the poem.

_____

_____

_____

3. What memories of places, people, events, senses does the poem call to

mind? _____

_____

_____

_____

4. What idea or thought is suggested by the poem?

_____

_____

_____

5. What is the most important word in the poem? _____ Why?

_____

_____

_____

6. What sort of person do you imagine the author to be?

_____

_____

_____

7. What image from the poem stands out the most in your mind?

_____

_____

_____

8. Do you think the author still hunts? _____ Explain.

_____

_____

_____

9. The author says he "sinned." Would you call what he did a sin?

_____

_____

_____

10. Explain briefly a time in your past when you did something for which you still feel guilty and will always carry with you.

_____

_____

_____

Discuss these answers in class. There are no right or wrong answers to these, although some may be more thoughtful than others. It's important to see how others responded to these questions. (To tell the truth, your author feels questions such as the preceding one are more important than trying to answer questions such as "What does the poem mean?")

VOCABULARY CHECK

Directions: Try to state in literal terms what the following affective language is saying or describing.

1. "The air ran blue as the flowers"

_____

_____

_____

2. "They cried like two sorrowful high flutes"

_____

_____

_____

3. "Two airy things forever denied the air!"

_____

_____

_____

4. "Ran like quicksilver on the golden sand"

_____

_____

_____

5. "…on golden legs slim as dream things"

_____

_____

_____

Discuss these responses in class, comparing your literal, critical, and affective interpretations with those of others.

CHAPTER 10

READING AFFECTIVELY EFFECTIVELY

A. Reading Short Stories

When you go to a football game or some other sports event, you go knowing that there will be traffic problems, parking problems, that you will be surrounded by thousands of people, that you will have to put up with all types of people and noises, and that you will probably sit far from the action. Yet, you accept all that in order to become a part of the event itself. When you watch television, you know that you are going to have programs interrupted by commercials, yet in spite of these breaks, you are willing and able to get back into the program after several minutes. When you go to a movie, you are willing to sit in the dark surrounded by three walls and a big screen as light filters through moving film. In each case you are willing to go along with what is expected of you so that for a time you can get involved in what you are seeing and feeling.

To read imaginative literature (novels, short stories, and poems), you need to be willing to go along with what is expected of you, too. In this case, you are expected to enter the world of the author who may want you to go back in the past, or forward to the future, or to share the present as the writer sees it. You must be willing to enter the imagination of the writer and attempt to see how he or she sees and feels life. In order to do this, you must understand how to read the form the writer chooses to use. Just as you have learned to identify a thesis in an essay, to identify paragraph forms and structure, to separate fact from opinion, to recognize how language creates tone and reveals attitude and intent, so, too, do you need to understand how to approach the reading of imaginative literature.

The last chapter introduced you to affective language used in short stories and poetry. You saw how important it is to read beyond the words and to relate to the "secret power" of language. Here's part of a short story by Jay McInerney, "Story of My Life." Read it, then answer the questions that follow. Feel free to reread the passage if needed in order to answer the questions.

The party goes on for three days. Some of the people go to sleep eventually, but not me. On the fourth day they call my father and a doctor comes over to the apartment, and now I'm in a place in Minnesota under sedation dreaming the white dreams about snow falling endlessly in the North Country, making the landscape disappear, dreaming about long white rails of cocaine that disappear over the horizon like railroad tracks to the stars. Like when I used to ride and was anorectic and I would starve myself and all I would ever dream about was food. There are horses at the far end of the pasture outside my window. I watch them through the bars.

Toward the end of the endless party that landed me here I am telling somebody the story of Dick Diver. I had eight horses at one point, but Dick Diver was the best. I traveled all over the country jumping and showing, and when I first saw Dick, I knew he was like no other horse. He was like a human being—so spirited and nasty he'd jump twenty feet in the air to avoid the bamboo of the trainer, then stop dead or hang a leg up on a jump he could easily make, just for spite. He had perfect conformation, like a statue of a horse dreamed by Michelangelo. My father bought him for me; he cost a fortune. Back then my father bought anything for me. I was his sweet thing.

I loved that horse. No one else could get near him, he'd try to kill them, but I used to sleep in his stall, spend hours with him every day. When he was

From Jay McInerney, "Story of My Life," *Esquire*, August 1987, p. 112.

poisoned, I went into shock. They kept me on tranquilizers for a week. There was an investigation, but nothing came of it. The insurance company paid off in full, but I quit riding. A few months later, Dad came into my bedroom one night. I was like, uh oh, not this again. He buried his face in my shoulder. His cheek was wet, and he smelled of booze. I'm sorry about Dick Diver, he said. Tell me you forgive me. He goes, the business was in trouble. Then he passed out on top of me, and I had to go and get Mom.

After a week in the hatch they let me use the phone. I call my Dad. How are you? he says.

I don't know why, it's probably bullshit, but I've been trapped in this place with a bunch of shrink types for a week. So just for the hell of it I go, Dad, sometimes I think it would have been cheaper if you'd let me keep that horse.

He goes, I don't know what you're talking about.

I go, Dick Diver, you remember that night you told me.

He goes, I didn't tell you anything.

So, okay, maybe I dreamed it. I was in bed after all, and he woke me up. Not for the first time. But just now, with these tranqs they've got me on, I feel like I'm sleepwalking anyway, and I can almost believe it never actually happened. Maybe I dreamed a lot of stuff. Stuff that I thought happened in my life. Stuff I thought I did. Stuff that was done to me. Wouldn't that be great. I'd love to think that 90 percent of it was just dreaming.

1. Besides "a place in Minnesota," there are clues that let us know where the narrator is. Where do you think the person is? _____

_____

2. Is the narrator a male or female? What makes you think so? _____

_____

3. Describe the narrator. _____

_____

_____

_____

4. Who killed Dick Diver and why? _____

_____

_____

5. What kind of life do you think the narrator has led? _____

_____

_____

Considering that the narrator is "under sedation" and is looking out at horses through a window with bars on it, we can infer that the narrator is in a hospital, perhaps the psychiatric ward or a rest home for drug addicts. Again, we assume the storyteller has taken a drug overdose because of the reference to a three-day party, the "long white rails of cocaine," and because of the need for a doctor on the fourth day.

It's not immediately apparent that the narrator is a female, but it becomes more probable as we read. The references to starving herself, being anorectic, and riding horses certainly don't mean she is a female, but by the time we've read more, especially her reference to being her father's "sweet thing," it's a good assumption. We hear of more young women being anorectic than young men.

The narrator is probably in her late teens or early twenties, based on her language: "He goes ... ," "I go ... ," "He goes ..." is the vernacular of a younger person. Her father is apparently still responsible for her, since he is the one she calls, and he is the one who called the doctor and had her institutionalized. We can assume that she comes from a wealthy family, since she had eight horses at one time and "traveled all over the country jumping and showing." Happy when she had her horses, she certainly is unhappy now, wishing she had "maybe dreamed a lot of stuff" that happened in her life, "stuff that was done to me." Her father drinks too much, and we gather that because his business was failing at one point, and he killed her favorite horse for the insurance money. We see her as a child who had plenty of material things, but not the kind of love and attention she wanted or needed. She hints she was spoiled: "Back then my father bought anything for me." The death of her horse was probably a turning point in her life, especially after learning her father's role in it. She has turned to drugs and is now in some type of hospital on tranquilizers—not a happy person.

Rather than tell us all these things literally, the author has asked us to enter the world of the girl/woman telling the story. If we are alert to the clues the author provides, we read beyond the words and begin to understand things that perhaps even the character telling the story doesn't understand or say directly. We enter the life of a fictional character, but we see reality as we know it must be for some—and sometimes for ourselves.

Now let's say that you have been assigned a short story to read in an English class. You start reading it, but you don't know exactly what you are expected to look for. You feel a bit uncomfortable because you are not used to reading imaginative literature. Here is a set of guide questions you can use with any story or novel to help you get a little more from your reading.

Literal Questions

1. Who is the main character? What is she or he like?
2. Who are other important persons in the story? What is their relationship to the main character?
3. What is happening?
4. Where and when is everything happening?

Critical Questions

5. What seems to be the point of the story (called *theme*)? If the author were writing an essay instead of a story, what would the thesis be?
6. How does the title relate to the theme?
7. What events, scenes, and/or characters are used to develop the theme?

Affective Questions

8. Explain your feelings for the characters in the story.
9. What passages seem particularly well written or effective?
10. Why do you like or dislike the story?
11. What aspects of yourself or others do you see in the story?

These questions are certainly not the only ones, nor necessarily the best ones. But they give you a starting place, a direction toward understanding what it takes to enter into imaginative literature and get something from it.

The following drills will give you a chance to get more familiar with reading and understanding imaginative literature.

Drill A-1

Directions: As a way to direct your thinking as you read the following short story, answer the questions that appear at various points. Some questions require predicting or guessing what you think will happen. Write your answers on a separate sheet to be turned in to your instructor.

1. Read the title of the story below. What do you think this story will be about? What will happen? Why?

THE STORY OF AN HOUR

Kate Chopin

1   Knowing that Mrs. Mallard was afflicted with a heart trouble, great care was taken to break to her as gently as possible the news of her husband's death.

2   It was her sister Josephine who told her, in broken sentences; veiled hints that revealed in half concealing. Her husband's friend Richards was there, too, near her. It was he who had been in the newspaper office when intelligence of the railroad disaster was received, with Brently Mallard's name leading the list of "killed." He had only taken the time to assure himself of its truth by a second telegram, and had hastened to forestall any less careful, less tender friend in bearing the sad message.

3   She did not hear the story as many women have heard the same, with a paralyzed inability to accept its significance. She wept at once, with sudden, wild abandonment, in her sister's arms. When the storm of grief had spent itself she went away to her room alone. She would have no one follow her.

2. Which of your ideas in answer to question 1 can still be correct?
3. Now what do you think will take place? Why?

4   There stood, facing the open window, a comfortable, roomy armchair. Into this she sank, pressed down by a physical exhaustion that haunted her body and seemed to reach into her soul.

5   She could see in the open square before her house the tops of trees that were all aquiver with the new spring life. The delicious breath of rain was in the air. In the street

below a peddler was crying his wares. The notes of a distant song which someone was singing reached her faintly, and countless sparrows were twittering in the eaves.

6   There were patches of blue sky showing here and there through the clouds that had met and piled one above the other in the west facing her window.

7   She sat with her head thrown back upon the cushion of the chair, quite motionless, except when a sob came up into her throat and shook her, as a child who has cried itself to sleep continues to sob in its dreams.

8   She was young, with a fair, calm face, whose lines bespoke repression and even a certain strength. But now there was a dull stare in her eyes, whose gaze was fixed away off yonder on one of those patches of blue sky. It was not a glance of reflection, but rather indicated a suspension of intelligent thought.

9   There was something coming to her and she was waiting for it, fearfully. What was it? She did not know; it was too subtle and elusive to name. But she felt it, creeping out of the sky, reaching toward her through the sounds, the scents, the color that filled the air.

10   Now her bosom rose and fell tumultuously. She was beginning to recognize this thing that was approaching to possess her, and she was striving to beat it back with her will—as powerless as her two white slender hands would have been.

4. Which of your ideas about what will happen are still possible?
5. What new ideas do you have about what will happen now?

11   When she abandoned herself a little whispered word escaped her slightly parted lips. She said it over and over under her breath: "free, free, free!" The vacant stare and the look of terror that had followed it went from her eyes. They stayed keen and bright. Her pulses beat fast, and the coursing blood warmed and relaxed every inch of her body.

12   She did not stop to ask if it were or were not a monstrous joy that held her. A clear and exalted perception enabled her to dismiss the suggestion as trivial.

13   She knew that she would weep again when she saw the kind, tender hands folded in death; the face that had never looked save with love upon her, fixed and gray and dead. But she saw beyond that bitter moment a long procession of years to come that would belong to her absolutely. And she opened and spread her arms out to them in welcome.

14   There would be no one to live for her during those coming years; she would live for herself. There would be no powerful will bending hers in that blind persistence with which men and women believe they have a right to impose a private will upon a fellow-creature. A kind intention or a cruel intention made the act seem no less a crime as she looked upon it in that brief moment of illumination.

15   And yet she had loved him—sometimes. Often she had not. What did it matter! What could love, the unsolved mystery, count for in face of this possession of self-assertion which she suddenly recognized as the strongest impulse of her being!

16   "Free! Body and soul free!" she kept whispering.

6. Were you right? How do you know?
7. Now what will happen?

17   Josephine was kneeling before the closed door with her lips to the keyhole, imploring for admission. "Louise, open the door! I beg; open the door—you will make yourself ill. What are you doing, Louise? For heaven's sake open the door."

18   "Go away. I am not making myself ill." No; she was drinking in a very elixir of life through that open window.

19   Her fancy was running riot along those days ahead of her. Spring days, and summer days, and all sorts of days that would be her own. She breathed a quick prayer that life might be long. It was only yesterday she had thought with a shudder that life might be long.

20   She rose at length and opened the door to her sister's importunities. There was a feverish triumph in her eyes, and she carried herself unwittingly like a goddess of Victory. She clasped her sister's waist, and together they descended the stairs. Richards stood waiting for them at the bottom.

> **8.**   How close were your ideas to what happened?
>
> **9.**   What will happen now and why do you think so?

21   Some one was opening the front door with a latchkey. It was Brently Mallard who entered, a little travel-stained, composedly carrying his grip-sack and umbrella. He had been far from the scene of the accident, and did not even know there had been one. He stood amazed at Josephine's piercing cry; at Richards' quick motion to screen him from the view of his wife.

22   But Richards was too late.

23   When the doctors came they said she had died of heart disease—of joy that kills.

> **10.**   Irony is defined as an inconsistency between what might be expected and what actually occurs. Discuss any irony you see in this story.

Turn your answers in to your instructor.

Drill A-2

Directions: Here is another story. This time there are no questions to interrupt your reading. Sit back and read it straight through. Don't even try to be consciously aware of what you are supposed to do as a reader. Just read and enjoy the story.

A & P

John Updike

1   In walks these three girls in nothing but bathing suits. I'm in the third checkout slot, with my back to the door, so I don't see them until they're over by the bread. The one that caught my eye first was the one in the plaid green two-piece. She was a chunky kid, with a good tan and a sweet broad soft-looking can with those two crescents of white just under it, where the sun never seems to hit, at the top of the backs of her legs. I stood there with my hand on a box of HiHo crackers trying to remember if I rang it up or not. I ring it up again and the customer starts giving me hell. She's one of these cash-register-watchers, a witch about fifty with rouge on her cheekbones and no eyebrows, and I know it made her day to trip me up. She'd been watching cash registers for fifty years and probably never seen a mistake before.

2   By the time I got her feathers smoothed and her goodies into a bag—she gives me a little snort in passing, if she'd been born at the right time they would have burned her over in Salem—by the time I get her on her way the girls had circled around the bread and were coming back, without a pushcart, back my way along the counters, in the aisle between the checkouts and the Special bins. They didn't even have shoes on.

There was this chunky one, with the two-piece—it was bright green and the seams on the bra were still sharp and her belly was still pretty pale so I guessed she just got it (the suit)—there was this one, with one of those chubby berry-faces, the lips all bunched together under her nose, this one, and a tall one, with black hair that hadn't quite frizzed right, and one of these sunburns right across under the eyes, and a chin that was too long—you know, the kind of girl other girls think is very "striking" and "attractive" but never quite makes it, as they very well know, which is why they like her so much—and then the third one, that wasn't quite so tall. She was the queen. She kind of led them, the other two peeking around and making their shoulders round. She didn't look around, not this queen, she just walked straight on slowly, on these long white primadonna legs. She came down a little hard on her heels, as if she didn't walk in her bare feet that much, putting down her heels and then letting the weight move along to her toes as if she was testing the floor with every step, putting a little deliberate extra action into it. You never know for sure how girls' minds work (do you really think it's a mind in there or just a little buzz like a bee in a glass jar?) but you got the idea she had talked the other two into coming in here with her, and now she was showing them how to do it, walk slow and hold yourself straight.

3   She had on a kind of dirty-pink—beige maybe, I don't know—bathing suit with a little nubble all over it and, what got me, the straps were down. They were off her shoulders looped loose around the cool tops of her arms, and I guess as a result the suit had slipped a little on her, so all round the top of the cloth there was this shining rim. If it hadn't been there you wouldn't have known there could have been anything whiter than those shoulders. With the straps pushed off, there was nothing between the top of the suit and the top of her head except just *her,* this clean bare plane of the top of her chest down from the shoulder bones like a dented sheet of metal tilted in the light. I mean, it was more than pretty.

4   She had sort of oaky hair that the sun and salt had bleached, done up in a bun that was unravelling, and a kind of prim face. Walking into the A & P with your straps down, I suppose it's the only kind of face you *can* have. She held her head so high her neck, coming up out of those white shoulders, looked kind of stretched, but I didn't mind. The longer her neck was, the more of her there was.

5   She must have felt in the corner of her eye me and over my shoulder Stokesie in the second slot watching, but she didn't tip. Not this queen. She kept her eyes moving across the racks, and stopped, and turned so slow it made my stomach rub the inside of my apron, and buzzed to the other two, who kind of huddled against her for relief, and then they all three of them went up the cat-and-dog-breakfast-cereal-macaroni-rice-raisins-seasonings-spreads-spaghetti-soft-drinks-crackers-and-cookies aisle. From the third slot I look straight up this aisle to the meat counter, and I watched them all the way. The fat one with the tan sort of fumbled with the cookies, but on second thought she put the package back. The sheep pushing their carts down the aisle—the girls were walking against the usual traffic (not that we have one-way signs or anything)—were pretty hilarious. You could see them, when Queenie's white shoulders dawned on them, kind of jerk, or hop, or hiccup, but their eyes snapped back to their own baskets and on they pushed. I bet you could set off dynamite in an A & P and the people would by and large keep reaching and checking oatmeal off their lists and muttering "Let me see, there was a third thing, began with A, asparagus, no, ah, yes, applesauce!" or whatever it is they do mutter. But there was no doubt, this jiggled them. A few houseslaves in pin curlers even looked around after pushing their carts past to make sure what they had seen was correct.

6   You know, it's one thing to have a girl in a bathing suit down on the beach, where what with the glare nobody can look at each other much anyway, and another thing in the cool of the A & P, under the fluorescent lights, against all those stacked packages, with her feet paddling along naked over our checkerboard green-and-cream rubber-tile floor.

7   "Oh Daddy," Stokesie said beside me, "I feel so faint."

8   "Darling," I said. "Hold me tight." Stokesie's married, with two babies chalked up on his fuselage already, but as far as I can tell that's the only difference. He's twenty-two, and I was nineteen this April.

9   "Is it done?" he asks, the responsible married man finding his voice. I forgot to say he thinks he's going to be manager some sunny day, maybe in 1990 when it's called the Great Alexandrov and Petrooshki Tea Company or something.

10   What he meant was, our town is five miles from a beach, with a big summer colony out on the Point, but we're right in the middle of town, and the women generally put on a shirt or shorts or something before they get out of the car into the street. And anyway these are usually women with six children and varicose veins mapping their legs and nobody, including them, could care less. As I say, we're right in the middle of town, and if you stand at our front doors you can see two banks and the Congregational church and the newspaper store and three real-estate offices and about twenty-seven old freeloaders tearing up Central Street because the sewer broke again. It's not as if we're on the Cape; we're north of Boston and there's people in this town haven't seen the ocean for twenty years.

11   The girls had reached the meat counter and were asking McMahon something. He pointed, they pointed, and they shuffled out of sight behind a pyramid of Diet Delight peaches. All that was left for us to see was old McMahon patting his mouth and looking after them sizing up their joints. Poor kids, I began to feel sorry for them, they couldn't help it.

12   Now here comes the sad part of the story, at least my family says it's sad, but I don't think it's so sad myself. The store's pretty empty, it being Thursday afternoon, so there was nothing much to do except lean on the register and wait for the girls to show up again. The whole store was like a pinball machine and I didn't know which tunnel they'd come out of. After a while they come around out of the far aisle, around the light bulbs, records at discount of the Carribbean Six or Tony Martin Sings or some such gunk you wonder they waste the wax on, sixpacks of candy bars, and plastic toys done up in cellophane that fall apart when a kid looks at them anyway. Around they come, Queenie still leading the way, and holding a little gray jar in her hand. Slots Three through Seven are unmanned and I could see her wondering between Stokes and me, but Stokesie with his usual luck draws an old party in baggy gray pants who stumbles up with four giant cans of pineapple juice (what do these bums *do* with all that pineapple juice? I've often asked myself) so the girls come to me. Queenie puts down the jar and I take it into my fingers icy cold. Kingfish Fancy Herring Snacks in Pure Sour Cream: 49¢. Now her hands are empty, not a ring or a bracelet, bare as God made them, and I wonder where the money's coming from. Still with that prim look she lifts a folded dollar bill out of the hollow at the center of her nubbled pink top. The jar went heavy in my hand. Really, I thought that was so cute.

13   Then everybody's luck begins to run out. Lengel comes in from haggling with a truck full of cabbages on the lot and is about to scuttle into the door marked MANAGER behind which he hides all day when the girls touch his eye. Lengel's pretty dreary, teaches Sunday school and the rest, but he doesn't miss that much. He comes over and says, "Girls, this isn't the beach."

14   Queenie blushes, though maybe it's just a brush of sunburn I was noticing for the first time, now that she was so close. "My mother asked me to pick up a jar of herring snacks." Her voice kind of startled me, the way voices do when you see the people first, coming out so flat and dumb yet kind of tony, too, the way it ticked over "pick up" and "snacks." All of a sudden I slid right down her voice into her living room. Her father and the other men were standing around in ice-cream coats and bow ties and the women were in sandals picking up herring snacks on toothpicks off a big glass plate and they were all holding drinks the color of water with olives and sprigs of mint in them. When my parents have somebody over they get lemonade and if it's a real racy affair Schlitz in tall glasses with "They'll Do It Every Time" cartoons stencilled on.

15   "That's all right." Lengel said. "But this isn't the beach." His repeating this struck

me as funny, as if it had just occurred to him, and he had been thinking all these years the A & P was a great big dune and he was the head lifeguard. He didn't like my smiling—as I say he doesn't miss much—but he concentrates on giving the girls that sad Sunday-school-superintendent stare.

16   Queenie's blush is no sunburn now, and the plump in plaid, that I liked better from the back—a really sweet can—pipes up, "We weren't doing any shopping. We just came in for the one thing."

17   "That makes no difference," Lengel tells her, and I could see from the way his eyes went that he hadn't noticed she was wearing a two-piece before. "We want you decently dressed when you come in here."

18   "We *are* decent," Queenie says suddenly, her lower lip pushing, getting sore now that she remembers her place, a place from which the crowd that runs the A & P must look pretty crummy. Fancy Herring Snacks flashed in her very blue eyes.

19   "Girls, I don't want to argue with you. After this come in here with your shoulders covered. It's our policy." He turns his back. That's policy for you. Policy is what the kingpins want. What the others want is juvenile delinquency.

20   All this while, the customers had been showing up with their carts but, you know, sheep, seeing a scene, they had all bunched up on Stokesie, who shook open a paper bag as gently as peeling a peach, not wanting to miss a word. I could feel in the silence everybody getting nervous, most of all Lengel, who asks me, "Sammy, have you rung up their purchase?"

21   I thought and said "No" but it wasn't about that I was thinking. I go through the punches, 4,9,GROC,TOT—it's more complicated than you think, and after you do it often enough, it begins to make a little song, that you hear words to, in my case "Hello (bing) there, you (gung) hap-py *pee*-pul (splat)!"—the *splat* being the drawer flying out. I uncrease the bill, tenderly as you may imagine, it just having come from between the two smoothest scoops of vanilla I had ever known were there, and pass a half and a penny into her narrow pink palm, and nestle the herrings in a bag and twist its neck and hand it over, all the time thinking.

22   The girls, and who'd blame them, are in a hurry to get out, so I say "I quit" to Lengel quick enough for them to hear, hoping they'll stop and watch me, their unsuspected hero. They keep right on going, into the electric eye; the door flies open and they flicker across the lot to their car, Queenie and Plaid and Big Tall Goony-Goony (not that as raw material she was so bad), leaving me with Lengel and a kink in his eyebrow.

23   "Did you say something, Sammy?"

24   "I said I quit."

25   "I thought you did."

26   "You didn't have to embarrass them."

27   "It was they who were embarrassing us."

28   I started to say something that came out "Fiddle-de-doo." It's a saying of my grandmother's, and I know she would have been pleased.

29   "I don't think you know what you're saying," Lengel said.

30   "I know you don't," I said. "But I do." I pull the bow at the back of my apron and start shrugging it off my shoulders. A couple customers that had been heading for my slot begin to knock against each other, like scared pigs in a chute.

31   Lengel sighs and begins to look very patient and old and gray. He's been a friend of my parents for years. "Sammy, you don't want to do this to your Mom and Dad," he tells me. It's true, I don't. But it seems to me that once you begin a gesture it's fatal not to go through with it. I fold the apron, "Sammy" stitched in red on the pocket, and put it on the counter, and drop the bow tie on top of it. The bow tie is theirs, if you've ever wondered. "You'll feel this for the rest of your life," Lengel says, and I know that's true, too, but remembering how he made that pretty girl blush makes me so scrunchy inside I punch the No Sale tab and the machine whirs "pee-pul" and the drawer splats out. One advantage to this scene taking place in summer, I can follow this up with a clean exit, there's no fumbling around getting your coat and galoshes, I just saunter into the

electric eye in my white shirt that my mother ironed the night before, and the door heaves itself open, and outside the sunshine is skating around on the asphalt.

32   I look around for my girls, but they're gone, of course. There wasn't anybody but some young married screaming with her children about some candy they didn't get by the door of a powder-blue Falcon station wagon. Looking back in the big windows, over the bags of peat moss and aluminum lawn furniture stacked on the pavement, I could see Lengel in my place in the slot, checking the sheep through. His face was dark gray and his back stiff, as if he'd just had an injection of iron, and my stomach kind of fell as I felt how hard the world was going to be to me hereafter.

On another sheet of paper, answer the following questions the best you can. Reread the story if you need to do so. Your instructor may want you to turn in your answers.

Literal Questions

1. Who is the main character? What is he like?
2. Who are other important persons in the story and how are they used to help develop the main character?
3. What is happening in the story that is unusual?
4. Where and when is everything happening?

Critical Questions

5. What seems to be the point (theme) of the story? If the author were writing an essay instead of a story, what would the thesis be?
6. How does the title relate to the theme or point of the story?
7. What events or scenes are used to develop the theme?

Affective Comprehension

8. Explain your feelings for the main characters in the story.
9. What passages seem particularly well written or memorable?
10. What aspects of yourself or those you know do you see in the story?

Here is another set of questions to be used for class discussion. They are not as general as the previous set of questions. If you have trouble answering any of them, look over the story again. A reader rarely has a full understanding of any story of merit after just one reading, so don't feel dissatisfied with yourself if you can't answer all the questions now.

1. Why does John Updike call his story "A & P"?

_____

_____

_____

2. What does Sammy's description of the people in the store tell you about Sammy himself?

_____

_____

_____

3. How accurate do you think Sammy's view of the world is? Do you agree with his attitudes and observations? Why?

_____

_____

_____

4. While Sammy is first attracted to the three girls by their physical appearance, what does he finally become concerned with?

_____

_____

_____

5. What does Queenie and her world represent to Sammy? How do you know? Cite some examples from the story.

_____

_____

_____

6. Do you agree with Sammy's decision to quit his job? Why? Would you do the same thing under similar circumstances?

_____

_____

_____

7. Is Sammy a strong or weak character? Do you admire or dislike him? Give specific reasons based on events in the story.

_____

_____

_____

8. Is the story merely about a young man who quits his job because of the way his boss treats the girls? What makes you think so?

_____

_____

_____

Drill   **A-3**

Directions: Sam Spade, Mike Hammer, Philip Marlowe—do you know these names? They are fictional "private eyes" from widely read detective stories. They have appeared in books, radio and TV programs, and movies. The story you are about to read satirizes these characters, especially Mickey Spillane's *I, The Jury*. Without this prior knowledge, you might miss some of the humor. As you read the story, notice how much of the satirical humor depends on the reader's knowing certain names, character types, and incidents that have appeared in many other detective stories.

THE WHORE OF MENSA

Woody Allen

One thing about being a private investigator, you've got to learn to go with your hunches. That's why when a quivering pat of butter named Word Babcock walked into my office and laid his cards on the table, I should have trusted the cold chill that shot up my spine.

"Kaiser?" he said, "Kaiser Lupowitz?"

"That's what it says on my license," I owned up.

"You've got to help me. I'm being blackmailed. Please!"

He was shaking like the lead singer in a rumba band. I pushed a glass across the desk top and a bottle of rye I keep handy for nonmedicinal purposes. "Suppose you relax and tell me all about it."

"You . . . you won't tell my wife?"

"Level with me, Word. I can't make any promises."

He tried pouring a drink, but you could hear the clicking sound across the street, and most of the stuff wound up in his shoes.

"I'm a working guy," he said. "Mechanical maintenance. I build and service joy buzzers. You know—those little fun gimmicks that give people a shock when they shake hands?"

"So?"

"A lot of your executives like 'em. Particularly down on Wall Street."

"Get to the point."

"I'm on the road a lot. You know how it is—lonely. Oh, not what you're thinking. See, Kaiser, I'm basically an intellectual. Sure, a guy can meet all the bimbos he wants. But the really brainy women—they're not so easy to find on short notice."

"Keep talking."

"Well, I heard of this young girl. Eighteen years old. A Vassar student. For a price, she'll come over and discuss any subject—Proust, Yeats, anthropology. Exchange of ideas. You see what I'm driving at?"

"Not exactly."

"I mean, my wife's great, don't get me wrong. But she won't discuss Pound with me. Or Eliot. I didn't know that when I married her. See, I need a woman who's mentally stimulating, Kaiser. And I'm willing to pay for it. I don't want an involvement—I want a quick intellectual experience, then I want the girl to leave. Christ, Kaiser, I'm a happily married man."

"How long has this been going on?"

"Six months. Whenever I have that craving, I call Flossie. She's a madam, with a master's in comparative lit. She sends me over an intellectual, see?"

So he was one of those guys whose weakness was really bright women. I felt sorry for the poor sap. I figured there must be a lot of jokers in his position, who were starved for a little intellectual communication with the opposite sex and would pay through the nose for it.

"Now she's threatening to tell my wife," he said.

"Who is?"

"Flossie. They bugged the motel room. They got tapes of me discussing *The Waste Land* and *Styles of Radical Will,* and, well, really getting into some issues. They want ten grand or they go to Carla. Kaiser, you've got to help me! Carla would die if she knew she didn't turn me on up here."

The old call-girl racket. I had heard rumors that the boys at headquarters were on to something involving a group of educated women, but so far they were stymied.

"Get Flossie on the phone for me."

"What?"

"I'll take your case, Word. But I get fifty dollars a day, plus expenses. You'll have to repair a lot of joy buzzers."

"It won't be ten Gs' worth, I'm sure of that," he said with a grin, and picked up the phone and dialed a number. I took it from him and winked. I was beginning to like him.

Seconds later, a silky voice answered, and I told her what was on my mind. "I understand you can help me set up an hour of good chat," I said.

"Sure, honey. What do you have in mind?"

"I'd like to discuss Melville."

"*Moby Dick* or the shorter novels?"

"What's the difference?"

"The price. That's all. Symbolism's extra."

"What'll it run me?"

"Fifty, maybe a hundred for *Moby Dick.* You want a comparative discussion—Melville and Hawthorne? That could be arranged for a hundred."

"The dough's fine," I told her and gave her the number of a room at the Plaza.

"You want a blonde or a brunette?"

"Surprise me," I said, and hung up.

I shaved and grabbed some black coffee while I checked over the Monarch College Outline series. Hardly an hour had passed before there was a knock on my door. I opened it, and standing there was a young redhead who was packed into her slacks like two big scoops of vanilla ice cream.

"Hi, I'm Sherry."

They really knew how to appeal to your fantasies. Long straight hair, leather bag, silver earrings, no make-up.

"I'm surprised you weren't stopped, walking into a hotel dressed like that," I said. "The house dick can usually spot an intellectual."

"A five-spot cools him."

"Shall we begin?" I said, motioning her to the couch.

She lit a cigarette and got right to it. "I think we should start by approaching *Billy Budd* as Melville's justification of the ways of God to man, *n'est-ce pas?*"

"Interestingly, though, not in a Miltonian sense." I was bluffing. I wanted to see if she'd go for it.

"No. *Paradise Lost* lacked the substructure of pessimism." She did.

"Right, right. God, you're right," I murmured.

"I think Melville reaffirmed the virtues of innocence in a naïve yet sophisticated sense—don't you agree?"

I let her go on. She was barely nineteen years old, but already she had developed the hardened facility of the pseudo-intellectual. She rattled off her ideas glibly, but it was all mechanical. Whenever I offered an insight, she faked a response: "Oh, yes, Kaiser. Yes, baby, that's deep. A platonic comprehension of Christianity—why didn't I see it before?"

We talked for about an hour and then she said she had to go. She stood up and I laid a C-note on her.

"Thanks, honey."

"There's plenty more where that came from."

"What are you trying to say?"

I had piqued her curiosity. She sat down again.

"Suppose I wanted to—have a party?" I said.

"Like, what kind of party?"

"Suppose I wanted Noam Chomsky explained to me by two girls?"

"Oh, wow."

"If you'd rather forget it . . ."

"You'd have to speak with Flossie," she said. "It'd cost you."

Now was the time to tighten the screws. I flashed my private-investigator's badge and informed her it was a bust.

"What!"

"I'm fuzz, sugar, and discussing Melville for money is an 802. You can do time."

"You louse!"

"Better come clean, baby. Unless you want to tell your story down at Alfred Kazin's office, and I don't think he'd be too happy to hear it."

She began to cry. "Don't turn me in, Kaiser," she said. "I needed the money to complete my master's. I've been turned down for a grant. *Twice.* Oh, Christ."

It all poured out—the whole story. Central Park West upbringing. Socialist summer camps, Brandeis. She was every dame you saw waiting in line at the Elgin or the Thalia, or penciling the words, "Yes, very true" into the margin of some book on Kant. Only somewhere along the line she had made a wrong turn.

"I needed cash. A girl friend said she knew a married guy whose wife wasn't very profound. He was into Blake. She couldn't hack it. I said sure, for a price I'd talk Blake with him. I was nervous at first. I faked a lot of it. He didn't care. My friend said there were others. Oh, I've been busted before. I got caught reading *Commentary* in a parked car, and I was once stopped and frisked at Tanglewood. Once more and I'm a three-time loser."

"Then take me to Flossie."

She bit her lip and said, "The Hunter College Book Store is a front."

"Yes?"

"Like those bookie joints that have barbershops outside for show. You'll see."

I made a quick call to headquarters and then said to her, "Okay, sugar. You're off the hook. But don't leave town."

She tilted her face up toward mine gratefully. "I can get you photographs of Dwight Macdonald reading," she said.

"Some other time."

I walked into the Hunter College Book Store. The salesman, a young man with sensitive eyes, came up to me. "Can I help you?" he said.

"I'm looking for a special edition of *Advertisements for Myself.* I understand the author had several thousand gold-leaf copies printed up for friends."

"I'll have to check," he said. "We have a WATS line to Mailer's house."

I fixed him with a look. "Sherry sent me," I said.

"Oh, in that case, go on back," he said. He pressed a button. A wall of books opened, and I walked like a lamb into that bustling pleasure palace known as Flossie's.

Red flocked wallpaper and a Victorian décor set the tone. Pale, nervous girls with black-rimmed glasses and blunt-cut hair lolled around on sofas, riffling Penguin Classics provocatively. A blonde with a big smile winked at me, nodded toward a room upstairs, and said, "Wallace Stevens, eh?" But it wasn't just intellectual experiences—

they were peddling emotional ones, too. For fifty bucks, I learned, you could "relate without getting close." For a hundred, a girl would lend you her Bartók records, have dinner, and then let you watch while she had an anxiety attack. For one-fifty, you could listen to FM radio with twins. For three bills, you got the works: A thin Jewish brunette would pretend to pick you up at the Museum of Modern Art, let you read her master's, get you involved in a screaming quarrel at Elaine's over Freud's conception of women, and then fake a suicide of your choosing—the perfect evening, for some guys. Nice racket. Great town, New York.

"Like what you see?" a voice said behind me. I turned and suddenly found myself face to face with the business end of a .38. I'm a guy with a strong stomach, but this time it did a back flip. It was Flossie, all right. The voice was the same, but Flossie was a man. His face was hidden by a mask.

"You'll never believe this," he said, "but I don't even have a college degree. I was thrown out for low grades."

"Is that why you wear that mask?"

"I devised a complicated scheme to take over *The New York Review of Books,* but it meant I had to pass for Lionel Trilling. I went to Mexico for an operation. There's a doctor in Juarez who gives people Trilling's features—for a price. Something went wrong. I came out looking like Auden, with Mary McCarthy's voice. That's when I started working the other side of the law."

Quickly, before he could tighten his finger on the trigger, I went into action. Heaving forward, I snapped my elbow across his jaw and grabbed the gun as he fell back. He hit the ground like a ton of bricks. He was still whimpering when the police showed up.

"Nice work, Kaiser," Sergeant Holmes said. "When we're through with this guy, the F.B.I. wants to have a talk with him. A little matter involving some gamblers and an annotated copy of Dante's *Inferno.* Take him away, boys."

Later that night, I looked up an old account of mine named Gloria. She was blond. She had graduated *cum laude.* The difference was she majored in physical education. It felt good.

The following questions are not intended as a typical comprehension check. They are provided to help you get more from your reading—points to think about to enhance your affective comprehension.

1. The following names are taken from the story. In the blank following each name, write what you know about them (poet, novelist, musician, name of something they wrote, name of a school, and so on). Leave blank the ones you know nothing about.

    a. Proust _____

    b. Yeats _____

    c. Pound _____

    d. Eliot _____

    e. Melville _____

    f. *Moby Dick* _____

    g. *Paradise Lost* _____

    h. Alfred Kazin _____

    i. Brandeis _____

    j. Mailer _____

    k. Bartók _____

    l. Blake _____

    m. Kant _____

    n. Monarch College Outlines _____

    o. WATS _____

    p. Mensa _____

2. From the names of the people and books mentioned in the story, what can you

infer about the author Woody Allen? _____

_____

_____

_____

3. In order to understand the story, is it necessary for you to know who most of

the people mentioned in the story are? _____ Why? _____

_____

_____

4. In the blank in front of the following quotes from the story, write in *M* for
metaphor, *S* for simile, or *C* for cliché.

    _____ **a.** "shaking like the lead singer in a rumba band."

    _____ **b.** "pay through the nose."

    _____ **c.** "time to tighten the screws"

    _____ **d.** "hit the ground like a ton of bricks"

    _____ **e.** "a quivering pat of butter named Word"

    _____ **f.** "laid his cards on the table"

5. Define these slang terms.

    a. bimbos _____

    b. ten Gs _____

    c. house dick _____

    d. fuzz _____

    e. off the hook _____

    f. three bills _____

6. What is the point of the last paragraph?

_____

_____

7. What is it that makes this story familiar but different?

_____

_____

8. What is your affective reaction to the story?

_____

_____

B. Reading Poetry

Reading poetry usually requires more of a reader than probably any other type of writing. Reading a twelve-line poem, for instance, may take longer to understand than a forty-page chapter in a history textbook. Analyzing a poem for comprehension requires being alert to both denotative and connotative meanings of words, noticing the suggestion of meanings in images created by figurative language, and recognizing the mood or feelings the author intended. But as with any skill, the more you experience the reading of poetry, the easier it becomes.

Many freshman composition classes require that students not only read poetry and short stories, but write essays about them. Read the following passage from a typical freshman composition textbook. Read it carefully for advice on how to read a poem as well as how to write about it.

Analyzing a Poem

Suppose that you have been assigned to analyze the following sonnet by William Wordsworth:

THE WORLD IS TOO MUCH WITH US

1 The world is too much with us; late and soon,
2 Getting and spending, we lay waste our powers;
3 Little we see in Nature that is ours;
4 We have given our hearts away, a sordid boon!
5 This Sea that bares her bosom to the moon;
6 The winds that will be howling at all hours,
7 And are up-gathered now like sleeping flowers;
8 For this, for everything, we are out of tune;
9 It moves us not.—Great God! I'd rather be
10 A pagan suckled in a creed outworn;
11 So might I, standing on this pleasant lea,
12 Have glimpses that would make me less forlorn;
13 Have sight of Proteus rising from the sea;
14 Or hear old Triton blow his wreathed horn.

Many students, especially those who do not plan to be English majors, are needlessly intimidated by this assignment. Some students think that they do not like poetry, and even those who like it believe that they won't like analyzing it, especially not in a formal paper. Students object to "tearing the poem apart." But in this case, analysis involves looking at the parts only to get a better vision of the whole. Analysis means examining the parts and then putting them together, not tearing things apart.

Getting started

An analysis of a poem begins with a careful reading of it. Read the poem several times, at least once or twice aloud. Remember that the poet has taken great care in selecting and arranging these particular words in this

---

From Elaine P. Maimon, Gerald L. Belcher, Gail W. Hearn, Barbara F. Nodine, and Finbarr W. O'Connor, *Writing in the Arts and Sciences*, pp. 156–162. Copyright © 1981 by Little, Brown and Company, Inc.

special order to create a total effect of meaning, form, and sound.

Take a few minutes and jot down everything that you think of when you read the poem. You probably won't be able to use much of this material directly in your formal analysis, but the time you take to express your feelings about the poem will be important in the long run. A poem is written to reach you emotionally and intellectually. Even though your formal paper will be an intellectual discussion of the poem, your analysis will be more alive and meaningful if it has its roots in some feeling about the poem. Also, if you allow yourself to express feelings about the poem at first, you may find yourself more involved in the project than you thought you would be.

Although self-expression is important, your major purpose for this assignment is to think about the poem. But how does a person think about a poem? First of all, ask yourself what you know about this poem, from your textbook, from classroom discussion, from previous reading. The poem looks short, so you might as well count the lines, looking for the magic number fourteen. Sure enough, the fourteen lines indicate that you may be dealing with a special form, *a sonnet*. Now a trip to the library is in order, but not to look up other people's interpretations of the poem. Instead, look up "sonnet" in a glossary of literary terms, such as M. H. Abrams's *A Glossary of Literary Terms.*[1]

Here you will find a wealth of ideas for organizing your paper. You will learn, for example, that because of the way that Wordsworth's sonnet rhymes, it is an example of a Petrarchan sonnet, which usually discusses a problem or situation in the first eight lines and then presents some sort of resolution in the last six. Now you have something quite specific to put in your notes. You just have developed a possible structure for your analysis. But you have only the skeleton at this point. Most important in a poem are the words, and you have to find out much more about the words of this poem. As Donald Hall says in *Writing Well*[2] you have to get "inside" these words, to find out as much about them and their family relationships as the poet knew and felt.

Begin with the unfamiliar names, Triton and Proteus. A good desk dictionary will tell you something about these pagan sea gods. If you want to see them more clearly—as clearly as Wordsworth did on his pleasant lea—then look them up in the *Oxford Classical Dictionary* or in a dictionary of mythology.

Then look up "lea," "forlorn," "suckled," and other unfamiliar words in a good desk dictionary or, even better, in the *Oxford English Dictionary* (O.E.D.), which will give you the complete history of the word up to the time Wordsworth chose it. *The Oxford English Dictionary* is a particularly good place to look up familiar words like "world" and "nature," especially if you get interested in why Wordsworth uses those two words in opposition to each other. Doesn't nature include the world, and doesn't the world include nature?

While you are thinking about the poet's use of familiar words, also look to see what words go together in categories. Sometimes it helps to list all the verbs in a poem to see what kinds of actions the poem describes.

Another way to categorize the words in a poem is to see which ones relate in meaning. "Bosom" in line 5 should thus be associated with "suckled" in line 10 and "howling" and "sleeping" in lines 6–7, since all these words relate to the image of nursing a baby. Imagery means simply word patterns that make us see pictures or hear sounds. Whether you are an English major or not, a close look at words will help you to understand imagery.

---

[1] 3rd ed. (New York: Holt, Rinehart & Winston, 1971).
[2] 3rd ed. (Boston: Little, Brown, 1979).

If you are an English major, you may wish to extend your analysis to metrics and to other more technical elements of poetry. In that case, you may wish to consult a special text on the subject, such as James R. Kreuzer's *Elements of Poetry*[3]. Few freshman composition teachers expect you to write a technical analysis, and you should be able to create an A paper for most classes without consulting a special source on sophisticated poetic techniques.

You may want to find out something about the poet and about the time that the poem was written. Usually you do not have to look beyond your own textbook to find the date that the poem was first published—in this case, 1807. That piece of information will save you from talking about the poet's view of our materialistic nuclear age. The *Dictionary of National Biography* and other general reference works will tell you something about Wordsworth. You should consult these sources only to provide a context for your interpretation, not for research on other writers' views of the poem. You should use only those library materials that will help you to understand the words of the poem. You are then prepared to write your own interpretation.

[3] New York: Macmillan, 1962.

Now answer these questions.

1. How do you begin to analyze a poem? _____

_____

_____

2. Why should you jot down your feelings about a poem as you study it even

though you may not use the information in your essay? _____

_____

3. What is meant by getting "inside" the words of a poem? _____

_____

_____

4. What reference works are mentioned that would help you learn more about

reading poetry? _____

_____

_____

The answer to the first question is that you begin by carefully reading the poem several times, and aloud once or twice. Poems are structured the way they are because the poets want you to respond to not only the meaning, but the sound, form, and structure as well. Some poems rhyme, some don't. But generally the form and structure of a poem is used by a poet for some particular significance.

As to question 2, your first impressions may be important to your later analysis, and it helps to involve you emotionally as you read.

To get "inside" the words of a poem is to find out as much about them as the poet knew and felt. In a way, it's looking for the "secret power" of the words.

Several sources you may want to look into are mentioned: *A Glossary of Literary Terms, Writing Well, The Oxford Classical Dictionary, The Oxford English Dictionary, Elements of Poetry,* and *The Dictionary of National Biography.*

Use the following drills to help become more familiar with reading poetry.

Drill B-1: USING OUTSIDE SOURCES

Directions: Using the information you just read, write an evaluation or interpretation of the Wordsworth poem "The World Is Too Much With Us." Actually go to the library and find the sources mentioned or others the library may contain. The subject of your essay will be the poem. Your thesis will be whatever you want to say or feel about the poem. Use the lines and words from the poem itself to help support your thesis. Use what you have learned about reading an essay to help you write one.

Drill B-2

Directions: Read the following poem, looking specifically for the author's intent, attitude, and bias.

THERE IS NO FRIGATE LIKE A BOOK

Emily Dickinson

There is no frigate like a book
To take us lands away
Nor any coursers like a page
Of prancing poetry—
This traverse may the poorest take
Without oppress of toll
How frugal is the chariot
That bears the human soul.

Answer the following questions by circling the best responses.

1. The intent of the author is
   a. to compare a book to a frigate
   b. to praise the value of a book
   c. to compare a frigate with a chariot
   d. to discuss the value of the human soul

Reprinted by permission of the publishers and the trustees of Amherst College from *The Poems of Emily Dickinson,* edited by Thomas H. Johnson, Cambridge, Mass.: The Belknap Press of Harvard Univ. Press, Copyright 1951, © 1955, 1979, 1983 by the President and Fellows of Harvard College.

2. The attitude of the author is
   a. sarcastic
   b. humorous
   c. serious
   d. crusading
3. T/F   The bias of the author is that books are better than actual traveling because they are more accessible to more people.
4. In your own words, tell what each of the following refers to:

   a. coursers _____

   b. the chariot _____
5. What is your intellectual and emotional reaction to this poem?

   _____

   _____

   _____

   _____

   _____

   _____

Drill   **B-3**

Directions: Read the following poem once or twice. When you feel you have a good grasp of the poem, answer the questions. They require literal, critical, and affective reactions.

STATUS SYMBOL

Mari Evans

            i
Have Arrived
            i
   am the
New Negro
            i
am the result of
President Lincoln
World War I
and Paris

Reprinted by permission of Mari Evans from *I Am a Black Woman*, William Morrow & Company, 1970.

the
Red Ball Express
white drinking fountains
sitdowns and
sit-ins
Federal Troops
Marches on Washington
   and
prayer meetings ...
today
They hired me
it
is a status
job ...
along
with my papers
They
gave me my
Status Symbol
the
key
to the
White ... Locked ...
john

Check your comprehension

1. The tone of the poem is primarily
   a. joyful
   b. fearful
   c. ironic
   d. humorous

2. Why do you think the tone is what you circled in the first question?

   _____

   _____

   _____

   _____

   _____

3. What does each of the following represent symbolically in the poem?

   a. President Lincoln _____

   _____

   b. World War I _____

   _____

    c. Paris _____

_____

    d. Red Ball Express _____

_____

    e. white drinking fountains _____

_____

    f. Federal Troops _____

_____

    g. Marches on Washington _____

_____

4. What is ironic about the Status Symbol given to the "New Negro"? _____

_____

_____

_____

_____

_____

_____

_____

5. Why does the author capitalize "They"—those who hired her—and use the

lower case "i" instead of "I"? _____

_____

6. Do you think the author feels that the racial issue has really changed much?

_____

_____

_____

Why? _____

_____

_____

_____

7. What lines do you feel are particularly effective? _____

_____

_____

Why? _____

_____

_____

_____

8. Was the poem worth reading? _____

Why? _____

_____

_____

_____

C. Reading Practices

The following drills contain the usual comprehension and vocabulary practices. You may want to check your scores on the Student Record Chart to see what your scores were on the Practice Readings in the last chapter. Try to equal or better your scores on these. You or your instructor may want to time these drills.

Drill   C-1

Begin timing. Starting time: _____

SALVATION

Langston Hughes

1   I was saved from sin when I was going on thirteen. But not really saved. It happened like this. There was a big revival at my Auntie Reed's church. Every night for weeks there had been much preaching, singing, praying, and shouting, and some very hardened sinners had been brought to Christ, and the membership of the church had grown by leaps and bounds. Then just before the revival ended, they held a special meeting for children, "to bring the young lambs to the fold." My aunt spoke of it for days ahead. That night I was escorted to the front row and placed on the mourners' bench with all the other young sinners, who had not yet been brought to Jesus.

2   My aunt told me that when you were saved you saw a light, and something happened to you inside! And Jesus came into your life! And God was with you from then on! She said you could see and hear and feel Jesus in your soul. I believed her. I had heard a great many old people say the same thing and it seemed to me they ought to know. So I sat there calmly in the hot, crowded church, waiting for Jesus to come to me.

3   The preacher preached a wonderful rhythmical sermon, all moans and shouts and lonely cries and dire pictures of hell, and then he sang a song about the ninety and nine safe and in the fold, but one little lamb was left out in the cold. Then he said: "Won't you come? Won't you come to Jesus? Young lambs, won't you come?" And he held out his arms to all us young sinners there on the mourners' bench. And the little girls cried. And some of them jumped up and went to Jesus right away. But most of us just sat there.

4   A great many old people came and knelt around us and prayed, old women with jet-black faces and braided hair, old men with work-gnarled hands. And the church sang a song about the lower lights are burning, some poor sinners to be saved. And the whole building rocked with prayer and song.

5   Still I kept waiting to *see* Jesus.

6   Finally all the young people had gone to the altar and were saved, but one boy and me. He was a rounder's son named Westley. Westley and I were surrounded by sisters and deacons praying. It was very hot in the church, and getting late now. Finally

"Salvation" from *The Big Sea* by Langston Hughes. Copyright 1940 by Langston Hughes. Copyright renewed © 1968 by Arna Bontemps and George Houston Bass. Reprinted by permission of Hill and Wang, a division of Farrar, Straus and Giroux, Inc.

Westley said to me in a whisper: "God damn! I'm tired o' sitting here. Let's get up and be saved." So he got up and was saved.

7   Then I was left all alone on the mourners' bench. My aunt came and knelt at my knees and cried, while prayers and songs swirled all around me in the little church. The whole congregation prayed for me alone, in a mighty wail of moans and voices. And I kept waiting serenely for Jesus, waiting, waiting—but he didn't come. I wanted to see him, but nothing happened to me. Nothing! I wanted something to happen to me, but nothing happened.

8   I heard the songs and the minister saying: "Why don't you come? My dear child, why don't you come to Jesus? Jesus is waiting for you. He wants you. Why don't you come? Sister Reed, what is this child's name?"

9   "Langston," my aunt sobbed.

10   "Langston, why don't you come? Why don't you come and be saved? Oh, Lamb of God! Why don't you come?"

11   Now it was really getting late. I began to be ashamed of myself, holding everything up so long. I began to wonder what God thought about Westley, who certainly hadn't seen Jesus either, but who was now sitting proudly on the platform, swinging his knickerbockered legs and grinning down at me, surrounded by deacons and old women on their knees praying. God had not struck Westley dead for taking his name in vain or for lying in the temple. So I decided that maybe to save further trouble, I'd better lie, too, and say that Jesus had come, and get up and be saved.

12   So I got up.

13   Suddenly the whole room broke into a sea of shouting, as they saw me rise. Waves of rejoicing swept the place. Women leaped in the air. My aunt threw her arms around me. The minister took me by the hand and led me to the platform.

14   When things quieted down, in a hushed silence, punctuated by a few ecstatic "Amens," all the new young lambs were blessed in the name of God. Then joyous singing filled the room.

15   That night for the last time in my life but one—for I was a big boy twelve years old—I cried. I cried, in bed alone, and couldn't stop. I buried my head under the quilts, but my aunt heard me. She woke up and told my uncle I was crying because the Holy Ghost had come into my life, and because I had seen Jesus. But I was really crying because I couldn't bear to tell her that I had lied, that I had deceived everybody in the church, and I hadn't seen Jesus, and that now I didn't believe there was a Jesus any more, since he didn't come to help me.

Finishing time: _____

Starting time: _____

Reading time: ___4/5_____

Check page 501 for your reading rate: WPM: ___913 ?___

COMPREHENSION CHECK

Now answer these questions, applying a mixture of literal, critical, and affective comprehension.

1. What is the name of the main character in the story?

    Langston _____

2. He is ___twelve_____ years old.
    a. ten   c. twelve
    b. eleven   d. thirteen

3. Where does most of the story take place? _in his Aunt's Church_

___

4. Place a check mark in front of each statement that you believe is an example of figurative language:

___✓___ **a.** "bring the young lambs to the fold"

_____ **b.** "sat there calmly in the hot, crowded church"

___✓___ **c.** "old men with work-gnarled hands"

___✓___ **d.** "the whole building rocked with prayer and song"

5. T/F "The whole room broke into a sea of shouting…" is an example of a simile.

6. T/F "The membership of the church had grown by leaps and bounds" is an example of a metaphor.

7. The attitude of the author toward himself as a young boy is one of
    a. embarrassment
    b. slight amusement
    c. sarcasm
    d. hatred

8. Why does the boy wait so long to "get saved"? _He's waiting for something to really happen_

9. Why does the boy cry that night? _Because he lied and because he didn't believe in Jesus anymore._

10. What is the point of the story? _That not all people are "saved" in the same way_

___

___

Number correct: ___9___

VOCABULARY CHECK

Directions: Define the following underlined words from the story.

1. a big <u>revival</u> at my aunt's church

_____

2. bring the young lambs to the <u>fold</u>

_____

3. <u>dire</u> pictures of hell

_____

4. he was a <u>rounder's</u> son

_____

5. waiting <u>serenely</u> for Jesus

_____

6. swinging his <u>knickerbockered</u> legs

_____

7. surrounded by <u>deacons</u>

_____

8. <u>punctuated</u> by a few ecstatic "Amens"

_____

9. <u>ecstatic</u> "Amens"

_____

10. on the <u>mourners'</u> bench

_____

Number correct: _____

**Record the results on the Student Record Chart on page 495. Discuss the results with your
instructor.**

Drill **C-2**

Directions: Survey the article to see what rate you can apply to the reading of the selection while still obtaining good comprehension. Apply all the skills you have learned.

Begin timing. Starting time: _____

THE BARRIO

Robert Ramirez

1   The train, its metal wheels squealing as they spin along the silvery tracks, rolls slower now. Through the gaps between the cars blinks a streetlamp, and this pulsing light on a barrio streetcorner beats slower, like a weary heartbeat, until the train shudders to a halt, the light goes out, and the barrio is deep asleep.

2   Throughout Aztlán (the Nahuatl term meaning "land to the north"), trains grumble along the edges of a sleeping people. From Lower California, through the blistering Southwest, down the Rio Grande to the muddy Gulf, the darkness and mystery of dreams engulf communities fenced off by railroads, canals, and expressways. Paradoxical communities, isolated from the rest of the town by concrete columned monuments of progress, and yet stranded in the past. They are surrounded by change. It eludes their reach, in their own backyards, and the people, unable and unwilling to see the future, or even touch the present, perpetuate the past.

3   Leaning from the expressway or jolting across the tracks, one enters a different physical world permeated by a different attitude. The physical dimensions are impressive. It is a large section of town which extends for fifteen blocks north and south along the tracks, and then advances eastward, thinning into nothingness beyond the city limits. Within the invisible (yet sensible) walls of the barrio, are many, many people living in too few houses. The homes, however, are much more numerous than on the outside.

4   Members of the barrio describe the entire area as their home. It is a home, but it is more than this. The barrio is a refuge from the harshness and the coldness of the Anglo world. It is a forced refuge. The leprous people are isolated from the rest of the community and contained in their section of town. The stoical pariahs of the barrio accept their fate, and from the angry seeds of rejection grow the flowers of closeness between outcasts, not the thorns of bitterness and the mad desire to flee. There is no want to escape, for the feeling of the barrio is known only to its inhabitants, and the material needs of life can also be found here.

5   The *tortillería* fires up its machinery three times a day, producing steaming, round, flat slices of barrio bread. In the winter, the warmth of the tortilla factory is a wool *sarape* in the chilly morning hours, but in the summer, it unbearably toasts every noontime customer.

6   The *panadería* sends its sweet messenger aroma down the dimly lit street, announcing the arrival of fresh, hot sugary *pan dulce*.

7   The small corner grocery serves the meal-to-meal needs of customers, and the owner, a part of the neighborhood, willingly gives credit to people unable to pay cash for foodstuffs.

8   The barbershop is a living room with hydraulic chairs, radio, and television, where old friends meet and speak of life as their salted hair falls aimlessly about them.

9   The pool hall is a junior level country club where *chucos,* strangers in their own land, get together to shoot pool and rap, while veterans, unaware of the cracking, popping balls on the green felt, complacently play dominoes beneath rudely hung *Playboy* foldouts.

10   The *cantina* is the night spot of the barrio. It is the country club and the den where the rites of puberty are enacted. Here the young become men. It is in the taverns that a young dude shows his *machismo* through the quantity of beer he can hold, the stores of *rucas* he has had, and his willingness and ability to defend his image against hardened and scarred old lions.

11   No, there is no frantic wish to flee. It would be absurd to leave the familiar and nervously step into the strange and cold Anglo community when the needs of the Chicano can be met in the barrio.

12   The barrio is closeness. From the family living unit, familial relationships stretch out to immediate neighbors, down the block, around the corner, and to all parts of the barrio. The feeling of family, a rare and treasurable sentiment, pervades and accounts for the inability of the people to leave. The barrio is this attitude manifested on the countenances of the people, on the faces of their homes, and in the gaiety of their gardens.

13   The color-splashed homes arrest your eyes, arouse your curiosity, and make you wonder what life scenes are being played out in them. The flimsy, brightly colored, wood-frame houses ignore no neon-brilliant color. Houses trimmed in orange, chartreuse, lime-green, yellow, and mixtures of these and other hues beckon the beholder to reflect on the peculiarity of each home. Passing through this land is refreshing like Brubeck, not narcoticizing like revolting rows of similar houses, which neither offend nor please.

14   In the evenings, the porches and front yards are occupied with men calmly talking over the noise of children playing baseball in the unpaved extension of the living room, while the women cook supper or gossip with female neighbors as they water the *jardines.* The gardens mutely echo the expressive verses of the colorful houses. The denseness of multicolored plants and trees gives the house the appearance of an oasis or a tropical island hideaway, sheltered from the rest of the world.

15   Fences are common in the barrio, but they are fences and not the walls of the Anglo community. On the western side of town, the high wooden fences between houses are thick, impenetrable walls, built to keep the neighbors at bay. In the barrio, the fences may be rusty, wire contraptions or thick green shrubs. In either case you can see through them and feel no sense of intrusion when you cross them.

16   Many lower-income families of the barrio manage to maintain a comfortable standard of living through the communal action of family members who contribute their wages to the head of the family. Economic need creates interdependence and closeness. Small barefooted boys sell papers on cool, dark Sunday mornings, deny themselves pleasantries, and give their earnings to *mamá.* The older the child, the greater the responsibility to help the head of the household provide for the rest of the family.

17   There are those, too, who for a number of reasons have not achieved a relative sense of financial security. Perhaps it results from too many children too soon, but it is the homes of these people and their situation that numbs rather than charms. Their houses, aged and bent, oozing children, are fissures in the horn of plenty. Their wooden homes may have brick-pattern asbestos tile on the outer walls, but the tile is not convincing.

18   Unable to pay city taxes or incapable of influencing the city to live up to its duty to serve all the citizens, the poorer barrio families remain trapped in the nineteenth century and survive as best they can. The backyards have well-worn paths to the outhouses, which sit near the alley. Running water is considered a luxury in some parts of the barrio. Decent drainage is usually unknown, and when it rains, the water stands

for days, an incubator of health hazards and an avoidable nuisance. Streets, costly to pave, remain rough, rocky trails. Tires do not last long, and the constant rattling and shaking grind away a car's life and spread dust through screen windows.

19 The houses and their *jardines,* the jollity of the people in an adverse world, the brightly feathered alarm clock pecking away at supper and cautiously eyeing the children playing nearby, produce a mystifying sensation at finding the noble savage alive in the twentieth century. It is easy to look at the positive qualities of life in the barrio, and look at them with a distantly envious feeling. One wishes to experience the feelings of the barrio and not the hardships. Remembering the illness, the hunger, the feeling of time running out on you, the walls, both real and imagined, reflecting on living in the past, one finds his envy becoming more elusive, until it has vanished altogether.

20 Back now beyond the tracks, the train creaks and groans, the cars jostle each other down the track, and as the light begins its pulsing, the barrio, with all its meanings, greets a new dawn with yawns and restless stretchings.

COMPREHENSION CHECK

1. What is the thesis or main idea of this article? _____

_____

_____

2. What is a barrio? _____

_____

3. What is the author's attitude toward the barrio he describes? _____

_____

4. The phrase "...from the angry seeds of rejection grow the flowers of closeness between outcasts, not the thorns of bitterness..." is an example of a simile.

a. True, because _____

b. False, because _____

5. "...this pulsing light on a barrio streetcorner beats slower, like a weary heartbeat..." is an example of a metaphor.

a. True, because _____

b. False, because _____

6. Explain Ramirez's use of walls and fences to help develop his theme of

cultural isolation. _____

_____

_____

7. How does the author's use of words such as *closeness, home, family, refuge,* and *neighborhood* help us understand how those who live in the barrio feel

about it? _____

_____

_____

8. What is Ramirez describing when he says, "...the brightly feathered alarm clock pecking away at supper and cautiously eyeing the children ..."?

_____

_____

9. Ramirez states, "One wishes to experience the feelings of the barrio and not the hardships." What are some of those feelings and what are some of the hardships?

Feelings   **Hardships**

_____   _____

_____   _____

_____   _____

10. Does Ramirez give any evidence to indicate that the people in the barrio want

to leave? _____ Explain. _____

_____

_____

Number correct: _____

VOCABULARY CHECK

Directions: Define the underlined words from the article.

1. <u>paradoxical</u> communities, isolated from the town

_____

2. it <u>eludes</u> their reach

_____

3. to touch the present, to <u>perpetuate</u> the past

_____

4. a world <u>permeated</u> by a different attitude

_____

5. the <u>leprous</u> people are isolated from the rest

_____

6. the <u>stoical</u> pariahs ... accept their fate

_____

7. the stoical <u>pariahs</u> of the barrio

_____

8. <u>complacently</u> play dominoes

_____

9. thick, <u>impenetrable</u> walls

_____

10. an <u>incubator</u> of health hazards

_____

Number correct: _____

Record your scores on the Student Record Chart on page 495. Discuss your scores with your instructor.

D. Reacting on All Levels

By now you ought to have a deeper understanding of the meaning of, and the need for, developing reading versatility. Approaches to reading are as varied as the types of reading materials that exist and the reasons for reading them. This last chapter has shown you some approaches to reading imaginative literature. It brings together the general content of all three units in the book. As the Introduction told you, total comprehension is a combination of the literal, critical, and affective levels of understanding. Good comprehension brings everything you've learned separately into play. The diagram below shows the many facets of comprehension.

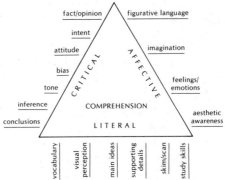

By now you should be aware, from doing previous drills, that a short poem may take longer to read and understand than a chapter in a textbook. You can read some materials quickly, even skim and scan them, whereas others require rereading. Good imaginative literature seldom communicates on a literal level only. It is necessary to use your imagination, to interpret symbols, and to breathe life into characters, settings, and situations.

Developing reading versatility requires more than reading this book. It requires a lifetime of reading and reacting, at all levels of comprehension.

Drill D-1

Directions: Answer the questions below. Then read the essay that follows. You or your instructor may want to time your reading.

1. If someone asked you what was meant by the phrase "the American Dream,"

what would you say? _____

_____

_____

2. What do you hope to have accomplished ten years from now? _____

_____

_____

Begin timing. Starting time: _____

THE AMERICAN DREAM

Betty Anne Younglove

The lament for the death of the American dream grows ever louder. And although the verses may vary, the chorus is the same: The American dream is out of reach, unattainable.

Some of the verses I hear most often:

• Young families cannot afford a three-bedroom house in the suburbs because the prices or interest rates or taxes are too high.

• The average family cannot afford to send its sons and daughters to "a Harvard" because the cost is equivalent to the total family income before taxes; moreover, there is not enough money to send the kids to a prep school to insure they can get into "a Harvard" even if they can come up with the money.

• Why, oh why, can't the young people of today be guaranteed the dreams their parents had?

First, let us get this dream business—and business it now seems to be—straight. The word *dream* is not a synonym for *reality* or *promise*. It is closer to *hope* or *possibility* or even *vision*. The original American dream had only a little to do with material possessions and a lot to do with choices, beginnings and opportunity. Many of the original American dreamers wanted a new beginning, a place to choose what they wanted and a place to work for it. They did not see it as a guarantee of success but an opportunity to try.

4 The dream represented possibilities: Get your own land and clear it and work it; if nature cooperates, the work might pay off in material blessings. Or the dream represented the idea that any citizen with the minimum qualifications of age and years of citizenship could run for President even if he were born in a humble log cabin. He had no guarantee he would win, of course, no more than the man clearing his land was guaranteed a good crop.

5 The preamble to the Constitution does not promise happiness, only the right to pursue it.

6 This new elegy, however, seems to define the American dream as possessions and to declare that material things, power and money are our rights; we not only deserve them but maybe a free lunch as well.

7 Whatever verse we have been listening to in this new song about the dream, we should recognize it as nothing more than a siren song leading us with Pied Piper promises. Let's go back to the original idea—a tune we can whistle while we work to achieve the goal of our choice.

Finishing time: _____

Starting time: _____ **(subtract)**

Reading time: _____
Check your rate on page 501.

WPM: _____

COMPREHENSION CHECK

1. The best statement of thesis for this essay is
    a. The original meaning of the American dream referred to an opportunity to try for something better, but today it seems to be equated with obtaining material possessions.
    b. The American dream that previous generations had is now unattainable even though the preamble to the Constitution promises the right to happiness.
    c. The word "dream" in the phrase "American dream" is synonymous with the words "reality" or "promise."
    d. The American dream is a myth and always has been

From "Rostrum," *U.S. News & World Report*, Dec. 8, 1986. Reprinted with permission of Betty Anne Younglove.

2. The author's attitude toward the concept of the American dream is
   a. cynical, because it is unattainable
   b. humorous, because it is misunderstood
   c. confused, because it no longer is relevant
   d. positive, if defined correctly

3. The intent of the author is to
   a. give examples of the American dream
   b. show how the definition of the American dream has changed
   c. provide the correct definition of the American dream
   d. both c and d

4. When the author says, "we not only deserve them [material things, power, and money] but maybe a free lunch as well," she is being
   a. truthful
   b. sarcastic
   c. hopeful
   d. humorous

5. T/F   The essay is mostly factual.

6. T/F   The fact that the average family cannot afford to send its sons and daughters to "a Harvard" because the cost is too high is an example of why the American dream is no longer possible.

7. T/F   The author equates "the American dream" with the words "hope," "possibilities," and "vision."

8. What is meant by the phrase "this new song about the dream"?

_____

_____

9. What does the author mean by "...let us get this dream business—and business it now seems to be—straight"?

_____

_____

10. T/F   We can draw the conclusion that the author would consider the right to attend college, obtain a good paying job, and own a house and car as good examples of achieving the American dream.

Number correct: _____

VOCABULARY CHECK

Directions: Define in context the following underlined words or phrases.

1. the lament for the death of the American dream

_____

2. although the verses may vary, the chorus is the same

_____

3. they can't get into "a Harvard"

_____

4. the preamble to the Constitution

_____

5. this new <u>elegy</u> seems to define the American dream

_____

6. a <u>free</u> <u>lunch</u>

_____

7. a <u>siren</u> <u>song</u> leading us with Pied Piper promises

_____

8. <u>Pied</u> <u>Piper</u> <u>promises</u>

_____

9. the <u>American</u> <u>dream</u>

_____

10. What do all the following words used in the essay have in common: <u>lament</u>, <u>verses</u>, <u>chorus</u>, <u>song</u>, <u>tune</u>, <u>whistle</u>?

_____

Number correct: _____

Record the results on the Timed Reading Chart on page 497. Discuss your scores with your instructor.

Drill **D-2**

Directions: Survey the reading selection quickly to decide how fast you should read it. Apply all the techniques you have learned in order to get the best possible comprehension.

Begin timing. Starting time: _____

WHAT SOAP OPERAS ARE TRYING TO TELL US

Carolyn See

1   To know about _General Hospital_ is doubly shaming now; first, because it's a soap opera; and second, because it's newly fashionable. But fashion or not, almost as many people know where they were when Luke and Laura finally made love during that summer they ran away to Beecher's Corners as where they were when the North Koreans swarmed down into the South. We'd known Luke and Laura were going to do it, but _when?_ I was at work that day, holding office hours with a student. My older daughter, Lisa, a freelance writer, was home keeping tabs. (My younger daughter would see it after school on her best friend's Betamax.) Lisa called me. "I think . . . Yes, I think . . . Oh, my God . . . _Oh, my God!_" It was later said that it had been the very hottest show on television ever; the most erotic, the most sensual.

From _Dial Magazine,_ April 1982. Reprinted by permission of Carolyn See, whose latest novel is _Golden Days,_ McGraw-Hill, 1987.

2   More people watch *General Hospital* than any other daytime show and many a nighttime show. This information can be "played" any number of ways. *Newsweek's* cover story on *General Hospital* mentioned other soaps, but last Christmas season the cute boutiques in Beverly Hills immediately sold out of "I ♡ *General Hospital*" coffee cups and were left with an embarrassing backlog of *Ryan's Hope* paraphernalia. Other "experts" muddy the waters by calling *Dynasty* and *Dallas,* even *Upstairs, Downstairs,* nighttime soaps, a contradiction in terms. (Or is anything about people instead of crime and cars a "soap"?)

3   Whatever is happening, soaps are enjoying extraordinary success just now, while, in a separate shrine, as it were, *General Hospital,* like the obscure madonna in the side altar of the cathedral who has all the power, goes on, month after month, demonstrating mythological perfection.

4   What are the soaps trying to tell us? First, that Dan Rather doesn't matter. He can dress up like an Afghan all he wants. It doesn't matter what awful chemicals the Russians may be using or how many Polish miners perish underground. *No news matters.* The larger world doesn't matter. Port Charles is a large city, but there has never been a strike there or a cyclone. That snowstorm existed only in relation to Monica's baby.

5   Culture is largely a vehicle, on the sidelines. A professor noodles on the piano he keeps in his office while he worries about a domestic problem. But did you ever see a concert violinist on a soap? Did you ever see Lesley with her nose in a book? Did you ever see anyone in the daytime holding a record album? Or painting a picture (unless with an ulterior motive)?

6   Sports don't matter much. Who goes to the homecoming game matters, but that's all.

7   On the other hand, Christmas matters; Easter matters. So do parties, dates, engagements, sickness (naturally), and—don't forget this—who murdered whom, who's in a coma, and who's in jail for a crime he/she didn't commit.

8   What soaps are trying to tell us is appallingly simple: People matter more than all the other stuff. The rest of it is window dressing. A soap opera confirms that one person is important. In fact, the soaps may be seen as an inner refutation of almost every other thing we see on commercial *and* public television. Forget the Cosmos! Forget the Bomb. But remember what it feels like to be in love, accused, betrayed. Remember what it's like to feel. Remember what strange fun it was when something you thought was one way in the world turned out to be another way entirely. (When Stephen on *Dynasty* turns out to be not quite as homosexual as he thought. When the emerald necklace is made of paste—or was it? When Fallon almost sleeps with her own father by mistake—no, wait!) Remember pain. Neighbors are impossible. People lie and cheat. Living hurts. Soaps refute the cliché that Americans care only about happy talk.

9   Try giving university sophomores an "opinion paper" to write. It is unutterably difficult for them, because their one opinion is: Richard/Marjorie may/may not sleep with/break up with me Saturday night.

10   Beyond all this, twinkling in the creamy, benevolent success of most of the soaps, *General Hospital* suggests daily to a huge public—and to its own cast, to actors, writers, directors—that it's *possible,* even now to have fun.

11   Why is it the most successful show on daytime television? Because it arrives at a perfect time. You watch it after a respectable morning's work, before the kids are home, long before it's time to start dinner. At work, you take a fashionably late lunch. In college, your morning classes are over, afternoon workouts not yet begun.

12   Of course, there's a lot of sex on soap operas, more than on nighttime programs. For students—men and women—watching soap operas is a social activity accompanied by cheers and laughter. Some colleges have incorporated watching *General Hospital* into their curricula, and New Jersey's Monmouth College offers a course in the psychology of the soap opera.

13   The direction on *GH,* the writing, the character development, are nearly flawless.

Many daytime soaps still content themselves with two-shots in living rooms and a lugubrious underwater pace; *General Hospital* is all over the place, with crowds, yachts, Richard Simmons. *GH* people talk like humans—perkily. The dialogue sounds good. Villains don't content themselves with one spiteful, doleful note. For as long as she was on, Tracy Quartermaine, with her turbans and manicures and thin, exasperated smiles, was a perfect bellwether of awfulness, her rage perfectly motivated—a combination of material greed and surprise at how continuously stupid good people could be.

14   Then the secret ingredient (optional, like the dollop of brandy in beef Bourguignon), what *GH* took a chance with when other soaps hung back, what *Dynasty* flirts with but hasn't quite embraced—fun.

15   Sometimes when two people are in love, they have fun. What a concept! During the past few years, a writer or a producer at *General Hospital* discovered that, and it was alchemy. Critics who groan that Luke and Laura's relationship began with rape—he assaulted her, eventually she fell in love with him, dumped her husband, ran away to join Luke—are taking a knee-jerk liberal position. Luke and Laura may have "started up" because of that four-letter word, but they carried the show because they had fun in each other's company; their time together was golden time. (Just as Alan and Monica *love* each other's company, even as they kick and bite and scratch.)

16   Fun. Not comedians or sequins or "variety," but fun from *hanging out.* It's catching. That's why kids watch these shows in groups—the two o'clock slot is becoming an endangered species in American universities. That's why Elizabeth Taylor called the producer of the show and asked to be on it.

17   "She showed up with a full-length mink and these huge bouquets of flowers, the limo and all. And Tony Geary, who plays Luke, kept banging his head and laughing. 'I can't *believe* I'm playing a scene with Elizabeth Taylor!' "

18   This word was smuggled from the set of *GH,* where security rivals that of the Rand Corporation and the fun spills out in every direction—not just through the tube. At the Actors' Fund Benefit of *The Little Foxes,* a sparkling event in Los Angeles, with almost everyone in the audience a celebrity, the orchestra seats were taken up by a sweet set of faces: Taylor bought tickets for everyone in the *General Hospital* cast and crew. They sat in their rented tuxes with smiles as dreamy as Laura's at her capitulation in Beecher's Corners.

19   Crime, yes. Freezing to death, why not? Adultery, *bien sûr!* But staying alive by being interested in "daily life" to the point of fanaticism, to the point of love, hate, fun—that's the message of the soaps.

Finishing time: _____

Starting time: _____ (subtract)

Reading time: _3rd5_ _____
Check your reading rate on page 501.

WPM: _____426_____

COMPREHENSION CHECK

1. According to the author, what are soap operas trying to tell us? _____

That people + fun are important in our daily lives

2. What "soap" is watched more than any other daytime show? _____

   G H

3. Based on the contents of the article, is your answer to question 2 a fact or an

   opinion? *fact* _____

4. We can infer from the article that the author is a teacher because _____

   She was with a student when Luke & Laura did it.

5. What is the "secret ingredient" of the soap *General Hospital*? *FUN*

6. What is the author's attitude toward soap operas? *She likes them*

   _____

7. Why, according to the author, is giving university sophomore students an

   "opinion paper" to write so difficult for them? *B they are worried*

   about a possible Date Friday night.

8. Why do you suppose someone such as Elizabeth Taylor would want to be on

   a soap opera? *fun* _____

   _____

9. Is this article biased toward any particular soap opera? *GH*

   If so, which one? *GH* _____

10. The author says soaps tell us to "Forget the Cosmos! Forget the Bomb." Do you

    think she advocates this herself? *Yes* _____

    Explain. *She's in favor of enjoying life.*

    _____

Number correct: _*100%*_

VOCABULARY CHECK

Directions: Define the underlined words from the article.

1. a <u>freelance</u> writer

   _____

2. the cute <u>boutiques</u> in Beverly Hills

   _____

3. a backlog of "Ryan's Hope" <u>paraphernalia</u>

   _____

4. like the <u>obscure</u> madonna in the side altar

   _____

5. seen as an inner <u>refutation</u> of almost everything

   _____

6. at a <u>lugubrious</u> underwater pace

   _____

7. villains don't content themselves with one <u>doleful</u> note

   _____

8. like the <u>dollop</u> of brandy in beef Bourguignon

   _____

9. smiles as dreamy as Laura's at her <u>capitulation</u>

   _____

10. was a perfect <u>bellwether</u> of awfulness

   _____

Number correct: _____

Record the results on the Timed Readings Chart on page 497. Discuss your scores with your instructor.

Drill **D-3**

Directions: Quickly survey the following essay, reading the title, the first paragraph, and the last paragraph. Then time yourself as you read the selection.

Begin timing. Starting time: _____

THE LANGUAGE OF FEELINGS

David Viscott

1   The world is a puzzle each of us assembles differently. But each of us can learn to deal with it by using our natural gifts in a more effective way—which includes learning to feel more honestly. The more honest you become the more energy you will have to deal with the problems you face. Being in touch with your feelings is the only way you can ever become your highest self, the only way you can become open and free, the only way you can become your own person. Seeing the world intellectually is as different from "feeling" it as studying a country in a geography book is from living there.

2   If you don't live in your feelings, you don't live in the real world. Feelings are the truth. What you do with them will decide whether you live in honesty or by a lie. Using defenses to try to manage feelings may distort your perception of the truth, but it does not alter that truth. Explaining feelings away does not resolve them or exorcise them. They're there. They have to be dealt with. Putting the blame on others does not take away their sting, or reduce their intensity. Feelings may be disguised, denied, rationalized, but a painful feeling will not go away until it has run its natural course. In fact when a feeling is avoided, its painful effects are often prolonged and it becomes increasingly difficult to deal with it.

3   To understand the emotional and psychological effects of pain it's helpful to understand its physical nature. Physiologically the sensation of pain is transmitted through specific nerve fibers and is perceived when any sensory receptor is overloaded beyond its normal capacity to receive and transmit information. When pressure becomes too severe or temperature too hot, or sound too loud the stimulus is no longer perceived as pressure, temperature or sound, but as pain. An electrical current, called the current of injury, is initiated in the nerve ending and is sent along to the brain. The painful impulse produces an avoidance response that causes us to remove the threatened part of the body from danger—a reaction that often occurs automatically.

4   This avoidance response is basic to the understanding of human feelings, because painful human feelings also produce a current of injury, telling us that we are in danger and that we must protect ourselves. Feelings can be overloaded just as any other energy system can.

5   When an emotional injury threatens, our natural reaction is to avoid it. If the injury is not avoidable, it should be accepted as a real threat in order to make preparations to reduce the extent of the injury so the best remedy can be decided on. Just as during the development of the child's independent striving, so too in the process of injury and healing there is a time for support and assistance and a time when a person by himself must help along the process of healing, which is also a period of growth.

6   Sometimes, though, we overreact to painful feelings and set up impenetrable defenses. When our feelings are altered by such defenses, separating us from pain, managing feelings can become difficult because we simply lose sight of the problem.

7   There is a time for defenses and a time when they should be put aside. The purpose of defenses is to protect against further injury by giving us some distance and time. When they are used too broadly to shield us from all pain, they use so much energy they have nearly the same depleting effect as the injury itself. The energy that's consumed by defenses goes into putting up and maintaining a barrier to reality. Each of us needs to find a balance between pain and defense and rely on his own experience as a guide. While we frequently have little choice whether to use a defense or not, we can lower our defenses by enduring as much pain as we can tolerate until most of the pain is gone. It's not easy, it takes courage, but it works.

8   Basically there are two general kinds of feelings, positive and negative. Positive feelings add to one's sense of strength and well being, producing pleasure, a sense of completion, life, fullness and hope. Negative feelings interfere with pleasure, use up energy and leave one drained, with a sense of truncation, emptiness and loneliness. Positive feelings are joyous, like the sexual expressions between two people who care for each other or like the feeling of being reunited with a friend or achieving a hard-sought goal. Negative feelings have the impact of loss, like the perception of little deaths everywhere one looks. Positive feelings often find their expression in creative works, such as a work of art or a new idea. Positive feelings can also be an act of love or kindness. They have a sense of renewal about them.

9   The purpose of understanding your feelings and allowing them to flow to their natural conclusion is to become as open and as free of negative feelings as possible so that you can become your higher, more creative and productive self. Higher, because you are increasingly free of the burden of defenses that have their roots in fear and pain. More creative, because your energy is being expressed outwardly in a positive way, enhancing whatever it comes in contact with in your own unique way. More productive, because your energies are no longer drained by the need to keep feelings from being expressed, and you gain strength by expressing them in a natural way.

10   When you suffer the emotional injuries that everyone occasionally must, you may be drained of energy and feel hurt and hopeless for a time. This is a natural result of being injured. If you allow yourself to experience the natural stages of emotional hurt without trying to avoid reality you will be able to resolve your pain more completely. Your energy will return sooner and with it your creativity and productiveness.

11   Feelings should reflect the present and provide a personal perspective on the events you are confronting. This doesn't mean there's no room in the present for memories of happy times or sad events. Rather it means that feelings should be derived primarily from what is happening now, not from the unsettled events of the past. Which is why, of course, we should try to settle the pain of the past and be free to look back at the details of our lives from the perspective of understanding—which opens the way to continuing growth. The past should not be bound down in a rigid memory that has been defensively maintained, for example, to support a favorable impression of ourselves. When we block out the parts of the past that are unflattering or embarrassing, we often lose more than we bargained for. The defenses that block unpleasant memories also block pleasurable ones. And that inability to remember what's positive robs us of energy and joy, and prevents us from forming and keeping an optimistic attitude. The ideal is to be free of the need to distort reality, so that if you wish you can recall feelings from the past and be free to reexamine them and settle them anew.

12   This process of solving emotional problems throughout life makes possible real growth and development. The developmental "issues" of childhood, for example, constantly reappear as conflicts in our lives and continue to shape us. If we remain open we can continue to grow. If we are closed and defensive, we waste our energy and never realize our potential. The issue of the earliest phase of development is dependency; the life goal is to achieve independence. The issue of the next phase is mastery and control; the life goal is to achieve freedom. The issue of the next phase is identity, including sexual; the life goal is simply to be comfortable being yourself and accepting your feelings without pretense.

13   Adolescence is the first opportunity to work through these earlier issues again, a chance to test the validity of previous conceptions, the strength of earlier defenses. It's also a time to reconsider compromises made out of fear of losing one's parents' love, out of fear of losing control of one's emotions, or out of fear of embarrassment. Typically adolescents display a wide and constantly varying pattern of defenses, bewildering the people around them by changing their stand on issues as well as self-image from one moment to the next. The adolescent is confronted with all of the lessons he was supposed to have mastered long ago—or at least that his parents *expected* him to have mastered. No wonder he seems bewildered.

14   As an adolescent's emerging sexual energies begin to seek expression they also tend to make him feel out of control. They create feelings and fantasies he may not find acceptable and he may act in a self-destructive way to punish himself. The adolescent sometimes feels crazy and often acts it. The classical picture of adolescent turmoil is all too familiar with its mood swings and acting out of feelings rather than "feeling" them.

15   The adolescent's behavior is his language for expressing his feelings. It's as valid for him as "talking out" feelings is for an adult. When a parent panics in the face of his adolescent's rebellion, he tends to reinforce his child's worst fears about himself. The parent then seems out of control to the adolescent, who now may believe *no one* can help him, and this can lead to severe testing of limits and encounters with the law.

16   Parents often try to quash feelings in their children that they feel uncomfortable about in themselves. Their dishonesty in refusing to admit their own feelings may make their child rebel even more—he can see through, or sense, their "adult" defense.

17   Some parents actually secretly encourage their children's acting up and live a life of vicarious fulfillment as their children do things they wish they'd had the courage to do either when they were adolescents themselves or at the very moment. A parent who feels trapped in a marriage, for example, may encourage his child to run away and then follow him in fantasy.

18   Just as adolescence provides a second chance for the child to master the unsettled issues of his earlier life, it often stirs up a second adolescence in the parent: The child may not only, as they say, be father to the man within, but to the parent without as well.

19   Try to keep in mind: If you don't treat your children's feelings as important, how can you expect them to act in their own best interests, which is in the best expression of their feelings? Postponing a child's assumption of responsibility for his own behavior and prematurely forcing that responsibility both cause problems—of seething anger and feeling stifled on the one hand, and feeling abandoned and overwhelmed on the other.

20   It's been said that an adolescent is grown up when he can do what he wants even if his parents are in favor of it. Good parents don't make that choice even more difficult by being opposed to something their children desire merely because they are afraid of their own feelings.

21   In the years that follow adolescence, the issues of the past continue to be brought up and at least partially resolved as age takes away the defenses of even the strongest resistance. In later years there is no use lying. The mirror tells the truth and we must accept it. This is not necessarily some painful "coming to grips" with things; it also means learning to enjoy what *pleases* us. Too bad we didn't know earlier what we know now about ourselves—that we are what we are and have been that all along. How difficult it is to learn simply to be.

Finishing time: _____

Starting time: _____ **(subtract)**

Reading time: _____
Check your reading rate on page 501.

WPM: _____

COMPREHENSION CHECK

1. T/F   The thesis of this article is that not being in touch with your feelings is the only way you can ever become your highest self, open and free, your own person.

2. T/F   When a feeling is avoided, its painful effects are often prolonged and become more difficult to deal with.

3. T/F   According to the author, seeing the world intellectually is as different from "feeling" it as studying a country in a geography book is from living there.

4. T/F   Unlike any other energy system, feelings cannot be overloaded.

5. The author's attitude and tone is
   a. serious
   b. sarcastic
   c. remorseful
   d. sad

6. There are two types of feelings, according to the author. What are they?

   _____

7. T/F   We can infer that the author believes that in order to achieve real growth and development we must learn to solve our emotional problems during all stages of life.

8. T/F   We can infer that the author believes some parents unknowingly damage their children emotionally.

9. Explain what the author means when he says, "It's been said that an adolescent is grown up when he can do what he wants even if his parents are in

   favor of it." _____

   _____

   _____

   _____

10. T/F   We can draw the conclusion that the author believes that many people don't know how to deal with their feelings.

Number correct: _____

VOCABULARY CHECK

Directions: Define the following underlined words as they are used in context.

1. feelings may distort your perception of the truth

   _____

2. explaining does not resolve or exorcise them

   _____

3. it's initiated in the nerve ending

   _____

4. produces an avoidance response

   _____

5. set up <u>impenetrable</u> defenses

_____

6. the same <u>depleting</u> effect as the injury itself

_____

7. with a sense of <u>truncation</u>, emptiness, and loneliness

_____

8. try to <u>quash</u> feelings

_____

9. "<u>coming to grips</u>" with things

_____

10. the <u>language of feelings</u>

Number correct: _____

Record the results on the Timed Readings Chart on page 497. Discuss your scores with your instructor.

Drill   **D-4**

Directions: Quickly look over the following essay by reading the title, the first

paragraph, and the last one. What do you think the title means? _____

_____

Begin timing. Starting time: _____

ULTIMATE DISCOURSE

E. L. Doctorow

1   When I was a boy everyone in my family was a good storyteller, my mother and father, my brother, my aunts and uncles and grandparents; all of them were people to whom interesting things seemed to happen. The events they spoke of were of a daily, ordinary sort, but when narrated or acted out they took on great importance and excitement as I listened.

2   Of course, when you bring love to the person you are listening to, the story has to be interesting, and in one sense the task of a professional writer who pub-lishes books is to overcome the terrible loss of not being someone the reader knows and loves.

3   But apart from that, the people whose stories I heard as a child must have had a very firm view of themselves in the world. They must have been strong enough as presences in their own minds to trust that people would listen to them when they spoke.

4   I know now that everyone in the world tells stories. Relatively few people are given to mathematics or physics, but narrative seems to be within everyone's

From *Esquire*, Aug. 1986, p. 41.

grasp, perhaps because it comes of the nature of language itself.

5   The moment you have nouns and verbs and prepositions, the moment you have subjects and objects, you have stories.

6   For the longest time there would have been nothing but stories, and no sharper distinction between what was real and what was made up than between what was spoken and what was sung. Religious arousal and scientific discourse, simple urgent communication and poetry, all burned together in the intense perception of a metaphor—that, for instance, the sun was a god's chariot driven across the heavens.

7   Stories were as important to survival as a spear or a hoe. They were the memory of the knowledge of the dead. They gave counsel. They connected the visible to the invisible. They distributed the suffering so that it could be borne.

8   In our era, even as we separate the functions of language, knowing when we speak scientifically we are not speaking poetically, and when we speak theologically we are not speaking the way we do to each other in our houses, and even as our surveys demand statistics, and our courts demand evidence, and our hypotheses demand proof—our minds are still structured for storytelling.

9   What we call fiction is the ancient way of knowing, the total discourse that antedates all the special vocabularies of modern intelligence.

10   The professional writer of fiction is a conservative who cherishes the ultimate structures of the human mind. He cultivates within himself the universal disposition to think in terms of conflict and its resolution, and in terms of character undergoing events, and of the outcome of events being not at all sure, and therefore suspenseful—the whole thing done, moreover, from a confidence of narrative that is grounded in our brains as surely as the innate talent to construe the world grammatically.

11   The fiction writer, looking around him, understands the homage a modern up-to-date world of nonfiction specialists pays to his craft—even as it isolates him and tells him he is a liar. Newsweeklies present the events of the world as installments in a serial melodrama. Weather reports on television are constructed with exact attention to conflict (high-pressure areas clashing with lows), suspense (the climax of tomorrow's prediction coming after the commercial), and the consistency of voice (the personality of the weathercaster). The marketing and advertising of product-facts is unquestionably a fictional enterprise. As is every government's representations of its activities. And modern psychology, with its concepts of *sublimation, repression, identity crisis, complex,* and so on, proposes the interchangeable parts for the stories of all of us; in this sense it is the industrialization of storytelling.

12   But nothing is as good at fiction as fiction. It is the most ancient way of knowing but also the most modern, managing when it's done right to burn all the functions of language back together into powerful fused revelation. Because it is total discourse it is ultimate discourse. It excludes nothing. It will express from the depth and range of its sources truths that no sermon or experiment or news report can begin to apprehend. It will tell you without shame what people do with their bodies and think with their minds. It will deal evenhandedly with their microbes or their intuitions. It will know their nightmares and blinding moments of moral crisis. You will experience love, if it so chooses, or starvation or drowning or dropping through space or holding a hot pistol in your hand with the police pounding on the door. This is the way it is, it will say, this is what it feels like.

13   Fiction is democratic, it reasserts the authority of the single mind to make and remake the world. By its independence from all institutions, from the family to the government, and with no responsibility to defend their hypocrisy or murderousness, it is a valuable resource and instrument of survival.

14   Fiction gives counsel. It connects the present with the past, and the visible with the invisible. It distributes the suffering. It says we must compose ourselves in our stories in order to exist. It says if we don't do it, someone else will do it for us.

Finishing time: _____

Starting time: _____ **(subtract)**

Reading time: __*1:30*_____

Check your reading rate on page 501.

WPM: _____

COMPREHENSION CHECK

1. The best statement of thesis for this essay is
   a. Fiction was more important in the past than it is in the present.
   b. Fiction is more important now than it was in the past.
   c. Fiction is the ultimate discourse, expressing what people do with their bodies and think with their minds.
   d. Nothing is as good as fiction.

2. **T**/F   The attitude of the author toward fiction might be described as reverent.

3. T/**F**   The essay is based mostly on facts.

4. The intent of the author is to
   a. praise fictional writings
   b. show how people are more interested in facts than fiction
   c. explain the value of fiction
   d. define fiction

5. **T**/F   We can infer that the author wants his readers to appreciate fiction as he does.

6. Circle any of the following statements with which the author would agree.
   a. Fiction is the ancient way of knowing.
   b. Even weather reports on television contain elements of fiction in their presentation.
   c. Fiction allows us to experience people and events we might not meet or want to meet in real life.
   d. Fiction is a valuable resource and instrument of survival.

Number correct: _____9_____

7. T/**F**   We can infer that some minds are not structured for storytelling, thus preferring scientific discourse.

8. Explain what the author means by the statement, "Stories were as important to survival as a spear or a hoe." *to distribute the suffering to share the burden is as important at growing the food*

9. The author says that religion, science, poetry, and the simple need to communicate "all burned together" in the past to create metaphors such as, "the sun was a god's chariot driven across the heavens." Explain what he means. *describing a scientific happening with colorful words*

10. T/**F**   We can conclude that the author would probably make the reading and study of fiction a requirement in college.

VOCABULARY CHECK

Directions: Define the following underlined words or phrases in context.

1. stories gave <u>counsel</u>

_____

2. when we speak <u>theologically</u>

_____

3. the total discourse that <u>antedates</u> all the modern vocabularies

_____

4. cultivates within himself the <u>universal</u> <u>disposition</u>

_____

5. the <u>innate</u> talent to construe the world grammatically

_____

6. the innate talent to <u>construe</u> <u>the</u> <u>world</u> <u>grammatically</u>

_____

7. it is <u>ultimate</u> <u>discourse</u>

_____

8. narrative that is <u>grounded</u> <u>in</u> <u>our</u> <u>brains</u>

_____

9. the <u>consistency</u> <u>of</u> <u>voice</u>

_____

10. modern psychology with its concepts of <u>sublimation</u>

_____

Number correct: _____
Record the results on the Timed Readings Chart on page 497. Discuss your scores with your instructor.

UNIT III
PROGRESS CHECK

Read the following short story and answer the questions that follow it. The purpose of the Progress Check is to compare the results with those on the Inventory you took at the beginning of this unit.

Begin timing. Starting time: _____

THE SOMEBODY

Danny Santiago (Daniel James)

This is Chato talking, Chato de Shamrock, from the Eastside in old L.A., and I want you to know this is a big day in my life because today I quit school and went to work as a writer. I write on fences or buildings or anything that comes along. I write my name, not the one I got from my father. I want no part of him. I write Chato, which means Catface, because I have a flat nose like a cat. It's a Mexican word because that's what I am, a Mexican, and I'm not ashamed of it. I like that language too, man. It's way better than English to say what you feel. But German is the best. It's got a real rugged sound, and I'm going to learn to talk it someday.

After Chato I write "de Shamrock." That's the street where I live, and it's the name of the gang I belong to, but the others are all gone now. Their families had to move away, except Gorilla is in jail and Blackie joined the navy because he liked swimming. But I still have our old arsenal. It's buried under the chickens, and I dig it up when I get bored. There's tire irons and chains and pick handles with spikes and two zip guns we made and they shoot real bullets but not very straight. In the good old days nobody cared to tangle with us. But now I'm the only one left.

Well, today started off like any other day. The toilet roars like a hot rod taking off. My father coughs and spits about nineteen times and hollers it's six-thirty. So I holler back I'm quitting school. Things hit me like that—sudden.

"Don't you want to be a lawyer no more," he says in Spanish, "and defend the Mexican people?"

My father thinks he is very funny, and next time I make any plans, he's sure not going to hear about it.

Reprinted by permission.

"Don't you want to be a doctor," he says, "and cut off my leg for nothing someday?"

"*Due beast ine dumb cop,*"[1] I tell him in German, but not very loud.

"How will you support me," he says, "when I retire? Or will you marry a rich old woman that owns a pool hall?"

"I'm checking out of this dump! You'll never see me again!"

I hollered it at him, but already he was in the kitchen making a big noise in his coffee. I could be dead and he wouldn't take me serious. So I laid there and waited for him to go off to work. When I woke up again, it was way past eleven. I can sleep forever these days. So I got out of bed and put on clean jeans and my windbreaker and combed myself very neat, because already I had a feeling this was going to be a big day for me.

I had to wait for breakfast because the baby was sick and throwing up milk on everything. There is always a baby vomiting in my house. When they're born, everybody comes over and says: "Qué cute!"[2] but nobody passes any comments on the dirty way babies act. Sometimes my mother asks me to hold one for her but it always cries, maybe because I squeeze it a little hard when nobody's looking.

When my mother finally served me, I had to hold my breath, she smelled so bad of babies. I don't care to look at her anymore. Her legs got those dark-blue rivers running all over them. I kept waiting for her to bawl me out about school, but I guess she forgot, or something. So I cut out.

Every time I go out my front door I have to cry for what they've done to old Shamrock Street. It used to be so fine, with solid homes on both sides. Maybe they needed a little paint here and there but they were cozy. Then the S.P. Railroad bought up all the land except my father's place, because he was stubborn. They came in with their wrecking bars and their bulldozers. You could hear those houses scream when they ripped them down. So now Shamrock Street is just front walks that lead to a hole in the ground, and piles of busted cement. And Pelón's house and Blackie's are just stacks of old boards waiting to get hauled away. I hope that never happens to your street, man.

My first stop was the front gate and there was that sign again, that big S wrapped around a cross like a snake with rays coming out, which is the mark of the Sierra Street gang, as everybody knows. I rubbed it off, but tonight they'll put it back again. In the old days they wouldn't dare to come on our street, but without your gang you're nobody. And one of these fine days they're going to catch up with me in person and that will be the end of Chato de Shamrock.

So I cruised on down to Main Street like a ghost in a graveyard. Just to prove I'm alive, I wrote my name on the fence at the corner. A lot of names you see in public places are written very sloppy. Not me. I take my time. Like my fifth-grade teacher used to say, if other people are going to see your work, you owe it to yourself to do it right. Mrs. Cully was her name and she was real nice, for an Anglo. My other teachers were all cops, but Mrs. Cully drove me home one time when some guys were after me. I think she wanted to adopt me but she never said anything about it. I owe a lot to that lady, and especially my writing. You should see it, man—it's real smooth and mellow, and curvy like a blond in a bikini. Everybody says so. Except one time they had me in Juvenile by mistake and some doctor looked at it. He said it proved I had something wrong with me, some long word. That doctor was crazy, because I made him show me his writing and it was real ugly like a barbwire fence with little chickens stuck on the points. You couldn't even read it.

Anyway, I signed myself very clean and neat on that corner. And then I thought, Why not look for a job someplace? But I was more in the mood to write my name, so I went into the dime store and helped myself to two boxes of crayons and some chalk

[1] *Due ... cop.* "You're an idiot" ("*Du bist ein Dummkopf*").
[2] *Qué how.*

and cruised on down Main, writing all the way. I wondered should I write more than my name. Should I write "Chato is a fine guy" or "Chato is wanted by the police"? Things like that. News. But I decided against it. Better to keep them guessing. Then I crossed over to Forney Playground. It used to be our territory, but now the Sierra had taken over there like everyplace else. Just to show them, I wrote on the tennis court and the swimming pool and the gym. I left a fine little trail of Chato de Shamrock in eight colors. Some places I used chalk, which works better on brick or plaster. But crayons are the thing for cement or anything smooth, like in the girls' rest room. On that wall I drew a phone number. I bet a lot of them are going to call that number, but it isn't mine because we don't have a phone in the first place, and in the second place I'm probably never going home again.

I'm telling you, I was pretty famous at the Forney by the time I cut out, and from there I continued my travels till something hit me. You know how you put your name on something and that proves it belongs to you? Things like school books or gym shoes? So I thought, How about that, now? And I put my name on the Triple A Market and on Morrie's Liquor Store and on the Zócalo, which is a beer joint. And then I cruised on up Broadway, getting rich. I took over a barber shop and a furniture store and the Plymouth agency. And the firehouse for laughs, and the phone company so I could call all my girl friends and keep my dimes. And then there I was at Webster and García's Funeral Home with the big white columns. At first I thought that might be bad luck, but then I said, Oh, well, we all got to die sometime. So I signed myself, and now I can eat good and live in style and have a big time all my life, and then kiss you all good-bye and give myself the best funeral in L.A. for free.

And speaking of funerals, along came the Sierra right then, eight or ten of them down the street with that stupid walk which is their trademark. I ducked into the garage and hid behind the hearse. Not that I'm a coward. Getting stomped doesn't bother me, or even shot. What I hate is those blades, man. They're like a piece of ice cutting into your belly. But the Sierra didn't see me and went on by. I couldn't hear what they were saying, but I knew they had me on their mind. So I cut on over to the Boys' Club, where they don't let anybody get you, no matter who you are. To pass the time I shot some baskets and played a little pool and watched the television, but the story was boring, so it came to me: Why not write my name on the screen? Which I did with a squeaky pen. Those cowboys sure looked fine with Chato de Shamrock written all over them. Everybody got a kick out of it. But of course up comes Mr. Calderón and makes me wipe it off. They're always spying on you up there. And he takes me into his office and closes the door.

"Well," he says, "and how is the last of the dinosaurs?"

Meaning that the Shamrocks are as dead as giant lizards.

Then he goes into that voice with the church music in it, and I look out of the window.

"I know it's hard to lose your gang, Chato," he says, "but this is your chance to make new friends and straighten yourself out. Why don't you start coming to Boys' Club more?"

"It's boring here," I tell him.

"What about school?"

"I can't go," I said. "They'll get me."

"The Sierra's forgotten you're alive," he tells me.

"Then how come they put their mark on my house every night?"

"Do they?"

He stares at me very hard. I hate those eyes of his. He thinks he knows everything. And what is he? Just a Mexican like everybody else.

"Maybe you put that mark there yourself," he says. "To make yourself big. Just like you wrote on the television."

"That was my name! I like to write my name!"

"So do dogs," he says. "On every lamppost they come to."

"You're a dog yourself," I told him, but I don't think he heard me. He just went on talking. Brother, how they love to talk up there! But I didn't bother to listen, and when he ran out of gas I left. From now on I'm scratching that Boys' Club off my list.

Out on the street it was getting dark, but I could still follow my trail back toward Broadway. It felt good seeing Chato written everyplace, but at the Zócalo I stopped dead. Around my name there was a big red heart done in lipstick with some initials I didn't recognize. To tell the truth, I didn't know how to feel. In one way I was mad that anyone would fool with my name, especially if it was some guy doing it for laughs. But what guy carries lipstick? And if it was a girl, that could be kind of interesting.

A girl is what it turned out to be. I caught up with her at the telephone company. There she is, standing in the shadows, drawing her heart around my name. And she has a very pretty shape on her, too. I sneak up behind her very quiet, thinking all kinds of crazy things and my blood shooting around so fast it shakes me all over. And then she turns around and it's only Crusader Rabbit. That's what we called her from the television show they had then, on account of her teeth in front.

When she sees me, she takes off down the alley, but in twenty feet I catch her. I grab for the lipstick, but she whips it behind her. I reach around and try to pull her fingers open, but her hand is sweaty and so is mine. And there we are, stuck together all the way down. She twists up against me, kind of giggling. To tell the truth, I don't like to wrestle with girls. They don't fight fair. And then we lost balance and fell against some garbage cans, so I woke up. After that I got the lipstick away from her very easy.

"What right you got to my name?" I tell her. "I never gave you permission."

"You sign yourself real fine," she says.

I knew that already.

"Let's go writing together," she says.

"The Sierra's after me."

"I don't care," she says. "Come on, Chato—you and me can have a lot of fun."

She came up close and giggled that way. She put her hand on my hand that had the lipstick in it. And you know what? I'm ashamed to say I almost told her yes. It would be a change to go writing with a girl. We could talk there in the dark. We could decide on the best places. And her handwriting wasn't too bad either. But then I remembered I had my reputation to think of. Somebody would be sure to see us, and they'd be laughing at me all over the Eastside. So I pulled my hand away and told her off.

"Run along, Crusader," I told her. "I don't want no partners, and especially not you."

"Who are you calling Crusader?" she screamed. "You ugly, squash-nose punk."

She called me everything. And spit at my face but missed. I didn't argue. I just cut out. And when I got to the first sewer I threw away her lipstick. Then I drifted over to the banks at Broadway and Bailey, which is a good spot for writing because a lot of people pass by there.

Well, I hate to brag, but that was the best work I've ever done in all my life. Under the streetlamp my name shone like solid gold. I stood to one side and checked the people as they walked past and inspected it. With some you can't tell just how they feel, but with others it rings out like a cash register. There was one man. He got out of his Cadillac to buy a paper and when he saw my name he smiled. He was the age to be my father. I bet he'd give me a job if I asked him. I bet he'd take me to his home and to his office in the morning. Pretty soon I'd be sitting at my own desk and signing my name on letters and checks and things. But I would never buy a Cadillac, man. They burn too much gas.

Later a girl came by. She was around eighteen, I think, with green eyes. Her face was so pretty I didn't dare to look at her shape. Do you want me to go crazy? That girl stopped and really studied my name like she fell in love with it. She wanted to know me, I could tell. She wanted to take my hand and we'd go off together holding hands. We'd go to Beverly Hills and nobody would look at us the wrong way. I almost said "Hi" to that girl and, "How do you like my writing?" But not quite.

So here I am, standing on this corner with my chalk all gone and only one crayon left and it's ugly brown. My fingers are too cold besides. But I don't care because I just had a vision, man. Did they ever turn on the lights for you so you could see the whole world and everything in it? That's how it came to me right now. I don't need to be a movie star or boxing champ to make my name in the world. All I need is plenty of chalk and crayons. And that's easy. L.A. is a big city, man, but give me a couple of months and I'll be famous all over town. Of course they'll try to stop me—the Sierra, the police, and everybody. But I'll be like a ghost, man. I'll be real mysterious, and all they'll know is just my name, signed like I always sign it, CHATO DE SHAMROCK with rays shooting out like from the Holy Cross.

Finishing time: _____

Starting time: _____ **(subtract)**

Reading time: _____

Check page 501 for your reading rate: WPM: _____

COMPREHENSION CHECK

1. About how old is Chato and how do you know? _____

   _____

   _____

2. T/F   The relationship between Chato and his father is one of mutual respect.

3. T/F   "The toilet roars like a hot rod taking off" is an example of a metaphor.

4. When Chato says his mother has "those dark-blue rivers running all over

   them," to what is he referring? _____

   _____

5. Chato says that when he holds one of the babies, "It always cries because I squeeze it a little hard when nobody's looking." What inference about Chato's

   character can be drawn from this statement? _____

   _____

   _____

6. T/F   We can infer that Chato is lying when he tells Mr. Calderón that the Sierra "marks" his house every night.

7. How does Chato intend to become famous? _____

   _____

8. Chato says he likes the German language and is going "to learn to talk it someday." Do you think he ever will? Explain. _____

_____

9. Explain why the author called this story "The Somebody" and not something like "Chato de Shamrock." _____

_____

_____

10. What kind of future do you predict for Chato? Why? _____

_____

_____

_____

Number correct: _____

VOCABULARY CHECK

Directions: Define or explain the following underlined words and phrases as they are used in the story.

1. I still have our old <u>arsenal</u>.

_____

2. So I <u>cut out</u>.

_____

3. You could <u>hear those houses scream</u> when they ripped them down.

_____

4. I cruised on down <u>like a ghost in a graveyard</u>.

_____

5. I helped <u>myself</u> to two boxes of crayons and some chalk.

_____

6. I took <u>over</u> a barber shop.

_____

7. So I <u>signed myself</u>.

_____

8. So he goes into <u>that</u> <u>voice</u> <u>with</u> <u>the</u> <u>church</u> <u>music</u> <u>in</u> <u>it</u>.

_____

9. With some you can't tell, but with others <u>it</u> <u>rings</u> <u>out</u> <u>like</u> <u>a</u> <u>cash</u> <u>register</u>.

_____

10. <u>My</u> <u>other</u> <u>teachers</u> <u>were</u> <u>all</u> <u>cops</u>.

_____

Number correct: _____

Record the results on the record chart on page 493. Count 10 percent for every correct answer. If you are in doubt as to why any of your answers are wrong, check with your instructor.

NAME _____ SECTION _____ DATE _____

APPENDIX

Inventory Progress Chart

Student Record Chart

Timed Readings Record Chart

Timed Readings Conversion Chart

Timed Readings Conversion Chart

Directions: Your reading rate (WPM) can be found by locating the name of the article you read in the list below. Then look down that column. Stop at the number of minutes and seconds it took you to read the article. For example, if you read "Groups: The Sociological Subject" in 7 minutes and 45 seconds, your rate would be 280 WPM.

Unit I: LITERAL COMPREHENSION

Time	Inventory: "Groups: The Sociological Subject"	D-1 "Can Billions Buy Survival?"	D-2 "Using Drugs? You May Not Get Hired"	D-3 "Law of Social Cycles"	D-4 "In America, Fame Is an Open Door"	Progress: "Concepts for Cultural Analysis"
	WPM	**WPM**	**WPM**	**WPM**	**WPM**	**WPM**
1:00	2180	1170	1120	1350	1170	2300
1:15	1800	936	898	1086	936	1840
1:30	1453	780	733	905	780	1533
1:45	1300	669	628	779	669	1314
2:00	1090	585	565	675	585	1150
2:15	1000	520	505	600	520	1022
2:30	872	468	450	535	468	920
2:45	810	426	400	485	426	836
3:00	727	390	385	449	390	766
3:15	688	360	348	415	360	707
3:30	623	334	314	379	334	657
3:45	595	312	280	359	312	613
4:00	545	296	275	339	296	575
4:15	505	275	260	319	275	541
4:30	484	260	250	299	260	511
4:45	450	246	240	280	246	484
5:00	436	234	230	270	234	460
5:15	406	223	215	255	223	438
5:30	396	213	200	240	213	418
5:45	383	204	195	230	204	400
6:00	363	195	190	220	195	383
6:15	350	187	185	210	187	368
6:30	335	180	179	200	180	353
6:45	320	173	170	197	173	340
7:00	311	167	162	190	167	328
7:15	300	161	158	181	161	317
7:30	291	156	150	178	156	306
7:45	280	151	145	170	151	296
8:00	273	146	140	168	146	287
8:15	263	131	129	160	131	278
8:30	256	126		153	126	270
8:45	250	118		150	118	262
9:00	242			144		255
9:15	236			138		248
9:30	229					242
9:45	223					235
10:00	218					230
10:15	−215					−224

Unit II: Critical Comprehension

Time	Inventory: "Why I Want a Family" WPM	"Birth" WPM	"Splice of Life" WPM	"Ad Proves Baby Boomers..." WPM	Progress: "The Trouble with Television" WPM
1:00	1090	700	980	700	1090
1:15	872	560	784	560	872
1:30	727	467	653	467	727
1:45	623	400	560	400	623
2:00	545	350	490	350	545
2:15	484	311	436	311	484
2:30	436	280	392	280	436
2:45	396	255	356	255	396
3:00	363	233	327	233	363
3:15	335	215	302	215	335
3:30	311	200	280	200	311
3:45	291	187	261	187	291
4:00	273	175	245	175	273
4:15	256	165	231	165	256
4:30	242	156	218	156	242
4:45	229	147	206	147	229
5:00	218	140	196	140	218
5:15	208	133	187	133	208
5:30	198	127	178	127	198
5:45	190	122	170	122	190
6:00	182	117	163	117	182
6:15	174	112	157	112	174
6:30	168	108	151	108	168
6:45	161	104	145	104	161
7:00	156	100	140	100	156
7:15	150	97		97	150
7:30	145				145
7:45	141				141
8:00					
8:15					
8:30					
8:45					
9:00					
9:15					
9:30					
9:45					
10:00					
10:15					

Unit III: AFFECTIVE COMPREHENSION

Time	Inventory: "Love" WPM	"Salvation" WPM	"The Barrio" WPM	"The American Dream" WPM	"What Soap Operas Are Trying to Tell Us" WPM	The Language of Feelings WPM	"The Ultimate Discourse" WPM	Progress: "The Somebody" WPM
1:00	1400	913	1350	443	1170	2300	913	3500
1:15	1120	730	1086	354	936	1840	730	2813
1:30	933	609	905	295	780	1533	609	2344
1:45	800	522	779	253	669	1314	522	2009
2:00	700	457	675	222	585	1150	457	1758
2:15	622	406	600	197	520	1022	406	1563
2:30	560	362	535	177	468	920	362	1406
2:45	509	332	485	161	426	836	332	1279
3:00	466	304	449	148	390	766	304	1172
3:15	430	281	415	136	360	707	281	1082
3:30	400	261	379	127	334	657	261	1005
3:45	373	244	359	118	312	613	244	938
4:00	350	228	339	111	296	575	228	879
4:15	329	215	319	104	275	541	215	827
4:30	311	203	299	98	260	511	203	781
4:45	294	192	280		246	484	192	740
5:00	280	183	270		234	460	183	703
5:15	266	174	255		223	438	−174	670
5:30	254	166	240		213	418	166	639
5:45	243	159	238		204	400	159	612
6:00	233	152	220		195	383	152	586
6:15	224	146	210		187	368	146	563
6:30	215	144	200		180	353	144	541
6:45	207	141	197		173	340	141	521
7:00	200	140	190		167	328	140	502
7:15	193	138	181		161	317	138	485
7:30	186	135	178		156	306	135	469
7:45	180	130	170		151	296	130	454
8:00	175		168		146	287		440
8:15	169		160		131	268		426
8:30	164		153		126	270		414
8:45	160		150		120	262		402
9:00	155		144			255		391
9:15	151		138			248		380
9:30	147					242		370
9:45	145					235		361
10:00	140					230		352
10:15	−136					−224		343
10:30								335
10:45								327
11:00								302
11:15								285
11:30								273
12:00								262
13:00								244
14:00								227